ROBERT HARVEY is the author of many books of both current affairs and history. He is a former MP and Member of the House of Commons Foreign Affairs Committee, was an assistant editor of *The Economist* and foreign affairs leader writer and columnist for *The Daily Telegraph*. He has covered the Middle East, Southern Europe and Latin America. He was one of the first writers to note the rise of Saddam Hussein and has reported on the Iran/Iraq War, Soviet occupation of Afghanistan, the Gulf War and Central America's wars. The book was the lead on Andrew Marr's BBC *Start the Week* and featured both on Adam Boulton's Sky Television books programme and on Fox News in the US.

D0004584

Also by Robert Harvey

The Return of the Strong: The Drift to Global Disorder
The Undefeated: The Rise, Fall and Rise of Modern Japan
The Fall of Apartheid
Fire Down Below: A Journey of Exploration from Mexico to Chile
Portugal: Birth of a Democracy

GLOBAL DISORDER

ROBERT HARVEY

CARROLL & GRAF PUBLISHERS
New York

Carroll & Graf Publishers
An imprint of Avalon Publishing Group, Inc.
245 W. 17th Street
New York
NY 10011
www.carrollandgraf.com

First published in the UK by Constable,
an imprint of Constable & Robinson Ltd 2003

First Carroll & Graf edition 2003

This revised paperback edition published by Carroll & Graf 2003

Note: Part III of this book contains substantial material revised and updated
from an earlier work by Robert Harvey, *The Return of the Strong*,
published by Macmillan London, 1995

ISBN 0-7867-1289-9

Printed and bound in the EU

Library of Congress Cataloging-in-Publication Data is available on file.

'I dread our being too much dreaded . . . We may say that we shall not abuse this astonishing and hitherto unheard of power. But every other nation will think that we shall abuse it. It is impossible but that, sooner or later, this state of things must produce a combination against us which may end in our ruin.'

Edmund Burke

For Jane and Oliver

CONTENTS

ACKNOWLEDGEMENTS

I owe an incalculable debt to the many parliamentarians, diplomats, authors and journalists, economists and security development specialists around the world who have given so freely of their time in discussing these issues with me. I cannot possibly name them all, and to name a few would be invidious and, worse, might embarrass them by linking them to the views in this book which, of course, are mine alone.

However, I must place on record the colossal debt I owe to my assistant, Jenny Thomas, for her painstaking and indefatigable work, to my enthusiastic editor, Nick Robinson, and wise and encouraging agent, Gillon Aitken, to my mother and my sister Antonella and her family, and, as always, to the love, endurance and devotion of Jane and Oliver.

INTRODUCTION

Has the Fourth World War broken out? (The Cold War was the Third World War – a sprawling and sporadic global conflict to be sure, but one which resulted in millions of casualties and the defeat of communism.) There are signs that it has: the terrorist outrage on September 11, 2001, and the lesser attacks across the world in Bali, Kenya, Morocco and Saudi Arabia, accompanied by the smouldering Israeli–Palestinian confrontation, have been countered by the American invasions of Afghanistan and Iraq, involving hundreds of thousands of troops and ten times as many deaths as were inflicted on Nine-Eleven.

On the one hand President Bush spoke in September 2003 of Iraq as the 'central front' in the war against global terrorism; on the other it has been suggested that the United States is behaving no differently from other young mighty military and economic powers at a similar stage in their development – Great Britain in the eighteenth century, France under Napoleon, Germany and Japan in the first half of the last century, Russia in the second half.

The enormous and critical difference is that the United States, at this moment of unparalleled power, unlike any of its predecessors is a full-fledged democracy: thus it is answerable to the people and the nation's course can be guided and reversed without the full-scale upheaval necessary in a non-democratic state. Another difference is that the world has changed. The 'old' imperialist powers withdrew from their colonies not for altruistic reasons, but because of the cost in casualties and money which was unacceptable to domestic public opinion. The pattern was identical in Britain, France and Russia; in the case of Germany and

Japan, it took horrendous defeats for the lesson to be learnt. In a world where weapons of micro destruction are so widely diffused – small arms, machine guns, rifles, grenades, handmade bombs – empire is quite simply unsustainable against large populations. As one of Britain's wisest former foreign ministers, Geoffrey Howe, has said: 'America may be trying to act as an imperial power in a post-imperial world'.

The invasion of Iraq marks a massive break with America's usually cautious foreign policy based on furthering commercial interests without messy foreign entanglements abroad. First, it is an invasion unjustified by an actual act of present-day aggression, a massive and pressing humanitarian problem, or a direct threat to America's national interests. Second it has been taken in concert with only one of its major traditional allies, Britain, and the passive support of a few others, of which Italy, Spain and Australia are the most prominent. Mexico and Canada on the North American mainland and Germany joined more traditional American detractors like France, Russia and China in opposition to the war.

Third, this was the largest undertaking without the actual sanction of the United Nations and international law since the Vietnam War – and that particular precedent is not at all encouraging. The Bush administration has undertaken a radical departure from the politics of its predecessors, a reaching out halfway across the world into the heart of another region with incalculable consequences.

Intervention in Vietnam could at least be justified on the grounds of the worldwide struggle against the expansionist totalitarian menace of international communism. No such justification can be found for the invasion of Iraq. Unlike fundamentalist Afghanistan, which harboured the terrorists who carried out Nine-Eleven, the country was a closely controlled secular dictatorship which had taken no part in the atrocity – indeed on all the evidence was bitterly opposed to Islamic extremism (one analogy is Hitler's Germany and Stalin's Russia: both were evil dictatorships. But Stalin was Hitler's bitter enemy and an ally we needed: it obviously would have made no sense at all to attack the former for the aggressions of the latter in the 1930s).

The initial justifications given by the Bush administration for the attack on Iraq have been all but abandoned in the face of an overwhelming lack of evidence. No convincing evidence has emerged of any connection between al-Qaeda and Saddam. No weapons of mass destruction have been found. They may yet be – but the interrogation of hundreds of leading members of Saddam's regime has revealed none so far. Neither has the search of the relatively small area of Iraq likely to harbour such weapons.

Most of the chemical and biological weapons unaccounted for by UN inspections are likely to have deteriorated over the years, and the means of delivery – such few Iraqi al-Hussein missiles as the country possessed – threatened no more than Iraq's immediate neighbours, none of which asserted Saddam was planning to attack. They certainly posed no threat to American or British forces stationed in the Middle East – they were not even used against the invaders. As for a nuclear capacity, Iraq had been given a clean bill of health by UN weapons inspectors immediately before the invasion. There was no smoking gun, just a rusting one with a few damp old cartridges which might, or might not, have been fireable.

The issue of weapons of mass destruction mattered to the Bush administration only in the context of an attempt to secure UN approval of the invasion. It mattered a great deal more to the British government which would not have been able to persuade parliament and the people to back the war unless the invasion had been legally justified by UN resolutions. Hence the extraordinary farrago of 'spin', half-truths and unsupported allegations concocted by the Blair government in support of the war. While all the minutiae of the tragic Kelly affair were earnestly debated in the press during the summer of 2003, one glaring mega-truth towers over them: that the British Prime Minister misled parliament in the runup to the war, not just over the 45-minute claim, which was based on a single Iraqi informant – when before have great democratic nations gone to war on the probably false evidence of a single enemy national? – but in asserting that he knew the Iraqis had weapons of mass destruction (which presumably he couldn't share out of consideration for his informants).

If he knew, why have they not been found? Why has the evidence not been presented after the war? He did not know, and therefore he was either misled or he lied. In either case, as he has acknowledged, this is a resigning matter. There can be no graver charge against a government than that it embarked on an unprovoked war on the basis of false information to parliament and the public. An illegal war exposes British soldiers to unnecessary casualties and authorizes the mass murder of the opposition. The precedent was set by Anthony Eden's resignation at Suez – and that war was originally provoked by Nasser's blatant aggression, although a key aspect (Anglo–French co-operation with Israel) was concealed.

Whatever Tony Blair's motives for entering the war on America's side – whether a genuinely misplaced idealism or a cold calculation of Britain's interests as an ally of the United States – the Bush administration itself was largely unconcerned about weapons of mass destruction. Instead, reflecting a profound debate within the administration, the invasion of Iraq may have been staged for any one of a number of unadmitted other reasons relating to America's perceived national interest – or a mixture of them.

The administration has shifted its public justification of the war to the need to remove a monster regime, one which had tyrannized its people and had invaded its neighbours in the past – although there was no sign of its doing so again. Again, this is not a convincing motive. Many well-intentioned people would profoundly agree with this as a justification for international military intervention. Later in the book I try and suggest ways in which 'humane' interventions might exceptionally be justified and approved by all of the international community. But the issue is a long debated and complex one. If Iraq, why not Zimbabwe, much of Africa, several of Russia's southern neighbours, most of the Middle East, Burma, or even China? Obviously we can't do them all, comes the reply, but why not one, and a particularly nasty one at that? To which the retort must be, why Iraq now, rather than more dangerous violators of human rights such as North Korea and Iran, both further advanced along the road to developing nuclear weapons and already clearly possessing chemical and biological ones?

Moreover, was not attacking Iraq a dangerous diversion from the war against the real enemy – al-Qaeda and global terrorism? Instead, has the deposing of Saddam not actually opened up Iraq to penetration by al-Qaeda and other types of Islamic fundamentalism? Ah – but if Iraq was not actually co-operating with terrorists it might have done so one day, furnishing them with men and materials. About this British Prime Minister Tony Blair's own intelligence chiefs were unequivocal: shortly before the invasion they assessed that any invasion of Iraq would 'increase the risk of chemical and biological warfare technology or agents finding their way into the hands of terrorists'. This finding was suppressed by Tony Blair before the war. With the disappearance of radioactive material immediately after the war and the puzzling inability to find even those few weapons the Iraqis still might have possessed, the danger is now all too real that these have indeed found their way into the hands of terrorists. On all three counts, al-Qaeda has been helped, not hurt, by the invasion of Iraq.

A second possible motive is oil. This is not as despicable a reason for military intervention as many believe. Great powers have always intervened when essential national interests were at stake, and what could be more vital to America's economy than Middle Eastern oil, with dependency actually increasing rather than diminishing? The rest of the world should share these concerns: during the oil shortages and price hikes of the 1970s, hundreds of millions of people were plunged into poverty, debt and even starvation in the developing world: cheap oil is even more of a priority to industrializing Asia, Africa and Latin America than to the West.

There are huge concerns about the stability of Saudi Arabia, the biggest oil producer, which is a hotbed of Wahhabi Sunni Islamic extremism and the incubator of al-Qaeda (see chapters 8 & 17). Is the United States not merely acting in its own and the world's long-term enlightened self-interest in seeking to diversify its source of the world's lifeblood? Perhaps the motive cannot be stated, or it would arouse the ire of anti-imperialists everywhere. But it is at least understandable and even defensible. The issue then becomes whether invading Iraq is likely to lead to a more stable oil-producing Gulf, or a less stable one.

This elides into a third possible motive: that America's newly 'neo-conservative' lobby, allied to some (although by no means all) powerful pro-Israeli interests and Christian lobbies in the southern United States, is seeking fundamentally to redraw the map of the Middle East in America's image. Just as Eastern Europe is seen by some as a convert to American-style capitalism and democracy, now the structures of feudalism and authoritarianism astride the world's greatest oil lake should be reformed. Once again, where is the dishonour in this?

The issue, once more, is practicality. The concern is that eager foreign policy neophytes brought in by the Bush administration have secretly determined to redraw the map of the Middle East, as British governments once used to do. For the excellent reasons previously alluded to, the British got out with the task uncompleted, just as all the other European empires wound up their military and administrative occupations of other cultures and pursued their economic and humanitarian goals by other means. Eastern Europe shares a culture with the major European democracies, and was briefly hijacked by revolutionary communism. The Middle East has a very different culture, with Islam some 1400 years old, and will evolve towards political pluralism in its own way.

When the hardback version of this book was published in January

2003, shortly before the invasion of Iraq, I tried to list the practical arguments against intervention in a way that would not be seen as hostile to the Bush administration. The risks seemed so enormous, and the benefits so evanescent that I still hoped, against virtually overwhelming evidence to the contrary on the several visits I made to Washington after September 11, 2001, that the war could be averted. I always believed that the Americans and British would have little difficulty in overcoming Iraqi resistance – and indeed great credit is due to the bravery, speed and efficiency with which the allies carried out the occupation. I feared, for the reasons outlined in detail on pages 63 to 70, that the long-term consequences might be disastrous – a fear not dispelled when a very senior member of the Bush administration told me 'it is right to go in, whatever happens afterwards'. But what if afterwards is much worse than before?

Following a visit to Iraq in the summer and my continuing contacts with the country, I wish I could say that my initial fears were ill-founded. Sadly, I found the situation worse than I expected. The country, in my opinion, is not yet at the point of no return. Indeed it *must* be saved for the West not to have an apocalyptic disaster on its hands – a whirlwind of confrontation spinning across borders into Iran, Saudi Arabia, the Gulf, Syria and Turkey, and possibly across the rest of the Arab world, endangering oil supplies and proliferating terrorism across the globe. The Fourth World War would then truly have arrived and Osama bin Laden's greatest ambition would have been realized beyond his wildest dreams.

But saving Iraq will take a combination of American and Western resolve, restraint and good sense of a kind that has so far been sadly deficient in the current administration. Whoever becomes president in January 2005 – Bush or a Democratic successor – looks like having the mother of all international messes to clear up in the cities, deserts, marshes and mountains of Iraq.

On any balance sheet, there are positive aspects. Visitors to Baghdad might be surprised by the limited damage inflicted by the allies during the war, a tribute to their highly targeted bombing. There is a semblance of order, at least, although far too few police. Basic food supplies have been resumed, water and electricity exist at least intermittently and oil production is gradually climbing to prewar levels, although petrol supplies for the ordinary consumer remain appalling. Cholera has broken out in Basra and other poor areas, but not the widespread disease, malnutrition and migration feared by some in the immediate aftermath of the war.

There has been no general uprising against the Americans, particularly by the Shias in the south, and the Kurds are quiescent in the north, with fighting largely restricted to the central region around Baghdad, where Saddam loyalists and bandits, possibly helped by the men, money and weapons from foreign extremists pouring in, are still active. On the whole American and British troops have been courageous and restrained in difficult and dangerous circumstances, and individual administrators have been committed and hard-working.

But in other respects the occupation has been deeply flawed. It seems extraordinary that the Americans' smooth performance during the war was not followed up by the huge civilian relief and reconstruction operation that would obviously be needed after a war like this. There is scarcely any evidence that one was planned. A minimum of foresight would have averted the continuing interrupted electricity, water and food supplies so many months after the war. The 700 or so civilian administrators in Iraq are simply inadequate to the task. There should be thousands more.

If the reason was that security could not have been provided for more, there should have been a much larger American military presence to protect them and the water and oil installations that are being constantly blown up. Those in the Pentagon who urged a much larger military presence were right, and the American defence secretary, Donald Rumsfeld, was wrong. These things cannot be done on the cheap: it is far more expensive and difficult to increase numbers later than to get them right in the first place.

The problem is compounded by the American attitude to security. Understandably reluctant to risk casualties, the army of occupation tends to act in force, drive around in large well-protected convoys and carry out massive search operations or shelter in defended bases like the one at Saddam's former presidential palace in Baghdad – the headquarters of the occupation – and Baghdad International Airport, which shows only intermittent signs of being reopened for civilian use. American paranoia about security has prevented the re-establishment of a proper telephone system, domestic or mobile – only expensive satellite telephones can be used, and then only in the open, where the users are exposed to heat and attack. When the Bahrainis set up a telephone system, it was quickly closed down on security grounds. This may be a useful means of control, but it inhibits resumption of normal commercial and civilian life.

The (second) American administrator of Iraq, Paul Bremer, made the colossal mistake of disbanding the Iraqi army, much of the civil service, and the Baath party itself. As these between them comprise some 3 million people (along with their families more than a quarter of the population), and represent the only local forces of order and organization, the decision was not a sensible one. Ever since, this huge swathe of people has been sitting on its hands on a kind of work-to-rule basis, waiting for the call to return to its old status. These are the qualified men – engineers, civil servants, administrators, contractors, professionals, including teachers and doctors – needed to make the country work. At a lower level there is a huge network of law-abiding people waiting to be mobilized to keep order – many of them former informers yes, but waiting to be retrained, not alienated.

The lesson of successful limited military occupations in the past – in Germany, Italy and Japan after 1945 – was that it was necessary to work through established institutions. By all means purge the few hundred or maybe a thousand or two of those at the very top responsible for the worst atrocities: but even very senior people in Saddam's murderous administration were simply 'carrying out orders' – and probably faced execution if they didn't. Can they really be blamed for the atrocities? If the army had been kept on, it would today be carrying out the policing and security operations that are now unnecessarily putting American and British soldiers in the line of fire, or are simply not being carried out at all.

As it is, the security situation is much worse than the fragmented daily reports from Iraq suggest. The only firefights publicly acknowledged are those in which American soldiers have been killed. The fighting is widespread in the central region, although much rarer in the north and the south, and the number of American casualties being flown into Andrews air force base near Washington for treatment (some 8,000 between March and September 2003) suggests a much higher level of fighting than is acknowledged (and alarmingly is consonant with a larger number of American deaths than is being admitted): the Iraqi figures are unknowable. On the American side the number of deaths attributed to accidents is extraordinarily high by the standards of previous wars – higher even than combat deaths – and there are even (highly questionable) stories originating from mortuary attendants and suchlike that American combat troops are being buried quietly in the desert.

Security at night is deplorable. After curfew American patrols acting on tipoffs go out and open fire on suspected Saddamist guerrillas or criminals, which usually triggers off a gunbattle in which others open up on the troops. The shootout in which eight Iraqi policemen were killed in September 2003 is an extreme example which, rarely, occurs in daylight. I have heard too many reports from reliable sources of looting by American soldiers themselves as they go on search missions into houses to doubt them: they are entirely typical of conditions under an army of occupation, and it is hard altogether to blame ordinary GIs plucked from home comforts and stuck out in appalling heat and danger for months on end while the Pentagon gets its overstretched act together to find soldiers to replace them.

The trouble with these conditions is that they eventually breed intense local resentment. The level of continuing resistance in Iraq has surprised the Americans, as has the failure of the local population to greet them as liberators. They should remember that their decade of sanctions is blamed by most Iraqis for just as many deaths as the hated Saddam inflicted over the past dozen years. Another American mistake has been to proceed too slowly towards elections; instead a nominated governing council was appointed that lacks popular legitimacy and excludes important groups. Those on the council risk being tainted with colla-boration. The sooner elections are held, the sooner the Americans and the British can get out. America cannot control the outcome of the polls.

Much more dangerous is the potential for a far wider flareup. The flood of arms and money now pouring into Iraq comes from three principal directions: Saudi Arabia, Syria and Iran. It conjures up the danger of a regional conflagration of awesome proportions – a three-way civil war sucking in outside powers, as a fire does outside air, with the Americans and the British caught in the middle. It was precisely in order not to spark off this kind of bloodbath – red gold being spilt over black gold – that the United States and Britain were ill-advised to wade into Iraq.

It has long been a bedrock American and British policy in the region to use Iraq as a buttress against the much more dangerous nationalism and expansionism of Iran – hence the British arms-to-Iraq scandal and the original American decision not to invade in 1991. We believed that Iraq was a key deterrent to Iranian expansionism. We also believed that Saddam's secular fascism, repellent as it was, was a check on Shia extremism in Iran and Sunni extremism in Saudi Arabia. Those old policy saws were cavalierly chucked to the winds by the Bush and Blair governments, presumably because of the supposed weakness of the current Iranian regime.

Some American neoconservatives indeed see the invasion of Iraq as a prelude to the overthrow of the Iranian regime. This is mistaken and dangerous almost any way you look at it. Iran's internal power struggle is one between clerical conservatives and moderate reformists, the latter enjoying overwhelming public support, as shown in recent elections. It is a huge jump to believing that young Iranians, however frustrated they are with the conservatism of their elders, would support an American-imposed or -supported solution any more than Iraqis do. To hate Saddam or the mullahs is not to embrace America.

Reformist Iranians want an Iranian solution, albeit a democratic (Iran has evolved the rudiments of democracy) and much more liberal one in its enforcement of Islamic mores. The still powerful Iranian army holds the same views. All too slowly the popular moderates have been gaining ground. For the Americans to intervene would allow the hardline mullahs to portray their opponents as American stooges and crack down hard, or provoke a civil war which could kill tens of thousands, or both. It would be another gamble, another huge throw of the dice which have already landed badly in Iraq, against far larger odds.

The Gulf states, Israel and other countries are rightly deeply concerned about the evidence that Iran is developing a nuclear capability. The obvious reasons are that Iran is seeking to defend itself from a pre-emptive American strike in the short run, and may want to intimidate its much smaller Gulf neighbours in the long run. Acquisition of such a nuclear capacity can best be impeded through American assurances that they have no wish to interfere in Iran, the application of measures by the International Atomic Energy Authority, and pressure from Iran's chief allies, the Russians. Only if Iran goes ahead should military action be considered.

Now back to Iraq. The Iranians have been restraining their allies, the great majority of Iraqi Shias, through the application of intense pressure on what is a very hierarchical clerical movement. The supreme Ayatollah al-Sistani is in fact Iranian, and the assassinated Ayatollah Baqir al-Hakim was prevailed upon by Iran to appoint representatives to the American-nominated governing council. Even after the assassination, presumably by Saddam supporters or Wahhabi-backed Sunni fundamentalists, the Shia mullahs have kept their angry followers in line – in accordance with Iranian pressure.

Why, of all people, are the Iranians being so helpful to the Americans? Because they fear American action against their own country, and because they believe they have a lever to prevent it: the threat to unleash a Shia uprising in Iraq should America intervene in Iran. This arm-wrestling between the Americans and the Iranians is for the moment holding. The problem is that the Iranian-sponsored Iraqi Shia religious leaders may not be able to hold down the discontent of their supporters for ever: they are seething at shortages, the humiliation of the American–British occupation, and the occasional clashes. The longer the Americans stay, the greater their anger is likely to be. The southern radical young cleric Muktada al-Sadr may at any time call his followers onto the streets.

Over to the Saudis. Owing to decades of the West turning a blind eye to the deficiencies of that regime while pocketing lucrative contracts there, the United States is only now becoming aware that the regime is built on a marriage of convenience between pro-Western but corrupt al-Saud princes and anti-Western religious extremists, descendants of the puritan Wahhabi Ikhwan, fanatical warriors who carried out the actual unification of the Arabian peninsula. Al-Qaeda is a kind of advance scouting party for this sect. It is sending probing missions into Iraq with the intention of attacking Americans, radicalizing the country's huge Sunni minority, stirring up the Shia majority against the Americans through assassinations and provocations, and fighting for turf if necessary against the Shias.

Some of these men have even established links with Saddam's loyalists. Saddam's men are largely yesterday's news: their continuing attacks stem from the huge dollar reserves of the Saddam family, which enable them to buy killers in a desperately impoverished country. The Americans, not for the first time, are going for the wrong target.

Hence the growing long-term danger of a Saudi-financed extremist movement fighting for turf with an Iranian-financed one with the Americans and the British, hated by both sides, caught in the middle. Iranian-supported Shias in the Gulf states and Saudi Arabia's oil-rich eastern region could also rise up in such a confrontation. Meanwhile the extremists may have helped themselves to such Iraqi radioactive, chemical and biological material as they could, making the danger of the spread of critical weapons from Iraq into terrorist hands against the West self-fulfilling. The implications of all this for the rest of the Middle East, not to mention the Western countries in which these weapons may be used by terrorist recruits from Iraq, are extremely serious. With its huge commitment of troops in Iraq, America has its hands tied in dealing with terrorism elsewhere and with more dangerous regimes like North Korea. A further danger is of Kurdish secession from such an imploding state, which would inevitably prompt massive Turkish intervention and a war in the north.

Is there anything to be done to arrest this quasi-1914 buildup to a much more dangerous confrontation in the region? Fortunately, yes.

While the component parts of the explosive device are moving together, critical mass has not yet been achieved. Iraqis are an educated, likeable and on the whole unexcitable people and it will take a few more months to reach combustion point.

The American and British governments have to move quickly to acknowledge past mistakes and take remedial action as follows. President Bush's $21 billion civilian reconstruction programme for Iraq is a small start. First, it is necessary to begin the process of readmitting the Iraqi army, equipped with a new British-style code of conduct (it was after all initially a British creation), to its former status and to becoming the front-line police force for the occupation. Second, all but the worst offenders in the civil administration of Iraq and in the former Baath grass roots should be welcomed as allies in the process of national reconstruction, subject to the acceptance of democratic norms and legal methods (which will take time to implement).

Third, the American-appointed governing council should be either scrapped or enlarged to make it representative, and a quick timetable put into place for democratic elections for a constituent assembly followed by a parliament under a complex system of checks and balances while protecting the rights of Kurds, Sunnis and Shias. This would provide an upper chamber for the minorities and a lower one on a one-man-one-vote basis, and ensure a parliamentary government so that no Saddam-style strongman can take over again. This should also avert the danger of a Shia Islamic republic.

On the constitutional front, there is a temptation for the Americans to support a Kurdish-Shia 'deal' over the heads of the previously dominant Sunni minority. This should be resisted. However culpable some Sunnis were in the past, many of the country's best talents are drawn from that community. Any settlement which seeks to exclude a group, or which is based on sectarian or racial lines (other than protecting community rights), risks arousing hatreds of the kind that flared up in Lebanon or Ulster. Iraq has no history of such hatreds and can avoid them. Iraq's new government should be based on the democratically expressed will of all the people. Similarly, the demand of some Kurds for virtual self-government for Kurdistan alone could presage a break-up of the country. Federalism should apply to other administrative units in Iraq as well: the best example might be Spain, where the Basque country and Catalonia enjoy considerable autonomy, along with other regions.

Fourth, to reinforce this, a constitutional monarchy with limited powers should be established to guarantee the unity of the country, the freedoms of the people and the neutrality of the army. Iraq's immensely respected Hashemite dynasty, under the young, modern and energetic Sharif Ali, which was forcibly removed by the 1958 revolution and, because of its descent from the Prophet, revered by Shias, Sunnis and Kurds alike, is the obvious candidate.

Fifth, the American and British occupation forces should then seek to extricate themselves with as much speed and dignity as possible from Iraq, inviting in a multinational force of countries possibly under UN auspices (but the UN is regarded with suspicion by many Iraqis) if necessary merely to do peacekeeping and relief duties, not as an army of occupation; it is the job of Iraqis to police themselves and to govern themselves. There are only a few months to act.

The alternative is a Vietnam-style whirlpool, sucking in neighbouring countries, a terrorist Tet offensive against the American and British forces in Iraq and the spread of global terrorism to an extent so far undreamt of. In Saudi Arabia, the Americans should be looking to persuade the princes to open up the regime to a moderate middle class. In Iran, America should confine itself to invocations to democracy.

Finally, the leaders of Congress, the people and not least the military of the United States should look long and hard at the lessons to be drawn from this salutary experience. In particular they should reflect on the fate of previous empires and consider whether America really has the capacity, resources, stomach and willpower to act as the world's sole policeman over the coming century, or whether it would do better to invite the overwhelming mass of humanity that wants to keep the world at peace, to trade and get on with their normal lives, to share the burden. Any neighbourhood has a few bad guys who need to be controlled; but a neighbourhood in which the policeman has no friends and is himself the chief object of hatred is a dangerous one indeed.

The enormous goodwill and sympathy the United States enjoyed after September 11, 2001, has been dissipated in an astoundingly short space of time by crass actions of reckless adventurism. Now the people of the United States should resolve to return to the original idealism, deployment of force as a last resort and friend-winning ways of the Founding Fathers.

This book is not intended to be in any way alarmist. On the contrary, if the radically new issues at the start of this millennium are addressed, a better age for humanity lies ahead. But those issues need addressing. I wrote *The Return of the Strong* in 1994 to draw attention to what I termed the 'new global disorder', the danger, as I saw it, that with the welcome end of the Cold War, the restraining hand of the superpowers upon their client states had been withdrawn as a result of the collapse of the Soviet bloc and the triumphal disengagement of the United States from the rest of the world.

I pointed to three specific threats: first, that the United States, as sole remaining global superpower, would soon become an object of envy and vilification across the globe; second, that in place of superpower rivalry, a variety of lesser, but lethal and certainly more unstable, security threats would raise their heads ranging from Islamic fundamentalism to terrorism, nuclear proliferation and biological and chemical warfare stockpiles, 'rogue' states, the renewal of nationalist self-assertion among newly industrialized countries and, conversely, the disintegration of some states into warring ethnic, tribal or warlord-led factions, as well as those four grim old horsemen – poverty, hunger, debt and migration; and third, that the globalization of uncontrolled free-market capitalism would inevitably lead to a global anti-capitalist backlash.

The book sparked something of an intellectual controversy. In the *New Statesman* Fred Halliday, Professor of International Relations at the LSE, comparing my theories to those of Francis Fukuyama, Alain Minc and Samuel Huntington, declared flatly that my overall claim 'that the world is a more dangerous place now than it was during the Cold War is, though much repeated, simply untrue'. My view, argued Halliday, was simply 'too bleak'. Another commentator from the left, Will Hutton writing in the *Guardian*, was more charitable, describing the book as 'a brutal and challenging assessment of the post-Cold War era'. He broadly embraced the analysis while taking me to task for 'hovering uneasily between a Conservative anxiety to praise markets and privatisation and a recognition of their instability'. Jan Aart Scholte, in *International Affairs*, thought I was too kind on capitalism.

For the right, Michael Vlahos in the *Times Literary Supplement* denounced my 'fire-and-brimstone pessimism' from the viewpoint of an economic libertarian: 'Harvey's real anxiety is chaos, because chaos means change, the end of the world he has known. All of its comfortable contours, its many pleasures and rewards, are on the chopping block. Harvey hopes to stop change dead in its digital tracks by creating a crisis that will give the Cold War ruling class the clout to leash an economic revolution that can't be stopped.' After this pounding of mixed metaphors it was a relief to be accused of complacency towards the post-Cold War world by Godfrey Hodgson in the *Independent*. Noel Malcolm in the *Sunday Telegraph*, while finding my analysis 'intriguing' and my 'arguments against a new American isolationism unanswerable', took me to task for overstating the impact of global capitalism and for advocating 'collectivist' controls on the latter (specifically by a 'European super-state'). I would defend myself against all these charges, but confess I was delighted to have provoked such a debate.

Alas, the debate has been anything but completed. Six years after the book was published, all three of my central 'fire-and-brimstone' predictions have been fulfilled beyond my worst expectations. September 11 marks the most graphic demonstration yet of the hatred in which the United States is unjustly held by much of the world (as well as the urgency of the Islamic and terrorist problems). Even prior to that, global capitalism had become the target of a disparate but potentially huge worldwide protest movement, especially among the young; and the post-Cold War scene is littered with the wreckage of conflagrations that were allowed to catch and burn on for too long, Bosnia, Rwanda, Chechnya, Algeria, Kosovo, Afghanistan, to name only a few. The list of bigger potential eruptions: India–Pakistan, North Korea–South Korea, North Korea–Japan, China–Taiwan, China–Japan – is almost as daunting.

As Geoffrey Howe, the former British Foreign Secretary, wrote re-cently of *The Return of the Strong*, 'the sad thing is not that [its] diagnosis or prescriptions were inaccurate, but that so little has effec-tively been done to implement any significant part of [its] advice. There seems to be a real shortage of intelligent political leadership in most, if not all, of the leading democracies today.'

In the light of September 11, I decided to reissue the book. Although its central message is unchanged, so much new material and updating has been added as to make it, in effect, a new book. I have modified my arguments to take account of my critics' most valid points, although I feel myself at least partly vindicated by events. If September 11 has at last punched through the complacency of the 'phoney peace' following the collapse of communism, then some real good will have come from that terrible event. Chapter 12 outlines the seven key recommendations for a new global security architecture.

There may be those who, in the aftermath of September 11, will consider my first section on United States foreign policy after the Cold War overly critical. I make no apology other than to acknowledge that the candid friend who says 'I told you so' is only mildly less irritating than those gifted with the wisdom of hindsight! I would only point respectfully to my credentials: all my political and journalistic life I have been a passionate, although not uncritical, supporter of the United States and its foreign policy.

When I first joined the staff of *The Economist* in 1974, it was apparent that the Vietnam War was lost, and with significant reservations I respected the skill with which the Nixon administration succeeded in extracting the United States from its commitment, as well as in playing the China card that defused the potentially disastrous global consequences of America's defeat. I supported Henry Kissinger's policy of damage limitation, which continued under President Ford (while disagreeing with some over-the-top extensions of that policy, particularly in Latin America and with regard to Italy). While often critical of the Carter presidency, I thought his injection of human rights into the global agenda was hugely positive, particularly its application to the Helsinki accords, which helped to bring about the downfall of the Soviet Union.

After allowing for some serious mistakes, I was on the whole a supporter of United States policy towards Central America and was from the beginning deeply sceptical about the democratic intent and likely success of the Sandinista revolution in Nicaragua. I was, however, heavily critical of American policy towards global debt. I was an unabashed admirer of President Reagan's superbly managed policy towards the Soviet Union which, I believe, abruptly brought to an end a Cold War that could have taken decades to unwind.

Apprehension about the course of American foreign policy set in under Reagan's Republican successor, George Bush, who in my opinion singularly failed to grasp the historical opportunities on offer after the fall of the Berlin Wall, and whose initial leadership in the Gulf War fizzled out with its disastrous dénouement, 'snatching defeat from the jaws of victory'. America's mistakes in Bosnia also began at this time.

Outright disillusion set in under President Bill Clinton, who arguably presided over America's worst foreign policy era since that of Calvin Coolidge in the 1920s. This was marked by the failure to intervene in Bosnia until appalling carnage had occurred, the decision to stay out of Rwanda, where genocide arguably could have been avoided, the complete absence of long-term strategic thinking, band-aid diplomacy in the Middle East and the missed opportunity for dealing with Osama bin Laden and the al-Qaeda terrorist network. Only towards the middle of Clinton's second term did any improvement take place: he should not be denied the sincerity of his efforts to defuse the Middle East and Ulster conflicts, although these met with half-success.

The purpose of this litany is not self-justification; I was often wrong in my judgements. It is to demonstrate that as a staff correspondent on *The Economist* and the London *Daily Telegraph* (both of them staunchly pro-American newspapers), and a former Conservative member of the House of Commons Foreign Affairs Committee, I have a track record of more than a quarter of a century of continuous support for and admiration of the United States, which I believe rescued Western Europe during the Second World War and saved it from tyranny in the Cold War. Equally, I consider it the duty of America's friends to point out when that great country has gone astray, and to seek to avert serious mishaps which could lead to disaster for the United States and the world. This is not a rallying cry against the Americans; it is a call for the United States to re-embrace the enlightened, altruistic and simultaneously self-interested foreign policy that characterized the nearly half-century between 1941 and 1989.

Meanwhile, the introduction I gave to the 1995 edition seems almost as pertinent now as then. I wrote that at the close of the nineteenth century more self-confidence and exuberance emanated from the capital of the world's largest empire, London, than at any time in history. The industrial world, while far from free of war, appeared more tranquil than at any time for centuries. The global economy was in a state of sustained expansion, with Britain's Industrial Revolution being imitated in the United States, Germany, France and, to a lesser extent, Russia. Capitalism was at its zenith, bestriding the major economies and their colonies. The volume of international trade had multiplied twenty-five times in a hundred years. It was an era of growth, progress and self-reliance.

The great European wars had washed past earlier in the century; the American Civil War was over. It was possible to believe in a new world order where civilization would gradually clothe the less developed parts of the world in peace and material advance. While Britain began to indulge in social reform to cushion the excesses of capitalism, the United States was experiencing the first huge benefits of railways, mass production and thrusting entrepreneurship. When the twentieth century began, there was little reason to fear the future. As the strait-laced energy of the Victorian age mellowed into the comfortable respectability of the Edwardian, security, prosperity and progress seemed assured.

Within two decades the whole booming, peaceful, bourgeois scene was transformed as the wave of prosperity was dashed on to the jagged rocks of nationalism and, a little later, communism. The First World War plunged Europe into an almost entirely futile slaughter of nationalist ambition and destroyed the old order.

Meanwhile communism seized control in Russia in 1917, and threatened to spread across much of the globe. The second great chapter of the twentieth century had begun. The capitalist world went on an economic roller coaster, from post-war recession to boom in the 1920s to protracted recession in the 1930s, dazing millions of people into seeking extremist solutions. As a reaction against the threat of socialism in Europe, but also against the coldly impersonal forces of capitalism plunging the globe into economic tumult, Fascism took power in Italy in 1922, Nazism in Germany in 1933 and Francoism in Spain in 1939. In the Far East, an increasingly militarist Japan embarked on a policy of imperialist expansionism that culminated in war with China and, eventually, America and Britain.

In Europe, German expansionism ignited war with France, Britain and eventually Russia, drawing in the United States. The three decades between 1914 and 1945 were times of trouble, marked by some of the most unstable political and economic conditions the world has ever known. The twin ogres of nationalism and communism bestrode continents, putting millions to the sword and enslaving hundreds of millions. While nationalism was to some extent self-generating, communism arose almost entirely out of extreme economic conditions that had been neither understood nor addressed.

But they had a common source: the first wave of 'globalization' in the late nineteenth century, in which impersonal international capitalism was seen as a threat to the assertive nation state by militarists, Fascists and Nazis, and as an oppressor of the global poor by socialists and communists. The resemblance to today's world is not coincidental. History does repeat itself, albeit in the context of new terminologies, technologies and ideological lexicons.

After the defeat of Germany, Italy and Japan, two global superpowers – the United States and the Soviet Union – were left straddling the ruins of post-war Europe. Almost by historical accident, the third chapter of the twentieth century began. The world settled into a gridlock where East and West confronted each other under threat of nuclear annihilation, each with client states over which they exerted some control. For the first time since the late nineteenth century a kind of global political and economic order and an unprecedented surge of prosperity and development were restored. Between 1945 and 1990 the volume of trade increased some twelve times while world output jumped six times.

In place of world war there were frequent confrontations, often by proxy, in the developing world. The first was Korea in the early 1950s, where the superpowers drew back from the brink of world war. The superpowers circled each other angrily over Berlin in 1948, Hungary in 1956, Cuba in 1961, Indo-China throughout the 1960s and early 1970s, Czechoslovakia in 1968, Angola and Ethiopia in the mid-1970s, Afghanistan and Central America in the 1980s, and successive Middle Eastern crises. But the unspoken rules of the game kept them from conflict.

Between 1987 and 1991 the Soviet empire fractured spectacularly, and the triumph of good over evil seemed complete. Poland, Czechoslovakia, Hungary, East Germany, Bulgaria and Romania fell like skittles as it became apparent that the Soviet Union would no longer shore up their unpopular bureau-dictatorships. The Baltic republics, the Ukraine and the southern republics broke away from the weakening embrace of Russia. The Soviet system was exposed for the bureaucratic, incompetent, authoritarian mastodon that it was. To some, Western liberal democracy and free-market values reigned supreme. The 'end of history' had arrived.

In fact it was the end of the struggle between rival ideologies and the beginning of the fourth and last chapter of twentieth-century history (the first of the twenty-first century). For within months the hounds of ethnic nationalism were unleashed again, vigorously, destructively and murderously; and global capitalism was displaying the same kind of insensitivity towards ordinary people as at the beginning of the last century.

As the new millennium dawns, the same seeds of global disorder, even anarchy, that grew into the years 1914–45 are being sown. Racialism and ethnic nationalism are already on the rampage on a small scale. Bigger powers show signs of going their own way. America is disengaging from Europe and vice versa, Germany and Japan are becoming more politically assertive and China is rearming.

Security challenges are springing up across the world: Iraq, Iran, North Korea, Pakistan–India. Global chaos is entirely avoidable, through the kind of longsighted security policies that kept the post-1950 era from holocaust, and the economic imagination and vigour that led to a half-century of unprecedented growth.

On global strategy, we face a dangerous period of lowered guards and an escalating possibility of conflict. As Eugene Rostow has written: 'in the short term the Soviet collapse, like the fall of any empire in history, has radically destabilised world politics'. A new era of petty, and not-so-petty, nationalisms among newly industrialized countries has begun. Economically, global capitalism may be at a stage not far different from that of national capitalism at the end of the last century: its authoritarian nature, disregard for national and personal sensitivities, enormous power and – as the world debt crisis in the 1980s showed – incompetence could give rise to a perilous reaction: the birth of a new communism.

The old communism collapsed because it was imbued with the same faults on an even bigger scale as the old capitalism. The modern capitalist corporation more nearly resembles the communist corporation than it would like to think, and is in danger of going the same way. Communism, a truly monstrous system, was created by the inhumanity of early capitalism. An equally deformed global changeling could be born of today's capitalist failings. Global capitalism shows the same tendency to escape international control that it did in the 1920s and the 1930s.

The major powers at the end of the millennium, as Cold War memories faded, exuded the same complacency and self-congratulation as at the end of the nineteenth century. The twin spectres of extreme nationalism and communism can be discerned again. Unless action is taken as the warm glow of sunset on the twentieth century is replaced by the pale dawn light of the twenty-first, we will gaze towards the same horizon of global horrors as our great-grandfathers, this time through a nuclear haze. The world is a much more dangerous place than it has been for nearly half a century.

PART I

MEGAPOWER

CHAPTER I

PARADISE LOST: NINE-ELEVEN

S ince September 11, 2001, the thorns of conflict have spread alarmingly across the world. Iraq has been accused of seeking to develop nuclear weapons, while North Korea has admitted doing so and Iran may be going down the same road. Two existing nuclear powers, India and Pakistan, have nearly gone to war. Saudi Arabia and Pakistan, two key if authoritarian Western allies, are being undermined from within by Islamic fundamentalists. Iraq has been invaded. This represents no fewer than four radical departures for the world we live in.

Primarily, it is an act of American assertion, albeit buttressed by the sanction of the world community represented in the UN. It represents a statement by the world's only megapower that it can, and will, enforce its concept of international law anywhere in the world if it feels that global peace or its interests are threatened. It is a demonstration of power, aimed in this case at a potential nuclear proliferator, but potentially at a state harbouring terrorists, or contemplating aggression, or permitting major criminal activity such as drugs trafficking. America is conveying a message: don't tangle with us, we have the power and we will use it, whenever and whatever, with or without the support of our friends. If we can take out a major offender like Iraq, we can make our will felt almost anywhere in the world.

Second, the pressure is as much punitive as intended to stop Iraq arming itself with weapons of mass destruction. It is being punished for past misdeeds – its taunting the international community, its failure to change regime, the aggression against Kuwait, its internal atrocities against the Kurds and its Shia population in the south.

Third, it is a first exercise of America's new doctrine of pre-emptive defence – we will go to you before you come to us – the most far-reaching change in international strategy since the doctrines of deterrence and national self-defence, now superseded.

Fourth, it is a formal declaration of a borderless world. Respect for national sovereignty is no longer the guiding principle of the relationship be-tween states, where the world community has the right to intervene only if one country attacks another. We, the United States is saying, have the right to intervene overwhelmingly on behalf of the world community (whether or not other members of it agree), if we believe somebody's actions are harmful to the world, as we define this. Our overwhelming military power, coupled with our sense of rightness, endows us with the moral authority.

All of this overturns centuries of balance-of-power politics and pains-taking international legal construction. There are huge immediate risks involved and it could, in the view of America's friends, including myself, prove highly counter-productive in the long run. But it does reflect the reality of the world at the dawn of the twenty-first century – a world in which a single unprecedentedly powerful democratic state confronts a host of smaller but potentially dangerous challengers. On the one hand, it shines a great beam of hope – that the new world disorder into which the world had been slipping while America looked the other way in the nearly decade and a half since the end of the Cold War is coming to an end. On the other hand, it sends a shiver of fear – that the global policeman may use his power as much to promote its own interests as to keep order, and that the world may one day unite in simmering resent-ment against its overmighty enforcer.

This book is about this seismic change in our world, and about the ways in which the global giant can hope to keep order in a field teeming with potential enemies: by showing steely resolve when necessary; but also by offering to make friends and share its decision-making with the great majority; and by returning to simple human values that the world's 6 billion people can accept and respect.

The First and Second World Wars were both declared by defined enemies on definite dates: 4 August 1914 and 3 September 1939. The Cold War (the Third World War) by contrast had a much more elusive beginning. Did it start when the communists seized power in Czechoslovakia on 25 February 1948, in violation of the Yalta agreement? Or with President Truman's defiant speech to Congress on 17 March? Or with the Berlin

Blockade of 24 June? Or with North Korea's invasion of South Korea on 25 June 1950? The Cold War was to prove a shadowy conflict, not a matter of huge armies confronting one another (except in a few instances like Korea and Vietnam), but one of flare-ups, revolutions, coups, the manipulation of pawns, proxy wars, intelligence and counter-intelligence, nuclear bluff and counter-bluff.

A Fourth World War will be the same, only more so. We may not know it is under way until some time after it has started. It did not begin on September 11, 2001, even though the number of people killed from terrorist attacks between 1990 and 1996 was some 50,000 – double as many as in the whole of the previous fourteen years – and some thirty local armed conflicts rage unchecked today around the world. World war has to be on a much larger, more continuous and more dangerous scale, threatening the survival of whole nations and systems, to qualify.

Some of the following will have to feature: a serious escalation in terrorist activity, placing Western societies under constant threat and requiring countermeasures that erode fundamental liberties, as well as the more frequent use of civilian targets in existing conflicts around the world; an escalation in the current edgy relations between the West and some Arab countries to a more general confrontation with Islam; a serious interruption in oil supplies from the Middle East, damaging the world economy.

Other possibilities include a spread in the disintegration of states like the Congo and those in the Horn of Africa, the southern former Soviet republics and Afghanistan, or further strife in the Balkans; intensified Arab–Israeli confrontation following the invasion of Iraq which could trigger a chain reaction of hostility towards the West, reinforce hostile regimes like Syria, Libya and Iran, so resulting in the fall of pro-Western regimes, in particular Saudi Arabia and the Gulf sheikhdoms, and also endanger Egypt, Jordan, Tunisia, Algeria and Morocco; a hardening of the regime in Iran which could send new waves of Shia terrorism and Islamic fundamentalism across the Middle East; a breakdown in negotiations with North Korea which could result in a nuclear or large conventional attack on the South and would initially sweep all before it, requiring a massive commitment of American troops and bombing to stop it. It would be no coincidence if some of these things happened simultaneously: when American forces are overstretched in one theatre, there is a strong temptation for adversaries in another to strike.

There are further dangers: Libyan and Sudanese re-engagement in large-scale destabilization of neighbouring states; the use of nuclear weapons in a confrontation between India and Pakistan, China and

Taiwan, or Japan and China; the spread of nuclear capability to Iraq, Iran, North Korea or Libya; and in Latin America a major offensive against old-fashioned Marxist guerrillas allied with drugs traffickers could lead the United States into a quagmire.

While coping with these multiple choices the United States might find itself bereft of allies, if Europe remains divided, inward-looking and deeply resentful of American megapowerdom. To round off the picture, across the globe and within America itself, anti-capitalist, anti-globalization and anti-American revolutionary movements could turn the streets into battlegrounds.

Fortunately, all of this is still an apocalyptic nightmare. September 11 occurred and some of these things are happening, but most of the world is at peace, there is probably greater prosperity than ever before, the global economy for the most part has survived last year's shocks, most of the Islamic world remains friendly to the West, oil prices bounce about within just reasonable limits, and Pakistan has not gone to war with India, nor China with Taiwan.

There is no new world war yet, nor need there ever be one, but if some of the things described above *do* happen, mankind's fourth great global conflict may well have begun. Doubtless historians then will earnestly debate whether to call it the War of Multiple Challenges, or the Hydra War (after the monster of many heads that Hercules fought in ancient Greece), and doubtless they will argue as to when exactly it started. But the essential point is that it need not start. This book attempts to set out how an endemic state of global conflict might be prevented.

The evil symbolism of the terrorist attacks on the World Trade Center and the Pentagon was of a cruelty so pure as to astonish even, it appears, the instigators themselves. Turning harmless passenger aircraft into lethal missiles, the terrorists wiped the most potent symbol of American capitalism in the heart of New York's financial district off the face of the earth, while the diamond-shaped core of American military might was badly damaged, and the strongest air defence system in the world powerless to stop it.

The diabolical nature of the attacks carried out in the name of a 'merciful' god scarred all those alive and cognizant on September 11. The conscription of innocent passengers with many minutes to contemplate their own horrific approaching deaths, the incineration of office workers going about humdrum early morning tasks, the rain of people preferring to jump to death rather than be incinerated, the awesome absolutes of collapsing towers engulfing brave volunteers who had rushed to the scene – all seared themselves on the mind more than previous disasters or wartime sufferings that were on a far larger scale. It was also the first major act of war on American continental soil since the Civil War, and the first by a foreign 'aggressor' since the war of 1812. Truly, there was a sense of paradise lost, of innocence irreparably violated, under the most gruesome circumstances imaginable.

Yet the peculiar horror of the September 11 attacks should not obscure the need to put them into perspective, or to understand precisely what they were. Were they, as one American senator promptly commented, a new Pearl Harbor? Were they the first act of a new war, as President Bush's declaration of his own 'war against terrorism' immediately implied? Were they the worst single act of terrorism in history, the worst atrocity so far inflicted upon innocent civilians? What did the attacks really represent: just a single action by a group of astonishingly well-organized fanatics, or did they say something much deeper about America's relationship with the rest of the world? To ask and answer these questions coolly is essential to formulating the proper responses and to restoring a sense of proportion.

To answer Senator Chuck Hagel first, who saw in September 11 a new Pearl Harbor – an event which was to plunge America into nearly four years of global warfare involving hundreds of thousands of its troops and which caused tens of thousands of American casualties, creating a radically altered world that placed America firmly on the road to superpowerdom for the second half of the twentieth century. By some eerie coincidence, as the number of deaths on September 11 inched slowly downwards from the initial overblown estimates of around 7,000 to under 3,000, the figure has almost come to rest level with that of the number of Americans killed at Pearl Harbor.

That aside, to pose the question is instantly to recognize its absurdity. Pearl Harbor was a massive military attack against sovereign US territory by a major power threatening to dominate eastern Asia – and was in any case only one of a series of calculated and murderous acts of aggression across half the continent of Asia. September 11 was the act of a handful of desperate men without state backing, operating on a shoestring budget and taking advantage of virtually non-existent security to slaughter unprotected civilians. The only real parallel is as a potential 'wake-up call' for America's sluggish foreign-policy makers of a kind similar to the jolt Pearl Harbor provided to a country mired in two decades of isolationism.

Initial reactions are not encouraging. While the United States has certainly replied with speed, overwhelming force and precision against the perpetrators of the September 11 atrocity, a wholesale re-evaluation of America's post-Cold War foreign policy seems as distant as ever. The war in Afghanistan, as it has been carried out in practice, marks little departure from the type of limited campaign that America has prosecuted in recent years in places like Kosovo (as noted in the introduction, the invasion of Iraq was different). When the distinguished British military historian and strategist Sir Michael Howard lamented that the declaration of war against the terrorists was according them a legitimacy they did not possess, he was missing the point. The declaration was legalistic and rhetorical, not real.

To pass to question three: quite possibly September 11 was the worst single terrorist attack in modern history, if we define terrorism (as this book will), to mean an unprovoked attack against civilian non-combatants away from any theatre of war by men or women not working for a power openly at war with the victims' country. (A great deal of harm comes from looser definitions of terrorism: using the above definition a terrorist can never be a 'freedom fighter' and political motives cannot validate an act of terrorism.) Certainly the numbers eclipse any single episode in, for example, the long-running campaign of terrorist attacks by the Irish Republican Army in Britain (although more have died violently in total since the Troubles began, in a country with a quarter of the population of the United States, than in the Twin Towers attack), Eta in Spain, attacks by Chechen separatists in Russia and Tamil terrorists in Sri Lanka, to name only a few.

If terrorism is enlarged beyond this strict definition (as the terrorists themselves, in their perversity, would wish, thus reclassifying their innocent victims as 'collateral damage', which is inevitable in war, or civilians caught up in a war for the greater good) to the targeting of civilians in war or for a political cause, the numbers killed on September 11 become a drop in the ocean besides the tens of thousands of civilians killed in the bombing of Dresden, the 100,000 killed in the firebombing of Tokyo or the 300,000 eventual victims of the atomic attacks on Hiroshima and Nagasaki, let alone the tens of millions of civilians killed by the totalitarian regimes of Russia, China, Nazi Germany and imperial Japan during the last century.

Back in the present day, however unspeakable the evil and suffering caused by September 11, sympathy may be tempered a little in many Third World countries where thousands of people die in natural disasters every few years without undue anguish on the part of the rest of the world. None of this is to diminish the suffering and shock represented by the attacks, yet perspective suggests that September 11 was not quite as unique, overwhelming and seismic an event as at first appeared. But, yes, it was the worst single act of global terrorism in the world to date, on the narrower, correct definition of the term.

Yet something of great international significance did happen on September 11, something that was indeed earth-changing in its implications and consequences. The sudden, tragically devastating spear thrust at the commercial and military heart of America by a handful of religious (although technologically educated) fanatics graphically demonstrated that the continental United States, for all its two-ocean barriers against the rest of the world, is no more insulated from its tragedies and struggles in an era of mass communication than it is from global economic shocks. The phenomenon of economic globalization is now well known. September 11 represented the 'globalization of politics'. Many of those who argued that with the globalization of free-market economics, politics would become all but redundant, have to reconsider. The political actions of a few men can still have a colossal economic impact – never mind the ability of all-out war to devastate the global economy for generations.

The globalization of politics is not new. Communism was a global phenomenon, as was nationalist-militarist aggression during the 1930s, but the lessons of both had been largely forgotten in recent years. Almost no one had calculated how an intensification of economic globalization would be followed by greater political globalization after a time-lag resulting in this case in a strike into the seemingly impregnable American mainland using such commonplace 'weapons' as civilian jet aircraft, computers, the Internet, faxes.

This leads to the second seismic significance of the attacks on New York and Washington. The immediate, understandable reaction of the United States has been to hit back at the perpetrators of the crime and those who harbour them. But longer-term reflection demands three things: an understanding of how the only superpower relates to, and is perceived by, non-Americans, who outnumber Americans by over 20:1 and occupy nearly twenty times as much territory around the world; calm consideration of whether the business of that superpower is merely to look to its own immediate interests, or whether it has a wider duty to try and make the world a more peaceful and prosperous place (and thereby also serve its own long-term interests); and careful analysis of how its commercial relations with the rest of the world might be managed to serve the mutual, enlightened self-interest of both and reduce the dangers of a political backlash which could be so destructive to the US's economic interests.

All three, in fact, became concerns immediately after the fall of communism during the milestone year of 1989. What happened on September 11 was that these challenges at last, and in the most horrific way possible, caught up with the United States after twelve years of phoney peace.

On a historical Richter scale, September 11 was no Pearl Harbor. Rather it was the first terrible warning of things to come, the first step along the path that leads to global conflict – in fact an echo, in a very different manner, of the Japanese occupation of Manchuria, which also started in September (18) exactly seventy years before. That unprovoked attack was, in retrospect, a clear signpost to the way the world was going over the coming decade.

Similarly, September 11 more visibly, because closer to home, is a clear indication that much worse is to come if the United States and its allies fail to learn the necessary lessons and apply them. As in 1931, there have already been a dozen tragic indicators around the world of the dangers, and, as then, a decade has already been lost. But the situation by the beginning of the 1930s was by no means irretrievable, although time was running short; nor is it now. The Second World War began two decades after the First, and the Third (Cold) only a couple of years after the Second. However, unless the right lessons are learnt from September 11, and evasive action is taken now, we may not even have a decade at our disposal.

There are three things that are completely different about the geopolitics and economics of the world today than anything in past human experience. The first is the overwhelming, cascading, all-embracing reality of American power: no power in human history has enjoyed such unchallenged global dominance, and this creates entirely new problems of managing power and success, which are just as difficult as managing failure, and which have far wider consequences. It is also vital for America not to equate this colossal power with omnipotence, which of course it does not have (more than three decades of trying to broker a Middle East peace settlement provides a clear indication of the limits of its power).

The second is the integration of the world community. Information reaches the other side of the world at almost the speed of light. Decisions involving billions of pounds can be communicated across the globe at the touch of an electronic keyboard. Humans can travel from one hemisphere to another faster than the speed of sound. Conference calls link decision-makers thousands of miles from each other. Hundreds of millions of computers talk to each other every day from Tierra del Fuego to Kamchatka, from Cape Town to Calgary. An economic storm in Buenos Aires affects shares in Berlin. A political crisis in Kabul shakes decision-makers in the White House in Washington. Culturally, *Sex in the City* is watched in Hong Kong as well as New York, while Kung Fu movies are appreciated in New York as well as Hong Kong. The world is interconnected as never before.

Third, the spread of technology and the growing wealth of many new nations has resulted in the simultaneous emergence of a host of new middle-ranking military political and economic powers across the world. Where only twenty-five years ago the world was basically divided between two superpowers, a small number of rich, middle-ranking European powers and Japan, and the rest, now it is a vastly more intricate quiltwork. There are dozens, if not scores, of countries capable of throwing their military weight about in their region, if not the world, many of them at very different stages of political development – some burgeoning mature democracies, many of them having shot to riches and serious military power within the space of a generation or two and still retaining the basic political instincts that have governed them for centuries, lagging far behind their economic evolution. All these factors are profoundly destabilizing and immensely complex, making the world a more difficult place to manage than in the clear us-versus-them confrontation of the Cold War, and calling accordingly for much more sophisticated systems of crisis management and diplomacy today.

If the United States and its allies among the democratic countries fail to respond, a war based on prolonged global disorder is indeed in prospect. It will be unlike any that has occurred before. It will not be a general global conflict between major powers. Rather it will be one of constant friction between middle-ranking powers, occasionally flaring into open conflict involving huge numbers of casualties, and even possible nuclear exchanges. The futile Iran-Iraq War, in the dying days of the Cold War, set the scene. There will be sporadic, murderous terrorist attacks on a potentially huge scale; ethnic and nationalist clashes sometimes leading to genocide; periodic economic crises, social discontent, and a growing anticapitalist backlash; a single, hugely powerful, world policeman, distrusted and envied in much of the world, occasionally intervening where its interests are most seriously threatened, but unable to keep the general peace, then retreating back to the fort. The prospect is altogether too grim and antediluvian a state of nature for responsible powers to permit it to happen.

The principal security recommendations in this book are outlined in detail in Part II, Chapter 12. They are:

1. Recognition of the overwhelming position of the United States as underpinning the world's security.
2. A new security relationship between the United States and Europe (including possibly Russia) and Japan.
3. Reaching out for the support of the four-fifths of nations outside this grouping that also seek security and freedom.
4. Reform of the UN to permit it to play a full role in authorizing international peacekeeping.
5. Reform of Nato to enable it to become the enforcement arm of the international community.
6. Establishment of a structure of regional security alliances across the globe.
7. Creating an early warning system for potential global flash-points.

The principal economic recommendations are in Part III. They can be summarized as:

1. The regulation of the global economy through co-operation between the three economic superstates of the next few decades – North America, Europe and Japan – in co-operation with regional groupings from the rest of the world.
2. A co-ordinated 'Marshall Plan' for the three-quarters of the developing world so far untouched by globalization.
3. Reform from within of the modern corporation.

CHAPTER 2

THE UNITED STATES OF THE WORLD

Any first-time visitor to Washington DC knows that he or she is calling in on the capital of the free world. A capital where government is balanced evenly between the executive, legislature and judiciary, where freedom of speech and the rule of law are enshrined in a constitution that carefully protects the rights of the individual and the relationship between central and state governments. Yet when I first arrived in the 1970s I was struck by the similarity with a city I knew well: the ruins of Ancient Rome. There are the same self-assertive pillars and domes best exemplified by the Lincoln Memorial and the Capitol Building (named after the Roman original), a Roman-style Senate and popular assembly (the House of Representatives), the same wide triumphal boulevards laid out in straight lines, the same criss-cross grid of symmetrical streets dividing blocks, even the same penchant for Egyptian-style needles and luxurious, if deceptively modest, suburban villas housing the powerful, epitomized by the White House itself. The ubiquitous white, and often marble, American public buildings complete the impression.

All this seemed troublingly ironic: for Rome in its glory had become an empire, and did not the United States pride itself on being the antithesis to empire? Indeed, it prided itself on being the slayer of the European colonial empires that a century ago dominated the planet. The more troubling question still was whether a country of such colossal global reach as the United States could be described as anything other than an empire. Yet is not American power and world domination much exaggerated by outsiders, a paranoid construct of envious countries conscious of their own faded glories and current limitations?

For the answer to this, it is necessary to turn to an eminent American, Raymond Seitz, a former ambassador to Britain and the only state department official so qualified that he beat the customary political nominees to the post. Thoughtfully, eloquently and by no means uncritically, he spoke of the reality of American power at the Churchill Lecture in Guildhall, London, in November 1999.

The United States has accumulated a magnitude of power without precedent in the twentieth century. To find a comparison, you would probably have to look to the British Empire in the nineteenth century, but in terms of sheer, concentrated power you could argue that you have to go all the way back to Rome to identify a source of such commanding sway, so great is American power today.

There is, for example, much more going on in the American economy now than all the breathless, daily speculations about share prices and interest rates. With a dip or two along the way, the United States has been growing steadily for the last twenty years and the value of our remarkably productive economy is fast approaching $9 trillion. But this isn't the important point.

Behind the statistics, a fundamental metamorphosis is taking place, a re-making of how the American economy works. We all read about the Information Revolution, but in America it is tangible and intrinsic and real. There are more personal computers in the United States than in all of the rest of the world combined, and if you look at a map of internet traffic, the pulsating switch is in America. Young people today, full of imagination and energy, are flooding into this adventuresome, profoundly democratic cyberfrontier. We have already become a channel-surfing, hot-linking, down-loading, internetting, megabyting society.

The accelerating pace of change is so rapid and exponential that no one really knows where it's headed. But one thing is sure: it is transforming everything we do. I can't tell whether this remarkable economy is a new paradigm, as some economists claim, and information technology is hardly an American monopoly. But I don't think it is too outlandish to say that the economic future of the world revolves around what is happening today in America.

Beyond the economy – and partly because of it – American military power today is unassailable. This is true in both nuclear and conventional capability, and if nothing else Kosovo proved that the United States now plays in a military league of its own. In strictly military terms the exercise of NATO power was astonishing, and largely American. Moreover, it seems the United States has learned to conduct a kind of stand-off techno-war which is designed to be virtually risk-free, provided we apply that power against a target which is little able to resist it. I was most struck by the use of the B-2 bomber – at a billion dollars a copy, incidentally – taking off from its base in Missouri, flying 5,000 miles to release its ordinance over Belgrade and then returning to base in time for dinner. Now, it seems, we Americans can go to war without ever leaving home. However one assesses this military prowess, it remains unrivalled in today's world and virtually unique.

Beyond the economic and military, American cultural influence, broadly defined, is almost too obvious to describe: movies, television, pop music, gimmicks and gizmos, fast-food, fashions and fads. This pervasive American influence on the simple pace of daily life everywhere is frequently decried. American popular culture is nonetheless exuberant and contagious, especially for the young, and I was struck by an example the other day at Gatwick Airport when I was waiting in a queue at immigration.

I glanced over my shoulder and saw a gaggle of teenagers tumbling along the broad corridor. They were dressed according to the generally accepted uniform of youth: colourful sweatshirts emblazoned with The University of Something or Other; baseball caps turned backwards in good old home-boy fashion; baggy trousers; unlaced Nike look-alikes; and back-packs. Oh, I said to myself, I wonder where these kids are from – Chicago? Dallas? No. Bucharest.

And finally, there is an ideological component to this American accumulation of power. The end of the Cold War meant that the free-market world doubled in size almost overnight. And at roughly the same time, developed nations started to release into the private sector critical parts of their own economies, such as telecommunications or transportation or energy.

There are indisputably different kinds of capitalism, and one size will never fit all. But freer markets do mean freer societies. This broad de-nationalization of the world's economies and their easy integration through electronics has created a new economic world more congenial to American thinking than we have ever known before.

And attached to this, naturally, the concepts of democracy and freedom and universal human rights are widely accepted as the standards by which governments are to be judged, and however imperfectly we may practise these values at home, the American expectation is to look at the world and see a clouded version of our own image.

Just a glance at these measurements of power – the economic, military, cultural and ideological – makes me conclude that it is incorrect to call the United States a superpower. The United States is a super-duper power.

In the natural progression of history, such huge, disproportionate power in the world would produce an equal and countervailing power. This may happen eventually, but there is now no state or plausible combination of states that seems capable of seriously challenging American predominance. The proponents of balance-of-power theory will have an awkward time in the next decades.

It is hard to quarrel with his view. With 1.4 million troops, four major fleets, global air power including airlift capability, rapid reaction projection, a nearly total domination of both the military and peaceful uses of space, and a military budget as big as those of all its allies put together, American dominance is actually more absolute, and extends over a much wider global canvas, than that of the Roman Empire.

America's strength cannot, of course, be measured by military means alone, or even primarily. After decades of warnings from eminent academics about the inevitable decline of great powers, America during the 1990s exhibited a truly awesome economic strength, its GDP reaching the $10 trillion target after 107 months of unbroken economic expansion, a record, its share of total world economic output rising from a quarter to a colossal 30 per cent. The United States economy is bigger than those of Japan, Germany and France, the three next biggest, combined. In the cutting-edge industries for future growth, in particular microprocessors, software and the Internet, the Americans have left the competition, particularly high-tech Japan, standing. The latter, once touted as America's most dangerous competitor, has fallen a long way behind.

The European Union as a whole has an economy comparable to that of the United States, and is steadily progressing towards greater integration. But in terms of growth, cutting-edge technology and most key economic indicators, it continues to lag behind, although this state of affairs may not continue indefinitely. Economic integration remains a long way behind that within the United States.

In political and military clout, of course, both the European Union and Japan are several laps behind. While America is thus way out ahead of even its own free-market partners, its old communist rivals have been left standing, with former 'superpower' Russia and burgeoning 'superpower' China between them possessing an economy around one-sixth of the American. This author would venture to predict with confidence that, although China has bounded forward, forecasts of it eventually catching up with America are even further fetched than the old ones about Japan and Russia.

American military power, far from diminishing, is growing by leaps and bounds. While European defence budgets have been cut since the end of the Cold War, with only Britain and France spending more than 2 per cent of their GDP, the American defence budget is more than 3 per cent of a much larger GDP.

Early in 2002, President Bush announced an increase of $48 billion in military spending – a whopping 15 per cent rise, taking it to nearly $380 billion, only a little less than the Cold War record, with further increases planned to take the total to more than $450 billion by 2007 – more than 10 per cent higher than during the Cold War. A further $37 billion extra is to be spent on 'homeland security' – civil defence, including $11 billion on precautions against biological warfare attacks.

Priority will be given to spending on precision weapons, surveillance drones, and high-tech equipment for ground troops, in particular special forces, airlift capacity and missile defence. Even allowing for bureaucratic inefficiency (some 70 per cent of American defence spending goes on overheads and infrastructure), these are staggering figures, amounting to more than the GDP of a medium-sized country. Next year's total will be eight times as much as Russia spends on defence, nineteen times as much as China officially does (although the real figure is probably closer to six times as much), nine times as much as Japan, more than ten times as much as Britain, fifteen times as much as France and sixteen times as much as Germany or around the same as the whole lot put together (even allowing for China's underreporting of its spending).

This year's increase alone is almost equivalent to the combined defence budgets of Britain, Canada, Belgium and Greece. The United States spends around $27,000 on research and development for each member of its armed forces, compared with a European average of $7,000. The Americans will spend five times as much on equipment next year as

Britain. The United States has a total manpower of 1.4 million – nearly seven times more than Britain.

The Secretary-General of Nato, Lord Robertson, seems justified in warning that the other members of the alliance look like 'a military pygmy' compared with the United States. As the American Defense Secretary Donald Rumsfeld put it, 'We're going to find it very, very difficult to work with some of these countries.' In key areas such as precision weaponry and long-range airlift, the Americans have a virtual monopoly. Small wonder they have been reluctant to work alongside allies during the Afghan war.

American use of high-tech weaponry has improved dramatically in Afghanistan, as compared with even the Kosovo war. Special forces are able to communicate target co-ordinates with digital equipment to long-range B-52 and B-2 bombers. Such aircraft, capable of carrying huge payloads in missions which can thus be restricted to just a couple of aircraft, are equipped with Joint Direct Attack Munitions (JDAMs) fitted with satellite guidance systems and directional fins which can be dropped within twenty minutes of a target being spotted.

Unmanned drones meanwhile can be pointed to seek out targets and fire missiles at them from any direction, which make them much less easy to intercept than more predictable ground-hugging cruise missiles. Some 70 per cent of the bombs dropped in the Afghan campaign were precision-guided, compared to 30 per cent in Kosovo and 10 per cent in the Gulf War. The drones can hover for twenty-four hours over a target, too high to be seen or heard, using high resolution and video cameras to pinpoint targets, then firing Hellfire missiles and landing on short airstrips. They are expensive (at around $3 million apiece) and have a fairly high accident rate, but pilots are not endangered. In November 2002, the killing of a senior al-Qaeda leader and his entourage by a 25-foot-long, 45-foot-wide Predator robot 'drone' armed with a hellfire missile in Yemen was a striking display of their power.

More awesome still, in terms of America's global reach, is the projected new generation of ten to twelve spy satellites, 'future imagery architecture' in the jargon, which will cost $25 billion over the next two decades, and which will start orbiting in 2005. These are designed to track objects as small as a baseball at any time of day or night, anywhere in the world, and relay the information to operational units, bypassing layers of current bureaucracy. Definition is set to increase by between eight and twenty times. The 2,000-mile-high satellites will be able to observe objects for twenty minutes at a time, instead of the current ten, making them much harder to dodge.

Other countries' military satellite programmes are puny by comparison. Japan will have four up in 2004, France two, Germany, Canada, Israel and India one apiece, while Russia's existing satellites are now deteriorating. In addition, America's Echelon satellite-based electronic eavesdropping system will be able to pick up not just intercontinental undersea calls but local calls anywhere on the planet. Thus America will technically soon have the power to 'see' anyone, anywhere, listen to their telephone conversations, and despatch sophisticated unmanned aircraft to track them, or manned aircraft with huge 'smart' bombs guided by ground teams, to follow them and destroy them. It is control on an all-encompassing, global scale.

In June 2002 President Bush unveiled his new doctrine of pre-emptive deterrence at West Point Military Academy. He declared: 'We must take the battle to the enemy, disrupt his plans and confront the worst threats before they emerge. In the world we have entered the only path to safety is the path of action. And this nation will act.' Old-fashioned deterrence, he argued, 'means nothing against shadowy terrorist networks with no nation or citizens to defend'. 'Containment,' he said, 'is not possible when unbalanced dictators with weapons of mass destruction can deliver those weapons on missiles or secretly provide them with terrorist allies. If we wait for threats to fully materialize we will have waited too long.' He spoke of the need to uncover terrorist cells in sixty or more countries.

This has been seen as a new strategic doctrine, on a par with the Truman 1947 doctrine of containment, Eisenhower's 1954 'rollback' doctrine, Kennedy and Johnson's aggressive containment doctrine, the Nixon, Ford and Carter doctrines of détente, and the Reagan doctrine of supporting anti-communist movements, all of them aimed at the communist countries. President Clinton never elaborated a doctrine. The first President Bush spoke of a new world order, but never elaborated on it.

The Bush doctrine has been widely criticized on the grounds that it represents a departure from the international order that has prevailed since the Treaty of Westphalia in 1648, which recognized the absolute sovereignty and legal equality of states. US Secretary of State Daniel Webster in 1837 established that pre-emptive hostile action could only be justified where there was an 'instant, overwhelming [necessity] leaving no choice of means and no moment for deliberation'. 'Pre-emptive war' was specifically treated as a war crime at the Nuremberg trials. The UN charter outlaws the 'threat or use of force against the territorial integrity or political independence of any state'. Article 51 of the Charter allows self-defence only 'if an armed attack occurs' against a nation, not before.

In a sense, Bush is merely stating the obvious: America has often resorted to pre-emptive or at least covert action within the boundaries of unfriendly nations it was not at war with. Yet it has always sought to hide this, or at least to find a legal justification when exposed. Ironically, Japan claimed to be making a pre-emptive attack on America at Pearl Harbor. But the danger of elevating pre-emption to the level of a doctrine is that other countries could do so as well – for example, India or Pakistan in their nuclear confrontation. As former US Secretary of State Henry Kissinger has said, 'It isn't in the American national interest to establish pre-emption as a universal principle available to every nation.' Pre-emption also requires extremely good intelligence and a high degree of certainty as to the other side's preparations or intentions, neither of which are usually readily available. It also requires success; otherwise the other side can strike back in legitimate self-defence. It seems likely that President Bush's doctrine will have to be rethought considerably when spelt out in detail. In December 2002, the administration explicitly stated that it would act pre-emptively or retaliate with small-scale nuclear weapons in the event of chemical or biological attacks against America or against American troops abroad.

Even stronger was the President's declaration of US military supremacy. 'It is time to reaffirm the essential role of American military strength. Our forces will be strong enough to deter potential adversaries from pursuing a military buildup in hopes of surpassing, or equalling, the power of the United States.' The document states that 'the President has no intention of allowing any foreign power to catch up with the huge lead the United States has opened up since the fall of the Soviet Union more than a decade ago.' As there is no such competitor anywhere in the world, the statement seems at best redundant, although possibly aimed at China, and domineeringly arrogant at worst.

But does dominant power amount to empire? The triumphal parades and the humiliation of subject peoples brought as captives to Ancient Rome are of course absent. So too is the cumbersome machinery of civil administration of the empires administered in the last century by the British and the French, or the often offensive trappings of power, the titles, plumage, pom-poms, military bands, the extravagant and inbred colonial societies, the self-consciously superior hordes of settlers enjoying their uprooting from the dismal terraces of England to lording over large houses maintained by racially 'inferior' servants.

American power is visibly none of these things. It more nearly approximates to seventeenth-century British power based on commercial outposts dotted along coasts, or the old Portuguese and Dutch trading empires which rarely penetrated further inland, than their nineteenth-century Anglo-French equivalents. America's military presence, while that of an all-seeing eye and all-hearing ear, is rarely visible. American servicemen are usually restricted to bases, enclaves or offshore islands in places like Britain, Germany, Naples, the Gulf and the Far East, although some new bases are being established in Central Asia, Kyrgyzstan, Uzbekistan, as well as Kandahar.

The absence of a settler class can perhaps be explained by America's own continental dimensions: ordinary Americans can migrate west or south in search of a better climate or life within the United States itself, unlike their European imperial counterparts. Americans abroad are those who really wish to travel, or to make money there.

It is perhaps in the buildings (the self-confident American embassies and the ubiquity in the Third World of skyscrapers) that the American 'colonial' influence shows itself most visibly; but the latter at least are usually constructed by local governments and businesses in homage to the American model. Some affect to see in the ubiquitous McDonald's outlets or Starbucks coffee houses the marks of empire, but these are outposts of commerce, not of American government control.

Indeed, Americans traditionally define their power as the antithesis of empire. As Henry Adams wrote:

. . . believing that in the long run interest, not violence, would rule the world . . . [the founding fathers] were tempted to look upon war and preparations for war as the worst of blunders; for they were sure that every dollar capitalized in industry was a means of overthrowing their enemies more effective than a thousand dollars spent on frigates and standing armies. The success of the American system was, from this point of view, a matter of economy. If they could relieve themselves from debts, taxes, armies, and government interference with industry, they must succeed in outstripping Europe.

As the political scientist David Fromkin writes:

It was a debate that had gone on since the time of Washington, Jefferson, and Adams. British leaders found it hard to believe that in the twentieth century – for was not the war of 1776 finished yet? – Americans could still harbour such sentiments and indeed take anticolonialism seriously. But they were wrong to underestimate the tenacity with which such views were held. Antifascism and anticommunism might come and go, but anticolonialism was the principal political plank in the enduring foreign policy of the United States. The fact that in exercising hegemony within the Western Hemisphere, or in occupying territories abroad in pursuit of military and commercial advantage, the United States itself practised what looked to others like imperialism was something the Americans at mid-century usually chose not to notice.

After Suez the American Revolution of 1776 had come to fruition. Its goals had been fully achieved at last. The era of European world domination had come to an end, it was perhaps the most important happening of the twentieth century . . .

Yet for all that American power is not empire, it is undoubtedly power, power of the most globally pervasive and overwhelming, if discreet, kind that the world has ever seen. Whatever the semantics, imperialism and global power projection are easily confused, especially by those of different cultures.

That this has not yet turned into a widespread global rejection of American dominance is owing to the way in which the latter is exercised in a very different way to those of all previous such hegemonies. As already noted, it is not a territorial domination involving administrations, occupying armies and district commissioners but one which leaves government and policing largely to local people. It is wedded to a hugely attractive concept – that of free-market economics – which, in theory at least, permits anyone freely to compete with American companies. American economic domination is not prescribed.

American dominance is also wedded to democratic political freedoms, rights and the rule of law which to those that embrace them seems the very opposite of colonial enslavement – even, indeed, represents liberation in many cases from undemocratic regimes that often oppress their people; connected with this, American political and economic values are, or purport to be, universal – that is, common to, and indeed desirable for, all the peoples of the world, whatever their race, colour or religion (as Francis Fukuyama has eloquently argued).

Further, partly because of America's own history in bringing together all races, cultures and religions, the United States can project itself as a quasi-global state gradually embracing the diversity of the globe itself (this is explicitly argued by some American theoreticians): from the United States of America to the United States of the World? Finally, its popular culture self-evidently has an extraordinary global reach, with Coca-Cola appealing to Chinese, rock music to Russians, jeans to Afghans, McDonald's to Italians and so on. Richard Cohen, in the *Washington Post*, has exulted: 'For the time being, America is the world's only superpower – both military and culturally as well. From jeans to music, America is Number One.'

William Pfaff in the *Los Angeles Times* has commented:

The world begins 2002 in a situation without precedent in human history. A single nation, the United States, enjoys unrivalled military and economic power, and can impose itself virtually anywhere it wants.

Even without nuclear weapons, the United States could destroy the military forces of any other nation on earth. If it should so choose, it could impose complete social and economic breakdown on almost any other state.

Its own weapons are mostly invulnerable, deployed under and above the oceans, or in hardened sites inside the United States. The nation's cities, if Washington's current ambitions are gratified, are to be defended by anti-missile systems.

It seems to many Americans and others that the United States is already potentially head of a modern version of universal empire, even of a willing empire whose members are volunteers . . .

It is hard, certainly for Americans, not to be caught up in the exuberant embrace of this certainty of the universality of their values. If such values are indeed liberating, have appeal to all peoples and reflect common and universal fundamental human aspirations to freedom, self-fulfilment, a better life and so on, why then, American dominance is not dominance at all but liberation – liberation to make a better life, to consume more, to compete economically, to be free politically.

This is a heady brew and perhaps the most attractive of the three universalist ideologies that have swept across mankind's borders since history was recorded – religion (the promise of a better afterlife), Marxism (the promise of equality in this world) and American-style economic and political freedom (the promise of a better life in this world, however unequal). Small wonder that the American liberal dream has comprehensively seen off the Marxist one, although not the more subtle and older religious one. In short, the ideology of America and its values are immensely attractive to huge numbers of people across the globe, and this makes America's current dominance quite different to anything that has gone before.

There is another crucial difference between this kind of hegemony and previous ones. It is the domination of a democratic state, elected by the people. One can grumble that only half of the Americans vote in presidential elections or that in the last (extremely unusual) contest constitutional quirks meant that the man who polled the most votes actually lost. But by any rational standard, America is in the front rank of free and democratic societies while even the British Empire, except in its dying days, was run by a ruling class elected by a limited franchise, while the Soviet empire, of course, was not democratic at all.

This, together with the continental nature of the United States itself, has resulted in a dominant power that is full of quirks and behaves unlike any that has ever gone before. First, the ultimate source of power, the people, while capable of great resolve in international affairs when stirred, are not primarily, or even particularly, interested in the exertion of American power abroad provided it delivers the goods – ever-increasing living standards and peace and stability at home.

Second, America's global power projection is often at the mercy of America's domestic institutional wrangles between President and Congress, for example, or merely petty partisan squabbling. It still seems incredible that for months near paralysis descended on American foreign policy over the issue of whether or not a president had engaged in intimate acts with a young student, and whether or not those acts could be defined as sexual.

Third, when America does choose to project its power, more often than not this is out of consideration for some particular sectional interest or domestic lobby than out of any grand strategy. All of these often combine to provide the impression of a giant with its shoelaces tied together stumbling over its feet and sometimes falling flat on its face in its dealings with the world it is supposed to run. The very things that make tolerable what might otherwise seem an insupportable overmightyness by a single power – its democracy, pluralism and lack of interest in conquering or running other nations – also often make it seem uniquely flat-footed, insensitive and confused in its global policies. Seitz has a fine passage on this:

> The irony of course is that America has accumulated all this power without any discernible plan for how to use it. If there is an emerging hegemony, it is largely accidental. Our exercise of power today is episodic, responding not to any identifiable scheme of things but instead to whatever the issue of the moment happens to be, or whatever CNN tells us it is. Feeling good about something or feeling bad about something is not a sound basis for a coherent foreign policy, and often today America's foreign policy seems more about other people's domestic policies than about relations among states.

> An erratic foreign policy only serves to stir the disquiet of others. Our stop-start relations with Russia and China are two important examples. And I have to confess that I worry when I see that in the course of ten months in 1998–99 the United States managed to bomb four different countries on three different continents.

> What seems to be missing in America is the capacity to exercise our power comprehensively and responsibly. And here the obstacles are many. In our federal system, the post-Cold War presidency is itself less critical to our national well-being than it used to be, and this has been compounded by the incumbency of the only elected president ever to have been impeached. Moreover, the old congressional coalition that used to allow a president to act with some latitude in foreign affairs has broken down in a welter of small-mindedness. Our splendid constitution is designed for the separation of powers, not the fragmentation of them.

> Because there is little strategic context, each foreign policy issue today becomes a proxy for domestic partisan brawling. So it has been on the question of Chinese membership in the World Trade Organization. So too on granting fast-track authority to the president for another trade round. Our contributions to the United Nations have been similarly ensnared. As wealthy as our nation is, the budget for foreign affairs is way less than one per cent of the national budget.

> A year ago the senate majority leader accused the President of manipulating national security in order to cover up his own domestic tribulations. And last month the Senate voted down the Comprehensive Test Ban Treaty. The issue was never really

argued out on the basis of America's long-term strategic requirements nor whether CTB enhances our security or diminishes it. The
issue was who could embarrass whom, with scant regard for the
global ramifications.

The failure of CTB is difficult to reconcile with the proposal for
an Anti-Ballistic Missile system, but both are troubling examples of
a contrarian America. The truth is that exceptional power can make
you lazy and much less inclined to search for common ground.

The American public is on the whole uninterested in most of this.
For Americans, Washington has always been a suspect city, an
attitude exacerbated by the impression that the nation's capital is
driven by special interests and big money. Moreover, the American
media, especially the electronic media, seems to conspire in trivia-
lizing international events and in turning foreign affairs into a series
of cartoons. In our noisy, media-driven society of celebrity and
image and flash and fifteen-minutes-of-fame and hyper-everything,
it is hard to take anything seriously.

Americans, however, are not isolationist – remember that 20 per
cent of our GDP depends on foreign markets, that one in ten
Americans was born abroad and that our alliance commitments
overseas have easily survived the end of the Cold War. Nor are
Americans naturally unilateralist or chauvinistic or triumphalist,
nor are they even particularly aware of the immensity of American
power. In truth, the world is less compelling than it used to be, and I
do wonder just how outward-looking other peoples really are. But
Americans simply don't pay much attention to these things mainly
because they aren't asked to.

The end result, however, is that serious foreign policy has been so
marginalized in the United States that we no longer seem to have
much appreciation for the consequences of our own actions. The
problem is not isolationism. The problem is indifference. And this is
what worries our friends abroad.

I would add two further reasons for the 'multiple personality' America
seems so often to display in foreign affairs. First, short-termism: with
important legislative elections every two years and presidential ones
every four, policies are often under pressure from, or changed for, short-
term electoral advantage. Second, a pluralism of power control within
the buraucracy itself. The eminent Venezuelan diplomat and intellectual
Alfredo Toro-Hardy, in his *The Age of Villages* exaggerates only slightly

when he writes of Washington as 'the most fragmented political ambient that you can imagine'.

The unique, contradictory, even bizarre nature of the world's 'super-duper-power' now becomes clearer: its primary purpose is economic domination. Political and military intervention exist largely to further this. Its political, economic and cultural values have, it believes, universal appeal, and its very pluralism limits aggressive intent, while encumbering the rational exercise of foreign policy. Given that all states act primarily out of their own perceived self-interest – the most elemental of all foreign policy maxims – it would be hard to imagine a more benevolent mega-power than the one which emerged from the smoke and rubble of the collapse of communism at the end of the Cold War.

Why, then, is America so widely suspected of bad intentions, distrusted and even hated? No one who travels extensively would say that America is much loved, or even much respected, except for its power, however much ordinary people enjoy the fruits of pax Americana, from democracy to Coca-Cola.

The evidence, while fragmentary, is pretty overwhelming. Professor Robert Jervis, the former President of the American Political Science Association, says that much of the world sees the United States as 'the prime rogue state . . . today'. In February 2002 the then French Foreign Minister Hubert Vedrine attacked American policy as 'simplistic for reducing all the problems in the world to the struggle against terrorism'. America, he said, was acting 'unilaterally, without consulting others, taking decisions based on its own view of the world and its own interests'. This can be dismissed as the ranting of an inveterate anti-American. More recently the deputy director of the French Institute of International Relations, Dominique Moisi, has argued that 'for the first time since 1947 a mutual decoupling of the United States from Europe is possible'.

An opinion poll published by the *International Herald Tribune* in association with the respected Pew Research Center and the US Council on Foreign Relations just days before September 11 made alarming reading for Americans. A staggering 85 per cent of those polled in France considered that President Bush made decisions 'based entirely on US interests' compared with 8 per cent who thought he took European interests into account as well; the percentages in such traditional American allies as Britain (79 per cent to 14 per cent), Italy (74 per cent to 15 per cent) and Germany (73 per cent to 18 per cent) were only marginally better. Eight months later the figures were barely changed.

Some 65 per cent of Germans, America's most important allies in Europe, disapproved of President Bush's foreign policy, with only 23 per cent in favour. The figures were nearly as lopsided in France (59 per cent to 16 per cent) and only marginally better in loyal Britain (49 per cent to 17 per cent) and Italy (46 per cent to 29 per cent). There was a small but significant improvement eight months later, perhaps reflecting the impact of September 11.

America's renunciation of the Kyoto Protocol on the environment was overwhelmingly opposed in Britain (93 per cent to 10 per cent), Italy (80 per cent to 12 per cent), Germany (87 per cent to 10 per cent) and France (85 per cent to 10 per cent), while the proposed Missile Defence system found only 10 per cent approval in Germany (83 per cent were opposed), 14 per cent approval in France (against 75 per cent opposed), 20 per cent approval in Britain (against 66 per cent opposed) and 24 per cent approval in Italy (against 65 per cent).

These figures are far in excess of polls taken regarding controversial American initiatives during the Cold War, such as Intermediate Nuclear Forces, and show how the existence of a single megapower has served as a lightning conductor for hostility. Not too much should be read into a poll, but the results suggest not just strongly felt opposition to the United States on key issues, but a sense of hostility towards American dominance.

A look at the global reaction to the September 11 attacks bears this out. Horror and solidarity were expressed, naturally, by the European allies as well as all humane observers around the globe, even those opposed to American policies. Moderate Arabs were appalled. A cartoon showed the fugitive Saudi dissident Osama bin Laden inside a dark cave 'somewhere in Afghanistan', using a flute to charm a mushroom cloud out of a basket, as a serpent recoiled in horror. The cartoon, by Mahmoud Kahil, a Lebanese, appeared in the English-language Saudi daily, *Arab News*. In Egypt's semi-official *Al Ahram* newspaper, Nabil Luka Bibawi, a professor of criminal law, cited extensive passages from the Koran preaching religious tolerance and prohibiting attacks against innocent non-Muslims, calling them attacks against the Prophet Muhammad and God:

> Terrorists don't know the methods of rational, calm debate. Terrorists impose darkness on the climate of the intellect because they try to force their backward ideas on public opinion under the veil of religious correctness . . . They construe religious thought to suit

their political objectives to reach power . . . There can be no worse distortion of religion than that. If world Zionism spent billions of dollars to tarnish the image of Islam, it will not accomplish what the terrorists have done with their actions and words.

Jamal Khashoggi, the deputy editor of Saudi Arabia's *Arab News*, wrote of bin Laden's 1998 fatwa sanctioning the killing of American and British civilians:

There is no respected Islamic scholar here in Saudi Arabia or anywhere else in the Muslim world who would support such a fatwa. With bin Laden's religious upbringing, he should know that only the most knowledgeable Islamic scholars have the right to issue fatwas. It seems that bin Laden has become a revolutionary in a world of his own imagination. He would not hesitate to break any taboo. How did he come to create this fantasyland of terror?

Even the spiritual leader of Hezbollah, Sheikh Fadlallah, declared the September 11 attacks 'not compatible with Islamic law'.

The rejoicing in some Palestinian streets was not unexpected. But there was also joy quickly suppressed in the streets of Riyadh and Beijing. Saudi intelligence figures suggest 95 per cent of Saudis between the ages of 21 and 40 admired Osama bin Laden after the attacks. Elisabetta Burba, in the *Wall Street Journal*, reported from Beirut:

The café's sophisticated clientele was celebrating, laughing, cheering and making jokes, as waiters served hamburgers and Diet Pepsi. Nobody looked shocked or moved. They were excited, very excited. Ninety per cent of the Arab world believes that America got what it deserved [I was told]. An exaggeration? Rather an understatement.

Newspapers in Cairo and throughout the Middle East gave ample space to the ludicrous theory that Israel had been behind the attacks in order to find a pretext for striking hard against the Palestinians. President Mubarak of Egypt, who receives some $2 billion a year in American subsidies, did not feel strong enough to rebut these reports.

The *International Herald Tribune*, again in conjunction with the Pew Research Center, polling 275 opinion leaders around the world, found that an alarming 58 per cent of non-Americans believed most ordinary people in their countries thought that American policies and actions in the world were 'a major cause' of the September 11 attacks, while 29 per cent believed some people felt this, and only 9 per cent thought that hardly any did. In America, 32 per cent thought that hardly any did, 48 per cent that only some did, and 18 per cent that most did.

Of the non-Americans polled, 42 per cent thought that many or most people felt the United States was overreacting to the attack (56 per cent thought hardly any did), compared to none in America who shared the former opinion. Some 70 per cent of non-Americans believed that most or many people in their countries felt that it was 'good that Americans now know what it's like to be vulnerable'. A poll of 38,000 people in 44 countries published by Pew in December 2002, produced even more alarming results: only 6 per cent of Egyptians and 10 per cent of Pakistanis viewed America favourably, compared to around 70 per cent who did not. Around the world, particularly in Germany, Turkey and America, there was a striking decline in American popularity.

While the American action in Afghanistan was broadly supported, there were large majorities against intervention in Iraq, Somalia or other countries. The same poll suggested that of the reasons why people outside America disliked the United States, the major factors were resentment of US power in the world (52 per cent) and US policies which 'may have contributed to the growing gap between the rich and poor' (52 per cent), followed by the power of multinational corporations (36 per cent) – the latter interestingly being a view held overwhelmingly, however, in Western Europe, Eastern Europe and Russia, and Latin America.

Finally, those polled did not feel that most people in their countries thought America did a lot of good in the world (76 per cent to 21 per cent), an astonishingly negative perception, although 69 per cent had a mostly favourable perception of the United States compared to 28 per cent who did not (falling to a 46/32 per cent split in the Islamic world). These figures should be deeply troubling to Americans. They are hardly surprising: America allocates less than 0.2 per cent of its GDP to foreign aid – the lowest in the major industrial world, less than a cent of every dollar in its budget for 2003. At a time when military spending is increasing by $48 billion, foreign aid is up by just $200 million – although refreshingly President Bush is proposing substantially to increase this.

There are many other indications of the underlying hostility. One Nanjing university student wrote after September 11: 'What makes me despair is that at the same time these terrorist hijackers were gleefully smiling, at least half of our compatriots were loudly laughing.' Wei Jing

Sheng, the prominent Chinese exile, recently drew attention to the nationalist anti-Americanism of young Chinese today – even among those who support the dissident movement – partly because they view the Americans as having sold out to the Beijing regime, and partly because of America's hostile acts towards China. In Russia opinion polls have long shown opposition to the United States and disillusion with the free-market values it has been seen to promote in Moscow. In South Africa, American pharmaceutical companies, allegedly refusing to sell anti-Aids drugs at affordable prices, have become targets of popular ire.

While governments across the world continue to reiterate the benefits of friendship with the only global superpower, at street level and even among the relatively prosperous middle classes, America's stock is dangerously low. Ivo Daalder of the Brookings Institution reflects American bewilderment:

A very significant thing for Americans is the realization that our view of ourselves is not widely shared. Americans are in general totally convinced of our own essential goodness – that we are the most democratic, most liberal, most just people in the world and that we assume everybody else sees it the same way. We are not very good at putting ourselves in the shoes of others, and therefore we don't necessarily understand that people don't share the view of us that we have ourselves.

An American journalist Mark Hertsgaard writes, in *The Eagle's Shadow* (Bloomsbury, 2002):

In the wake of September 11, the question obsessing Americans about the Muslim world was, 'Why Do They Hate Us?' But Muslims had long wondered the same about Americans. In a sparkling exception to most American news coverage, Sandy Tolan reported on National Public Radio in January 2002 that nearly everyone he had interviewed during six weeks of recent travel through the Middle East resented the negative stereotypes attached to Muslims and Arabs by American movies, television, and news coverage. In Europe, stretching back to the novels of Goethe and the operas of Mozart, there had long been respect for the great achievements of Islamic civilisation in culture, astronomy, architecture, and more. America, by contrast, regarded Muslims as primitive, untrustworthy fanatics, worth dealing with only because they had oil.

'You are dealing here with people who are almost childlike in their understanding of what is going on in the world,' Gerald Celente, director of the Trends Research Institute in Rhinebeck, New York, told the *Financial Times* shortly after September 11. 'It's all: "We never did anything to anybody, so why are they doing this to us?"'

For the minority of Americans who do concern themselves with foreign affairs, the question 'why do they dislike us?' must be of major concern (although a minority of the foreign policy establishment led on the Republican side by Richard Perle and on the Democratic side by isolationist-protectionist interests professes not to give a damn. Perle's analysis is that America only wins friends abroad through displays of strength, not ingratiation. Better to be feared and respected than to be liked).

The answers to the question are, in truth, pretty obvious. There is the simple sea-change already referred to that, with the collapse of Soviet communism, the bad guys against whom the Americans could rally their allies have left the scene. As Madeleine Albright, the former Secretary of State, put it, 'It was very different when you had two superpowers, and observers could divide their animosity between one or the other.' Now resentment was focused on 'the big guy on the block'. Michael Lind, Senior Fellow at the New America Foundation in Washington, puts it another way:

There's an anti-bourgeois, anti-capitalist and ultimately anti-modern theme that always emerges to criticize the dominant power of the day. It was directed at the cities of northern Italy, then in the seventeenth century at the Netherlands, then at Britain when she picked up the torch of capitalism, and now it's the US.

It was always surprising how much support the Soviet Union could attract for its policies of vicious repression and upside-down economics from many Third World countries in its old Cold War rivalry with the United States. While some of those countries have grudgingly espoused American free-market economics, residual resentment often remains. Meanwhile, many of those who once united behind the United States during the Cold War in their loathing of communism are now free to take a much more critical view of their overmighty ally. This does not apply just to moderate Third World regimes but also to countries like Germany, which are gingerly formulating a more autonomous role for dealing both with East and West and, symbolically, the Pope, whose standard-bearing anti-communism has been replaced by an equally staunch anti-materialism not quite explicitly aimed at the United States. A Russian journalist recently remarked: 'During the Cold War, half the world could hate the Soviet Union and the other half could hate the United States. Your problem now is you're the only ones left to hate. Anyone anywhere who is unhappy with his life will blame the United States.'

A further, crucial aspect of this consequence of the end of the Cold War is that for many of its supporters the United States was fighting a crusade of good versus evil against the Soviet Union. America was visibly fighting for freedom and justice against a tyranny that enslaved a huge section of mankind, occupied Eastern Europe, suppressed uprisings with tanks and imprisoned and tortured dissidents. With the Soviet bloc's disappearance, the United States no longer appeared to be a crusader for good: it simply seemed to stand for its own self-interest, but on a much larger scale than any other country. It appeared to have lost its moral purpose, beyond the making of money. It had lost a role, and found an empire. The crusade against terrorism may be an attempt to rediscover such a role, but as so few outsiders view the problem in such alarmist tones, perhaps because they have long experienced terrorism and wars on their own territories, it seems unlikely to work.

America could rediscover a moral role by going back to its founding principles, and standing as a beacon of light for democracy and freedom around the world. Instead, immediately after the Cold War, the United States appeared to sink into a surprising moral lethargy, even torpor. America was heavily criticized even during the Cold War for backing unsavoury despots against communism – summed up in Roosevelt's phrase about Nicaragua's Anastasio Somoza the First, 'He may be a son of a bitch, but he's our son of a bitch.' But at least America could argue, rightly or wrongly, that the communist alternative was worse.

Since 1989, the United States has remained bedfellows with a host of repellent regimes without any such excuse other than the need to continue to do business with them. Alongside initial toleration for Serbia's Milošević, Rwanda's mass murderers (and indeed Saddam himself) until galvanized into action by television and popular opinion, can be set America's extraordinary rapprochement with China (in many ways an even more evil empire than Russia, although with few missiles) under President Clinton, the cultivation of the crude emergent dictator-ships of Central Asia, for commercial and strategic reasons, and continuing close relations with the dark-age barbarism of Saudi Arabia's alliance of corrupt princes and religious flagellants, without any attempt to reform this. The lessons of the past seem unlearnt: cosying up to Saddam Hussein against Iran and supporting Islamic extremists in Afghanistan are 'blowback' mistakes that have come to haunt the Americans.

Only Congress's statutory human rights certifications appeared to force the administration to take any interest in human rights issues at all. But the human rights issue was ready-made for a fresh American global moral crusade, founded on the principles of its own 1776 revolution – handled, obviously, with sensitivity so that the United States could not be accused of neo-colonialism. Yet empowering the people of other nations to rise up against their despots is hardly an act of imperialism.

America is also accused by many of economic imperialism under the guise of free-market economics. Professor Robert Hunter Wade of the London School of Economics expresses this in eloquent, if extreme, terms:

> Suppose you are a modern-day Roman emperor, leader of the most powerful country in a world of sovereign states and international markets. What international political economy do you create so that, without having to throw your weight around too much, normal market forces bolster the economic pre-eminence of your country, allow your citizens to consume far more than they produce, and keep challengers down?
>
> You want autonomy to decide on your own exchange rate and monetary policy, while having other countries depend on your support in managing their own economies. You want to be able to engineer volatility and economic crises in the rest of the world in order to hinder the growth of centres that might challenge your pre-eminence. You want intense competition between exporters in the rest of the world to give you an inflow of imports at constantly decreasing prices relative to the price of your exports.
>
> You want to invite the best brains in the rest of the world to your universities, companies and research institutes. You befriend middle classes elsewhere and make sure they have good reasons for supporting your framework.
>
> What features do you hardwire into the international political economy? First, free capital mobility. Second, free trade (except imports that threaten domestic industries important for your

reselection). Third, international investment free from any discriminatory favouring of national companies through protection, public procurement, public ownership or other devices, with special emphasis on the freedom of your companies to get the custom of national elites from the management of their financial assets, their private education, healthcare, pensions, and the like.

Fourth, your currency as the main reserve currency. Fifth, no constraint on your ability to create your currency at will (such as a dollar-gold link), so that you can finance unlimited trade deficits with the rest of the world. Sixth, international lending at variable interest rates denominated in your currency, which means that borrowing countries in crisis have to repay you more when their capacity to repay is less. This combination allows your people to consume far more than they produce (and it periodically produces financial instability and crises in the rest of the world). To supervise the international framework you want international organisations that look like cooperatives of member states and carry the legitimacy of multilateralism, but are financed in a way that allows you control.

A third problem is a perceived American arrogance. The petty retaliation against Germany for daring to disagree with President Bush's Iraq policy is calculated to inflame even America's allies. Public contracts with German firms were quickly cancelled in the land of free enterprise for purely political reasons. The head of Germany's foreign trade association said that: 'German firms now face the prospect of being simply cut out of deals in America.' The kind of nationalism rarely seen outside a totalitarian state also grates on outsiders. In what other country would a popular – and usually witty – syndicated cartoon devote a repeat strip to its national flag, as Beetle Bailey did in April 2002?

More seriously, there are fears, post-'nine-eleven' that America is undergoing one of its periodic outbreaks of illiberalism (seen for example with the anti-Bolshevism of the 1920s, the anti-Japanese feeling during the 1940s, and the McCarthyism of the 1950s.) The American liberal journalist Mark Hertsgaard, again with some overstatement, points to American media uniformity after the attacks and subsequent legislation:

The climate of intimidation was such that the most radical assault mounted on the United States Constitution in decades became law with scarcely a peep of protest from either the political class or the general public. On October 25, 2001, President Bush signed into law the 'USA Patriot Act', an Orwellian phrase if ever there was one. Among its many extraordinary provisions, the law cancelled habeas corpus rights for non-citizens (which amounted to twenty million people in the United States); the attorney general was now authorised to detain indefinitely any non-citizen that he and he alone deemed a threat to the national security. The act allowed government agents to search a citizen's house without notifying that citizen and expanded the government's ability to wiretap not only telephone but Internet communications, giving the government access to a person's e-mail, bank and credit card records. Federal agents could also seize public library records to check what people were reading. Separately, the Justice Department asserted the right to monitor conversations between criminal suspects and their lawyers. Other new laws gave the CIA the right to spy on Americans, authorised the attorney general on his sole discretion to designate domestic groups as terrorist organisations, and lowered the legal threshold for obtaining a search warrant from 'probable cause' to 'relevant to an ongoing criminal investigation'. Meanwhile, the President declared by executive fiat that any non-citizen he considered a suspected terrorist could be tried by a military tribunal.

A fourth source of rancour, opposition and sometimes ridicule is also, ironically, one of America's most successful exports: its popular culture. It is hard to overstate the contempt and anger this inspires in guardians of 'higher' and traditional cultures allegedly at risk. There are many who fear older cultures are being overcome, particularly among the young, by American mores. There are those traditionalists who deeply object to the sexual freedom flaunted in American culture. There are those, such as filmmakers, who fear their more traditional products are swamped by lowest-common-denominator Hollywood sex-and-violence epics. Some American intellectuals such as Samuel Huntington have been berated for seemingly declaring war on the whole of a religion and a civilization.

Finally, the conduct of American foreign policy since the end of the Cold War must itself shoulder a part of the blame for the dangerous and exponential growth of anti-Americanism across the globe over the past decade – as we shall see in the next chapter.

CHAPTER 3

THE MAKING OF A MEGAPOWER

At the end of the Second World War, American policy-makers were determined to avert the 'dark valley' that followed the First – the mistakes that rendered another global confrontation virtually inevitable within just two decades. The main errors were American disengagement from Europe; a naked pursuit of economic interests, 'the business of America is business' – with no corresponding sense of responsibility for managing the world economy, which was to culminate in the disastrous crash of 1929 and world recession thereafter; a washing of America's hands with regard to ominous developments in the Far East and Europe – the rise of Fascism, Japanese militarism and Nazism were other peoples' business, not America's; and the boycotting of such toothless institutions – the League of Nations, for example – as other countries tried to cobble together support to guarantee international security. The results were sadly predictable: global conflict broke out again and the United States was dragged in at enormous cost to itself amid worldwide suffering.

After the Second World War the United States had learnt its lesson. In a brilliant series of foreign policy initiatives, made all the more so by the rapid unfolding of events after 1945, the Americans created a new world order. Europe was rebuilt through the Marshall Plan, perhaps one of the greatest examples of enlightened altruism and self-interest in history, laying, through government pump priming, the foundations for private-sector economic growth that survived until the Vietnam War-generated inflation and oil crises of the 1970s. The creation of Nato established a new, if tense, stability in Europe. America made clear its international commitments around the world and lent its support to the new institutions of collective responsibility: the United Nations, Nato itself, the World Bank, the IMF. This was a stinging repudiation of the post-1918 experience.

Serious mistakes were undoubtedly made: America's relentless campaign against British and French 'colonialism' alienated its European allies and led the United States into dangerous engagements, particularly in Asia. But the Cold War was the heyday of American engagement with the world and ushered in four decades of security and economic development unprecedented in a terrible century of suffering, and even in history. (It is often forgotten how recent the concept of a secure and peaceful existence is for the overwhelming majority of humanity, even in the developed world: for most, life before was insecure, dangerous, constantly at the mercy of disease or violence, and characterized by backbreaking, life-threatening poverty). Fundamental rules were set down for maintaining the peace: an arms race with precisely defined mathematical parameters; doctrines of mutual assured destruction and flexible response in Europe; a proxy war in the Third World involving flexible responses to Soviet-bloc offensives; and so on.

In March 1946 Churchill arrived in Fulton, Missouri, to make his 'iron curtain' speech. Truman felt obliged to dissociate himself from it. Yet, prodded by George Kennan, the most eloquent American diplomat in Moscow, and the Navy Secretary, George Forrestal, Truman was now to undergo a complete conversion to the idea not just that Russia was an inherently nationalistic, expansionist empire (which was true) but that its communist ideology threatened to subvert the world. In fact after the Second World War its ideology was no more than the tool of its nationalist interests, as events were repeatedly to show.

The disintegration of Europe now appeared imminent – in the summer of 1946 the UN Economic and Social Council was told that 100 million Europeans were starving and some 40 million barely subsisting. Britain had also made the decision to withdraw from India, Burma, Egypt and Palestine, and was now about to start leaving the eastern Mediterranean. The Americans – who had been pressing for that withdrawal – decided to step into the breach.

In June 1947 Secretary of State George Marshall announced the most imaginative American initiative in diplomatic history in conciliatory terms, as far as Russia was concerned: 'Our policy is directed not against any country or doctrine, but against hunger, poverty, desperation and chaos. Its purpose should be the revival of a working economy in the world so as to permit the emergence of political and social conditions in which free institutions can exist.' Some $12.5 billion was sent (around $75 billion at today's values) catalysing eight or nine times as much investment from within Europe itself.

In April 1948 the Russians cut off western rail access to Berlin; the blockade of the city had begun, circumvented by the West through an airlift. This was the midwife to Nato, America's other great contribution to post-war security. After the disputes and dissimulations at Yalta, it was its finest hour.

While policy towards Europe was now to be relatively stable and mature over the next four decades, in Asia the pattern of a somewhat erratic policy was set for the rest of the world. It began with General Douglas MacArthur's shogunate of Japan which, while idealistic, enlightened and well-intentioned, was partly wrecked by an unholy alliance between the Japanese right and big business interests in the United States.

The next stage was the Korean War. The invasion of South Korea took place after Mao's victory in the Chinese civil war, which had provoked an outcry that America had somehow 'lost' China to the communists (in fact America could not have propped up the corrupt regime of Chiang Kai-Shek even if it had tried and Mao, though a communist, was barely supported by Russia, which at the time favoured Chiang).

American troops had already abandoned South Korea as being of very limited strategic significance. The Americans had made clear that South Korea was outside the sphere in Asia that they were prepared to defend against aggressors, which was the chain of islands stretching southwards from Japan.

MacArthur, the commander in the East, had made clear his opinion that South Korea was not the place to make a stand. But John Foster Dulles, the state department chief in the area, whose influence was to dog American foreign policy for a generation, made clear that 'US force should be used even though this risks Russian counter-moves. To sit by while Korea is overrun by unprovoked armed attack would start a disastrous chain of events leading most probably to world war.'

So MacArthur was despatched to stop the invasion. He did so brilliantly, striking behind enemy lines during the Inchon Landing, which drove the North Korean forces back over the 38th parallel. He pursued the communists in a furious offensive up to the Yalu river boundary with China. At that moment the Chinese chose to invade, and the Americans were thrown back. Only after a long retreat was the line held, and the tide began to turn again. At that stage MacArthur launched a fresh offensive, threatening to strike into China, and was dismissed. The war then dragged on in an indefinite stalemate, and a truce was reached on the old 38th parallel.

It was a conflict that was to bear an uncanny resemblance to some of the ones that followed: the misleading signals that the United States did not care about the territory about to be attacked; the belated deployment of large forces; the refusal to back local commanders when victory was in their grasp; the subsequent overwhelming by an army backed by vastly superior local numbers across the border. In this case the peace reached amounted to no more than the *status quo ante*.

The Korean commitment fathered the Vietnam commitment. The Americans pledged themselves to easing the French out of Vietnam and replacing them in fighting the Vietminh guerrillas. Indo-China, one state department mission insisted, was 'the keystone of a South East Asia defense order'. One American diplomat, Charles Ogburn, wrote of the choice America faced: '[we could] wash our hands of the country to allow the Communists to overrun it; or . . . continue to pour treasure (and perhaps eventually lives) into a hopeless cause in which the French have already expended about a billion and a half dollars and about fifty thousand lives – and this at a cost of alienating vital segments of Asian public opinion.'

The joint chiefs of staff, however, feared that control of Vietnam 'would bring about almost immediately a dangerous condition with respect to the internal security of all of the other countries of southeast Asia, as well as the Philippines and Indonesia, and would contribute to their probable eventual fall to communism. Even India and Pakistan would be threatened.'

When the French departed in disorder, the United States took on the burden of fighting the 'communist' onslaught on Vietnam – which was in fact principally a nationalist uprising. Learning nothing from Korea, the Vietnamese escalation again showed the Americans sliding into a mire in defence of a nation of little strategic value. Massive aerial attack proved to be inadequate against land infiltration from a vastly more numerous foe. Slowly and inexorably the Americans were driven back, with the loss of 58,000 men and the commitment of more than 500,000 troops.

Vietnam was certainly America's greatest overseas defeat – indeed its only overseas defeat, if Korea is regarded as a standoff – and had a shattering effect on the country's psyche. Like Korea, it was probably an unnecessary war and one which led to humiliating American withdrawal and defeat for its allies.

Vietnam marked a turning point in America's attitude to military engagement abroad. Just as the country's confidence after 1945 had engendered Nato, Korea and Vietnam, so for a while the United States was to retreat into its shell, incapable of supporting its allies around the Third World except in the most token way.

After Dulles and the stop-communism era, there now began the Kissinger era, with an executive embarked upon a policy of realpolitik and a Congress determined to prevent any further overseas entanglement. Unsurprisingly, the executive began to find ways of trying to circumvent the legislature. Kissinger's realpolitik, while credited with the withdrawal from Vietnam, albeit at the expense of Cambodia, failed to secure support for such American allies as the anti-communist movement in Angola.

Policy in Latin America suffered from many of the same deficiencies as that in Asia: over-concern about the communist threat; an identification of homegrown insurgencies with communism; glossing over the deficiencies of these societies that nurtured revolution; support of unappealing anti-communist dictatorships; long periods of neglect followed by sudden over-interest as matters got out of hand; and – specific to Latin America – reliance upon a military/business lobby within the United States which was closely aligned with its much less appealing brothers in the southern hemisphere.

It was Cuba that sparked the obsession with hemispheric communism, and was to bedevil relations with Latin America for two decades. Fidel Castro's revolution in Cuba was homegrown and against a manifestly corrupt dictator, Fulgencio Batista. In an effort to preserve his power, Castro blatantly espoused the communism of America's enemy, Russia, spearheaded by Carlos Rafael Rodriguez, the leader of Cuba's Communist Party. The Caribbean island embarked on a David and Goliath confrontation which has continued to this day, as a section within the American establishment refuses to recognize the end of the Cold War.

With Russian money, weapons, and Cuban military support, insurgencies in Latin America took on a host of local regimes backed by the United States. The latter won the war for the continent – as was not the case in South East Asia – but only at the expense of aligning with some of the most brutal and unappealing oligarchs in the world, sometimes unnecessarily. The crudeness of this approach was to erode the United

States' underlying appeal among the democratic middle classes that are now in the ascendancy throughout Latin America.

Middle Eastern policy has on the whole been more measured: a balance has been struck between America's much-criticized support of Israel and its concern to retain the goodwill of Arab oil producers. Thus the United States has usually played the role of peacemaker: from the Camp David Treaty accords to the White House agreement that facilitated the Israeli-Palestinian get-together resulting from the Oslo agreement, the United States has shown an astonishing capacity to retain credibility on both sides of the regional conflict. Both Israel and Egypt are two of the largest recipients of American aid.

With the end of the Kissinger era, the Carter presidency represented the innocent idealist in foreign affairs. Carter's formidable peacemaking skills were fully on display during the Camp David agreement between Israel and Egypt; and his fight for human rights reclaimed the moral high ground against the Soviet Union, which had arguably been compromised during the Johnson, Nixon and Ford presidencies. But he appeared a novice beside the battle-hardened cynicism of the Brezhnev era in Russia, and the Soviet invasion of Afghanistan and the Iranian revolution combined, somewhat unfairly, to make him appear a symbol of weakness and naïvety.

The Reagan administration, with its combination of tax-cutting deficit spending at home and huge increases in military expenditure, as well as military adventurism abroad against Libya, Lebanon and the Iran-for-contras scandal, at first appeared headed for the rocks. But its robustness towards the Soviet Union coincided with the collapse of that country's old guard and the ascent to power of an elite which preferred economic modernization to military confrontation and repression, symbolized by Mikhail Gorbachev. With his decision to relax repression at home, withdraw from Eastern Europe and Afghanistan, the Soviet empire collapsed.

At the end of the Cold War, the United States deserved the heartfelt thanks of the world. For more than forty years it had confronted a totalitarian and repressive superpower possessed of a huge nuclear arsenal, and had stood its ground. Terrible mistakes had been made, nuclear war had threatened on occasion, but the world had survived and a huge swathe of humanity had emerged from political enslavement. America had undeniably won the Cold War.

The largest military intervention since Vietnam was in the Middle East, and occurred through another Korea-style misjudgement. The United States did not believe Saddam Hussein was preparing to occupy

Kuwait in 1990. The American ambassador to Iraq, April Glaspie, gave the impression that the administration did not much care if it did. Only after the invasion had taken place did President Bush, believing the Saudi oilfields to be under threat, declare that it would be reversed.

As in Vietnam, massive American firepower was deployed, using 'smart bombs' and other weapons. The Iraqi First World War-style military machine was defeated in open desert under the impact of the most effective in late twentieth-century tanks and equipment. On the brink of a victory that would almost certainly have toppled Saddam Hussein – hated in his own country, which was also impossible territory for guerrilla operations – the allies called a halt. The dictator was allowed to stay in power and wreak misery on his own people, if no one else.

These decisions were dictated largely by domestic opinion – mainly though prime-time television – although there were some logical reasons behind them, in particular the fear of Iraq breaking up, leaving Iran dominant in the Gulf. In terms of the failure to send the necessary signals to aggressors, and in snatching stalemate from the jaws of victory, the episode was uncannily reminiscent of the Korean War.

The Gulf War was not the last battle of the Cold War era (the Third World War, one might say). It was the first of the post-Cold War period. What it revealed was immensely important, for it defined America's new strategic approach. To most external analysts this appeared to be incoherent, a series of ill-thought-out, ad hoc, often last-minute interventions dictated by domestic priorities, as Seitz argues, rather than a clear strategic programme. The consistency lay in the pursuit of self-interest. What is chilling is that the policy much more nearly resembled the calamitous one adopted after the First World War than the successful one immediately adopted after the Second – although for rather different reasons. Post-1919, Americans could see no reason to involve themselves in overseas commitments – and were proved disastrously wrong. Post-1989 they considered the principal foe vanquished and no other worthy of attention except on an occasional basis. The post-1945 sense of emergency was missing.

So the old policies threatened to return – not quite American disengagement from Europe, but much less engagement accompanied by griping; less of a sense of responsibility for managing the world economy and more of representing American business interests (as if the two were distinct); not quite a washing of hands towards mass-murder and potential conflicts not directly involving American interests, but of a watching brief; and a growing contempt for toothless multilateral institutions, in particular the UN.

This policy was not isolationist, in the classic sense of the term. Americans, when they saw their interests threatened, were prompt to engage in the world. But it was broadly unilateralist, not in the sense that the Americans spurned allies, but that they saw no need for them; and it was self-interested, in that only flashpoints of immediate concern for American interests called for actual intervention.

It could thus be defined as one of unilateral self-interest. It was a perfectly coherent international stance although one, I would argue, which was fraught with danger and could ultimately be self-defeating. It was the opposite of a world policeman, which means acting under defined rules acceptable to the international community to maintain world order. On the contrary, the United States was in danger of acting as world vigilante, venturing out into a dangerous neighbourhood when its interests were visibly threatened. *New York Times* columnist Thomas Friedman made one of the most telling comments after the Twin Towers horror: 'If anything has been learned from September 11, it is that if you don't visit a bad neighbourhood, it will visit you.'

The post-1989 policy was one of often doing good for others by beating up the bad guys, but was principally motivated by its own concerns and it was not too bothered whether it carried its friends along with it. There is a perfectly good American defence of this attitude: the world out there is a jungle, full of bad people who don't respect the rule of law; when we venture out we do so in force, fight by the rules of our adversaries to secure the safety of our borders and, along the way, do what we can to help the innocent, and withdraw. To which the riposte must be that even if vigilante law is often necessary, it should be accompanied by efforts to establish an international order so that it will no longer be necessary; the Wild West was eventually tamed. The current doctrine of unilateral self-interest is perfectly coherent, even defensible in the short term; but in the long term it is dangerous, even to American interests.

Meanwhile, the United States passed up the chance to capitalize on its huge reservoir of post-Cold War authority and goodwill to build an entirely new international order capable of deterring major threats to world peace and of eventually extending the rule of law to many areas of the world from which it is sadly absent today. It is not yet too late; but ten years is a long time to waste in international politics, and the goodwill towards America that blossomed across the globe after 1989 has been largely frittered away, while a new generation has grown up dominated by hatred of the world 'hegemonist'.

CHAPTER 4

THE LOST DECADE

A quick glance at America's post-1989 interventions abroad underlines the striking consistency rather than erratic nature of the United States' policy of unilateral self-interest over the past decade. With the departure of the enemy from outside the gates, six core principles have come to govern any military intervention abroad:

Is it vital to our interests?

Can a clear objective be defined?

When the objective is achieved, can we get out smoothly?

Will it involve a limited commitment of resources (defence policy has been predicated on the assumption that it can tackle only two major regional conflicts simultaneously)?

Closely related and most important, will the operation be almost casualty-free for America?

And how will it play on prime-time television?

A glance at each of the military interventions since the end of the Cold War bears out the bizarre selections that this policy imposed. In place of a commitment, Nato-style, to intervention in the event of attack – flexible response – a policy of flexible non-response has been substituted. The chief deterrent to potential regional aggressors was the possibility, rather than the certainty, that the United States would react. Astonishingly, since the end of the Cold War, the State Department moved into the position of advocating intervention, while the Pentagon, in spite of having to justify a military establishment of around 1.4 million men and women and a budget of between $250–300 billion, vigorously resisted military entanglement abroad (This has now reversed).

The 1990 invasion of Panama was a textbook case of post-Cold War intervention. The vital interest at stake was the cocaine traffic corrupting America's youth. The clear objective was the removal of the country's ruling gangster clique clustered around its dictator, General Manuel Noriega. The Americans were able to withdraw smoothly and completely. The force used was overwhelming, but limited. The invasion caused just a handful of American casualties, and looked good on television.

The 1991 Gulf War may have been the last of the old Cold War-style commitments, in that it mobilized most of America's allies and involved the largest deployment of forces since Vietnam. However, it also passed all six tests (except perhaps the fourth: the United States would have had trouble simultaneously coping with another major crisis). America's oil interests in the Gulf were easy to champion before Congress and the public. The clear and limited objective was the expulsion of Saddam Hussein from Kuwait, after which most American forces could be withdrawn. Thanks to the awesome softening-up campaign and the supremacy of the allies' desert blitzkrieg, the level of American casualties was remarkably low. Finally, with a short, sharp, surgical victory, the campaign played beautifully on prime-time television, to the extent that the time of withdrawal was dictated by the need to limit the duration of the offensive to a soundbite-friendly '100 hours' (as was wryly remarked by American ground forces commander Norman Schwarzkopf).

The moral cost was the decision to maximize Iraqi casualties through the allied bombardment and then, having permitted Iraq to escape half-defeated, to stand by as an uprising in the south was brutally suppressed, while imposing sanctions which have killed thousands through malnutrition and impoverished millions. There was little sign that this moral dimension was of much concern to planners. What mattered was a conflict virtually free of American casualties – bloodless war on one side, however bloody the consequences might be on the other.

The United States' decision to impose a no-fly zone in northern Iraq to protect the Kurds there in 1992 met five of the six tests, failing only that of overriding national interest. It was public concern at the spectacle of elderly refugees fleeing Saddam's poison-gas attacks into the mountains that prompted the move. For once, prime-time television had prompted intervention abroad: the tail had wagged the dog. Later strikes against Iraq – in 1993, following the discovery of an assassination plot against former President George Bush, and in 1996 after Iraqi troops violated the no-combat zone in northern Iraq, and again in 1998 – met all the six criteria for intervention.

The expedition to Somalia in 1992 was prompted by the humanitarian impact of mass famine caused at least in part by a civil war. Unusually, it failed four of the six tests (it was not vital to American interests, there was no clear objective, ultimately it did not play well on television, and the level of casualties, although fewer than fifty, was deemed unacceptable). The Somali intervention was regarded as a failure (although it averted famine) and put America off even small military commitments, particularly in Africa – for example an attempt to separate the warring sides in Rwanda–Burundi.

The United States steered vigorously away from military intervention in Bosnia as the problem escalated from a containable local Balkan confrontation – which American threats would probably have quenched – to all-out civil war. Between 1991 and 1993 some 1 million people were rendered homeless, around 200,000 died and 50,000 women were raped.

These cold statistics masked stories of individual tragedy, like that of a forty-year-old woman who told of dozens of women and guards being shepherded into the hall of a building where:

> they tore off their clothes, pulled their hair, cut their breasts with their knives. They would cut the belly of the women who wore the traditional Muslim baggy trousers. Those who screamed would be killed on the spot.
>
> In front of a few hundred prisoners they raped women and girls for days. It was unbearable to watch girls being raped in front of their fathers. In the evening, after heavy drinking, the Chetniks would come in the hall with lamps. Stepping on us, they would look for girls, not older than 12, 13. The girls cried, holding on to their mothers. As they were taken, pieces of their mothers' clothes remained in their hands. While doing that, the Chetniks would shoot at us.
>
> Later they would leave the girls' dead bodies in the hall, so we had to see them. We cried until morning. Then they would throw the bodies in the river. Every day the same picture was repeated; they would rape and kill in front of hundreds of us.
>
> Once a young woman with a baby was taken in the middle of the hall. It was in June. They ordered her to take off her clothes. She put

the baby on the floor next to her. Four Chetniks raped her; she was silent, looking at her crying child. When she was left alone she asked if she could breastfeed the baby. Then a Chetnik cut the child's head off with a knife. He gave the bloody head to the mother. The poor woman screamed. They took her outside and she never came back.

Horrific as such descriptions are, they are nothing new. Man, since the beginning of time, has shown how little encouragement he needs to return to bestiality, particularly in times of war. The aggression of Serbia and the opportunist savagery of Croatia were nothing new either: petty tyrannies and ethnic hatreds are phenomena as old as human history. What was missing, in the last decade of the twentieth century, was the will of outsiders to deter them, as though they had learnt nothing from every previous conflict in the century. One by one, the excuses for appeasing evil were reasserted with the kind of stubborn ingenuity that suggested that international relations had taken a giant leap back into the 1930s.

The conflict within Yugoslavia was initially described by the non-interveners as a 'civil' war. In fact Yugoslavia had always been an artificial creation and the aggression of its strongest component, Serbia, against first the Croats and then the Bosnians was plain from the first. Once Tito died and the Eastern bloc crumbled, there was no possibility of holding Yugoslavia together. The only issue was how much of it would be run by Serbia, which controlled the bulk of the country's armed forces. There could be no excuse for dismissing the war as an 'internal' affair when the international community had already granted recognition to such 'internal states' as the Baltic republics and even acknowledged an obligation to protect the stateless Kurds.

There was then an attempt to equate the three communities. It was said that this was an ethnic war between three sides equally guilty of atrocities. The fact that some appalling acts were carried out by Bosnia's Muslims could hardly obscure the overwhelming aggression and racial war – 'ethnic cleansing' – carried out against them; even the Croats, helping themselves to a piece of Bosnia, had themselves been victims of major Serbian attack. As early as November 1992, Tadeusz Mazowiecki, the respected former Prime Minister of Poland, reported to the United Nations Commission on Human Rights that 'the collective evidence leaves no doubt as to who is responsible for the horror [in Bosnia]: the Serbian political and military leaders in Bosnia-Herzegovina, supported by the authorities of Serbia.' The West pointed to the undiplomatic manner in which the Croats, and then the Muslims, had voted to secede from Yugoslavia. Thus the overwhelming desire of a people to be free through their own democratic choice was cynically dismissed by the democratic powers (Germany excepted).

The military establishments of the Western nations, in particular the Pentagon, were soon wheeled in to assert that military intervention in Bosnia was impossible, requiring an overwhelming commitment and small possibility of exit. In fact there was little evidence that the Serbs were particularly effective fighters. They were mainly successful in terrorizing civilians and shelling cities without retaliation. On the few occasions that well-equipped UN troops were allowed to retaliate against Serbian attacks, the effect was devastating. While the nature of Bosnia's terrain would certainly not render intervention a quick or casualty-free operation, it was no Vietnam either. Intervening forces would have had the vehement support of a clearly defined ethnic section of the population which, because of the policy of ethnic cleansing, was geographically concentrated; unlike Vietnam, the enemy would thus be visible and in front, not invisible and behind; the country was rough, but not jungle.

There must be some doubt that UN troops in Bosnia were really so exposed: heavily armed British tanks, for example, proved virtually invulnerable to the firepower of irregular Serb forces – as in attacks on convoys near Tuzla. The UN force at Vitez would have been within range of Serbian 155 mm guns in the hills, but the Serbian guns, if they had opened fire, would have been quickly subject to observation with advanced radar and heat-sensing equipment that could pinpoint them for air strikes. Moreover, artillery could have been provided to shore up UN positions. Playing up the threat of Serbian retaliation against 'vulnerable' UN forces seemed principally an excuse for staying out of the conflict.

The Serbs, effective at murdering unarmed civilians though they were, did not have an impressive record in real fighting. During the battle of Vukovar in 1991, for example, around 1,500 Croats, equipped only with rifles and handguns, held off 25,000 Serbs equipped with tanks, MiGs and heavy artillery for three months, until they ran out of ammunition. Far from being effective hand-to-hand fighters or guerrillas, the Serbs relied heavily on tanks and artillery in old-style Soviet fashion: some nine-tenths of the casualties they inflicted were from artillery and tank guns. Although some of the guns could be hidden, they had to emerge to fire, and the number of available sites – flat areas near roads – were limited in the mountains.

If Serbian firepower was exposed, so were their supply lines, across just half a dozen bridges spanning the Danube and the Drina. It is worth noting that the war between Serbia and Croatia only stopped when it reached a military stalemate – 'level killing fields'; tilted ones provide every incentive for the more powerful to continue to take territory. This, of course, is not a new doctrine, but one which dominated all Cold War planning, based on mutual assured destruction or, more simply, 'deterrence'.

Short of major intervention, other options existed, such as air strikes against Serbian artillery and the interception of supplies from Serbia into Bosnia. Neither was ever threatened or tried until too late. Publicly aired doubts about the difficulty of intervening, before Serbian aggression really got under way, sent a repeated message to the beast of Belgrade, President Milošević, that there would be no retaliation.

George Kenney, acting chief of the Yugoslav desk at the State Department, who resigned in protest at American inaction as far back as August 1992, angrily alleged that it was cold political calculus that explained why the Americans had kept out of Bosnia. 'The administration, I believe, made a basic decision at the highest levels that politically it had more to gain from not getting involved in a very messy foreign conflict where it cannot count on an easy or quick solution but risks getting the blame for failure.' He argued convincingly for limited military intervention:

Would US military involvement lead to a quagmire? Unless we were extraordinarily inept in our deployment of force, I doubt it. Although I am not a military expert, I believe that the forces in Bosnia are poorly disciplined, loosely organized and to a large extent nothing more than wild young men who have gone on a mass killing spree. These are the disgruntled who have no stake in what was normal society in Bosnia or in Serbia. But they have the guns and, for now, face only weak opposition. I am convinced that they would not stand up to a strong attack.

We do not have to take the ground and hold it. That is the Bosnian government's problem. But we could undertake a number of limited military actions that would greatly support the Bosnian government in its efforts to reclaim its territory.

All these suggestions were considered when it was too late to save tens of thousands of lives. Kenney's analysis had an uncomfortable ring of truth.

The prime movers behind the policy of non-intervention were the military establishments. In the United States, a post-Vietnam policy of non-intervention, except where American forces could be overwhelmingly deployed at very little risk, was still in force. The Gulf War had been a confirmation, rather than a departure, from this. In Western Europe, military establishments still in rivalry with one another, incapable of co-ordination except against a now-departed Soviet threat, proved unable to rise to any other occasion. America and Europe swapped recriminations about where responsibility for Bosnia lay.

America's Secretary of State, Warren Christopher, in an almost exact echo of Chamberlain's famous comment about Czechoslovakia on the eve of Munich, spoke of 'a humanitarian crisis a long way from home in the middle of another continent'.

The United States departed from years of precedent in suggesting that it would recognize Bosnia's new, shrunken boundaries. In 1931 the then American Secretary of State elaborated what became known as the Stimson Doctrine: America would not recognize political or territorial changes made by force – in this case China's occupation of Manchuria. This was later applied to Nazi and Soviet conquests from 1938 on, as well as to the Baltic republics seized by Russia in 1940.

The Europeans retorted that it was the global superpower America that should give a lead. On Bosnia Britain – America's traditional ally in conflict – provided the clear lead for the forces of cringe, blindness to evil and isolationism. By the time there was some will to act, particularly on America's part, the presence of UN forces with a major humanitarian mission provided another let-out: these would be attacked by the Serbs, it was asserted, if the West intervened.

Certainly the UN forces saved possibly hundreds of thousands of lives in the winters of 1992–3 and 1993–4, but their capacity to resist attack was never tested, and the right kind of intervention could anyway have protected them. Military intervention would have been difficult, cost lives and perhaps lasted years. But to assert that the West had no business to be where these appalling conditions applied was to rule out intervention in nine-tenths of the globe, to give aggressors everywhere a blank cheque.

It was asserted that the Balkans were of no strategic significance to the West, and that the war was a small, local one which would not spread. Aside from the flagrant immorality of this assertion – the Second World War broke out over Poland, after all, another country of no great strategic interest to the Western powers – contravened the facts. Serbia's war against Croatia had already spread to Bosnia, and Kosovo and Macedonia were tinder dry for conflagration to the south, with the further possibility of drawing in the Greeks and the Turks. The wider implications of permitting potential aggressors around the world to believe they could succeed, like the Serbs, were never addressed. For any European government to assert that aggression within Europe was of no strategic importance seemed remarkably short-sighted.

Finally, in as classic a statement of appeasement as was ever heard before the last war, worthy of the 1930s British politicians Sam Hoare, Kingsley Wood or Lord Halifax, Western policy-makers asserted that, with no military intervention contemplated, we could not even arm Bosnia's Muslims to resist the aggressor Serbs, who were fighting with the arsenal of the Yugoslav army behind them. Better to continue to twist the arm of the victim (Bosnia) to accept dismemberment than to help him fight back. In virtually every post-war conflict from which the West has decided to abstain, it has armed its own side or the perceived victims of aggression: Afghanistan's mujahidin and Angola's non-communist guerrillas are examples.

The West's attitude to Bosnia seemed to suggest that it was preferable that one side, the aggressor, applier of systematic ethnic cleansing and atrocities, be given the freedom to win, so as to get the killing over as quickly as possible. The new doctrine was to apply pressure on the loser to stop fighting. The consequences of such thinking being applied in the Second World War, or any other conflict, do not bear thinking about. What if Roosevelt had decided not to level the killing fields between Germany and Britain by denying the latter lend-lease in 1941? Thus the victims were starved of military help, the aggressors rewarded.

Truly, Western policy towards Serbia represented the very bottom of the barrel in international relations, a combination of cravenness, selfishness, inertia, immorality and tolerance of pure evil that will for ever besmirch the reputations of those principally responsible for it.

In July 1993, Eugene Rostow, the Reagan administration's Director of the Arms Control and Disarmament Agency, devastatingly attacked American inertia over Bosnia (other critics included Reagan himself and George Shultz, his Secretary of State):

> The Gulf War was fought not only to ensure America's access to the oil of the region but to defend a far more fundamental national security interest – that of resisting aggression. Mr Bush has said many times that if aggression is allowed to stand, the practice

spreads until it threatens the general peace; and, therefore, that the world community must enforce the rule even against relatively small violations.

This has been the basic theme of American foreign policy since the time of President Harry Truman.

Enforcing the rule of international law against aggression does not require the United States to send in the marines every time a leaf falls . . . But the major powers and the world community should take all substantial acts of aggression seriously, and move decisively against those that threaten regional or world stability.

Serbia's aggression against the former Yugoslav republic more than meets that standard. The most vital goal of U.S. security policy is to help build a system of world public order managed by the major powers in accordance with the rules of the United Nations Charter.

In an effort to escape from the challenge of the Yugoslav tragedy, some now contend that the collapse of the Soviet Union makes it less important for the Western allies to enforce the law against aggression than in the days of Soviet Union expansionism. A few even argue that because of the recent changes in Russian policy, the rule against aggression has become 'optional'.

This view is in error. A scrupulous respect for the rule against aggression is more important to the Western allies today than it was before the Soviet collapse began in 1989. In the short run, the Soviet collapse, like the fall of every other empire in history, has radically destabilized world politics. It will take an alert, perceptive and flexible Western foreign policy to make sure that the system emerges with a structure favourable to America's abiding national interests.

During this period of transition, hostile or unfriendly combinations of states may come into being, threatening to become hegemonies – combinations between Russia and Germany, for example, between China and Japan, or between Russia and China. This is no time to behave as if the end of the Soviet Union has guaranteed perpetual peace. A reasonably peaceful world order can only be built on the foundation of a favourable balance of power or, even better, a true concert of the major powers.

Fortunately, there is reason to believe that what happened in Bosnia will not set the pace for international relations: the West was caught on the hop by the end of the Cold War without the necessary deterrent structures for defusing regional conflicts and it misjudged the extent of the problem. But if Bosnia was the pointer to the future, global anarchy threatens to become reality indeed.

The cruel farce of Western policy towards Bosnia reached its nemesis on 5 February 1994. A mortar shell was lobbed into Sarajevo market, killing sixty-eight people, from a distance of less than a mile (leading to suggestions that the Muslims had acted to provoke Western retaliation against the Serbs). The television pictures of the carnage were ghastly, shocking even to Western publics that had become blasé about the suffering in Bosnia. That single massacre – a drop in the ocean of a slaughter that had claimed maybe 200,000 lives – prompted Western governments to go into fast reverse on policies of pusillanimity dressed up as sage and statesmanlike caution. The West had found a leader at last, by the improbable name of prime-time Television.

President Clinton was suddenly persuaded of the need for air strikes – but not of American ground troops – as was the French government. Britain went along reluctantly: we were at least consistent in our disdain. Miraculously, in a 180-degree change, the marketplace massacre had altered Western policy from do-nothing to do-something (the exact policy so long derided). It was decided that the previous objections to allied air strikes on Bosnian-Serb artillery outside Sarajevo no longer stood up. The risk to UN forces on the ground was no longer an overriding reason for staying out. Military action was no longer seen as dangerously open-ended. Nato was no longer deemed to lack the authority to act 'out-of-area'. Serbian artillery was no longer seen as untargetable, Serbian fighters as an overwhelming foe, air attacks as risking too many civilian casualties.

Unlike, say, finance ministers forced to put their policies into reverse by events, their diplomatic counterparts were finely skilled at chocolate-coating the total abandonment of a policy as an effortless progression towards an always-consistent goal. Nato, with a tough new British commander on the ground, General Sir Michael Rose, finally summoned the will to issue an ultimatum against Serbia to withdraw its artillery from a 12-mile exclusion zone around Sarajevo, under threat of air strikes. President Clinton sought to strengthen Western resolve after the massacre with the Churchillian rallying cry: 'Until those folks get tired of killing each other over there, bad things will continue to happen.'

A remarkable thing did happen as the ragged Chetnik militia of civilian slayers faced the threat of massive attack from the most sophisticated air forces in the world. The Serbs complied, their crumpled, amiable, double-crossing and mendacious leader, Radovan Karadžić, admitted that they were 'not so stupid' as to take on Nato. Not a single serviceman was required to die to achieve what had been declared unachievable only days earlier. A show of Western resolve, of the kind that had characterized the post-war decades, which over the previous three dog years of Western diplomacy had been entirely lacking, proved effective. Of course this was but a beginning, and many more trials lay ahead. But it was an enormous step forward for those who had long argued that Western political and military leaders should be less spineless. And it begged the question – how many lives might have been saved if Nato had acted a year or two earlier?

Sarajevo settled into an uneasy semblance of normality; the war slackened elsewhere. The high hopes aroused early in 1994 began to dissipate as it became clear that Western forces would retaliate only if public anger back home was aroused. The Bosnian Serbs taunted the UN by helping themselves to military supplies early in the summer, provoking a token response. In the summer of 1994 the devious Milosevič abruptly imposed an embargo on Bosnian Serbs for refusing to agree to the latest Western plan for carving up the country; it seemed that sanctions were at last having an effect on Belgrade.

Congress prodded President Clinton into setting a deadline for lifting the arms embargo on Bosnia's Muslims – which the Europeans argued would set off a new phase in the war. Certainly the timing would be wrong if it resulted in renewed fighting and a withdrawal of UN forces before the onset of winter; a delay past the winter was essential. Yet, failing Bosnian-Serbian acceptance of the plan – itself a nauseating legitimization of many of Serbia's conquests – lifting the embargo in the long term, particularly if UN forces were withdrawn, seemed the only course likely to give the Muslims a fighting chance.

In late 1994, under intense Congressional pressure, President Clinton announced that American forces would no longer help enforce the arms embargo on Bosnia. Nato air strikes against Serbian positions were also stepped up. Bosnian forces staged their first major effective offensive on all fronts of the war. This triggered a savage Serb counter-attack, and fierce fighting at Bihac.

Western policy-makers could not argue that their damage limitation exercises had shortened the war. The Bosnian crisis, in truth, served as an awful – if limited – example of the dangers of appeasement and the failure to install proper post-Cold War security structures: 'one that got away', as Sir Jim Lester, senior member of the House of Commons Foreign Affairs Committee, aptly defined it. Would that it were the only one.

By early 1995 the outlook was bleak indeed. With President Clinton and the new Republican majority in Congress united in continuing to rule out the despatch of large numbers of ground forces, and the Europeans insisting that they would send only peacekeepers in America's absence, the UN force had become the flimsy railing that prevented Bosnia from hurling itself over a cliff: a decision to withdraw would inevitably lead to all-out conflict.

The policy of sending UN peacekeepers, instead of a Western intervention force with a mandate to act against aggression, had been wrong from the beginning. But peacekeepers were better than no force at all. No foreign minister, understandably for once, would wish to be responsible for a decision to withdraw that could spark all-out war. The new Republican majority in Congress pressed for such a withdrawal, then quietened down as it began to realize the consequences. Britain's Defence Secretary, Malcolm Rifkind, let it be known that withdrawal was under active consideration, possibly as a tactic to concentrate the minds of the warring factions.

For the issue was not so much whether the UN should withdraw, but whether the warring factions would allow its forces to stay. The Serbs had always disliked and harried the peacekeepers, but permitted them to remain out of fear of Western military retaliation. By 1995 the prospects of any but limited Western air attacks were fading, which loosened the restraints on Serbian forces to behave themselves. The Croat President, Franjo Tudjman, threatened to force out the 12,000 UN peacekeepers between his forces and the Croat Serbs who had seized the enclave of Krajina in order to absorb it into Greater Serbia. Inevitably, Milosevic would come to their defence against the Croats. Only the Bosnian Muslims had an interest in retaining the UN presence; however, their demand for the lifting of the arms embargo would, if met, probably trigger an all-out Serbian offensive which would require the withdrawal of UN forces under fire.

Western policy-makers were thus boxed into a corner of their own making. It seemed clear that they should take no action – withdrawing UN forces, lifting the arms embargo – which at this stage might precipitate all-out conflict. The only sensible course was to prepare plans for the enforced evacuation of UN troops, itself a tricky and dangerous operation likely to take up to a year and involving the commitment of American ground forces.

Prospects for a settlement looked forlorn, with the Serbs refusing to talk and the Croats threatening to attack the Serbs. In repressed Kosovo, meanwhile, the pot, in early 1995, reached boiling point while the throttling embargo on Macedonia was bringing Greece and Turkey to the edge of conflict. Barring a determined effort by both the Americans and the Russians to force the three sides to a settlement backed up by the threat of military action, all-out war in the Balkans seemed in prospect. If the UN forces were forced out, the West would have no further excuse for denying the Bosnians the arms they sought against aggression. At last, faced by the prospect of further full-scale bloodshed, the West acted, threatening outright invasion. President Clinton secured the Dayton Agreement and Nato peacekeepers were sent in five years too late. The peace in Bosnia has been kept ever since. The United Nations mission handed over to 9,000 European peacekeepers at the end of 2002, leaving a democratic Bosnia with only 22,000 under arms compared with nearly half a million in 1995, and 250,000 refugees back in their homes. It was a remarkable success for international peacekeeping, and a model for elsewhere.

This deeply reluctant deployment of troops met four out of six of the Pentagon's criteria for intervention – the objective was clearly defined, limited in scope, almost wholly casualty-free, and defensible on television. The Bosnian deployment did not have such a clearly defined end or a vital interest – but it did belatedly patch up a deep rift with the rest of Nato and restore the rule of international law, which are key American concerns.

The 1994 invasion of Haiti met five out of the six criteria. The national interest at stake might seem negligible, although the country's plight had excited the concerns of the black caucus in Congress. Yet there were elements of deep farce: after an ultimatum from former President Carter, American troops were invited in by the very military junta they were supposed to overthrow, although they were initially instructed not to intervene as government thugs attacked the country's democratic forces. Pentagon spokesmen announced with relief that 'massive bloodshed' had been averted – which hardly seemed likely in any confrontation between overwhelming American military force and Haiti's ramshackle 7,000-strong militia, which possessed only six artillery pieces, one propeller plane, one helicopter and four working armoured personnel carriers.

Another one that got away, with even worse consequences, was Rwanda, a holocaust of near-Cambodian proportions. Following the death of

Rwanda's President in a suspicious air crash in April 1994, its Hutu majority turned on the smaller, but dominant until 1960, Tutsi minority and slaughtered up to a million people. The local UN commander, General Romeo Dallaire, said, 'we didn't need overwhelming force, but punctual and appropriate use of force to stop the slaughter.' He asked for more men and authorization to use them. By July, however, the Ugandan-supported Rwanda Patriotic Front, dominated by Tutsis, had seized control of the capital, Kigali, precipitating a massive exodus by Hutus fearing revenge. Altogether, some 2 million of Rwanda's 7.7 million population fled their homes, into Tanzania, Burundi, Uganda and Zaire, subsisting in horrific refugee camps, where some 40,000 quickly died of cholera. The new regime installed Hutus as president and prime minister and gave assurances that the refugees would be allowed to return peacefully; as Hutus made up 85 per cent of the population, reconciliation was in the Tutsis' interests – although few of the refugees trusted their promises.

The West stood inertly by as the bloodbath got under way, its belated intervention restricted to an inadequate, although welcome, refugee aid present of some $250 million primarily co-ordinated by the United States, and a well-intentioned French attempt to protect one section of the refugees. Many local observers believe that limited outside military intervention, before the rebels reached Kigali, might have provided the Hutu regime there with the security not to embark on the massacres and would have led to a negotiated settlement. When the massacres began, there were 2,500 UN observers present. Instead of being reinforced, most were withdrawn. In May President Clinton refused a UN request to send troops after nearly 500,000 people had been massacred. As a direct result, nearby Congo was plunged into war. Some 350,000 were killed there in three years, while more than 2 million died of disease or starvation, and 1 million lost their homes.

What cannot be disputed is that, in the absence of any outside interest whatever, the most horrific sequence of events possible followed, leading to vastly more expenditure and a more enduring refugee problem than a 'stitch in time' intervention would have entailed in the first place. President Clinton's reluctance to re-engage in another Somali-style quagmire and America's wish not to lose a single casualty, even when the lives of hundreds of thousands of non-Americans were at stake, must be judged in the harshest possible light.

Rwanda, of course, was precisely the kind of Third World killing ground that the post-Cold War West has been least equipped and least concerned to prevent. Only the existence of a volunteer, rapidly deployable UN intervention force, or of regional powers acting under UN auspices, as suggested later in this book, might have prevented the massacre. Following the UN's experience in Somalia (which, however, was a notable humanitarian success – the mistake was to be drawn into the country's internal politics), neither was on the cards. Another yawning gap in the post-Cold War security structure was exposed by Rwanda; Kigali and Goma were added to the 1990s' hall of shame and horror alongside Sarajevo and Gorazde.

One of the saddest postscripts of the Bosnian war came in 2002, when the entire Dutch government of Wim Kok resigned in honourable acknowledgement of the failure of 400 largely Dutch UN peacekeepers to stop the worst single massacre of the entire conflict, the slaughter of 7,000 men and boys at Srebrenica in July 1995. The peacekeepers actually helped the Serbs to separate the men from the women and children. The American Assistant Secretary of State for Human Rights John Shattuck wrote at the time of 'credible reports of summary executions and the kidnapping and rape of Bosnian women in Srebrenica', but the Clinton administration did absolutely nothing and has not similarly acknowledged responsibility.

The former southern states of the Soviet Union became a region of sporadic, almost unceasing, turmoil and bloodshed, with some thirty separate conflicts at the last count. There was, of course, the brutal pounding of Chechnya. In Georgia, rebellions in Abkhazia as well as by the followers of former strongman Zviad Gamsakhurdia left the country's President Eduard Shevardnadze on the ropes and provided a pretext for Russia to intervene to prop him up on its terms (almost certainly, the Soviet army helped the rebellions with this end in view).

To the south-east, Armenia lay blockaded by its neighbour Azerbaijan as punishment for its support for the Armenian enclave inside Azerbaijan, Nagorno-Karabakh. To break this President Levon Ter-Petrossian had to beg for Russian help – which the Russians were willing to grant provided a new Transcaucasian federation, consisting of Armenia and Georgia and Azerbaijan, was set up. With Russian bases and border forces this amounted to little less than a reconstruction of the Soviet Union in this area.

Azerbaijan itself lost about a fifth of its territory to the Georgians, who opened a salient up to Nagorno-Karabakh in years of savage fighting; tens of thousands were killed and up to 1 million Azerbaijanis displaced by the war – a slaughterhouse nearly on a par with Yugoslavia, although more remote from Western attention. The Azerbaijani leader, Geidar Aliev, sought Russian help and was prepared to join the Commonwealth of Independent States – but not to have Soviet occupying forces in his country. The presence of oil complicated the strategic calculation here, with some Western companies eager to move in.

To the east lies the vast province of Kazakhstan, more than a third of whose people were Russian, with large reported reserves of oil and gold, as well as part of the Soviet nuclear arsenal. So far the Russians have not interfered much in Kazakhstan, which has been flirting with the Americans. Its President, Nursultan Nazarbayev, has been closely allied to the fiercely repressive regime of President Islam Karimov in smaller Uzbekistan to the south.

Karimov's main objective has been to stop Islamic fundamentalism, and in this he enjoys warm Russian support. Further south still, in Turkmenistan on the very borders with Iran, another strongman, Sapurmurat Niyazov, also relentlessly repressed his Islamic movement and all expressions of dissidence. The most frontline state of all against Islam is Tajikistan, to the east, where moderate Islamic forces were driven out of power in December 1992 by a pro-Soviet regime backed by 20,000 Russian troops bent on suppressing Islamic guerrilla incursions across from Afghanistan. As with Turkmenistan and Uzbekistan, the regime is ferociously repressive: glasnost might as well not have occurred. President Yeltsin stated baldly that 'this border is in effect Russia's, not Tajikistan's'.

The belated incursion into Bosnia was followed by the intervention in Kosovo. Once again, the dangers had long been apparent, and the United States had many times hinted that it might intervene – which only served to encourage the Serbs into believing that no such intervention would take place. A series of threats followed by last-minute negotiating fudges only served to reinforce Serb scepticism.

Then the West suddenly began bombing, with the stated intention of forcing the Serbs to the negotiating table within a matter of days. Instead the Serbs accelerated the occupation of Kosovo, creating an appalling humanitarian crisis. The Western allies must be given the benefit of the doubt. The Serb occupation would probably have taken place anyway, even had the allied bombardment not begun, although the latter certainly accelerated the process, but this was little excuse for not having acted much earlier. The bombardment of Serbia itself may even have stiffened

Serbian opinion in favour of Slobodan Milosević. Only after weeks of this, the threat of ground intervention by allied troops caused the Serbs abruptly to withdraw, their forces surprisingly intact, and the chain of events began that led to Milosević's downfall. The operation could be judged a belated success. However, the Kosovo Liberation Army was soon to become a serious problem in its own right through its harassment of the Serbs.

Once again the six tests can be applied: Kosovo was not vital to American interests but public opinion on American television could no longer stand idly by as the massacres in Kosovo escalated and the refugee flow swelled. A clear objective was defined – keeping the Serb army out of Kosovo – but in this case there was no smooth exit. The commitment was limited and virtually casualty-free for Americans. But it was a near call: for had ground intervention occurred, significant casualties would have been incurred and, to repeat, it was only the threat of ground intervention that drove the Serbs out. It had been a very close-run test of America's post-1989 strategy.

CHAPTER 5

AFGHANISTAN, IRAQ,
THE MIDDLE EAST AND EUROPE

So to September 11 and Afghanistan. Has American strategy changed in the wake of nine-eleven, 'the last week of the world as it was', as one writer for the London *Guardian* put it, a day compared by some not just with Pearl Harbor but with 4 August 1914 or 3 September 1939? Some 78 per cent of American opinion formers and 79 per cent of those abroad, according to a poll three months later, considered that September 11 opened up a new chapter in world history. The determination with which the United States took the fight to al-Qaeda and the Taleban in Afghanistan would seem to suggest a new era. After a prolonged period of intense bombing, the collapse of the Taleban regime proved surprisingly swift, with the local forces of the Northern Alliance and their allies doing the great majority of the fighting.

But a quick glance down the familiar checklist shows that the Afghan operation conforms closely to the pattern of post-1989 interventions. The American assault on Afghanistan was obviously prompted by American national interests – punishment of those responsible for the September 11 massacre. The objective was clear and limited – to destroy al-Qaeda and its bases and the Taleban regime harbouring them. President Bush has repeatedly made it clear that America will withdraw as soon as its objectives are achieved; they have no intention of lingering, whatever their allies, who are urging completion of the job – 'nation-building' – might say.

The commitment has been a limited one, and no other major operations against other theatres have been undertaken while this one has been under way. The operation has once again been almost casualty-free for America, involving aerial bombardment, the use of limited numbers of highly trained, highly equipped special forces and large numbers of surrogates. Finally, it has been hugely popular in America, as the necessary expiation of the horrors of September 11.

There are other familiar aspects to the Afghan campaign. The Taleban, who until September 11 had been of minor concern to American policy-makers, were suddenly elevated to the status of major enemies although the evidence suggests that the regime, repressive as it was (although little more so than the murderous Northern Alliance regime it had supplanted) had little choice but to harbour al-Qaeda, whose financial means and military strength made it unassailable inside Afghanistan. The Taleban itself, like Saddam Hussein, had been strongly encouraged in the past by the United States as a counter to the Soviet occupying forces during the 1980s.

The United States' reluctance to commit its own ground forces even after so many Americans had been killed has been all the more striking. One senior European former minister puts the whole episode in starker terms: 'The Americans bomb from great heights and are getting better at it, while using local forces to carry out ground operations and incur the casualties.' The morality of using advanced technology and local surro-gates to inflict the maximum number of casualties on the enemy so as to preserve one's own forces casualty-free is debatable.

A year after the capture of Kabul, there are many disturbing signs that American goals have not been achieved. Both Osama bin Laden and the Taleban leader, Mullah Omar, have escaped capture. Taleban fighters, who fled into Pakistan and who largely control its frontier province, are infiltrating back into Afghanistan. Meanwhile the country's weak leader, Hamid Karzai, is locked in a power struggle with Defence Minister Mohammed Fahim, and has to be protected by American special forces. Warlords remain in control of most of the country outside Kabul. Although the al-Qaeda camps have been destroyed, Afghanistan is reverting to its lawless state, while neighbouring Pakistan has been destabilized by the war. America now hopes to build a 70,000-strong Afghan National Army. But the limits of megapowerdom are evident.

[The following was written and published shortly before the American invasion of Iraq; but in the author's opinion remains highly relevant.] With Afghanistan seemingly 'in the bag', Iraq has become the next suitable case for intervention. This author believes that Iraq presents a far more difficult challenge than Afghanistan. The American Secretary of State, Colin Powell, initially said as much when he pointed out in November 2001 that Saddam's military was far stronger than the ill-equipped Taleban forces and that the Iraqi opposition was not comparable to the Northern Alliance in Afghanistan:

> They're two different countries with two different regimes, two different military capabilities. They are so significantly different that you can't take the Afghan model and immediately apply it to Iraq.
>
> Everybody is focusing on Iraq as if it is the only thing out there, or it is time for us to do something beyond what we are doing. There are lots of Qaeda cells around throughout the world that we're going after, and there are other countries that are of concern to us besides Iraq.

No firm Iraqi connection has been established behind September 11 but America believes now is the time to deal with a country developing weapons of mass destruction and obstructing international inspection (which begs the question of North Korea and Iran) and, more plausibly, that Saddam's crimes against his own people require his removal by the international community – which perhaps should have been considered last time around, in 1991, when the prospects of removing him were vastly better. Other possible targets for intervention include Somalia, Sudan and Yemen.

The UN-authorized Security Council resolution in November 2002 put the ball squarely back into Iraq's court. The United States has not gone down a unilateralist route – it has sought and received the sanction of the world community: whether military action ensues depends on Iraq's compliance. This is a giant step forward for America: no country, however powerful (indeed being so powerful it has to set the example of obeying legal norms) can act outside the framework of global legitimacy which over the centuries has evolved to mark out that behaviour which is acceptable from that which is not. Nazi Germany was the most powerful nation in Europe, but that did not justify its actions.

Moreover, intervention against Iraq presents particular difficulties. First there is the issue of justifying invading a country which for ten years has taken no aggressive action against an outside power. It is in breach of a host of UN resolutions, but has complied with many others and many other countries are engaged in similar breaches; that is not reason enough. It is a country with a record of appalling repression of its own peoples but, again, so are a host of other countries (although, as I later argue, the world community should consider 'internal aggression' when serious enough as justifying international intervention as much as external aggression); but that is not justification enough today – particularly as many Western powers, including the United States, not only ignored but connived in this misbehaviour in the past. Perhaps the worst example was continuing United States Defense Department co-operation with Iraq even as chemical weapons were being used against the Kurds at Halabja. Indeed, Colonel Rick Francona saw the evidence of Iraqi gas attacks against the Iranians in the battle for the Fao Peninsula. The United States at the time did not view this as of 'deep strategic concern'.

Iraq possesses chemical and biological weapons and is developing nuclear ones – but so do other countries, which are deemed acceptable because they are 'friendly' (but, as for example Pakistan, they may not be so tomorrow). Iraq has long been deterred from using such weapons as it has by the threat of a nuclear reaction strike by outside powers, and there is no reason to believe this has changed. The case can be made that the combination of all three, plus Iraq's record of previous aggression, makes it uniquely dangerous; yet the argument is far from overwhelming. There is no convincing evidence linking Iraq to al-Qaeda or September 11. The CIA has just officially graded Iraq a 'low' threat to US interests, and Senator Bob Graham of the Senate Intelligence Committee has warned that Iraq could deflect America from the far more immediate threat posed by al-Qaeda.

Second, there is the issue of practicability. The expulsion of the Iraqis from a fellow Arab and Islamic country, Kuwait, in an unpopular war was accomplished by America and its allies with ease. But an outright invasion of the Iraqi heartland runs the risk of arousing a nationalist reaction among the Iraqi people. The Iraqis were stoic in resisting Iranian attacks when that long war in the 1980s started to go wrong; and history has frequently shown that bloody tyrants can be transformed into defenders of the fatherland when this is attacked – Stalin in 1942, Hitler in 1945 being the obvious examples. There is a strong possibility that the Iraqi people will turn on their oppressors and welcome the Americans as liberators; there is an equal possibility that the climate of fear in Iraq and the existence of strong vested interests and military forces that support the regime will lead to intense resistance, with ordinary people standing to one side to see which way the fight is going. The 450,000 or so Iraqi army, drawn up in 10 divisions, three of them armoured, and militia might crumble. The 80,000-strong elite Republican Guard, equipped with 600 tanks, and the 15,000-strong Special Republican Guard, with its 100 tanks and anti-tank Jagger guided missiles might fight to the bitter end.

There can be no doubt that the Americans will win any war against Iraq if they bring their overwhelming strength and technology to bear; indeed, once started, they cannot afford not to win; but the war could be messy and could involve significant American casualties if Saddam's forces prove capable of significant house-to-house fighting in the cities. The example of Khorramshahr, the shattered town on the Shatt-al-Arab, which I visited during the Iran-Iraq War, provides a horrifying display of what could go wrong (the Chechen capital of Grozny, which twice resisted Russia before being flattened at a high cost to both sides, provides a more recent example). To cope with this, American tactics are now based on seizing key targets in cities, rather than fighting for whole neighbourhoods.

Third, there is every prospect that a cornered Saddam would seek to widen the war by using chemical or biological weapons against his attackers and against Israel. The Israelis are confident that their defence systems could cope with the twenty-four or so Scud missiles Saddam is still believed to possess, and can be expected to behave with restraint in response, although Ariel Sharon has made clear that he would retaliate. Certainly, if significant casualties are inflicted on Israel the pressure for retaliation would be overwhelming, and could widen the war into an Arab one against Israel.

Saddam has long been deterred from using his weapons of mass destruction against Israel and the West by the threat of mass retaliation. Indeed former British Prime Minister John Major has made clear that the allies threatened to use tactical nuclear weapons – his phrase was 'immediate and catastrophic consequences' – against Iraq during the 1991 Gulf War should it deploy chemical or biological weapons against them. This deterrent has been highly effective up to now (and indeed begs the question of why Saddam, after a decade of being deterred, is considered likely to resort to them now if he is not attacked). But if he has his back to the wall, he may consider he has nothing to lose. If he uses chemical weapons in southern Iraq, as General Wesley Clarke has pointed out, up to 14 million people will be at risk, creating huge problems for the invading armies. Again, it is for the military planners to judge the extent and acceptability of the risk.

The fourth chief concern relates to the impact on Iraq's neighbours. The United States has a very small front on which to operate – only Kuwait and some of the tiny Gulf statelets have shown any enthusiasm

– although others can be cajoled or bribed, and America's sea and air projection make up for some of this deficiency. But Saudi Arabia, long facing internal calls for the expulsion of the 6,000 or so American troops on its territory, could be destabilized if conscripted into helping, as could Jordan, which was so concerned in 1991 that it sided with Iraq.

Turkey, a key ally, is deeply reluctant to get involved. Turkey's former Prime Minister Bulent Ecevit stated bluntly before his departure, 'We know that the United States cannot carry out this operation without us. That is why we are advising that it abandon the idea.' He claims that 'a de facto Kurdish state is already being formed'. His successor is even more opposed to the idea. The huge financial costs of the last invasion are still remembered, quite apart from the knock-on effect of autonomy for the Iraqi Kurds. The Turks are quietly threatening to invade Iraqi Kurdistan; the Kurds reply that the region would become a 'graveyard' for the Turks.

September 11 provides no justification for an attack on Iraq, as despite intensive intelligence research, only the most tenuous links have been established between Iraq and al-Qaeda. Indeed, it would be unusual for Saddam's ruthlessly disciplined regime to have any but intelligence-gathering relations with a disparate and decentralized organization that it could not control such as al-Qaeda. Saddam practises a ruthless secular socialism which pays only lip service to Islam, and is the polar opposite of obscurantist conservative Islamic fundamentalism. To bracket al-Qaeda with Saddam is on a par with equating Nazism and Soviet communism during the inter-war period in Europe as examples of European extremism, and represents the kind of quasi-racist dismissal by Washington of differences between Arab countries and political movements that most irks people in the region.

The fifth chief concern is that an unprovoked assault against a second Islamic country after September 11 – and one which has no obvious connection with that attack – could precipitate precisely the kind of rolling confrontation between Islam and the West which the United States is so anxious to avoid, and so play directly into al-Qaeda's hands. In terms of Islamic terrorist recruitment, it could swell the ranks of young suicide bombers. On a 'street' level it seems certain to increase anti-Americanism and opposition to the unpopular regimes the West is seen as buttressing in the Arab world. At an elite level it increases the pressure on those regimes to radicalize or grow more hostile to the West. This is perhaps truest of the most important vulnerable regime, Saudi Arabia.

There are many in the West who dismiss these fears with

generalizations. The Arabs, it is said, respect strength and no such upheaval, although much predicted, occurred in the last Gulf war. The last proposition is true – but the West at the time was acting to defend an Islamic nation against aggression by a neighbour – which is a very different matter to invading an Islamic nation currently at peace with its neighbours.

Some theorists in Washington even think that an attack on Iraq will cause the regimes in other Middle Eastern countries to collapse in a glorious outbreak of regional democracy and goodwill. Condoleeza Rice, the President's national security adviser, has talked of a 'march of democracy'. Ali Dessouki, Egypt's Minister of Youth, who is grooming the young Gamal Mubarak for power, remarked of this: 'Cinderella. How nice of her. Is she dreaming?' No seasoned observer of the region could share this opinion or view any such collapse, if there is one, without the utmost apprehension in view of the extremist forces likely to rise to the surface. With America failing to take action against North Korea, most Arabs believe Iraq has been singled out in an effort to take control of its oil.

The sixth chief worry is the endgame. A host of theories has been bandied about as to what would replace the Iraqi government in the event of Saddam's overthrow, ranging from a MacArthur-style occupation of Japan to democracy, federation and dismemberment. After visiting Iraq several times, it seems to me the dangers are all too real. The Shia majority, more than 60 per cent of the population, is not going to accept continued domination by the Sunnis – just 22 per cent – after several decades of tyranny, whether in a federation or not, and the Sunni people of the centre, fearful of vengeance, seem unlikely to lie down under Shia rule. Since 1998 a series of top Shia clerics have been gunned down by Saddam, including the Grand Ayatollah Mohammed Sadiq al Sadr in an ambush on a road near Najaf, and Hussain Bahr al Uloom last year, probably in revenge for the 1996 attack on Saddam's son, Uday, which crippled him.

One plausible scenario is an American-backed Sunni government in the centre vying with an Iranian-supported Shia majority in the south – not a pleasing prospect for the Americans. Both the main eixile groups, the Iraqi National Accord and Iraqi National Congress, are both predominantly Sunni. In the north the Kurds, some 20 per cent, who already enjoy great autonomy under the no-fly zone, may be enticed to enter a federation. Equally, they may prefer to seek outright independence and grab the Mosul-Kirkuk oilfields – which will almost certainly invite

Turkish and Iranian intervention, as both would be fearful of the establishment of an embryo Kurdish state that could dismember their own countries. The Turks, indeed, have threatened a thrust into Iraqi Kurdistan to control a rush of refugees in the event of war – which is widely expected to be a pre-emptive strike against a fledgling Kurdish republic.

Immediately after the war, uprisings and revenge killings, particularly in the south, seem all too likely. In 1991 hundreds of Baathists were hacked to death and buildings burnt and looted. The MacArthur solution seems preposterous except in the very short term: he ruled through the office of the Emperor and the existing Japanese government, not after the collapse of the regime. At a minimum, 75,000 US troops would have to be stationed there at a cost of some $16 billion a year for several years – an insupportable burden. The casualties would be even more insupportable if the Americans found themselves confronted with widespread Iraqi opposition and an Iranian-backed Shia insurgency in the south.

It is not impossible that the Iraqis, who are still one of the more highly educated, developed and urbanized peoples of the Middle East, would embrace a messy democratic federation with power-sharing and checks and balances to ensure that no single group – not even the 60 per cent Shia one – would gain power. If so a constitutional monarchy under the respected Hashemites to unite the country might be by far the best option. But more likely Saddam's overthrow would soon trigger widespread conflict within the country that could be stopped only by another iron hand (just as Nasser's rule in Egypt was followed by Sadat), which would run directly counter to American goals in the country. As former US Vice-President Al Gore put it: 'The resulting chaos in the aftermath of a military victory could easily pose a far greater danger to the US than does Saddam.' The danger of instability in Iraq spreading to neighbouring countries such as Turkey, Syria, Jordan, Saudi Arabia, Kuwait and Iran is also serious.

Last and least is the cost. The 1991 Gulf War cost some $60 billion ($80 billion in today's dollars), only a fifth of it paid by America, and probably precipitated the American recession that followed. This one may cost as much, and four-fifths of the cost will be borne by America. If it recovers the money from Iraq, it will incur bitter opprobrium.

A list of dangers of this length should make any country, no matter how powerful, pause for thought. The danger is one of a botched intervention which massively sets back American objectives in the region, and indeed the cause of civilized and peaceful government in the world. The containment policies of the last decade have for the most part worked well, preventing further Iraqi aggression and reducing its imports of military equipment to a few spare parts, but no tanks and aircraft. Only chronic defiance by the Iraqi government regime of the UN-mandated inspections, and continuing development of, in particular, nuclear weaponry should force America to war. It is to be hoped that the Iraqis come to their senses, preferably with the overthrow of Saddam into the bargain (although his ruthless skill at survival makes this far from easy, as dozens of executed conspirators would testify if they could).

One prominent American academic recently went so far as to assert that the United States has no need to construct a coalition of allies in its overseas interventions: 'If allies want to join us, fine, you have permission to join us [sic] but this is an American war and we do not need you. We don't need the UN, the EU or Nato.' This insensitive, pugnacious, patriotic, we-don't-need-friends attitude (which is constantly reflected in Hollywood films where allies are at best dispensable and at worst untrustworthy) is in a sense part of America's strength. As a people they will not be cowed.

But calmer voices are also desperately needed. As Seitz puts it, 'looking back, I cannot think of anything of substance we have achieved internationally without the validation of allies.' America not only desperately needs its traditional friends, but it must reach out to make new ones. If only a handful of terrorists can wreak such havoc, just consider the dangers posed by one or more genuinely hostile states – never mind the more than 1 billion Muslims some American commentators rashly embrace as natural enemies.

The American scholar Joseph Nye in *The Paradox of American Power*, has thoughtfully introduced the notion of 'soft power' in contrast to 'hard power' into the debate about America's global dominance. This is hugely important. While, he argues, America is unquestionably possessed of more hard power than any nation in history, it is losing the argument in terms of soft power – diplomacy, winning friends across the world, public opinion and the ability to get 'others to want what you want'. Nowhere is this more self-evident than with the Arab-Israeli conflict, which is so extensively covered elsewhere that I do not propose to examine its tragic complexity here in any detail, save to make two observations relevant to this book.

As an illustration of Nye's point, it is truly astonishing how a power possessed of the unparalleled military and economic strength of the

United States has proved unable in the thirty-five years that have elapsed since the 1967 Middle East War to make any other than limited progress towards the resolution of this seemingly intractable dispute. The notion of American omnipotence is quickly dispelled by a glance at the size of the problem – Israel, a territory with the size and double the population of Wales or a smallish American state, Palestine with a still smaller territory and people.

The impact of the problem of course spreads much further afield, but the main Arab players nearby have actually been remarkable for their reluctance to be dragged directly into the dispute, in spite of Palestinian anger and unrest in their own countries. Egypt seized the first opportunity for peace after the Yom Kippur War in 1973, militant Syria has respected the ceasefire on the Golan Heights (although Lebanon has for long been a running sore between the two countries), Jordan has been scrupulously well behaved, and Iraq, while resorting to strident invective and a handful of Scud missiles against Israel during the Gulf War, has not gone to full-scale war against Israel. Although there are many extremists in the Middle East who see advantage to be derived from unceasing Israeli-Palestinian turmoil, most countries in the region are desperately keen for a resolution of the conflict.

The dispute has caused more difficulty than any single global issue, and taken up more man-hours of America's State Department than any other. Yet after the short-lived euphoria of the Camp David and Oslo agreements, the region has settled back into a tit-for-tat slugfest of escalating turmoil. The United States has showered economic assistance on two of the main players, Egypt and Israel, and military assistance to the latter in an effort to keep the peace. Yet with the current Palestinian intifada, the recent wave of Palestinian suicide attacks into Israeli territory, and the massive armed intervention by the government of Ariel Sharon into the West Bank and Gaza, prospects have rarely been as bleak since the Oslo accords, which some observers argue have unravelled altogether. If the world's first megapower cannot achieve peace between these two muleheads, who can? Indeed, one might ask, what is the purpose of possessing such power to so little effect?

In fact, the United States has shown a remarkable diffidence about using the power at its disposal to bring the warring parties together. Some argue that this is because of the powerful pressure of the Jewish lobby in Washington, others because of Arab oil power, others still because of the sheer danger and volatility of a region with so many potential sources of conflict. Yet with the end of the Cold War, one of

America's greatest fears – that the Soviet Union would take advantage of any American missteps in the Middle East – has vanished. Still America has not lost its caution.

More than two decades of observing the conflict has not deflected this author from the conclusion I reached on my first visit to Israel in 1979 – that unless the United States, perhaps alone, perhaps with its allies, is prepared to send in a serious peacekeeping force to divide the two combatants in the region, there will be no peace. A situation in which one country, Israel, is overwhelmingly preponderant militarily and in occupation of another's territory, while yet retaining a justified sense of insecurity and encirclement, is inherently unstable, offering constant temptations and provocations to both sides to continue the fighting.

Only the United States and its allies (not the UN, which is regarded with deep suspicion in Israel and has no real military authority) has the power to deliver a peace that will be trusted and respected on both sides. It is understandable why America has been deeply reluctant to assume such a responsibility, which could entail a very long haul and the risk of losing lives (although this is perhaps exaggerated in the context of an Arab-Israeli peace agreement). But as with their eventual incursions into Bosnia and Kosovo, America's global responsibilities now require action to stop the two sides continuing to toss firecrackers at each other across the powder dump of the Middle East.

The British experience in Northern Ireland is not an encouraging demonstration of the cost of responsibilities involved in such peace-keeping; it has been a huge burden for the British, who have little real sympathy for either side. But who can doubt that without the British military presence in the province, the toll of the past thirty years would have been much, much worse? Responsibility comes with power, and the United States, if it wants to be treated with global respect, must exercise one with the other.

A peacekeeping force presupposes, of course, agreement, which seems as remote as ever, as carnage in Israeli cafés and at bus stops alternates with Israeli tanks smashing their way through Palestinian neighbour-hoods. Yet, as Oslo and Camp David Two showed, the two sides are really not that far apart when the dynamic repulsive forces of internal Israeli and Palestinian politics do not drive them apart. My under-standing is that Prime Minister Ehud Barak of Israel did privately offer most of the territory demanded by the Palestinians at the second Camp David talks (although this is a matter of public wrangling); that the Palestinians are privately prepared to drop their formal demand for the right of return of refugees expelled in the first Arab-Israeli wars in exchange for the dismantling of most of the Israeli settlements on the West Bank; and that the issue of Jerusalem, while nitpickingly tricky, is not insurmountable.

I remember on my first visit, those two old stalwarts of Israeli politics Abba Eban and Yitzhak Rabin carefully drawing a line for my benefit delineating the boundaries of Israeli and Palestinian statehood, which hardly differs from the line proposed by Barak. How many thousands have died and tens of thousands of lives been ruined – and how many will continue to be so – to get back to the same line as twenty years ago?

There are of course still fanatics on the Palestinian side who would wish to drive the Israelis into the sea and extremists on the Israeli side (including Ariel Sharon when I talked to him twenty years ago) who speak of regaining the lands of Judaea and Samaria and driving the Palestinians to form a state across the River Jordan. But in view of Israel's military strength, the former view is utterly unrealizable, and in view of demographic patterns, the latter also futile. On current birth rates a 'greater Israel' would inevitably result in a majority Arab population of Israel – unless Israel embarked on a policy of mass population expulsion or a denial of Arab voting rights, which is surely unacceptable in today's world. Thus, ironically, the 'greater Israel' policy would actually overwhelm the Jewish majority and achieve the traditional Palestinian objective of ending the Jewish state – which cannot be acceptable to the great majority of Israelis.

The lines of a settlement are clear. The very security that an American and allied military presence would give the Israelis would be the best stimulus towards such an agreement – and the best deterrent against Palestinian violations of the settlement. The current combination of bribes and diplomacy may not achieve a settlement of this vicious, dangerous dispute for many years yet, if at all. The logic of American megapowerdom dictates that the United States sends an effective peace-keeping force to separate the combatants as well.

The growing rift between the United States and its traditional Western European allies is often glossed over because 'we share the same culture and fundamental values' – liberal democracy, free trade, economic prosperity and so on. In fact, this is a seriously mistaken view. The gap has grown wider with the end of the Cold War – we have lost our common enemy – and is growing wider still, for a variety of reasons. That this is regrettable does not mean that it is not happening. It is bad for Europe, which still depends on American military protection and can also lend a restraining hand. It is bad for America because while the current temptation is just to shrug the matter off, the world's only megapower will need all the friends it can get in a hostile world. East Asia, which does not share much of the culture and fundamental values, and is sliced up between a number of competing powers which share no common defence or economic alliance, is no substitute. This Atlantic quarrel is one of the most serious developments in the post-Cold War era.

Living on different parts of the planet, we have divergent interests and perceptions of danger. Western Europe is much closer to the main sources of global instability – in particular the Middle East. It does not share America's commitment to Israel to anything like the same degree, believing that the continuing occupation of the West Bank is providing the prime obstacle to a settlement there and generating turmoil in the region. Regional threats from places like Iraq, Algeria, Libya or even Iran could provide physical dangers to parts of Europe within missile range, as well as exposing European countries, which have much larger Islamic populations than the United States, to major terrorist attack. Europe, too, is vastly more dependent on Middle East oil than America.

With North Africa gradually emerging as a major, if still unstable, trading and population bloc of its own, Europe is deeply concerned about its trade and relations immediately to the south, much more so than the United States. Western Europe is hugely affected by migration both from these countries and from the East. Now that the Cold War is over, European relations with Russia and the former Soviet bloc countries are much closer than those the United States enjoys. America often seems surprised that with our 'common values' Europeans should feel they have differing interests: yet this is no more surprising than, for example, Western Europe's failure to show the same degree of alarm at the threat that Cuba allegedly poses to the United States.

Europe's history, in spite of the common cultural background, has been vastly different from that of the United States, which more nearly resembles that of Australia, Russia or Brazil, other countries with moving frontiers that have recently colonized vast continental interiors. Obviously a new and highly unified continental nation of immense economic power with a common language has very different perceptions to an ancient continent of – until the last sixty years or so – usually warring nation states, which has twice in the last century experienced the ravages of total conflict across much of its territory, and has only recently embarked upon a unique experiment in political and economic co-operation.

Americans tend to belittle the advances made towards these goals, none more so than the common currency which many in Washington repeatedly asserted would never happen; and it remains true that Europe remains primarily a union of separate and distinctive nation states with a sometimes spidery and convoluted bureaucratic structure of co-operation between them. Yet it took the United States a civil war and some hundred years of territorial expansion to fashion the great political and economic union it has become; and a further half century to become a formidable military power (as late as the early 1930s America had only the sixteenth largest army in the world).

Europe, which once bristled with warring and competing military powers, has not set itself up as a military union but as an economic one to rival the United States, partly out of a sense that only by doing so will it be accorded equal treatment from across the Atlantic. That the Europeans have done so under the umbrella of American military protection understandably causes considerable resentment in the United States – which, however, is reciprocated in Europe whenever its attempts to develop common foreign policy and military institutions run into a volley of criticism and ridicule from America. The Americans seem reluctant to make up their minds whether they want Europe to do its own fair share of defending the peace around the world, or whether they want to keep Europe dependent on the American defence umbrella.

Some Americans believe that the mid-Atlantic rift is more fundamental still. Richard Perle, a senior Pentagon adviser, claims that Europe 'Has lost its moral compass . . . Germany has subsided into a moral-numbing pacifism.' A powerful, and at times provocative statement of American concerns was recently published by Robert Kagan of the Carnegie Foundation in Washington (*Prospect*, August 2002). According to Kagan:

It is time to stop pretending that Europeans and Americans share a common view of the world, or even that they occupy the same world. On the all-important question of power – the efficacy of power, the morality of power, the desirability of power – American and European perspectives are diverging. Europe is turning away from power or, rather, it is moving beyond power into a self-contained world of laws and rules and transnational negotiation and cooperation. It is entering a post-historical paradise of peace and prosperity, the realisation of Kant's 'perpetual peace'. The US, meanwhile, remains mired in history, exercising power in the Hobbesian world where international laws and rules are unreliable and where true security and the defence and promotion of a liberal order still depend on the possession and use of military might . . .

Europeans could provide peacekeeping forces in the Balkans – indeed they eventually provided the vast bulk of those forces in Bosnia and Kosovo. But they lacked the wherewithal to introduce and sustain a fighting force in hostile territory, even in Europe. The European role was limited to filling out peacekeeping forces after the US had, largely on its own, carried out the decisive phases of a military mission and stabilised the situation. As some Europeans put it, the division of labour consisted of the US 'making the dinner' and the Europeans 'doing the dishes' . . . Rather than viewing the collapse of Soviet power as an opportunity to flex global muscles, Europeans took it as an opportunity to cash in the peace dividend. Average European defence budgets gradually fell below 2 per cent of GDP and European military capabilities steadily fell behind those of the US throughout the 1990s . . .

Today's transAtlantic problem, in short, is not a George Bush problem. It is a power problem. US military strength has produced a propensity to use that strength. Europe's military weakness has produced an understandable aversion to the exercise of military power. Indeed, it has produced a powerful European interest in inhabiting a world where strength doesn't matter, where international law and institutions predominate, where unilateral action by powerful nations is forbidden, where all nations, regardless of their strength, have equal rights and are equally protected by internationally agreed rules . . .

Americans are 'cowboys', Europeans say. And there is truth in this. The US does act as a sheriff, perhaps self-appointed but widely welcomed nevertheless, trying to enforce some peace and justice in what Americans see as a lawless world where outlaws need to be deterred, often through the muzzle of a gun. Europe, by this analogy, is more like a saloon-keeper. Outlaws shoot sheriffs, not saloon-keepers. In fact, from the saloon-keeper's point of view, the sheriff trying to impose order by force can sometimes be more threatening than the outlaws who, at least for the time being, may just want a drink . . .

The 'essence' of the EU, writes Seven Everts, is 'subjecting inter-state relations to the rule of law', and Europe's experience of successful multilateral governance has in turn produced an ambition to convert the world. Europe 'has a role to play in world governance', says Romano Prodi, a role based on replicating European experience on a global scale. In Europe 'the rule of law has replaced the crude interplay of power politics' . . .

Given that the US is unlikely to reduce its power and that Europe is unlikely to increase more than marginally its own power or the will to use what power it has, the future seems certain to be one of increased transAtlantic tension. The danger – if it is one – is that the US and Europe will become positively estranged. Europeans will become more shrill in their attacks on the US. The US will become less inclined to listen, or to care. The day could come, if it has not already, when Americans will no more heed the pronouncements of the EU than they do the pronouncements of Asean or the Andean pact.

To those of us who came of age in the Cold War, the strategic decoupling of Europe and the US seems frightening. If Americans were to decide that Europe was no more than an irritating irrelevancy, would American society gradually become unmoored from what we now call the west? It is not a risk to be taken lightly, on either side of the Atlantic.

Kagan's arguments are worth quoting at length because they reflect much current American intellectual and government thinking. What really is frightening is the conception of America as an international power not bound by the rule of law. Clearly, in any structured global system, there is a need for both law making and its enforcement. To take the saloon-bar analogy, if America is the sheriff, Europe (and indeed the American people) resembles more the peaceful burghers of the town on whose behalf the sheriff acts, not a shady saloon-keeper. To separate the two functions is a prescription for lawlessness: for if the sheriff does not obey the law, does he not quickly become a vigilante or even an outlaw himself? Surely the Soviet Union, possessed of huge military power unmatched by its economy, also saw itself as a sheriff of Eastern Europe, if not the world?

Where Kagan is absolutely right is his stress on the need for continuing military strength among the democracies to cope with the multiple threats to peace from around the world. As he says, Europe must spend more on defence and bear its fair share of the burden of defending freedom: greater European defence integration should also play its part in this (although many senior American officials over the years have objected to both). Clearly, if America has possession of the gun, it is for the peaceful inhabitants of the town (including Americans) to set down the laws and rules of engagement in which it can be used.

For a town as big as the world, it would be nice to have two sheriffs and even a posse. It is hard to look at countries like Britain, France, Spain, and even Germany and Italy, both of which are showing a growing disposition to perform 'out-of-area', and sincerely conclude that they have declared a farewell to arms. But they do have different interests and perceptions of danger and its proximity, particularly in North Africa, the Middle East and Eastern Europe. The Americans should sometimes consider that not everyone in the world sees other countries exactly as they do. America has much more sense of proximity and of responsibility – despite being an ocean away – towards the Far East and South Asia. A division of labour, as suggested later in this book, is called for. And yes, Europeans should spend more on defence if they wish to have an equal say in enforcing the law.

Yet it would be premature to rush to judgement. The Bush administration, more than most, has shown two faces to the world, reflecting the character of the powerful axis of Vice-President Dick Cheney and Defense Secretary Donald Rumsfeld on the one hand, and Secretary of State Colin Powell on the other, with the President acting as final arbiter. So far President Bush's rhetoric has been forthright and unambiguous, more so than any predecessor since Ronald Reagan, and has certainly matched the determined mood of the American public. The President's condemnation of the 'axis of evil' in his 2002 State of the Union address escalated the rhetoric beyond what was wise (although concrete proposals were vague). It is not clear that Iraq, Iran and North Korea had any connections with al-Qaeda, or much with each other, and whether similar solutions were proposed for all of them; subsequently this was softened.

But the Bush administration's actions have become much more deliberate, particularly since the abandonment of a unilateralist approach to Iraq in the summer in favour of a UN-approved one. War with Iraq, although probable, is not yet inevitable. The decision to go to war now rests with the Iraqi regime itself, if it refuses to abide by the properly authorized ultimatum of the global community to eliminate its weapons of mass destruction.

All of this is the proper conduct of a great power, which should wage war only if a country presents an overwhelming or immediate danger. The Bush administration's elaboration of new doctrines of pre-emption rather than deterrence, and of overwhelming power, are much more dubious, although it remains to be seen whether it amounts to anything in practice. Some other controversial initiatives – initial hostility towards China, the imposition of steel tariffs – have been sharply watered down, while others – repudiation of Kyoto, the scrapping of the ABM Treaty – represent no more than a bowing to American domestic political reality, and others still, such as Missile Defence, may indeed be the right policy. Still others – such as the scrapping of the Test Ban Treaty and the decision to mothball, not eliminate, excess nuclear warheads – are clearly ill-judged.

But, apart from the controversial Iraq policy, it is the rhetoric that marks a break with the past, and is losing friends. To paraphrase Teddy Roosevelt, 'Speak loudly and wave a big stick' seems to be the watchword of the Bush administration. The slight Republican edge in the mid-term congressional elections suggests cautious, but not enthusiastic, popular approval.

CHAPTER 6

THE BENIGN EMPIRE

There are three proper American responses to September 11: to seek out the perpetrators and bring them to justice; to try to prevent such outrages through the necessary security measures; and to isolate the killers in their own societies through securing the broadest possible consensus for the international rule of law and for American policies. It is the third that has been conspicuously lacking. Why does so much of the rest of the world hate Americans so? Americans searching for the answer could do worse than look to the debate within their own country as to their place in a unipolar world. Some commentators are not so much triumphalist as outright imperialist.

This holds that, in the words of respected *Washington Post* columnist William Pfaff, 'America has always identified the national interest and universal human interests.' Two respected commentators, William Kristol and Robert Kagan, wrote in *Foreign Affairs* in 1996 that 'the appropriate goal' of American foreign policy was to preserve world hegemony 'as far into the future as possible' through a policy of military supremacy and moral confidence. 'The more Washington is able to make clear that it is futile to compete with American power' the less likely it is that others 'will entertain ideas of upsetting the present world order'.

Joshua Muravchik's book, *The Imperative of American Leadership*, argues that 'aside from perhaps the French, the only people averse to American leadership are Americans'. The world, he suggests, is grateful for American hegemony as it knows 'that they have little to fear or distrust from a righteous state'. Daniel Deudney, of Pennsylvania University, goes further. The West, he says, should be turned into an

American-led world federation: 'The allies are now in a position comparable to the American states in the constitutional debate in 1787–8 over centralized federal power. In other words, Washington should in name as well as in fact become the capital of the Western world.' Thomas Donnelly, Senior Fellow at the Project for the New American Century, is an unabashed imperialist who believes in 'policing the American perimeter in Europe, the Persian Gulf and East Asia . . . I think Americans have become used to running the world and would be very reluctant to give it up, if they realised there were a serious challenge to it.' Charles Krauthammer, the American conservative, openly presses for a new American unilaterism 'because we run a uniquely benign imperium'. Charles Fairbanks of Johns Hopkins University says that America is an 'empire in formation'. Robert Kaplan speaks approvingly of the emperor in Ancient Rome combining 'diplomacy with the threat of force to preserve [the peace].'

A magisterial new analysis of global affairs, warfare and international law was published in 2002 by a Washington insider, Philip Bobbitt. His historical sweep and vision are remarkable and his central thesis groundbreaking and intriguing: this is that the world is at one of half a dozen turning points in its history. To risk over-simplifying an erudite and complex argument, the old-fashioned nation state, which came into being primarily as a defensive unit for the prosecution of war against its neighbours, has had its day. Now that nuclear weaponry, terrorism, cyber-warfare and biological and chemical weaponry can so easily penetrate its defences at a fraction of the cost of the mass-mobilization of states needed to win the last century's conventional wars, the nation state is virtually obsolescent. It was heading that way anyway because of its replacement by the 'market-state', a porous shadow with little autonomy of its own in a world dominated by the global market, which is partnered by transnational institutions wielding as much or more power.

Bobbitt's initial conclusion – most of the book was finished before September 11 – seems almost uncannily prophetic:

National security will cease to be defined in terms of borders alone because both the links among societies as well as the attacks on them exist in psychological and infrastructural dimensions, not on an invaded plain marked by the seizure and holding of territory . . . There will be no final victory in such a war. Rather victory will consist in having the resources and the ingenuity to avoid defeat.

Bobbitt's faith in the global free market if unoriginal, is unquestioning, even missionary:

> the market-state promises a 'virtuous' circle to those states that copy its form and obey its strictures. The privatisation of state-owned firms brings immense capital gains to the state as it liquidates vast monopolies; this windfall supplements the savings from cuts in welfare programs and thus lowers deficits, which leads to less inflation, which attracts capital and lowers the borrowing costs required to finance deficits, which in turn lowers the deficits still further, which permits lower taxes, which can produce more savings, which can enable more investment, which produces more funds for research and development, which enhances productivity, which lowers prices thus making exports more competitive, which creates jobs while lowering the cost of living for the consuming public. In the underdeveloped world, such policies mean higher growth owing to comparative wage advantages, which growth leads to a more educated population, which brings more women into the workplace, which leads to lower birth rates, which enhances political stability, which means greater macro-economic prudence, which leads to more foreign investment, which finances still more growth, which tends to liberalise authoritarianism, which encourages personal autonomy.

But this leads to some startling geo-strategic conclusions. In common with other observers of 'asymmetric' warfare, Bobbitt believes that 'states will have to reconfigure and retrain their forces to function in ambiguous environments, where the threat may come not from another state or even an identifiable aggressor, and where the line between war and crime has been smudged'. He argues:

> Deterrence and assured retaliation, as well as overwhelming conventional force, which together laid the basis for the victory of the coalition of parliamentary nation-states in the Cold War era, cannot provide a similar stability in the era of the market-state to come because the source of the threats to a state are now at once too ubiquitous and too easy to disguise. We cannot deter an attacker whose identity is unknown to us, and the very massiveness of our conventional forces makes it unlikely we will be challenged openly. As a consequence, we are just beginning to appreciate the

need for a shift from target, threat-based assessments to vulnerability analyses. A target or threat-based strategy depends upon retaliating against enemy assets. The threat of retaliation against known targets keeps the peace. A vulnerability-centred strategy employs various defences to keep the peace when the targets for retaliation are unknown.

Where does this lead?

Two tasks lie before us: to decide, as states, when it is appropriate to use force in this new world; and to determine, as a society of states, when to collectively sanction the use of that force in this world. This is a matter of creating precedents and case law. It amounts to deploying the habits of law on behalf of strategy, and of course vice versa.

These precedents and case law, however, are not those generated by courts. We may accomplish in Bosnia a successful, long-term intervention by the society of states on world-public-order grounds; if we do, then the Yugoslav Wars will become as much a precedent in the future as the Gulf War is now. The same is true of our war on international terrorism. The rules of collective engagement will be based on how the last similar problem was approached, and on what basis we would like to see the next, future problem resolved. I believe that the combination of improvised constitutional instruments with increasingly settled case law is the appropriate method for the society of market-states. This combination is a reversal of the method of the nation-state (and to that extent may take place outside the U.N.).

This is startling indeed, for an expert in constitutional law. It is in fact an ingenious and elaborate justification for consigning the painstakingly built structure of international law to the scrapheap and starting again with ad hoc interventions which would provide precedents and case-law for future invasions. Thus presumably an invasion of Iraq would provide a precedent for an occupation of Saudi Arabia, and so on, without the time-wasting business of achieving international legality or consensus. It is, in fact, a carefully crafted justification for precisely the policy the Bush administration may now have arrived at – creating international law through its own actions. Bobbitt glosses over the difficulty of getting other countries to accept the legitimacy of such unilateralist law –

making it up as we go along – but perhaps this doesn't matter for the lawgiver if he has overwhelming force on his side.

In an elegantly crafted inversion, Bobbitt sees al-Qaeda as 'a malignant and mutated version of the market-state.

> Like other emerging market-states, it is a reaction to the strategic developments of the Long War that brought forth cultural penetration, the liberalisation of trade and finance, and weapons proliferation, on an unprecedented scale. Like other states, this network has a standing army; it has a treasury and a consistent source of revenue; it has a permanent civil service; it has an intelligence collection and analysis cadre; it even runs a rudimentary welfare program for its fighters, and their relatives and associates. It has a recognisable hierarchy of officials; it makes alliances with other states; it promulgates laws, which it enforces ruthlessly; it declares wars.
>
> This network, of which Al Qaeda is only a part, greatly resembles a multinational corporation but that is simply to say that it is a *market-state*, made possible by advances in international telecommunications and transit, rapid computation, and weapons of mass destruction. Lacking contiguous territory, Al Qaeda is a kind of virtual state . . .

It would not be surprising if Bobbitt's book serves as a kind of legally empowering bible for the thinking behind part of the current American administration. Yet the wealth of erudition, historical analysis and stimulating and provocative constitutional and strategic theory do not sustain the extraordinary conclusions which appear grafted on to the work: that free markets and modern technology are destroying the old nation state, just as insidious and lethal methods of warfare are slipping past its borders; therefore entirely new strategies are needed to deal with these new enemies, including, for example, an invasive concept of homeland security and pre-emptive attack; and that therefore international law should be made up as we go along to deal with this new situation.

Bobbitt evidently has the United States in mind as the principal lawmaker. But isn't that also a nation state, as remain most of its enemies such as Iraq, Iran and North Korea? And is not the primitive nationalism of such states just as much of a threat as the terrorist hybrid of al-Qaeda, which may be something of a freak, dependent on a

combination of wealth and fanaticism (after all the idea of huge conglomerates of evil such as Smersh and Spectre has been around since
James Bond and *Man from Uncle* days, and this is the first that has
shown up)? And are not the time-honoured, tedious methods of better
intelligence, international co-operation and pressure on those that help
terrorists a better way of fighting non-state terrorists, rather than
elaborate new doctrines for striking across borders (most nations af-
flicted with terrorist incubuses would be delighted to co-operate to get
rid of them) and smothering limitations on freedom in the home country?

Is there not a political dimension to reducing the conditions that create
support for terrorists, something entirely unaddressed by the security
theorists? Are surveillance societies and pre-emptive strikes really likely
to be any more invincible than the clumsy old nation state's traditional
methods in stopping terrorists smuggling in anthrax or dirty bombs? Is
the nation state indeed really doomed? That is not entirely apparent from
the wealth of petty nationalisms that have sprung into being since the end
of the Cold War, and the nationalist and ethnic conflicts between them.

Indeed, the nation state only seems to be weakening under the impetus
of global free markets in the more sophisticated democracies of North
America and Western Europe, which are most likely to be the victims of
terrorism. Its instigators are likely to be intensely nationalistic or disintegrationist states which provide a handy bolt hole for terrorists, like
Somalia or Yemen, which America seems to have no legal inhibitions in
zapping from time to time, arousing an international outcry only when it
bombs the wrong targets. Mr Bobbitt's book is worth reading for the
journey, rather than the destination.

Consider, too, the most significant intellectual duel in post-Cold War
America, that between Francis Fukuyama and Samuel Huntington. Both
depart from the same premise – the innate superiority of American
values. For Fukuyama in *The End of History* this is already established:
the crushing defeat of Soviet collectivism – the alternative model – was
'the end of history'. For Huntington, there are other equally difficult
struggles to come: history, he believes, will continue as a clash of cultures
– specifically the one between Western Judaeo-Christian values and
Islam. Huntington is in no doubt of the superiority of the former over
the latter.

Fukuyama at least displays less ignorance of the world outside: it is
possible to argue that basic human rights, the free election of leaders
through the ballot box and even free enterprise are elemental human
rights with a universal application to all peoples.

Huntington's views, in particular, are dangerously simplistic. He makes the obvious point that divisions between civilizations are centuries old, and that with the world 'becoming a smaller place' these civilizations increasingly rub up against each other. However, such clashes were much worse in the past, when nations had fewer inhibitions about pursuing conquest. Huntington asserts that 'cultural characteristics are less easily mutable . . . than political and economic ones . . . Russians cannot become Estonians and Azerbaijanis cannot become Armenians.' Of course, all nationalities can become Americans! He continues:

The process of economic modernisation and social change through-out the world are separating people from long-standing local identities. They also weaken the nation state as a source of identity. In much of the world religion has moved in to fill this gap, often in the form of movements that are labelled 'fundamentalist'. Such movements are found in Western Christianity, Judaism, Buddhism and Hinduism, as well as in Islam. In most religions the people active in fundamentalist movements are young, college-educated, middle-class technicians, professionals and business persons. The revival of religion provides a basis for identity and commitment that transcends national boundaries and unites civilisations.

. . . The growth of civilisation-consciousness is enhanced by the dual role of the West. On the one hand, the West is at a peak of power. At the same time, however, and perhaps as a result, a return-to-the-roots phenomenon is occurring among non-Western civilisations. Increasingly one hears references to trends towards a turning inward and 'Asianisation' in Japan, the 'Hinduisation' of India, the failure of Western ideas of socialism and nationalism and hence 're-Islamisation' of the Middle East. And now a debate over Westernisation versus Russianisation in Moscow. A West at the peak of its power confronts non-Wests that increasingly have the desire, the will and the resources to shape the world in non-Western ways.

These generalizations lead him into some unfortunate convolutions: 'the success of the North American Free Trade Area depends on the con-vergence now under way of Mexican, Canadian and American cultures.' When have Mexican and American cultures ever been remotely regarded as even capable of converging, except in the sense that the United States occupied large parts of former Mexico and that huge numbers of Mexicans have now migrated to the United States?

In making both his additional points, Huntington unwittingly concedes victory to Fukuyama. In my view, it is because of the global transformations wrought by 'economic modernisation and social changes' and, moreover, as a reaction to Western industrial changes that old civilizations are returning to their roots. The more powerful, universalist phenomenon of modernization is impregnating the whole globe, hence the need to assert more traditional cultural values and defend them.

Obviously Huntington has a point: this need can take a violent, fundamentalist, anti-Western form. But it can hardly supplant Western progress. The Industrial Revolution and the technological revolution both come from the West. Islam, Buddhism and Hinduism have not made their own models of science: there is no such thing as an Islamic way of designing an aircraft engine. Instead these civilizations have adopted Western science and technology (just as the West once adopted 'Islamic' numerals and Chinese warfare manuals) while not abandoning their Eastern values – indeed, in some cases, reasserting them, as Huntington says.

There is no inevitability of a clash here (although some may occur), no inherent superiority of one over the other. Which is superior, a culture skilled in warfare, or one in the humanities, or one in the sciences? Each have prevailed at one time or another. Who is superior, the artist, the mathematician or the philosopher? The question is obviously meaningless. A Buddhist may argue that he has a religion that is more likely to lead to self-fulfilment and inner peace, a Muslim that his has a more complete way of life and social relations, or a Christian that his is the more charitable and tolerant. Cultures can argue ad nauseam about the merits of their different architectural styles without resolving which is superior (although intriguingly the dome of the main mosque in Qom is of the same proportion as that of the main basilica in Florence, suggesting some universal dimensional verity – but that is another argument!). The answer is that they all have equal value except to their followers.

If Huntington's clash of civilizations really is on the cards, then Armageddon beckons. Compared to around 2 billion Christians, there are now some 1.4 billion Muslims, more than three times as many as in 1960, largely owing to their higher birth rate. There are now Islamic majorities in forty-nine countries. A war against communism, a short-lived secular ideology, could be won; a war against the deep-rooted religious beliefs of hundreds of millions of people can never be won. Further, the schisms and divisions within both the Christian and Islamic worlds are so colossal that to view either as monolithic is simply untenable.

Fortunately, Huntington has confused the situation in the Middle East with the wider Islamic community in the world, most of which has no interest beyond a historic-religious one in the distant Middle East. Even there he ignores the emergence of an educated middle class in many nations and the fact that before September 11 Islamic fundamentalism seemed to be in retreat in its major enclaves – Iran, Algeria, Egypt, Sudan and Jordan.

Perhaps the worst aspect of Huntington's thesis is its quasi-racialist dismissal of the huge political differences across the Arab world (never mind the Islamic world as a whole) as irrelevant compared to the cultural identity of this huge swathe of mankind. The Baathist Socialists of Iraq and Syria have as much in common with the religious fundamentalists of Sunni Iran and Shia Saudi Arabia, the tolerant kingdom of Jordan or the democratic parties of Turkey as the 'Christian' Nazis and Fascists had with Christian liberal democrats in Europe before the Second World War. But they are all lumped together as 'Islamic'.

At the risk of indulging in a sweeping generalization of my own, the common confusion between the 'Arab' and the 'Islamic' worlds provides food for thought. Islam is seen as a uniquely authoritarian creed: yet it extends across entirely different ethnic and cultural groups thousands of miles apart. In Asia it blends in with traditional, highly organized hierarchical societies of peasant origin such as exist in Indonesia, Malaysia and on the subcontinent. In the Middle East, on the contrary, it orginally acted as a binding force for scattered groups of feuding, lawless tribesmen.

Is it a coincidence that the most militant expressions of Islamic fundamentalism today have emerged from the latter environment, originally an almost Wild West gun-law society compared with the respectful and ordered Asian Islamic tradition? Al-Qaeda, for example, flourishes precisely where there is barely any state authority at all – Yemen, Afghanistan, Sudan. Perhaps the shallowness of this argument itself exposes the absurdity of generalizing about the one-sixth of humanity stretching from Mindanao to Morocco.

As for the Israeli-Palestinian problem, the surprising thing is how little it influences the predominantly moderate Arab regimes in the Middle East, not how much; their own inter-Arab disputes are often just as bitter. Besides, is the Arab-Israeli quarrel really a clash of civilizations or religions? It is surely much more an argument over territory between ethnic groups claiming rival historical legitimacy.

In many respects, indeed, Israel is closer to its Middle Eastern roots and even to its Arab neighbours than it is to Western forms of Christianity that have mutated over 2,000 years in very different environments among different peoples. Fortunately Huntington's lurid scenario of a clash of civilizations is just that: a nightmare. There is no reason to believe that the world's great civilizations cannot continue for the main part to coexist by showing due respect for one another – with pockets of intolerance, of course. Fukuyama seems to have the last word:

There does seem to be something about Islam, or at least the fundamentalist versions of Islam that have been dominant in recent years, that makes Muslim societies particularly resistant to modernity. Of all contemporary cultural systems, the Islamic world has the fewest democracies (Turkey alone qualifies), and contains no countries that have made the transition to developed nation status in the manner of South Korea or Singapore.

There are plenty of non-Western people who prefer the economic part of modernity and hope to have it without having to accept democracy as well. There are others who like both the economic and political versions of modernity, but just can't figure out how to make it happen. For them, transition to Western-style modernity may be long and painful. But there are no insuperable cultural barriers to prevent them from getting there, and they constitute about four-fifths of the world's people.

Islam, by contrast, is the only cultural system that seems regularly to produce people like Osama bin Laden or the Taleban who reject modernity lock, stock and barrel. This raises the question of how representative such people are of the larger Muslim community, and whether this rejection is somehow inherent in Islam. For if the rejectionists are more than a lunatic fringe, then Huntington is right that we are in for a protracted conflict made dangerous by virtue of their technological empowerment.

. . . We remain at the end of history because there is only one system that will continue to dominate world politics, that of the liberal-democratic West. This does not imply a world free from conflict, nor the disappearance of culture. But the struggle we face is not the clash of several distinct and equal cultures fighting amongst one another like the great powers of nineteenth-century Europe.

The clash consists of a series of rear-guard actions from societies whose traditional existence is indeed threatened by modernisation. The strength of the backlash reflects the severity of this threat. But time is on the side of modernity, and I see no lack of US will to prevail.

This begs all kinds of issues: in particular whether the 'liberal-democratic West' is indeed an ideal goal or still has much further to evolve, a subject I will return to. As for Islam regularly producing people who reject modernity lock, stock and barrel, Fukuyama might do worse than to look at certain fundamentalist Christian sects in his own country. Yet on a more general level what the Fukuyama–Huntington debate does graphically show up is not just that the United States has a real problem in its new awkward position as sole superpower in relating to the rest of the world but that – even more seriously – it is unaware that it has a problem. Why are so many countries that share its very own Judaeo-Christian values among its bitterest critics?

Later, this book will offer suggestions as to how the United States can get to grips with this problem. But first if history has not in fact ended or become a life-or-death struggle between Christianity and Islam it is necessary to look at what is happening in the great world across the two oceans and below the Rio Grande. What are the security challenges in the new world disorder following the end of the Cold War and how should they be addressed? Has the world really become a more danger-ous place since 1989?

Many politicians and commentators in America, and a large swathe of public opinion there, believe that the only necessary response to September 11 is to punish those responsible in a fierce enough way to deter future terrorists, and to improve security within the United States to a level at which it is impossible for such attacks to recur. Even to state these propositions is to expose their absurdity. The terrorists that staged the attacks were suicide bombers, who are unlikely to be intimidated by normal forms of punishment. Certainly every possible weapon and deterrent should be employed against them and their support groups, as will be outlined later, but absolute security is not to be had.

As for creating a secure 'fortress America' – even if this could be done without an intolerable inversion of precisely those freedoms and open-ness that define the country's greatness – how could this be achieved for a nation with so many of its citizens working abroad, with so large a stake in the world, with so many vulnerable interests outside America, and with so many first-generation immigrants?

More significant still, the world is shrinking, in the old cliché. Technological and security developments make it less and less possible for any country to cut itself off from outside events. September 11 demonstrated graphically how small numbers of men equipped with the most primitive of technologies – crude knives, for example – can have a devastating impact. The new technology is even less secure, as the millions spent on security for computer systems testifies. While complete security is unattainable – and always has been – closing your eyes to the outside world provides no more than an illusion of security.

Commenting on *The Return of the Strong*, veteran British foreign-policy columnist Godfrey Hodgson wrote in the *Independent*:

Twenty years ago I interviewed Dr Benjamin Mays, a very wise black man who grew up in south Carolina at a time when he was lucky to be taught to read, and ended up the chairman of the Atlanta school board. He was reminiscing about the glory days of his pupil Dr Martin Luther King's march on Washington when people felt 'this is the time, and the things we've been struggling for for centuries are just about at hand'. And he looked at me and said, 'well, it's never so'. The collapse of the Soviet empire seemed another such moment . . . Well, it's never so.

Not only is it never so, it has not been less so for decades. The threats to global security are more varied in nature, more numerous in terms of the countries able to project them, above all more capable of being delivered from one side of the globe to another, than at any time in history.

PART II

SOURCES OF INSTABILITY

CHAPTER 7

TERRORISM AND
THE ISLAMIC QUESTION

Terrorism and Islamic fundamentalism now head the list of threats to global security in most people's minds. The former American Secretary of State George Shultz identified the problem as long ago as 1984:

> If the modern world cannot face up to the challenge, then terrorism, and the lawlessness and inhumanity that come with it, will gradually undermine all that the modern world has achieved.
> Democracies are vulnerable, because of their openness, their respect for individual rights and their difficulty understanding the fanaticism and apparent irrationality of many terrorists, especially those who kill and commit suicide in the belief that they will be rewarded in the afterlife.

The current fashion for suicide bombing creates an appalling new dimension because it neutralizes most of the usual deterrents – the death penalty, fear of being killed by security forces, life imprisonment. It is not, of course, new, as the kamikaze attacks on American ships in the Pacific War testify. But only dreary vigilance at all times and on all aircraft can stop it, and this means the time-consuming business of searches, X-ray machines, armed guards aboard aircraft and reinforced cockpits. Then what about trains, ships, shopping centres and buses?

Terror tactics have been with us for centuries. The targeting of innocent people to terrorize populations is one of the oldest ways of war, from the French atrocities during Napoleon's invasion of Spain (which were reciprocated with a vengeance) through to the Nazi massacre at Lidice following the assassination of the deputy Gestapo chief Reinhard Heydrich. A host of undeclared 'terrorist wars' have been ravaging parts of the world for decades, from those of Hezbollah, Hamas and Islamic Jihad in Israel, to Eta in Spain, to the IRA in Ulster, to the Tamil Tigers in Sri Lanka, to the Islamic groups in Kashmir and the Chechens in Russia.

The 1970s marked a particular high point, with the Red Brigades in Italy, the Baader-Meinhof Gang in Germany, the various Palestinian groups, the Montoneros in Argentina, the Tupamaros in Uruguay and so on. Terror waxes and wanes, as new techniques are discovered and as the intensity of society's negligence diminishes or increases. Anyone looking at the dismally lax state of security at many domestic airports can be in no doubt that there is much more to be done in terms of prevention.

But terrorism has recently shown a huge upsurge. Between 1968 and 1989, some 25,000 acts of terrorism were recorded around the world (1,670 a year). In the following seven years alone there were nearly 31,000 (nearly 4,400 a year). Some 50,000 people were killed in 1990–1996 – double as many as in the previous fourteen years. The number of civilian to military casualties is now 8:1 – an exact reversal of the pattern one hundred years ago. The ease of communications, the way in which people today can travel across the world without challenge and the existence of a global village through the media which makes, for example, someone living in a remote hamlet in Saudi Arabia familiar with the United States without ever having travelled there – apart from the issue of suicide bombers – make terrorist acts potentially commonplace.

There ought to be comfort in the thought that as people's standards of living improve, so they have more to lose and are less likely to engage in acts of mindless or suicidal nihilism. But the al-Qaeda attackers, whose pilots at least appear to have been well-educated professionals commanding rather more rudimentary cadres, offer little such consolation. As long as human discontent exists, fanatics and killers can be found among all classes. As is not the case in war, terrorists are a very small number of people, and misfits can always be recruited to their ranks.

As Archbishop Desmond Tutu and the British military analyst Sir Michael Howard have said, far better to describe these people as common criminals than to recognize them by declaring 'war' upon them. This used to be standard British practice in Ulster, and even the American government, in refusing to recognize al-Qaeda captives as prisoners of war, appears to be rethinking this (although there is, of course, another issue involved).

While the pool of potential recruits across the world may be huge, the methods have the potential to become increasingly dangerous: dirty bombs – conventional bombs capable of spreading radiation over a huge area, as al-Qaeda appears to have been developing – chemical weaponry of the kind employed by the Japanese terrorist organization Aum Shinriko to contaminate the Tokyo underground, biological weaponry, even exploding a small nuclear device are all horrendous possibilities in the near future. None can be prevented with any certainty.

According to the World Medical Association recently, bioterrorism

> could prove catastrophic in terms of the resulting illnesses and deaths, compounded by the panic such outbreaks would generate . . . The consequences of a successful biological attack, especially if the infection were readily communicable, could far exceed those of a chemical or even a nuclear event. Given the ease of travel and increasing globalisation, an outbreak anywhere in the world could be a threat to all nations.

Anthrax is difficult to vaccinate against, has a long life and in weapons form is very deadly, but cannot be spread easily. Smallpox and bubonic plague, on the other hand, can – but can be vaccinated against.

But, as with the campaign against crime, society simply has to improve its fightback. September 11 has sparked a new alertness to terrorists, with potentially enormously fruitful results. The campaign against the funding of terrorism has opened up a whole new front, and spectacular results are already being achieved. The intelligence war, which had gone into lamentable decline over the past two decades – the CIA had few operatives capable of speaking Middle Eastern languages, and had completely failed to penetrate the al-Qaeda network on the ground, becoming over-reliant on technological surveillance, while British intelligence had actually disbanded its section specializing in Islamic militancy – needs an enormous boost, and not just against Islamic extremists.

By using September 11 as a reason to target not just the terrorists themselves but countries that harbour them, the Bush administration has created a major precedent. This does not amount to a carte blanche for taking action against countries which involuntarily harbour terrorists;

but it does mean that the United States and other Western countries can oblige such countries to crack down on terrorists with real effect or, where they lack the means to do so, to step in. Somalia, Sudan and Yemen are obvious examples, while American forces are already helping the Philippine army in its war against Muslim separatists.

For countries like Iraq, Syria and Libya, whose governments may be permitting terrorists to train and operate from their soil, a clear warning is necessary, with a limited deadline given for expelling these groups; otherwise the United States and its allies would be justified in considering going in and 'taking out' camps and terrorist facilities whether through aerial or special forces operations.

For those who protest that these are 'freedom fighters' rather than terrorists the definition made earlier will do; in particular, those who deliberately target civilians, rather than military or official targets, to attain their objectives are terrorists – not soldiers. South Africa's African National Congress fighting apartheid provides a useful benchmark: while some splinter groups, and occasionally ANC combat units in error, did cause civilian casualties, the objective was military and strategic targets. The ANC thus qualified as a genuine liberation army; the IRA, whose targets were civilian as often as military, did not. Additionally, if the society in which an armed group operates is one in which political objectives can be achieved through the ballot box and one where the rule of law is respected, rather than a coercive one, then violence against even the forces of the state is criminal and terrorist. In a society based on coercion, armed action against the forces of repression is, in certain circumstances, justifiable (as in the ANC case).

But if terrorism, like crime, is with us to stay, that is no cause for despair. The author witnessed two major terrorist offensives at first hand as a journalist during the 1970s, one in Italy, the other in Argentina. In Italy the ferocity of the attack by the Red Brigades, the Armed Proletarian Nuclei and half a dozen splinters can hardly be overstated. Even Giovanni Agnelli, the respected president of Fiat, told me that he believed Italy was 'going the Argentinian way' towards ungovernability and endemic terrorism.

The prediction proved true of neither country. Through highly efficient police methods, including the penetration of terrorist cells and using 'pentiti' – penitent terrorists – to inform on their comrades, coupled with a humane refusal by the Italian state to resort to arbitrary methods, which would have swollen terrorist ranks, the whole offensive petered out during the first half of the 1980s.

In Argentina the same result was achieved through extreme brutality, including the murder or 'disappearance' of thousands of suspects, the suspension of civil rights for the whole nation and the widespread use of torture. There is no doubt which was the preferable method, the one which caused the fewest scars for the nation, and which worked soonest. But in both countries the scourge was eliminated.

'Separatist' terrorism, rather than ideological terrorism, has proved far harder to eliminate, possibly because it enjoys sympathy among a wider section of the population. Religious terrorism may fall into this category as well. The aim there should be one of containment and in particular limiting the appeal of the extremists to their likely sympathizers, even if total elimination may be unachievable.

The leap from fighting terrorism perpetrated by a handful of Islamic fundamentalists to considering all Muslims potential enemies is a vast one, but some, like Samuel Huntington, have made it. Even if Huntington's thesis is untenable, is there a specifically Islamic challenge to the West which repudiates its values, often resorts to violence and is likely to grow in strength? This is the second of the twelve security challenges apparently facing the world today.

At one extreme are those who argue that Islam is inherently anti-Western and expansionist. They point to verses in the Koran which suggest that Muslims have a duty to convert, to defeat other religions and to wage 'jihad' – holy war – upon them. Islam is also said to be clearly a 'way of life' affecting all aspects of a believer's earthly existence, including his political opinions and social behaviour. Islam is alleged to be a much more hierarchical and authoritarian religion than others, one inherently opposed to democratic ideas of personal rights. Finally, Islam is said to be inherently oppressive of women – and thereby by implication a more 'primitive' religion than others.

As Professor Ephraim Karsh of King's College London, puts it:

Unlike Christianity, which distinguishes clearly between God and Caesar, imperium and sacerdotium, Islam has historically combined the two first in the person of Prophet Muhammad, then in the form of the Sultan-Caliph; and even after the fall of the Ottomans, the last great Muslim empire, and the abolition of the caliphate in the wake of the First World War, the inextricable link between religion, politics, and society has remained very much alive.

This in turn means that there is no essential contradiction

between the 'greater' and 'lesser' forms of jihad. Quite the contrary, the concept of a 'holy war' against the 'infidel' has played a focal role in the history of Islam, from its rise in the seventh century to the present day. Participation in this endeavour can readily be considered an integral part of a Muslim's quest for personal self-enhancement . . .

There is no grassroots yearning in these societies for Western-style democracy, and any attempt to impose such a system is bound to encounter mass resistance and to be viewed by the local populations as neo-imperialism or a latter-day imposition of the 'white man's burden'.

Hassan Banna, who founded Egypt's Muslim Brotherhood in 1928, declared: 'It is the nature of Islam to dominate, not to be dominated, to impose its laws on all nations and to extend its power to the entire planet.'

In fact, it is heavily disputed whether the Koran advocates 'offensive' or merely 'defensive', or indeed personal, jihad. Nor does the Old Testament, interpreted literally, exactly shy away from supporting war in the cause of righteousness or the faith. Both Old and New Testament repeatedly insist upon religion as the guide to every aspect of life. Christ appears to advocate a detachment of religion from politics ('Give unto Caesar that which is Caesar's') but that is because He favours personal spiritual redemption, not material fulfilment. Christianity's rules are no less all-embracing than Islam's, however few actually fulfil them.

There is a strong patriarchal streak in the Koran which more resembles the Old Testament than the New, and the bias against women seems unmistakable; but this has to be viewed in the light of the society – the Arabian Peninsula – in which the Prophet lived and worked, where he was bringing order to a tribalistic and anarchic society, and actually establishing clear rights for women who were previously regarded as little more than slaves.

Just how uniquely different, paternalist, authoritarian, aggressive and misogynist is Islam from other religions? Fred Halliday does a fine job of demolishing some myths in his *Two Hours that Shook the World* (Saqi, 2001):

The Islamic tradition has a concept of 'legitimate' or 'just' war, *al-harb al-mashru'a* or *al-harb al-'adila*, just as Christianity has its concept of 'just' war. In contemporary Arabic there is a clear distinction between struggle that is legitimate, *jihad*, and that which is aggressive, illegitimate or motivated by robbery, *ghazu* or *'adwan*. The Quran (e.g. *suras* 9:13 and 22:40) contains legitimation for going to war, but also warns against the illegitimate use of force. 'Fight in the cause of God those who fight you. But do not transgress limits: for God loves not the aggressors (*mu'adun*) . . .'

Even the more pious would concede that the holy texts contain many ambiguities and possibilities for alternative interpretation, what the more secular among us would call contradictions. Most great works of human thought and literature do. Among Christians, 'Turn the other cheek' is juxtaposed with 'An eye for an eye, a tooth for a tooth', for example. The Quran enjoins that there should be no compulsion in religion (*la ikrah fi al-din*), but also makes clear in quite punitive terms, remote from freedom of choice, what will happen to unbelievers. Judaism is ambivalent on attitudes to gentiles. Hinduism contains much that can be used to enjoin an ethic of non-violence and tolerance, as Gandhi for one realised to great effect; it also has a mythology and language replete with the warlike and the blood-thirsty, as today's militants are quick to tell us. What the ideological interpretation would suggest is that the terminology, the injunctions, the very content of these texts are a resource that populist movements, consciously or not, use for contemporary purposes. There is, in this sense, no one 'true' Islam or Christianity or Judaism. It is possible in Islam to justify, for example, any general form of society – not just capitalism or socialism but also feudalism and slavery. It is possible to cite parts of the Quran that favour equality of men and women – it is also possible to cite plenty of passages that favour male supremacy.

Halliday points out that Ayatollah Khomeini's own interpretations of Islam and its role in the state are highly unconventional and controversial within the Shia community:

Khomeini's religious outlook was based not just on a literalist reading of the Quran, but on certain trends within Iranian Shi'ism: on the one hand, *irfan*, or mysticism, which enhanced a certain disdain for the immediate and the material, and on the other, the interpretation of Shi'ism, historically the sect of those in opposition to government, to mean not so much abstention from the world and from politics as a contestatory engagement with it. This included something that most theologians had previously rejected, namely the idea that there could be an Islamic government on this earth even before the return of the twelfth Imam. Khomeini's theory of *hokumat-i islami*, or Islamic government, rested on what was in effect a new, innovatory solution to the problem of how a sincere Muslim can affect politics in the absence of the Imam, namely his theory of the vice-regency of the legal authority, or jurisconsult, *velayat-i faqih*. In this theory, the legal interpreter, in the first instance Khomeini, was authorised to wield religious authority and establish an Islamic government, with an authority derived from god.

This apparently purely theological solution was of course to be understood not just as a theological breakthrough, but also as something that served a much more immediate, material concern, namely how to acquire and maintain political power. It justified the takeover of the Iranian state by the clergy and the depreciation or denial of other forms of authority.

If one looks at the terminology and policies enunciated by Khomeini, it all begins to look much more familiar, particularly in the light of third-world populist movements of the post-war epoch. Khomeini's central set of concepts, *mustakbarin* and *mustaz'afin*, literally 'the arrogant' and 'the weak', correspond to the people/elite couplet found in other populisms. Populist terms used to disparage the elite – corrupt, linked to foreigners, decadent, parasitic – all recur in Khomeini. The main political slogans of Khomeini – Islamic republic, revolution, independence, economic self-sufficiency – are the standard goals of nationalism in developing countries. His term for imperialism, *istikbar-I jahani*, 'world arrogance', is immediately recognisable the world over, and not a bad description at that. The denunciation of opponents as 'liberals' was taken from the communists. One might suppose that these borrowings would be subordinated to an other-worldly theological perspective, but what Khomeini actually said and did once he came to power illustrated, if nothing else, the primacy of Realpolitik. Thus, although he started by renouncing patriotism and the Iranian identity, he began invoking Iran and the concept of fatherland once the Iraqi invasion of 1980 had begun. Most interestingly of all, in the last months of his life, he enunciated a new principle of political behaviour, based on the primacy of *maslahat*, or interest: according to this, what mattered were the interests of the people and the state, not the formal prescriptions of religion. In situations of conflict between the two it was the interests of the state that prevailed even over basic religious duties such as prayer; no clearer enunciation of the implicitly secular principle of *raison d'état* could be given.

It is often said that in Islam there is no separation between religion and politics. In support of this, people quote the supposedly classical phrase, *al-Islam dinun wa dawlatun* (Islam is a religion and a state). Yet this is apparently a phrase invented in the nineteenth century. The history of any Muslim country reveals, not a fusion of temporal and spiritual powers, but a separation between the two. In the Ottoman empire, there was the Sultan and the *Sheyh-ul Islam*, representing two distinct centres of authority. In the titles of Suleyman the Magnificent, the world 'caliphate' did not appear: he regarded this as irrelevant to his authority. In Saudi Arabia there is the tribal family, Al Saud, and the religious family, Al Shaikh. So, the essentialists' assumption of continuity is mistaken and needs to be challenged . . .

Muslim fundamentalists make much of the Shari'a, despite the fact that Shari'a, in the conventional sense of legal prescriptions contained in the Quran, amounts to only about 80 verses out of 6,000 and covers only a few topics of potential legislation: the term itself, literally 'the right way', is mentioned but a few times. The invocation by Muslims of the early Islamic government of the Prophet is equally forced: even assuming that a system of government that evolved for seventh-century Arabian cities was appropriate for today, one would have to ask how valid it was, given that three of Muhammad's four initial successors died unconstitutional, violent deaths.

Jihad, usually taken to mean holy war, actually means, literally, 'effort', and can refer as much to struggle within the self as to military struggle.

At various moments in its history, Christianity has been belligerent, highly politicized, fiercely authoritarian and male-centred. The modification of these positions has come about in the last 300 years, largely in connection with various schisms, the scientific revolution and the Enlightenment. Is there any reason to believe that Islam, a faith more than 600 years younger, is incapable of reaching such an accommodation? Certainly, there is much in the Koran that suggests an 'enlightened' view, and there are many Islamic scholars who embrace this.

The real difference between the Christian and Islamic outlooks is that the societies in which they originate are at very different stages in their development today. Thus the Christian religions are based in relatively developed capitals like Rome, New York, Istanbul, Moscow and London, where accommodation has long had to be made to the forces of modernism and scientific scepticism. Islam's centres are Saudi Arabia and, for Shias, the holy cities of Iran, both countries which have experienced the dislocations of accelerated modernization beginning as recently as half a century ago. Small wonder that societies clinging to a very early interpretation of Islam take refuge in it against massive technological, social and economic transformations, or that clerics remain hugely powerful players in those societies in a manner that, in most of Western Europe, had faded by the middle of the nineteenth century. Imagine if the medieval popes or the Inquisition had been faced by television, the jet aircraft or the automobile.

Huntington is, of course, right in saying that people faced with the wrenching transformation of their traditional values within the space of a couple of generations cling to their religious bedrocks, and indeed assert them as a way of holding on to traditional identities in the face of the cultural, economic and technological assault from the West. But these are essentially defensive reactions, as even a cursory look at the ebbs and flows of Islamic fundamentalism in recent years shows.

Islamic fundamentalism is a worldwide phenomenon. There are fundamentalist movements in Indonesia, Malaysia, India, Pakistan, the Philippines, parts of sub-Saharan Africa, even the United States. Wherever there are Muslims there are fundamentalists, of very different sects, some in armed insurrection against regimes usually seen (if Islamic) as too lax and corrupt or (if non-Islamic) as downright hostile.

For the most part these movements have failed to gain much ground except where, for other reasons, the central authority was in crisis (as in Indonesia). Nor have these movements necessarily been anti-Western – for example in Malaysia, where they are primarily anti-Chinese, or India, where they are anti-Hindu. Some links have been established, however, between these movements, notably by al-Qaeda. A quick glance from East to West bears this out.

Islamic fundamentalism is becoming a force to be reckoned with in East Asia as well as North Africa, the Middle East and South West Asia. In terms of the proportion of Muslims to total population, it is obviously a much smaller problem. But it is increasingly affecting a number of countries. In particular:

- The Philippines, where more than 4 million of the country's 81 million people are Muslims. Kidnappings by Islamic insurgents, trained and equipped by sympathizers in Arab countries and Afghanistan, in the mountains and jungles have irrupted into the news. Al-Qaeda until recently had one, and possibly more, training camps in the Philippines.

  The government has recently launched a major offensive against the rebels, but their complaints of being treated as second-class citizens have resonance enough, although the government is unlikely to respond. The Philippines' current economic crisis is certainly a factor, as is support from al-Qaeda. American special forces are already in action against some of the extremists, and there is talk of increasing the commitment.

  Basilan has been the most troubled area, with some 250 guerrillas being killed by the security forces and nearly 750,000 Muslims driven from their homes during a government counter-offensive. Abu Sayyaf guerrillas kidnapped twenty tourists in 2001, releasing them after payment of a $15 million ransom. By contrast the Moro Islamic Liberation Front is in peace talks with the government.

- In Malaysia the Pan-Malaysian Islamic Party performed spectacularly at the last election, tripling its seats in parliament. It has taken advantage of widespread disillusion with the autocratic Prime Minister, Mahathir Mohammed, particularly after the trumped-up prosecution of a prominent Islamic leader, his former deputy, Anwar Ibrahim.

  The fundamentalist backlash is touching ordinary lives, with strict Islamic rules against alcohol and mingling between the sexes being enforced, particularly in the north-eastern state of Terenganu. As the leader of the Pan-Malaysian Islamic party puts it: 'Islam is not just meant for Arabs. It is meant for all peoples.' This is potentially a serious problem in a country with an ageing autocratic leader whose grip may be slipping at last.

- In Indonesia the Bali bombing in October 2002 tragically highlighted the extremist presence. The bombs, which killed more than 180 people, may have been the work of Riudan Isamuddin, better known as Hambali, an al-Qaeda operative originally based in the Philippines, rather than an Indonesian group. Until now the former Prime Minister Abdurrahman Wahid, a prominent

Muslim leader, has scrupulously tried to keep religion and politics separate. This infuriated Islamic activists who were previously repressed under the rule of General Suharto.

In Jakarta a vigilante group of young Muslims, the Front for the Preservation of Islam, has raided bars and brothels armed with swords and wooden poles, and threatened foreigners. The Laskar Jihad is another militant group largely based in the Moluccas, which has been contained by military action. Islamic fundamentalism has helped to fuel the independence movement in East Timor, which now seems on the verge of success with Western support. In the Moluccas some 4,000 people have been killed in the war between Islamic extremists and Christians over the past two years. The Christians may have been responsible for as many killings as the Muslims.

Economically, the threat is perhaps overstated. It is confined to patches of the countryside and parts of the capital. However bloody the fighting sometimes is, the moderate Islamic position seems likely to prevail. Under President Megawati, the expected Islamic backlash has so far not materialized. But the ripples of this problem are significant for all three countries concerned. And the Americans are now set to provide counter-terrorist training for Indonesia's notorious army.

- The largest Islamic community in the world is, of course, in India, which has coexisted with other faiths, well on the whole, since independence. However, ugly flare-ups occur from time to time, for example in March 2002 with the Muslim burning of a Hindu train, which brought immediate retaliation.

- Pakistan is an Islamic-majority state close to the very heartland of Islamic fundamentalism, on Afghanistan's borders. The country's pro-Western military ruler, General Pervez Musharraf, stands astride four galloping ponies: the remnants of the Taleban, many inside the lawless tribal area of the North West frontier and Baluchistan; his own fundamentalists, who did surprisingly well in the November 2002 elections, and are now in a precarious government with his third adversaries, the civilian parties; and pro-Islamic Kashmiri separatists. Although a skilful operator, his position is precarious to say the least. An Islamic takeover of Pakistan would be disastrous for the West – although they currently enjoy the support of about a third of the population. The Islamic wing of the military is also strong and, in alliance with the civilians, could depose Musharraf. The prospect of a militantly Islamic Pakistan is far from remote, the stuff of nightmares for Washington, particularly in view of its nuclear capability and past willingness to deal with North Korea and Iran (although Pakistan's ally China is a moderating influence on the Islamic Front).

What Islam-fearing alarmists really have in mind is not the Muslim world as a whole but the Middle and Near East – the old arc of crisis – or, as I would prefer, the E-shaped emergency extending from North Africa to the Arabian peninsula to Iraq, Iran, the southern republics of the old Soviet Union, Afghanistan and Pakistan. The issues here, far from being confined to Islam, are specific to the region but are nevertheless very varied, as you might expect for a territory some 6,000 miles from the tip of Morocco to the eastern tip of Pakistan. The surge of Sunni Islam in Afghanistan (and parts of Pakistan) took place as an initially American-, Pakistani- and Saudi-supported counter to the godless communism being imposed by the Soviet Union and its puppet regime. The evidence suggests that tribal loyalties are more powerful than religious ones as a political motivator, as the headlong collapse of the Taleban regime attests. But Islam remains a powerful force in both societies.

Travelling west to Shia Iran one encounters a society in which the Shah's reckless and headlong modernization crashed into a deeply traditional society, provoking a seizure of power by Islamic clerics. Two decades on, the Islamic revolution is floundering, as young people, the middle classes and the urban working classes all chafe under religious obscurantism, three-quarters of them awarding their votes at the last two presidential elections to the only cleric, Mohammed Khatami, who stood for reform and modernization.

To see the country that dubbed America 'the great Satan' sending messages of sympathy to the United States after September 11 was one of the more remarkable spectacles of recent months. It reflects the radical shift inside the country, however indistinguishable the grey beards and turbans may still seem from before. Perhaps the most devastating, and indeed poetic, condemnation of the September 11 attacks from the Middle East was expressed thus: 'the horrific terrorist attacks . . . were perpetrated by a cult of fanatics who had self-mutilated their ears and tongues and could only communicate with perceived opponents through carnage and devastation.' Who said this? Why, the President of Iran's Islamic fundamentalist regime.

With the moderate President Mohammed Khatami decisively re-elected in 2001 with 76 per cent of the vote, Iran is approaching a decisive showdown. Khatami proclaimed his support for 'freedom of speech, criticism and even protest within the law' but also counselled 'patience, moderation and prudence'. Nearly a quarter of a century after the revolution which overthrew the monarchy, a new generation of Iranians is becoming desperately weary of the conservatism of the ruling mullahs. The revolution was created by an improbable alliance between religious conservatives and country people fearful of the disruptions imposed by the Shah's rapid modernization programme, the private sector and the middle classes disillusioned by the centralization and corruption of the regime, and left-wing intellectuals seeking social revolution.

As the rule of theocracy proceeded, the mullahs, in alliance with the army and their own security forces, as well as the middle classes, vigorously suppressed the left to stave off the spectre of revolution; now, some fifteen years later, the middle classes and much of the armed forces (as well as the underground left) are bitterly disillusioned with leadership that has hobbled the country's economic development and enforces a nominally strict adherence to Islamic mores (although these are widely flouted in private and even prostitution is tolerated under the fig-leaf of 'temporary marriages'). Meanwhile the mullahs' most loyal supporters, the rural peasantry, are increasingly disenchanted, many blaming the clerics for what in most cases has been a steady decline in living conditions.

Faced by such widespread resentment, it was hardly surprising that at the previous presidential election, in 1997, Mohammed Khatami, a middle-ranking cleric widely identified as the regime's main internal dissident, secured election with nearly 70 per cent of the vote and then in February 2000 secured the biggest block of seats in the country's parliament before being overwhelmingly re-elected last year. But both Iranians and a hopeful world outside have been dismayed at the ease with which the popular president's momentum has been slowed by the hardline clerics. The hardliners hoped that, having disappointed his followers, his popularity would sharply decline. This has not happened.

Khatami, in spite of his popular mandate, was never going to dislodge the mullahs overnight. Iran's authoritarian power structure has tradi-tionally vested authority in a remote, above-the-battle emperor figure, previously the Shah, then Ayatollah Khomeini, then his successor Aya-tollah Ali Khamenei. The Shah sided with the modernizers in his regime who argued that political authoritarianism was necessary for the trans-formation of his country. The newly enriched classes rebelled at this – only to find that they had installed just as authoritarian a regime, and one that was economically illiterate.

Ayatollah Khomeini at least had the sense to stay above the battle; Ayatollah Khamenei, a far less prestigious clerical figure, has made the mistake of identifying with political hardliners against the overwhelming majority of the nation. Now he is being openly criticized not just in street graffiti but by senior Islamic scholars in the holy city of Qom – something unthinkable in Ayatollah Khomeini's time. If the lid is kept too tightly shut, sooner or later there will be an explosion that could sweep away the power of the mullahs altogether – although probably not before some-thing approaching civil war.

The conservative mullahs' reservoir of support is simply too narrow for them to survive indefinitely: it consists, apart from a majority of the clergy themselves, of part of the peasantry and a small part of the middle classes who fear the possibility of revolution. In political terms there is the formal authority of Khamenei himself, the Council of Guardians, whose role is to ensure that laws conform to Islam, the conservative judiciary, and the mullahs' own revolutionary guards.

True, the regime can always fall back on brute force to govern. But the loyalty of the armed forces is, to say the least, suspect: although heavily infiltrated by revolutionary commissars, most military men instinctively dislike the mullahs and reflect the aspirations of Iran's middle classes. Experience in most countries has shown that repression alone does not work for long. In particular the armed forces usually work in tandem with the propertied classes, traditional or emerging; they very rarely work against them. The mullahs have lost the support of the propertied classes as well as much of the peasantry and urban masses; they have too narrow a base.

The Iranian revolution is often compared to the Russian; on this assessment it still has half a century to run. But the Iranian revolution, whatever it may have been to begin with, is not a revolution at all: it is pure reaction. The Bolsheviks at least had the sense to identify themselves with the forces for change; the mullahs represent only regression, and one that is leaving Iran further and further behind; it is a miracle they have lasted this long. The more pressing issue is whether real revolution might follow the fall of the mullahs – and it is only the fear of this among sections of the armed forces and middle classes that keeps the mullahs in power. President Khatami thus runs the risk of becoming a Kerensky figure in a genuine revolution.

Over the past few months, Khatami has at last begun to direct the huge reservoir of popular support that brought him to power against the hardline mullahs. Most recently he told parliament, 'We have no choice but to succeed in establishing Islamic democracy. As long as the people want me, I will continue to serve, with the thought that I can move forward in the face of all problems.' Earlier Khatami explicitly warned of the dangers of social revolution if the mullahs failed to respond. He added: 'We must abide by principles of popular rule and pluralism in our constitution. We cannot backtrack. We are forced and doomed to make progress and do not have much time.'

The President appears to have emerged strengthened from a meeting – which may have been more of a showdown – with Khamenei, in which he is said to have agreed to support Khatami for the presidency and to seek to control the regime's hardliners: the Council of Guardians recently grudgingly permitted single women to go abroad to study and ordered the closure of a rabidly anti-Khatami newspaper, a couple of small signs of a change in climate.

Yet much more is required for any real evidence of improvement, following the muzzling of virtually all of the free press (some thirty publications) the imprisonment or harassment of most journalists, the vigorous persecution of the President's loyalists, including his brother, a prominent parliamentarian, the Deputy Interior Minister, Mostafa Taj-zadeh, who was charged with supervising the June election to prevent the mullahs rigging the vote, and the moderate Minister of Islamic Guidance, Ayatollah Mohajerani, whom Khatami was forced to dismiss.

Why did Khamenei compromise at all? Almost certainly because if he went into outright opposition, the country would be plunged into chaos and bloodshed, as the President has warned, with the mullahs by no means certain to win. Khamenei himself is a weak personality and may be dying of prostate cancer; it is by no means certain that his successor will be as easily manipulated by political hardliners; a much more spiritual leader is likely.

Khatami has long been criticized by his own supporters for failing to deliver reform. But he is playing a complicated political game. He is in effect saying to the hardliners that he is all that stands between them and revolution. In this context his much-denounced criticism of the student uprising in July 1999 becomes comprehensible. When a peaceful student protest was broken up by murderous Islamic toughs causing dozens of deaths and, in uncontrollable retaliation, spilt into the streets in five days of rioting, Khatami criticized the student uprising as too far, too soon and too radical: it threatened to frighten the middle classes and the armed forces into supporting the established order and would have resulted in his own downfall, had he gone along with it.

By coming out against his most enthusiastic supporters, Khatami was establishing his credentials as an upholder of established authority; in the run-up to last year's election he sought to prove that the hardliners were flouting the constitutional order and to isolate them. This complex manoeuvring may not succeed: but it seems certain that if the hardliners retaliate viciously, they risk the ire of the great majority of Iranians – something that the ailing Khamenei may have understood at last. If Iranians lose hope in Khatami, they will go for something more radical; Khatami is the last hope for the mullahs' survival – all that stands between them and the tumbrils. Political confrontation flared up again in autumn 2002 with the imposition of a death sentence against an eminent academic, Hashem Aghajari, who dared to criticize the authorities' interpretation of Islam. Student protests have spread; real confrontation may be next.

For the West, overwhelmingly the most sensible thing is to stay out of the power struggle. Whatever the temptation for the French and increasingly the British to rush in and secure contracts in the hope that Khatami will win, it is far better to stick to the American-led policy of selective sanctions. For it is precisely Iran's sense of isolation and lack of economic development that is turning Iranians against their brutal and obscurantist regime. If Khatami wins and opens up the country to democracy and reasoned dialogue with the West, that will be the time to reward good behaviour. This is not being achieved by American bombing. Much less is it suggestive of the triumphal onward march of militant Islam.

To Iran's south are a host of traditional Arab sheikhdoms whose political systems have been preserved in aspic by their colossal oil wealth, while similar absolute monarchies and tribal systems all over the world (even in Africa) have been replaced. Some of these, notably Saudi Arabia and Kuwait, are deeply wedded to traditional Islam. In the former's case, this is because the ruling al-Saud dynasty, which is less than a century old, having deposed the far older Hashemites (descended directly from the Prophet) from control of the holy cities of Mecca and Medina, espoused the obscurantist and extremist form of Sunni Islam advocated by the al-Wahhabi sect as an adjunct to its power.

It is wide of the mark, as much recent commentary suggests, to say that the Saudis are afraid of militant Islam. They have used militant Islam as a means of quasi-totalitarian control, as anyone who has been to the kingdom and witnessed the thousands of pettifogging rules that encumber ordinary people, and which are enforced by the country's 'religious police', can testify. The thousands of Islamic schools and the militants who volunteered to fight in Afghanistan emerged not in opposition to the regime but with its encouragement. The bloated, corrupt and probably deeply unpopular al-Saud dynasty is riding a tiger which could get out of its control. Islamic fundamentalism on the peninsula is the regime's own creation, an artificial construct. A more detailed analysis of the Saudi problem – which to me seems as pressing as Iraq, Iran or Afghanistan – is in the next section on oil. In nearby Yemen the government is seeking to crack down on fundamentalist tribesmen with open American assistance.

To the north, Iraq has been implausibly linked to the al-Qaeda attacks. The Iraqi dictator, Saddam Hussein, will not hesitate to invoke Islam occasionally if this suits his purpose: but he is part of the Baath Socialist movement which is defined by its secular rejection of extremist Islam and advocates rights for women, tolerance for alcohol and so on. The Sunni hierarchy in Baghdad has no power, and Shia rebels in the south have been ruthlessly suppressed. Similarly, while Iraq would certainly have no scruples about dabbling in terrorism, both the CIA and the Israeli Mossad have emphasized that there is no evidence it is doing so at present. Not much sign of an Islamic extremist revival there.

In next-door Jordan, an Islamic ascendancy in the elected consultative assembly soon ended as Jordanians grew tired of being preached at. In Palestine, in spite of Israeli occupation, extremist Islamic groups remain small minorities, the mainstream Palestinian movements being secular and socialist. Syria's secular Baathist regime was defined by its ruthless annihilation of an Islamic uprising in Hama in 1982.

In Turkey to the north, an endless confrontation between secular and Islamic camps persists, with the Atatürk-inspired army always ensuring that the balance is tilted the former's way. The barring of the latest popular Islamic leader, Recep Tayyip Erdogan, from standing in elections is yet another chapter. In November 2002, his party overwhelmingly won Turkey's general election, although because of the ban, Erdogan's deputy, Abdullah Gul, became Prime Minister. His goal is to prove that 'a Muslim identity can be 'democratic, transparent and compatible with the modern world'. If he succeeds, Turkey could become a model for countries like Iran and Saudi Arabia – and disprove the slander that Islam is incompatible with democracy. That would be a huge step forward in defusing fundamentalist Islam.

Egypt's often venomous Islamic extremists have been ruthlessly suppressed in recent years by President Hosni Mubarak's secular regime, and there are no signs that they enjoy even substantial minority support. The more moderate Muslim Brotherhood has seventeen seats in parliament. In Sudan the Islamic regime has been co-operating with the United States after the loss of 2 million lives through civil war and starvation. In Libya the 'Green Revolution' of Colonel Muammar Qaddafi, who espouses his own brand of Islamic socialism, probably enjoys the support of only a handful of Libyans and is Muslim in name only.

In Algeria, following the 1992 election victory of a pro-Islamic party, largely as a popular reaction against the corrupt clique that had run the country as a personal fiefdom since decolonization thirty years earlier, the army and the regime cracked down brutally. After a vicious civil war Islamic fundamentalists appear to have been defeated and to have lost their popular following, thanks to their own extreme brutality. Algeria's experience was not a pretty one.

Despite civil war, an outbreak of rioting by Berbers in Kabylie which resulted in eighty deaths, and a huge riot in Algiers in 2001, Algeria's dark decade of despair may be coming to an end. A turning point in its civil strife occurred in November 1995, with General Liamine Zeroual's election triumph, winning more than 60 per cent of the vote on a high turnout of 75 per cent, which dwarfed his moderate Islamic opponent and the hardline anti-Islamic candidate. With the Islamic Salvation Front (FIS) urging a boycott, abstentions were no more than 25 per cent, well below the 35 per cent the Front achieved in the 1992 election which triggered off the civil war in the country.

Today it can be seen that Zeroual's adoption of a twin-track approach of elections and an olive branch for moderates within the FIS, coupled with a continuing tough military response, has blunted the remorseless Islamic offensive. The military regime had a large responsibility for the ineptness, brutality and corruption that led to the wave of popular support for Islamic extremism a decade ago. Yet a policy of appeasement towards the Muslim fundamentalists would have resulted in another triumph for militant Islam, this time on the very Mediterranean doorstep of Europe.

In Algeria the combination of a brutal army, a significant and educated middle class opposed to Islamicization, the anti-Islamic Berber minority and less crude political leadership over the last year has knocked the fundamentalists off balance. It is at last possible to be hopeful about Algeria, which had seemed to be running headlong towards a cliff edge.

The pace of normalization has accelerated sharply since Zeroual was succeeded by the country's wily elder statesman Abdelaziz Bouteflika. His decision to give an amnesty to the Islamic Salvation Front's armed wing, the Islamic Salvation Army, was bitterly opposed by many leading army officers, but it seems to have helped dampen the embers of war, isolating the hardline terrorists. Scores of people are still being killed every week, particularly in the interior of the country and the suburbs of Algiers; but the widespread carnage that, according to Bouteflika, left 100,000 dead in the 1990s seems at an end. His 'civil concord', which provides an amnesty for guerrillas has been accepted by thousands. He is a moderate, but circumscribed by 'Le Pouvoir', the army-dominated military, political and business clique who are the real power brokers. Deaths are down from 2,000 a month to around 150. Antar Zouabri, the leader of the most ruthless Islamic guerrilla group, the Armed Islamic Group (GIA), was ambushed and killed in February 2002.

There are believed to be still around 3,000 Islamic militants in the field. The army's ruthlessness in prosecuting the war against them, and in its use of death squads to cull their sympathizers, is likely to be a matter of intense controversy in Algeria for years to come. Mothers of the 'disappeared' have already demonstrated in the capital. But a degree of normality currently appears to be returning. In fact, the recent explosion of popular discontent in Algiers against the country's economic management is a sign of ordinary life reasserting itself. With the recent oil price increase, the country's $5 billion trade surplus last year is expected to rise sharply this year, and French, German and American firms are returning to the country to explore the opportunities offered by the improving economy, even operating from Algiers itself after nearly ten years, when their presence was confined to heavily protected enclaves outside the capital.

Bouteflika presides over a group of ministers who are eager to pursue further decentralization and privatization of Algiers' previously crushingly state-controlled economy. The Energy and Mines Minister, Chakib Khelil, is a former World Bank privatization expert who oversaw Bolivia's and Argentina's successful energy privatization. The Finance Minister, Mourad Medelei Benachenhou, and the Minister of Trade,

Habib Temmar, are both committed to free-market reforms, particularly in the banking and telephone sectors. Fears of job losses are fuelling widespread labour protests in a country where unemployment is around 30 per cent and among under-25s around 80 per cent. Troops were needed to break up demonstrations at the obsolescent El Hadjer steelworks but the government's will seems likely to prevail.

In recognition of Algeria's emergence from its dark age, Bouteflika has been an increasingly welcome guest abroad, being received by President Chirac in France last summer, where he invited French companies to develop tourist resources in the country. The Algiers International Fair was a success. The French and American navies recently took part in joint exercises with the Algerian navy. Bouteflika's proposal to extend his presidential powers and his appeal for popular support for the move in a referendum have made it clear to the two outside powers most concerned that he is, for the moment, the dominant force in the country. His next objective must be to groom a successor and a political class capable of carrying on the nation-building after him.

With the hardline army chiefs on the sidelines – but always a potent force – the strongman is believed to be the Interior Minister, Noureddine Yazid Zerhouni, a former ambassador to Washington, who has so far successfully outmanoeuvred Bouteflika's chief opponent, the former Foreign Minister Ahmed Taleb Ibrahimi. If the privatization team can overcome the traditional obstructionism, bureaucracy and corruption of the Algerian state machine, the country has nowhere to go but up. Disastrously run by the post-independence socialist clique after France's withdrawal, and then traumatized by violence over most of the last decade, Algeria's wealth in natural gas, oil and tourism is more than enough to restore it to the delightfully cosmopolitan country of pre-independence days. Although returns are likely to be slow in the short run, owing to a lack of infrastructure and bottlenecks throughout the economy except in certain priority energy sectors, if the security improvement continues, long-term prospects for the country look good.

None of this exactly suggests that a tide of fundamentalism is sweeping the Middle East, although Western mistakes could conceivably stir up ripples. As everywhere else, it seems, the Middle East is being seduced by Western consumerism and a substantial middle class is emerging in some countries. In many cases, people vote for Islam simply as a reaction against governments perceived as corrupt and incompetent (Algeria,

Jordan). Except in Libya, Islamic parties are conservative, anti-socialist forces.

As for the issue of Israel, this continues to dog relations between Arab countries and the West, is a focus of intense popular unrest in some countries which could result in the overthrow of their rulers, and is often seen in the context of a Jewish-American conspiracy. Yet it is hard to discern a direct link between the growth of militant Islam and the Palestinian issue: Afghanistan, Iran and Algeria, all among the furthest away from Israel, are the most Islamic. The Palestinians, as already noted, are too developed a people to provide much support for Islamic extremists except as a useful spear in the war against Israel.

This idea of a new 'crusade' against a resurgent Islam seems far-fetched: the Turks are not about to reinvade the West, nor the Moors to cross the Straits of Gibraltar. There is no doubt that Western mistakes could make life deeply uncomfortable for their allies in the region, and even possibly reverse the current decline in the fortunes of Islamic fundamentalism (Algeria and Egypt lost to the extremists; Afghanistan now lost; Iran on the way out). But it seems unlikely. The real weak link in the chain is Saudi Arabia and the Gulf states, precisely because their societies are so fossilized. But this is a special case, affecting no more than 30 million out of 1.4 billion Muslims.

CHAPTER 8

OIL AND SAUDI ARABIA

The post-September 11 inquest has focused on a third great challenge to global security: the West's dependence on Gulf oil. After a steady increase due to cuts in production by the oil cartel the price began to decline, partly because of a global economic slowdown which reduced demand, and partly because of increased Saudi production. With the attack on September 11 the price soared as concerns grew about Middle Eastern security, then fell suddenly as the slowdown gathered pace. As US hostility towards Iraq gathers pace, the price is anticipated to increase.

Two strategies are commonly floated to reduce this dependence on Middle East oil: a cutback on consumption, particularly by gas-guzzling Americans, who with 5 per cent of the world's population consume a quarter of Middle Eastern oil; and a switch to alternative oil and energy sources. Realistically, there are limits to the possibilities of the first. Raising the low petrol tax in the United States and increasing dependence on renewable energy resources – although not nuclear power, which is expensive and opposed by many for safety reasons – would reduce American over-consumption. But this would be more than compensated for by the steady increase in consumption of newly industrializing countries like China and India. What happens when China itself, where the automobile remains the preserve of a small minority, acquires the car-a-family habit? The switch to alternative sources of oil and energy only becomes viable for the most part when average oil prices reach a certain level. This applies as much, for example, to the huge unexplored Venezuelan tar basin as to oil in Alaska or off the Brazilian coast.

However offshore oil in West Africa is beginning to look promising, if political problems can be overcome.

There is an exception: Russian oil, or, specifically, Caspian oil in view of the costs of exploration of the Siberian region. Although the potential of the region has been exaggerated, it is clear that substantial reserves exist that are commercially exploitable and competitive with the Middle East. The chief problem is bringing the oil to markets across territory that is almost as volatile as the Middle East – indeed skirts the northern part of the region across Afghanistan to India and China, and the restive southern republics and even possibly Iran through Turkey.

The West's biggest economic – as opposed to security – interest in the former Soviet Union is oil. The recent rise in oil prices has once again underlined the vulnerability of the West – and in particular the United States – to unstable Middle Eastern oil producers (plus Venezuela). Both in keeping oil prices down, and preventing interruptions to supply, it is hugely in the West's interest to develop an alternative major supply of oil.

A staggering $100 billion is pledged by Western companies over the next twenty years in what is loosely known as the Caspian region – the underbelly of the former Soviet Union which consists primarily of Kazakhstan, Azerbaijan and Turkmenistan. These, however, are the parts of the old Soviet empire that are most under challenge from Islamic fundamentalism. With that pretext in mind, Vladimir Putin's Russia itself is seeking to grab back some of its influence in the region in order to increase its share of the potential spoils with Western oil consortia.

After September 11, with the new security co-operation with Russia, this is not being entirely resisted by the United States. Some Westerners actually believe Russia's return would bring stability to the volatile and corruption-ridden region. They may think differently if Russia seeks to flex its oil muscle, or demands too much of the takings from the world's second Middle East.

The potential of the region has long been recognized. With Russia's withdrawal from the area, oil production, which ran at 11 million barrels a day for the Soviet Union as a whole in 1987, has fallen to 6 million barrels a day today, but is expected to rise by half in three years as a result of a 50 per cent jump in investment and a 30 per cent jump in pipeline capacity. Total Russian production could reach 10 million barrels a day, 2 million more than Saudi Arabia. Total Russian reserves are already 15 per cent more than Saudi Arabia. Lukoil, which is investing heavily in Iraq, Algeria, Sudan and Libya, and Yukos are likely to become global giants. Gas production from the region is also down. In addition to sitting astride one of the largest oil reserves, the Caspian has the largest natural gas reserves in the world. Caspian oil reserves are conservatively estimated at 18–20 billion barrels, with further recoverable reserves of 50 billion barrels. By 2010 the region should produce around 3 million barrels of oil a day at a cost of $12–$15 a barrel, falling later to $8–$10 a barrel.

The two with the biggest potential are the Shakh Beniz gas field off the Caspian coast in Azerbaijan, being developed by the BP/Amoco consortium, and the Kashagan oilfield, where an American-led consortium (the Offshore Kazakhstan International Operating Company) has been engaged in exploratory drilling. It is believed that both have the potential to begin to match Middle East oil and gas production.

The big problem, apart from the political instability of the areas concerned, has been the pipeline route out of the area, accentuated by the need to build a bypass through war-torn Chechnya. Azerbaijani oil production is expected to quadruple in just four years. Offshore and onshore production in Kazakhstan at the Tengiz oilfield may be even greater. In Kashagan and elsewhere in Kazakhstan, production is likely to increase dramatically to, some say, 4 million barrels a day in fifteen years.

All of this is likely to exceed by a long way the capacity of the 145,000 barrels a day pipeline from Baku to Supsa in Georgia, or the pipeline from Baku bypassing Chechnya to the Black Sea port at Novorossiysk. The Russians have therefore embarked on the Caspian Pipeline consortium route across the top of the sea from Tengiz. This is expected to convey 1.4 million barrels a day within a decade. But this will be insufficient, hence the American pressure for a pipeline from Turkmenistan and Azerbaijan through Georgia to the Turkish port of Ceyhan on the Mediterranean, with a capacity of 1 million barrels a day within five years, which also bypasses the Bosphorus bottleneck, where 50,000 ships transit a year, and an oil-spill disaster would be catastrophic.

That would also be the best route for gas from Turkmenistan and Azerbaijan to Turkey – a huge customer in its own right. However, the whole project seems to have stalled for the moment – for reasons of corruption and lawlessness. Both Russia and Iran are bitterly opposed. The region is a sink of misgovernment. Nursultan Nazarbayev of Kazakhstan was elected president with 99 per cent of the vote. President Islam Karimov's election in Uzbekistan was a similar farce which he won with more than 90 per cent of the vote. Thousands of Islamic 'terrorists' have been arrested and tortured in his country. President Sapurmurat

Niyazov of Turkmenistan has declared himself president for life. President Askar Akayev of Kyrgyzstan jailed his opponent in the last election on bogus charges. For how long the project will be suspended is a difficult question to answer. There are schemes being explored to export liquid natural gas to the east, bypassing the Gulf, where demand in China and India, in particular, are high across, of all places, Afghanistan, provided it can be pacified (Unocal, the American company, thought it had secured Taleban support for such a $2 billion pipeline – but this had to be abandoned).

The American objective had long been to keep the proposed route along the buffer region, away from both Iran and Russia. However, Russia's resurgent influence in the region threatened this. Russia recently signed an agreement with Kazakhstan to convey more of the latter's oil along the pipeline to Novorissiysk. This reflects Russia's growing influence in the region as a bulwark against Islamic fundamentalism from Afghanistan, whose militants have been infiltrating across the border into Uzbekistan, which regards itself as the region's leader. Some 25,000 Russian troops have been sent to Tajikistan, regarded as the weak link in resisting Islamic fundamentalism, and a Russian military base is now likely to be built there.

The race is now on between a resurgent Russia offering military protection against fundamentalists (before September 11 the Russians were considering their own air strikes on Afghanistan again) and the American offer of better-financed commercial development with more limited military protection. Russia's own obsession with Chechnya has to be seen in the context of its anti-Islamic crusade, and its determination to reassert its influence over the old Soviet republics and take the lion's share of the commercial proceeds from the huge oilfields and natural gas fields. Yet without Western technology and competitive market development free from the corruption that has so far dogged Russia's own dealings in private enterprise, the development of the oilfields and gas reserves may be far slower and more limited. Putin is probably realistic enough to do a deal – your development, our protection.

The economics of the price are also complex. As the development, extraction and transport costs of the Caspian oilfields are relatively high compared with the Middle Eastern ones, it will always be in Russia's interest to keep the oil price relatively high – say within OPEC's target band of $22–$28 a barrel. Until recently the Russians tried to have the best of both worlds by benefiting from OPEC restrictions on supply to force the price up, while they themselves, not being bound by OPEC quotas, overproduced to take maximum advantage of the price.

At last it seems that Saudi threats of flooding the market with oil and thereby creating a price collapse which would wreck the economics of Russian oil are beginning to have an effect, and Russia will either de facto or formally have to join the OPEC cartel. The Saudi aim of stable oil prices at a level only a little higher than before the oil shocks of the 1970s is not perhaps unreasonable. Western consumers have not entirely given up the idea of breaking up the cartel and sharply reducing oil prices. The market price for oil should, after all, be freely set.

The problem is that a wildly fluctuating oil price is in nobody's interest. Oil is a commodity with a unique number of potential market interferences. If prices go below a certain level, for example, Caspian oil becomes uneconomic, sharply restricting potential supply. A low oil price is likely to lead to greater global consumption, inducing shortages and, eventually, a higher oil price.

Above all, the security situation in the Middle East remains replete with potential bottlenecks. In other words, whatever the attractions of short-term pressures for a lower oil price, it may be in Western interests to keep the price stable within the OPEC bands, so as also to develop an alternative flow of Caspian oil and provide the kind of potential returns to Middle Eastern oil producers that would help to defuse tensions within their societies.

This raises a further key point. For all the pie-in-the-sky whimsy about reducing global consumption and finding alternative sources of energy and oil, the fact remains that for the foreseeable future there remains a colossal amount of cheap-to-produce oil in the Gulf region. During the 1970s, in an attempt to justify high oil prices, a lot of hogwash was talked about the world in general, and the Middle East in particular, running out of oil. In fact 'proven' reserves of oil have increased in almost symmetric proportion to consumption of existing oil. Countries like Saudi Arabia have merely brought new oilfields on line as and when necessary out of potentially awesome 'unproven' reserves. My survey of Saudi Arabia for *The Economist* argued this back in 1980.

But the Arabian peninsula is only part of the picture. Iranian oil exploration has been in the doldrums since the fall of the Shah but geologists speak of the potential of the country as being at least two or three times that of declared reserves and, with large areas unexplored, potentially many times that. It is also clear that two unexplored oilfields in southern Iraq could quadruple that country's existing reserves. In other words, the region's potential for cheap oil is, for all practical purposes, currently limitless, even taking into account expected increases in the global consumption of energy.

Two immediate consequences follow: it remains in the interest of Western consumers to preserve stability in the region to retain access to this cheap oil rather than develop more expensive alternative sources, except for emergencies (which the United States Strategic Petroleum Reserve was designed to overcome – although it is subject to political plundering, as by President Clinton before the last presidential election). And it remains in the producers' interest to keep the world hooked on their oil at least at relatively reasonable prices.

Provided OPEC displays some responsibility in not taking advantage of occasional crises and shortages to run up cheap get-rich-quick profits (and as this turns off customers in the long run this is not to their advantage), it seems reasonable for the West to acquiesce in oil prices around the $22–$28 a barrel mark to provide a stable framework for continued oil exploration and the producers' own development. To try and force down oil prices is crazy, undermining the economies of the moderate producers, indulging further in gas-guzzling and thereby increasing dependency, and creating the resentment that makes producers ratchet up prices whenever circumstances give them the chance.

So to the security problem. While this undoubtedly exists, it has been much exaggerated. Specifically, several of the worst-case scenarios for the Middle East have already come to pass and their impact, while often severe, has not been catastrophic. The worst, of course, took place in 1974–5 and 1979–80, caused by the Arab oil boycott in the first and the Iran-Iraq War in the second. Another such boycott cannot be ruled out, particularly if the Israeli-Palestinian dispute flares up sharply or another Middle Eastern war breaks out. But the short-term damage of such a boycott (lower incomes) to the oil producers themselves was so violent the first time round as to make it a largely self-defeating weapon of last resort. Moreover, it is hard enough today for OPEC to prevent its own members undercutting their own prices by overproducing on quotas. Policing a general boycott would be almost impossible.

With the Iran-Iraq War, two major producers for a short time virtually went out of production and then resumed at a much lower level than before. Yet the oil market survived the shock. With Iran's continuing revolution, one producer has had ferocious ideological reasons for denying the West its oil, but the need to generate revenue has frustrated these reasons even if oil production has fallen significantly.

With Iraq's invasion of another major oil producer, Kuwait, two major producers were put out of action. Prices rose, but the shock was bearable. Although most of Iraq's production has also been denied access to the world market for more than a decade, prices actually fell, not soared. The impact of September 11 has been less than feared. Since then America has been buying oil for its strategic petroleum reserve at the rate of 150,000 barrels a day, which has helped to keep prices up. The idea is to weather another calamity, such as a war with Iraq, with the reserve now at some two-thirds of its 900 million barrel capacity; some 4.2 million barrels a day could be provided in the event of a major oil shortage. Thus it seems the price will return to normal levels even in a calamity which puts two major producers out of action. Short of a blockage of the Straits of Hormuz themselves – which is a possibility but can probably be offset by using the pipelines across Saudi Arabia – most security crises in the Gulf, it seems, can be weathered. All but one.

An upheaval in Saudi Arabia which switches the largest producers' taps off can be far from discounted. (A fuller account of the problems of the kingdom begins on p. 280.) It is quite clear that Osama bin Laden's real goal in staging his attack upon the United States was not the greatest power on earth but a much more obvious target: the land of the holy cities of Mecca and Medina. And as the Saudi-born bin Laden well knew, his homeland is riddled with corruption and discontent, the rotten core of the Gulf oil edifice.

For bin Laden in his messages and videotapes, the greatest obscenity has always been the American presence in the holy land of Saudi Arabia not the Palestinian question. And for bin Laden, oil, 'stolen' from Saudi Arabia at gunpoint by knock-down prices, is the fuel of the West's economy. Control that and you control the world. The purpose of his terrorist feats is to bring home to the Saudi people that a new hero, tilting against the very might of the United States that sustains the country's obsolescent government in power, is at hand.

Al-Qaeda's project is nothing less than to seize control of the richest and most influential of the desert kingdoms and thereby obtain huge economic power. The al-Saud dynasty's hold on Saudi Arabia is dangerously frail and Western governments should be concentrating their attention on this issue which is one of the gravest security and economic concerns in the medium term.

As with Hitler's *Mein Kampf*, which few Western statesmen could be bothered to plough their way through in the 1930s, bin Laden has been disarmingly frank in his stated objectives. In 1996 he issued his first jihad – declaration of holy war – against 'America occupying the land of the two holy places. There is no more important duty than pushing the American enemy out of the holy land. A new caliphate is necessary to unite all Muslims.'

Two years later he issued a fatwa 'to America and their allies civilian and military all over the world', warning that the battle would 'inevitably move to American soil' and promising 'a martyr's privileges' to his followers – a hint at the suicide bomber tactic. According to letters discovered by the Italian authorities (although disputed by bin Laden sympathizers) he wrote:

> The greatest disaster that Muslims have suffered since the death of the Prophet is the occupation of the land of the two sacred mosques by the Christian armies of the Americans and their allies. For more than seven years the United States has occupied the land of Islam in the holiest of its territories, Arabia, plundering its riches, overwhelming its rulers, humiliating its people, threatening its neighbours, and using its bases in the peninsula as a spearhead to fight against the neighbouring Islamic peoples.

His main objective is to expel the Judaeo-Christian enemy from Saudi Arabia and then, intriguingly, to liberate Iraq, for 500 years the most powerful Islamic caliphate. A recently discovered training video drives home the same anti-al-Saud message.

Nothing could be clearer. Launching the attack on the Twin Towers was no more than a tactic, as bin Laden has no hope of defeating the Americans on their own soil. Its purpose was twofold: to invite American retaliation that would fuel radical Islamic opinion against the Americans in the Middle East, and to make him a hero of the Muslim 'street', in particular, Saudi Arabia, then Iraq (whose godless and secular Baathist regime led by Saddam Hussein is unlikely to be associated with his attacks). In Saudi Arabia bin Laden seems to be enjoying immediate success. Prince Nayef, the Interior Minister, in a very rare admission of dissent within the kingdom, remarked recently that 'we find, unfortunately, that in our kingdom there are those who are sympathetic with them.' He went on:

> we will not forget that those who are now in the caves and burrows, they are the ones who do harm to the kingdom, and unfortunately

Muslims are being held accountable for them although Islam is innocent.

There have been open demonstrations by groups of young men in Riyadh and other cities, celebrating the Manhattan attack and jeering at Westerners. Over the past few months, Western expatriates in Saudi Arabia have reported growing and widespread popular anger against them. As one worker who decided to leave reported, '[we] can feel a great deal of anger and antagonism towards [us], much more than normal. For [our] own safety, [we] have decided to hightail it.'

Most young Saudis now despise the United States, which increasingly reciprocates this hatred. This Saudi animosity stems in part from the vitriolic anti-Americanism of the clergy, and in part as a cultural assertion by a generation brought up on American consumerism. The evidence for this is overwhelming. According to a recent Saudi poll, 87 per cent of Saudis have an unfavourable view of the United States. As one put it: 'our people very much hate the US. The number one reason is that it supports Israel with no limits . . . now we hear that all Saudis in America will be fingerprinted.' Saudi Arabia's controversial former ambassador to Britain, who has now been recalled for his outspokenness, Ghazi Algosaibi, put it like this:

If you go around the Muslim world, you will find the vast majority of people will support Osama bin Laden, and this is more tragic than the attack itself. Why would such a crime like this find such support not just on the streets of Riyadh, but on the streets of Turkey, the streets of Tunis . . . people hate America.

The government has tried to rein back extremist Islamic teaching, to no avail. The schoolbooks are filled with invocations against the Jews and their allies. As one government official puts it, 'the fundamentalists have total control of the masses.' On a typical broadcast, the imam of the Mosque of Mecca, Sheikh Abdul-Rahmna al-Sudays, declared that God had turned Jews into 'pigs and monkeys' and condemned the 'poisonous culture and rotten ideas of the West'. One government official points out that 'you have hundreds of imams condemning the US at prayers every Friday. How can you stop that?'

These feelings are increasingly reciprocated. According to a briefing in July 2002 the Defense Advisory Board, a defence department think tank run by Richard Perle, the administration's archhawk over Iraq, 'the

Saudis are active at every level in the terror chain, from planners to financiers, from cadre to footsoldier, from ideologist to cheerleader.' 'Saudi Arabia is a problem,' says a senior American government official. He is understating it: there have been ten bomb attacks against Western nationalists in eighteen months. A prominent liberal dissident says gloomily, 'there is a time-bomb ticking away. The evidence points in one direction: the religious people are coming to power.' Others blame the government for not cracking down on the clergy sooner, when they had the opportunity. 'Now it is too late.'

The *mutaween*, the religious police, have become much more visible in stirring up young people's resentment against Westerners. A leading cleric in Burayda has issued a fatwa condemning the ruling al-Saud family. 'Whosoever supports the infidel against Muslims is considered an infidel . . . It is a duty to wage jihad on anyone who attacks Afghanistan.' Many young clerics are said to support bin Laden.

In spite of Saudi denials, the main recruiting ground for bin Laden is in south-western Saudi Arabia, near the old Sultanate of Hadramaut, now part of Yemen. Nine of the suspected airline hijackers come from this area. In addition, the Islamic University of Medina is proving a fertile recruiting ground for the terrorists. Why is the desert kingdom such a breeding ground for Islamic militancy? There are three reasons:

1. The West's failure to prod the inept ruling class into reform. It seems blindingly obvious that a state based on a tribal network and patronage and corruption as a way of life is not likely to survive long into the twenty-first century (this also applies to the emirates of the Gulf). Everywhere else in the Arab world, revolution has toppled the old monarchies, usually violently.

The only difference has been the oil wealth of Saudi Arabia and the Gulf, which has hitherto permitted the 'princes' (just an extended tribe, 8,000–50,000 of them, depending on whom you believe) to survive. Those who say that the sheer extent of the princely network provides greater stability than the Shah's one-man rule in Iran are wrong: all it means is that there are thousands of corrupt 'mini-Shahs' to resent. This is felt particularly strongly among the Saudi educated and wealthy non-princely class (from which bin Laden springs), barred from political power although of superior ability to the princes.

The Saudis have recently had a windfall, giving the impression that it is against their will that the oil price has been knocked up beyond the $22 a barrel mark. But the economy is taking time to revive. The almost total failure of the Saudis to open the regime up to democratic participation and debate over the past two decades has left them highly vulnerable to an extremist takeover. This was unnecessary. In Jordan and many Islamic states, progress is slowly being made towards establishing representative institutions. The Saudis have merely put in place a nominal *majlis al-shura*, a consultative assembly.

2. The sheer extent of United States involvement in the kingdom, about which even bin Laden has a point. The American military presence of some 6,000 troops and 35 aircraft is a small, visible sign of it. Commercially the American presence is huge – with some 45,000 American nationals in Saudi Arabia and investments of around $5 billion. Exxon is developing gas projects worth about $25 billion. Building contracts and arms supplies from the United States have been worth some $50 billion in just twenty years. It is no wonder that many young Saudis see America in the same light as bin Laden does.

3. The recent sharp decline in standards of living for Saudis. For a long time educated Saudis were virtually guaranteed an indolent and well-paid office job, while a colossal population of some 7 million foreign workers, who account for some 65 per cent of the workforce, did the menial work. With per capita income falling dramatically from $28,000 to around $8,000 over fifteen years and the population increasing to some 17 million (almost certainly an underestimate), thanks to a birth-rate of 37 per 1,000, unemployment rising to around a fifth of the workforce and only around half the entrants to the labour force being able to find good jobs, young Saudis are experiencing relative hardship for the first time. Crown Prince Abdullah has called for a massive cut in public spending, which was $11 billion over budget in 2001, saying the country is undergoing a 'suffocating' economic crisis.

These are powerful challenges to the Saudi regime. Are they necessarily lethal? It should be remembered that the south-west, where bin Laden draws his support, is an area regarded as backward by the more economically developed north-west, the centre around Riyadh, and the oil-rich eastern provinces. In addition the Bedouin tribes of the centre and the tribes of the far north are traditionally loyal to the regime.

In the west around the holy cities there is a traditional underlying loyalty to the Sharif of Mecca and the Hashemites, whom the al-Saud deposed, but certainly no real radicalism. The violence of bin Laden and his young supporters will have angered many more Saudis than the idealists and malcontents it will have attracted.

There is, however, no room for complacency. Islamic extremists could wage a terrorist war within Saudi Arabia which would find sympathizers in the armed forces and among some middle-class and working-class groups stifled by the obscurantism of the regime. A full-scale uprising in the short term seems likely because, however corrupt and unpopular, the al-Saud regime has failed to make the mistake of the Shah of Iran: that of alienating both traditionalists with a headlong drive towards modernization, and modernizers, through autocratic rule. While undoubtedly autocratic, the al-Saud family has gone out of its way to preserve its Islamic credentials. It is hard to see bin Laden gaining support among the moderate Islamic majority – as opposed to disaffected southern tribesmen linked to Yemen.

Reports of bitter divisions within the Saudi royal family are wide of the mark, including the allegation that the modernizing 'Sudeiri seven' (the sons of the founder of the dynasty, Ibn Saud, by his favourite wife) are hostile to their half-brother Prince Abdullah, now the effective leader of Saudi Arabia following the incapacitation of King Fahd. On the contrary, Abdullah would not survive without the support of his half-brothers, and was installed precisely because of the respect his Islamic simplicity inspires.

The intelligent but ailing Fahd inspires no such devotion. The ablest of the princes, the Defence Minister, Prince Sultan, has too many enemies. Abdullah is fully backed by the major powers in the land: the Interior Minister Prince Nayef, the governor of Riyadh, Prince Salman and the leader of the next generation, Prince Saud al-Faisal, who is being groomed as king (although he has just been slapped down for being too pro-American), who are in charge of the day-to-day running of the country. But Fahd, Abdullah and Sultan are all in their late seventies. Intriguingly, one junior member of the clan, Prince Walid ibn Talal, recently urged direct men-only elections for the country's 120-man consultative assembly, 'the faster the better', in line with Kuwait and now Bahrain, whose Sheikh Hamad called elections in October 2002 open to both sexes.

The al-Saud always unite against a foe: that is their strength. Abdullah's ascetic rule after that of the fun-loving Fahd has helped to defuse discontent. Of course there is no guarantee against a major terrorist attack, or even insurgency in parts of Saudi Arabia. American criticisms of Saudi Arabia's refusal to allow landing or even overflying rights for the attack on Afghanistan are wide of the mark. It is much more important to protect the al-Saud from charges of betraying Islam.

This is not to say there is no threat to the regime. The emergence of a genuine Saudi middle class and a discontented, more youthful educated class is posing a real and serious challenge. The al-Saud's wilful refusal to permit power-sharing, or a parliament with anything but rubber-stamp powers, will destroy them in the end.

The al-Saud survive by playing off two forces against each other. They say they protect Islam against the encroachments of the outside world, and they permit modernization to take place without the opposition of militant Islam. It is a delicate balancing act. But if they refuse to share power, curb their own corruption and become a constitutional monarchy, the dangers are vivid.

There is an immediate danger of terrorist attacks in Saudi Arabia, and a real medium-term one of the overthrow of the House of Saud – although not by bin Laden, so much as by an alliance of the emerging middle classes, youthful Islamic extremists and sympathizers in the armed forces. The disruption to oil supplies of any such process would, of course, be huge but, because the new regime would still have to rely on oil income for its survival, perhaps not devastating.

Even here – and Saudi Arabia is the weakest link in the whole terrorist/Islamic/oil equation – there is cause for immense concern, but not despair. Take even Saudi Arabia out of oil production, and other producers have the capacity to make up the shortfall, particularly if Caspian oil comes on line (which lends its development all the greater urgency). Moreover, however fanatic a Saudi regime, no shutdown could last for long. With around 90 per cent of Saudi Arabia's export income, 75 per cent of its national budget and 40 per cent of its GDP obtained from oil, the kingdom would quickly grind to a halt if the taps were turned off. A revolutionary regime would soon have to start exporting significant amounts again or risk overthrow.

Any interruption in oil production for Saudi Arabia would almost certainly be temporary, but in the short run it could have a devastating effect. Any revolution in Saudi Arabia would generate panic in the oil markets. A temporary interruption of Saudi supplies would create huge bottlenecks, and the domino effect on the smaller statelets that cling to the robes of the Saudi giant would choke off further supplies, although Iran and Iraq would probably take advantage of their rival's troubles to pump out more – provided they could get the oil out of the Gulf and along the pipelines. Certainly a Saudi revolution would prove a hammerblow to the world economy, and represents the single most dangerous threat highlighted by the events of September 11 (although hardly one caused by these, for the Saudi problem has long antedated Osama bin Laden and al-Qaeda).

What is American policy towards this potential global earthquake? I believe that the United States is for the first time considering 'writing off' the kingdom as unlikely to last more than a few years in its present form. Relations between the Americans and the Saudis have plunged to an all-time low ebb since September 11. Shortly before the terrorist attacks, Saudi Arabia's de facto ruler, Crown Prince Abdullah, confirmed his reputation in America for emotional instability by furiously castigating American policy on Israel. According to a senior Saudi, Abdullah declared, 'We believe that there has been a strategic decision by the United States that its main interest in the Middle East is 100 per cent based on Israeli Prime Minister Ariel Sharon.' This was America's right, but Saudi Arabia could not accept the decision. 'Starting from today, you're from Uruguay, as they say. You [Americans], go your way, I [Saudi Arabia], go my way. From now on, we will protect our national interests, regardless of where America's interests lie in the region.'

The Saudi ambassador, Prince Bandar, was instructed to cut off further discussion between the two countries. The time had come to 'get busy rearranging our lives in the Middle East'. Bush immediately sought to repair the damage with a conciliatory message, to which Abdullah replied positively. After September 11, Abdullah went further, secretly increasing Saudi oil production by 500,000 barrels a day and shipping it in Saudi tankers to force oil prices, which had jumped to $28 a barrel, down to $20.

But a backlash was already under way in the United States: fifteen of the nineteen terrorists who staged the September 11 attacks were Saudis. Saudi Arabia was blamed by some American officials for permitting bin Laden to build up his terrorist network and for setting up fanatical fundamentalist religious schools across the kingdom. Charles Freeman, a former American ambassador to Saudi Arabia, declared:

> The Sept. 11 attacks have raised many questions in the minds of Americans and others about Saudi Arabia and our relationship to it. Is there something rotten in the kingdom of Saudi Arabia? Is it still stable enough to be a reliable partner of the United States in the future? If one takes the President's question seriously, 'Are you with us or against us, where does Saudi Arabia really stand?'

The Saudis may have paid as much as $1 billion to fund the training of some 25,000 Saudi and Islamic fighters who had flocked to Afghanistan to combat the Soviet invasion there (although this was also American policy at the time), and also backed the Taleban seizure of power. Some

1,000 al-Qaeda fighters in Afghanistan are said to have been Saudi. Saudi Arabia refused to accept and try bin Laden when he was expelled from Sudan in 1998, preferring that he go to Afghanistan rather than upset the peace of the kingdom. 'Mistaken policy or an act of history – take your pick' was the delphic comment of the Saudi Foreign Minister, Prince Saud al-Faisal.

The architect of the policy, the Saudi Intelligence Chief, Prince Turki al-Faisal, has resigned, bitterly attacking his creation, bin Laden. 'God help us from Satan,' Turki wrote in the *Asharq al-Awsat* newspaper. 'You are a rotten seed like the son of Noah, peace be upon him. And the flood will engulf you like it engulfed him.' Even so, the Saudis and the Kuwaitis (along with Egypt and Jordan) refused to take part in the global freezing of bin Laden's assets. Turki further incensed the Americans by ruling out the use of American airbases in Saudi Arabia for staging operations against Iraq, and by insisting that there was no connection between al-Qaeda and Iraq. Bin Laden, said Turki, considered Saddam Hussein 'an apostate, an infidel, someone who is not worthy of being a fellow Muslim'.

Senator Carl Levin, chairman of the Senate Armed Forces Committee, replied chillingly: 'We need a base in the region, but it seems that we should find a place that is more hospitable. I don't think they want us to stay there.' The thinking seems to be that there is not much point in having an ally, and protecting a country, that is too timorous to range itself on America's side even in its own defence, as seems to be the case with Saudi Arabia.

Influential figures in Washington believe that the United States could get along without Saudi Arabia and the Gulf oil states by drawing on alternative oil sources such as Venezuela, Colombia, Alaska, the North Sea and, increasingly, Russia and the Caspian, as well as the Middle Eastern oil that would have to be pumped for the regimes there, of whatever hue, to survive economically. That would be a radical departure, but one worth considering in view of the consequences a revolution in Saudi Arabia would provoke, and the difficulty America would have of going to the Saudis' defence.

What can be done? The American defence department is believed to have three contingency plans for reacting to an emergency in Saudi Arabia: to land sufficient troops to buttress the regime in the event of civil disorder or an attempted coup; to seize military control of major cities, strongpoints and oilfields in the event of a revolution; and to occupy the Saudi oilfields in the eastern region as a last resort.

Of the three, only the third is remotely feasible. For American forces –
which can be airlifted en masse at a moment's notice on to airstrips
specifically designed for American aircraft – to fight on behalf of the
Saudi regime would utterly discredit it in the eyes of its own people and
bring about a bloodbath and the regime's inevitable downfall. If it is to
survive it must fight on its own. Similarly, an American occupation of
Saudi Arabia would invite a bloodbath on many times the scale of the
fighting in Mogadishu, unacceptable American casualties in street fighting, and would be unsustainable in the long term. The consequences of
American occupation of the holy cities scarcely bear thinking about.

An occupation of the oilfields in the eastern region is, however,
feasible. These are relatively well protected and form an enclave away
from the major cities. Indeed, even with the rest of the country plunged
into chaos, oil production could be maintained, although there would be
a danger of sabotage and/or missile attack. This would be a hazardous
operation but not unachievable.

The gaping hole at the heart of America's Saudi policy is political. All
America's prospects are based on the survival of the al-Saud, a not
particularly ancient tribal ruling group skimming the cream of the
country's oil wealth. They are not representative of the country, are
detested by the other tribal groups that they have conquered (who have
largely been bought off), and their rule is based on money, force and
religious intimidation. The emerging educated middle classes cannot,
however, ascend to serious power because of the political monopoly of
the 'princes'. The former therefore, have no particular love for the al-
Saud. If the Wahhabi clerical prop were to be taken away, only the
armed forces and national guard would be left. As the Shah of Iran
discovered, this is no guarantee of survival.

What the United States has to do is twofold: press the Saudi princes
into opening up their political system to allow a mature, moderate,
educated middle class eventually to form the core of an administration
capable of taking over the reins of government. This will be no easy task;
the al-Saud know that when a political and administrative elite is ready
they will have no choice but to step aside, their only hope of survival
being as a constitutional monarchy; and, second, to start training just
such an elite.

That way, even if a major challenge comes quite soon, the United
States would not be faced with the present appalling choice of supporting
the al-Saud or standing aside and leaving them to the mob. Instead they
might have an acceptable alternative to both the regime and its extremist

opponents ready to step into the breach. This is not pure pie-in-the-sky: Iran may be inching its way towards becoming an Islamic democracy – precisely the kind of regime the Saudis and many others fear most, because it will show that Islam, democracy and moderation can coexist, whatever Fukuyama and Huntington might say. This is a matter of urgency for American policy-makers, not the stuff of idle academic debate. A more detailed look at the politics of Saudi Arabia and the Gulf emirates begins on p. 276.

CHAPTER 9

THE NEW NATIONALISM

These three threats – terrorism, Islamic fundamentalism and the danger to oil supplies – were considered first because they are the ones most closely related to the attacks on September 11. But with the exception of the threat to Saudi Arabia, there are even more pressing problems still unaddressed in the 'phoney peace' of the post-Cold War world. Very prominent among them is one about which little comment is made at all: the newly aggressive nationalism of emerging economies.

Huntington might claim this is a reversion to ancient cultural divisions, but it is actually quite distinct and is not even a reaction against Western culture – for often the rivalries are between non-Western cultures (India–Pakistan, China–Japan) or even within cultural groups themselves (China–Taiwan). As formerly agrarian, impoverished and often colonial societies (sometimes deriving from ancient civilizations) have begun to emerge as substantial economic powers in their own right, so they have quite naturally begun to develop their own brands of nationalistic self-assertion.

Russia

This even applies to post-1989 Russia, which long disguised its nationalistic ambitions under the cloak of communist ideology; when the system of central planning itself crumbled, it could only feel sorry for itself for several years. Life expectancy in the decade to 1995 fell by seven years to 57 for men and 67 for women, and the population dropped by nearly 3 million. But as the country evolved its own brand of monopolist capitalism and the economic results began to show, so a nakedly renascent Russian nationalism is starting to motivate the system under President Vladimir Putin.

Nationalism has never been far beneath the surface, as the literary traditions of Alexander Solzhenitsyn or the radical nationalism of populists like Vladimir Zhirinovsky or the late Alexander Lebed suggest. But it is no longer unfashionable for the Russian state to be seen to be promoting Russia in a new 'great game' across the globe and specifically in Central Asia, notably in such countries as Afghanistan, Iran and Iraq.

There is also a major, and even perhaps healthy, rejection of American culture and free-market philosophies of the kind made so fashionable immediately after the end of the Cold War in Moscow. In Russia's case this mature reaction is not a threatening one. That is not to say that the West should not be deeply wary of Russian motives – such as, for example, its enthusiastic support for the 'war on terror'.

'With terrorism, we cannot come to terms. We must leave them no peace.' Thus Putin, commenting on September 11. This, of course, is deeply in Russia's interests, as the country faces a far greater immediate threat from Islamic fundamentalism than the United States. His charm, however, seems to have disarmed the initially sceptical President Bush.

Two errors have long blinkered Western analysts to the huge, brooding expanse of Russia. The first is what might be called a time-lag in understanding developments there. Thus when Mikhail Gorbachev came to power, most intelligence and political analysts expressed deep scepticism that anything would really change under this child of the Soviet system. To her great credit, Margaret Thatcher and her Foreign Secretary, Geoffrey Howe, immediately spotted his potential, but the Bush administration in America was seemingly caught by surprise by Gorbachev's sudden decision to withdraw from Eastern Europe, and had to admit that its earlier scepticism had proved unfounded.

A similar time-lag now exists in relation to Vladimir Putin's regime, although its direction has been all too consistent and clear. It is said that he is a pragmatist, and that the West must not rush to judgement about him. Tony Blair, whose earlier career involved virtually no experience of foreign policy, declared, after welcoming the leader of the regime responsible for one of the worst atrocities in the post-1945 world, the razing of Grozny to the ground, that he admired Putin: 'When he speaks of a strong Russia, he means strength not in a threatening way. When I am [asked] about Britain being strong, I don't mean that it threatens the outside world.' Thus Blair was the first Western leader to hurry to Russia after Putin's election, and Putin repaid the compliment by briefly visiting Britain and taking tea with the Queen. Blair, it seemed, had capped, or at least equalled, Mrs Thatcher's achievement in embracing a new Soviet leader. The two have now met several times, providing Putin with much-needed credibility. By contrast, he was initially treated frostily by the leaders of the United States, Germany and France.

Yet Gorbachev and Putin are somewhat different men. For Blair's sake, he had better not overstress his own resemblance to Putin. At least Britain's Prime Minister has not flattened a medium-sized city (like Bradford). Putin, elected overwhelmingly by the Russian people last time, is seen by Blair as a democrat and as a man the West can do business with. In fact his assumption of power represented another seismic change in Russian politics, although it is in his interests – and fully in accord with his old KGB training – to deceive the West that it should continue to think all is much the same for as long as possible.

The second error made by Western analysts is their failure to realize the one strand of continuity – indeed the backbone that runs through Russia's politics since the time of the Tsars: a ferocious prosecution of Russia's national interests at the expense of the country's own people, its near neighbours, or even its own ideology. The idealism of the early communists quickly gave way to the neo-feudal imposition of one-man rule (Stalin, a new Tsar) acting through a ruthless central state, security apparatus and, ultimately, the armed forces – particularly as the main check on the state, the power of the provincial nobility, had been destroyed.

What we are now witnessing is an attempt at exactly the same process of re-centralization after the democratic revolution ushered in by Gorbachev and Yeltsin has run out of steam in a welter of cynicism about crime, corruption and national disintegration. The difference this time is that communism was ultimately a shallow and easily manipulated ideology, while democracy is not, and it may have had time to lay real roots. But the attempt is being made, none the less.

Putin's succession to Yeltsin was a straightforward, old-fashioned Soviet palace coup of the kind that ousted Georgi Malenkov in the 1950s and Nikita Khrushchev in 1964 but was botched against Gorbachev in 1991. Such coups traditionally take place at the height of summer, when the political class is holidaying away from Moscow and the West's guard is lowered (the 1968 invasion of Czechoslovakia, the 1980 crackdown in

Poland, the coup attempt against Gorbachev) or close to Christmas (the invasion of Afghanistan in 1979); the Putin coup was of the latter kind. Yeltsin, contrary to the outside impression, was no buffoon. He manoeuvred expertly against his opponents in a system in which parliament and the regions had excessive power, and he was determined to frustrate a formidable alliance led by Yevgeny Primakov, a former prime minister, and the Mayor of Moscow, Yuri Luzhkov, who were seeking to force him out.

Only the most disingenuous can believe Yeltsin's assertion in his memoirs that Putin's 'lovely eyes' played a part in the succession. Putin represented the second and most politically astute generation of the KGB (now renamed the FSB), which had carried out its own internal coup against the old guard represented by Primakov, Putin's immediate predecessor but one. Putin was certainly Yeltsin's preferred successor; but the younger man decided to accelerate the process. Putin is believed to have confronted Yeltsin with the KGB's extensive dossier on the financial dealings of his regime (although not on him personally) and offered him honourable retirement in exchange for public acceptance of the coup, or disgrace for him and his associates. A spent force, Yeltsin chose to go quietly.

How did Putin assemble the necessary support for the coup? Since the 1917 revolution did away with the provincial nobility four chair legs of Russian power have dominated: 'the people', and the three existing power centres – the central bureaucracy, the army and the security forces. The combination of internal terror and external threats united all four to support Lenin and Stalin during the 1920s, 1930s and 1940s, with unity breaking down only in the power struggle between Beria, Malenkov and Khrushchev in the 1950s, which the latter won.

When Khrushchev successively lost the support of the bureaucracy, the armed forces, the KGB and even part of the party, he was overthrown. Under his successor, Brezhnev, the party and bureaucracy initially shared power, while the armed forces and the KGB were given free rein. When the combination of party corruption, bureaucratic inertia and military extravagance threatened to bankrupt the whole system (with the armed forces, in particular, demoralized by the unwinnable war in Afghanistan) a high-minded centralist, Gorbachev, was brought in by the bureaucracy, the KGB and the party to enforce the necessary economic disciplines, and sideline corruption and the armed forces.

When he ran up against a wall of obstruction, Gorbachev astonished everyone by opting for wholesale political reform and withdrawal from a

large part of the Russian empire. The rejuvenation of Soviet politics in
the heady days of Russia's new democracy proved strong enough to
frustrate the inevitable backlash by the armed forces, KGB and part of
the bureaucracy – and hastened the advent to power of a truly populist
president, Boris Yeltsin, who had acquired a wide following for his
attacks on the perks of the Soviet elite.

The third centre of Soviet power waited until Yeltsin over nearly a
decade dissipated his support through the corruption of his cronies and
the spread of a crime wave, while disillusion set in about the benefits of
Western-style free-market economics. These anyway were only half-
implemented – although contrary to outside impressions, a large part
of the modernized Soviet economy is now remarkably successful.

Putin and his young KGB associates judged the right moment to strike,
first buying the support of the armed forces by permitting them to go on
a rampage through Chechnya (which showed that none of the lessons of
Afghanistan had been learnt), then securing the assent of the bureaucracy
(most of which was heartily tired of the chaos of the Yeltsin years).
Although Putin had never been elected to office in his life, a popular
mandate had to be secured to keep political unrest to a minimum and to
assuage the West. This was achieved in 2000, with Putin installed as the
candidate of order by the Kremlin.

Putin owes his continuing popularity after his first two years in office
largely because his youth, energy and self-discipline have contrasted so
strongly with Yeltsin (although oddly they echoed Gorbachev) and
because his mission to make Russia great again chimed with the popular
mood of the moment. Capitalizing on this, he has pushed the Gorbachev
reforms into reverse in virtually every sphere except two: seeking to
retain the benefits of the free-market reforms that have affected at least
part of the Russian economy; and maintaining the goodwill of the West
for as long as the self-delusion of its leaders permits him to. Even
Gorbachev, who at first admired Putin for his discipline and for removing his arch-enemy Yeltsin, has now begun to express his doubts: 'the
main achievements of democratic reforms in the last fifteen years have
found themselves under threat,' he declared recently.

The aim is to put into place the structure of a national security state to
allow Putin to hold on to power when and if his regime becomes
unpopular and to pursue a vigorous prosecution of Russia's interests
abroad. As Sergei Markov, head of the Centre of Political Studies in
Moscow, puts it: 'Putin believes in democracy as a means to an end. If it
helps to make Russia great, fine. If not, he'll give it up.'

Popularly (although not among Russia's minority middle class of around 30 million people) there remains huge support for the traditional image of a Tsar-Stalin strongman in power, particularly during the current insecurity and lawlessness – at least until some major policy disaster. At home the trend of Putin's rule is unmistakable except to the more misty-eyed. In little more than two years he has dismissed the upper house of parliament, replacing it with a council of state staffed by his own placemen. The lower house, for the moment, is wholly intimidated and supports him. His supporters there recently pressed for a new government that would be even more compliant to the President. His old rival, Yuri Luzhkov, has been absorbed into Putin's Unity Party, giving Putin an effective majority in parliament.

He has marginalized the governors of the country's eighty-nine regions through the creation of seven super regions run by Kremlin appointees (five of them generals), in a nakedly anti-democratic move. Although in many regions the governors have outmanoeuvred the new 'eyes of the Czar', in St Petersburg, for example, Viktor Cherkesov has blocked 500 pieces of legislation and sacked 100 senior civil servants as he struggled against the governor, Vladimir Yakovlev.

He has established a network of state newspapers and television companies to bypass the independent network and two main channels, Boris Berezovsky's ORT and Vladimir Gusinsky's NTV. Berezovsky has been bullied into towing the line, while Gusinsky has been threatened with arrest. NTV's offices have been searched twenty-eight times by the authorities. Tatyana Mitkova, one of NTV's presenters, has been summoned to the state prosecutor's office to face what she describes as 'psychological pressure . . . this is going to happen to everyone. Everyone will be summoned. Everyone will be questioned.' While both of these men may be deeply flawed, they represent the diversity and pluralism that are minimal to guarantee democracy.

Putin's lackadaisical handling of the *Kursk* submarine disaster was criticized at first by his media foes, but as he started to fight back he skilfully turned the tables. This episode was widely misunderstood in the West. Putin did not get too closely involved at first so as not to offend his allies in the armed forces who blamed the *Kursk* disaster not on military incompetence but, rightly, on cuts in military spending. However, Putin did not take advantage of the *Kursk* disaster radically to reorganize the armed forces, although he has decided he wants them reduced by 350,000 over the next five years. He also says he wants to cut nuclear warheads from around 5,000 today to between 1,000 and 1,500 – while the United States wants to keep them at some 2,000–2,500. This is part of the fallout of an argument between the former Defence Minister, Marshal Igor Sergeyev, who favoured maintaining the nuclear deterrent, and the Chief of the General Staff, General Anatoli Kvashnin, who wanted a reduced deterrent and effective conventional force. When Putin did show up after *Kursk*, he scored points among the Russian public and used the occasion to berate his media critics: 'They are liars. The television stars people who have been destroying the state for ten years. They have been thieving money and buying up absolutely everything. Now they're trying to discredit the country so that the army gets even worse.' Putin went on that Berezovsky and Gusinsky had

> better sell their villas on the Mediterranean coast of France or Spain. Then they might have to explain why all this property is registered in false names under front law-firms. Perhaps we would ask them where they got the money.

This was pure Mussolini-style bombast.

Many of Putin's old KGB colleagues have been appointed to senior positions in his administration. Meanwhile the FSB has been unleashed against enemies of the Russian state. The jailing of Alexander Nikitin for his revelations about the danger of nuclear contamination from the submarines of the Northern Fleet is a case in point. Grigory Pasko, a journalist, has been jailed for twenty months for videotaping the discharging of nuclear waste into the Sea of Japan. Putin has denounced environmentalists as 'spies'. Raisa Isakova, a Jew, has been refused an exit visa in a rerun of the early years of the Brezhnev regime. Putin recently called the aims of the plotters who sought to overthrow Gorbachev in 1991 'noble', and their leader, former KGB chief Vladimir Kryuchkov, was invited to Putin's presidential inauguration.

In foreign policy, Putin has been energetically asserting Russia's traditional foreign policy interests. While wooing Presidents Clinton and Bush, he has made few concessions on arms control issues. Putin's visit to China was designed to reassure then- President Jiang Zemin that Russia would stand shoulder-to-shoulder with the country if the Americans brought pressure to bear on human rights. But he has also sought to court Japan, which is increasingly disillusioned with its traditional American ally. In the summer, a treaty of friendship was signed when Jiang Zemin visited Moscow.

As the first Russian leader in recent times to visit North Korea, Putin was placing his seal of legitimacy upon the embattled regime there. Both Germany's Gerhard Schröder and France's Jacques Chirac have been on the receiving end of Putin's charm offensive, designed to counter criticism of the war in Chechnya and to sow seeds of division among Western allies.

More recently Putin's visit to India, during which he toured the country's leading nuclear research centre, Bhabha, in Bombay, which he described as a 'temple of science and technology', sent an unmistakable signal that Russia was willing to help India with its nuclear weapons capability. Russia, already India's main arms supplier, is to sell India 310 T-90 tanks, as well as a refitted aircraft carrier, the *Admiral Gorshkov*, and to license production of 140 SU-30 fighter aircraft using Russian technology. Putin reiterated Russia's support of India over Kashmir. The warning to Pakistan and Afghanistan – 'those breeding grounds for religious extremism and international terrorism' – was unmistakable.

By also offering to resume natural gas supplies to Yugoslavia (which are desperately needed in a country with only half the fuel required for heating and electricity in winter) Russia is hoping to draw Serbia into its sphere of influence, too. Putin had been notably slow in supporting the overthrow of Milošević, although as President Kostunica said pointedly, the Soviet Foreign Minister, Igor Ivanov 'caught up with events' when he flew into Belgrade on 6 October, the day of the uprising.

Putin's last visit to Cuba was a downright singeing of Uncle Sam's beard. He and Cuba's dictator, Fidel Castro, denounced America's 'hegemony' and the American trade embargo on the island. He described Russia's policy of cold-shouldering Cuba for the past decade as 'not the right thing to do' and insisted it was time to 'regain our positions in Latin America'.

Russia has also now breached the 1995 secret pact with the United States not to supply military equipment to Iran. In November 2000 the then Russian Defence Minister, Marshal Igor Sergeyev, announced a farreaching programme of defence sales and training for Iranian officers in Russia as well as the supplying of patrol boats, submarines, rocket launchers, and Sukhoi-25-1 helicopters. Few people believe this will not extend to missile programmes or nuclear weapons. The Russians are still resisting pressure not to supply nuclear technology to Iran (see p. 181). In exchange for the deal, the Iranians are believed to be ready to seek to curb Islamic militancy in Russia's southern republics.

There is a price to pay for all this hyperactivity. Putin currently enjoys public support. This could be dissipated if results do not follow. His main prop remains the armed forces, to which he gave carte blanche to secure Chechnya. As with every such struggle against a well-entrenched and popularly supported guerrilla force, the Chechnya problem shows no sign of going away. However, in January 2001 Putin declared that the war was won and would now be reduced to a 'counter-terrorist' operation including a three-quarters cut in Russia's 90,000-strong army there. Russia's claims to have reduced the Chechen rebel army from 20,000 to 1,000 are widely ridiculed, as are its official casualty figures of 3,000 soldiers killed and 8,000 injured. The recent takeover by Chechen rebels of a Moscow cinema was resolved by Putin with characteristic decisive brutality and horrific casualties, although he may have had no alternative.

The *Kursk* disaster also reinforced the complaint of Soviet military chiefs about budget cuts going too far: already eighteen Russian nuclear submarines have been taken out of service, although only ten have actually been decommissioned because of the shortage of money. Putin has proposed cuts in Russia's armed forces from 1. 2 million to 850,000 in order to create a 'mobile, efficient, flexible and combat-capable' military machine.

The human cost and the unpopularity of the war in Afghanistan, coupled with the immense cost of the Soviet military machine, which absorbed a third of the national budget, helped lead to the collapse of the Brezhnev regime. If Putin continues fighting an unwinnable war in Chechnya and proves unable to ram through reform and cuts in the armed forces, he could quickly find his popular support evaporating. Then he would find himself a prisoner of the military and increasingly dependent on the repressive apparatus to support his regime.

By eliminating independent sources of power and stifling Russia's burgeoning pluralism, Putin may lose a power base independent of the army – and thus become its stooge – which could lead to a rerun of the mistakes that brought the Soviet Union to its knees in the 1980s. The West, by failing to condemn the horrors in Chechnya, is only adding to its reputation for opportunism and inconsistency in its policy towards Russia, which has helped to allow Russia's present leaders to blame it for the failures of the Yeltsin era.

There is a danger of 'losing' Russia twice over. First through insufficient and misguided economic support during the Yeltsin presidency, now for appeasing a man fundamentally opposed both to democracy and Western interests. 'What's in it for them?' is always a healthy question for Western policy-makers to pose about Russia. But it is highly unlikely to lead to armed confrontation because Russia has been down that route before – for forty years – and lost, amid near-bankruptcy.

Russia withdrew from Eastern Europe, the Baltic states, the 'near abroad' of Ukraine and its western and southern dependencies not from the goodness of its heart but because it could no longer afford to police and keep them – and that is all the more true today. Reoccupation would be even more difficult, if not impossible. Russia is slimming down its nuclear arsenals and armed forces not because it wants to, but because it has to – while still attempting to retain the most effective conventional force dispositions possible. Russia is a 'mature' emerging power, like most of Europe. It will pursue its aims through means other than armed aggression, colonization or violence.

China

China is much further behind, in several key respects. Its economic leap forward is, like Russia's, of comparatively recent vintage. This author is deeply sceptical of the claims that China will emerge as an economic superpower second only to the United States in the near future. The Chinese model has produced sharp economic growth in certain coastal provinces, but the statistics for the country's economic boom are grossly exaggerated according to recent studies, the key state industries remain hugely parasitical, and the strains of inequality between town and country, public and private sector, the few and the many, may prove too much for society to withstand. Some 25 million state workers have lost their jobs in four years, although a third are still employed in inefficient government companies, which still control over half of fixed assets but produce only a third of output. There are tens of thousands of strikes every year. Its political institutions remain those of a tightly knit communist autocracy which has recently been deprived of any ideological pretension that it is about the promotion of equality. Instead, inequality is the order of the day. Increasingly, therefore, the leadership has itself resorted to banging a nationalist drum to preserve its authority.

Worse, unlike Russia, the armed forces remain key power brokers at a time when the party has lost much of its authority, and the need to keep easily ruffled military feathers on side is a major inhibition on China's foreign policy, as was highly evident in the seizure of the American spy plane in 2001, when Chinese President Jiang Zemin took several weeks to persuade his generals of the only practical course of action – to hand the American crew back.

Worse still among young Chinese, nationalism is perhaps the most potent current ideology. This has nothing to do, *pace* Huntington, with the rediscovery of ancient Chinese civilization. It has to do with the *nouveau riche* self-assertiveness of a people who seek global political status to match their new-found global economic importance. With communist ideology laid bare as a sham, and with little sign of the rulers permitting democracy to make headway, nationalism is almost the only ideology that thrusting young Chinese can still rally around. 'Patriotic education' was launched by the government in 1946. It teaches that America used biological weapons against China in the Korean War, that it has 'inflicted' national humiliations – *guo chi* – on China, and that the Japanese are 'devils'. Such nationalism is often anti-American, because big brother so often seems to be looming over China's shoulder with the bombing of the Chinese embassy in Belgrade, with its spy planes patrolling just off the Chinese coast, with its arming and encouragement of Taiwan and support for Japan.

But it is by no means exclusively so. China's nationalism towards its neighbours can be even more bullying: in its oppression of Tibet and the Vighurs of Xinjiang (2,500 of whom have recently been arrested as 'Islamic terrorists' accused of killing forty people in a decade – hardly a serious threat); in its consistently uneasy relations with India and Vietnam; in its attempts to intimidate the Philippines over the Spratly Islands; in its claims to the South China Sea; in its steadily escalating war of words with Taiwan; and in its permanently uneasy relations with Japan. The Taiwanese stand-off could easily lead to war. Just because this has not happened after many decades of sabre-rattling does not mean that it won't. Taiwan is viewed as an ever-increasing political threat to the mainland. Some wars break out suddenly, or even by accident. Others build up slowly and inexorably, like steam in a pressurized container, so that the world is numbed into complacency by repeated threats and counter-threats, followed by climbdowns on both sides. China's confrontation with Taiwan falls into that category. Yet few people have noticed that the prospect of war between the two is ratcheting inexorably upwards. China is furious about President Bush's recent statement that America would do 'whatever it takes' to defend Taiwan – which is merely an outing of a long-established American policy.

China's reaction to the prospect of a major American arms sale to

Taiwan is the harshest yet. The Chinese Foreign Minister, Tang Jiaxuan, declared 'the United States should . . . rein in the wild horse riding on the side of the precipice.' China has announced a staggering 17.6 per cent increase in defence spending on a military budget officially said to be $20 billion but really believed to be around $60 billion. China's most dangerous recent action has been to order eight Project 636 Kilo-class submarines from Russia for $1 billion. These are so-called 'quiet' submarines, which would be able to deter American aircraft carriers from policing the Taiwan Strait. President Chen of Taiwan – which is also seeking such submarines for its defence – reacted by saying 'we must engage in a self-defensive act to prevent and deter a war.'

Following the election as President of Taiwan of Chen Shui-bian, who had openly advocated a formal declaration of Taiwan's independence in the past, which China said would inevitably lead to war, the confrontation cooled a little. China, which had threatened war if he was elected, made soothing noises and Chen made clear he had no intention of declaring Taiwan independent in the near future.

Indeed, he has been surprisingly conciliatory, even talking of integration, perhaps for fear of Chinese retaliation and because of his weak domestic base. Taiwan's stock market has slumped by a third since the last election, and economic growth has fallen. China's influential Deputy Prime Minister, Qian Qichen, also recently made soothing noises about the need for a 'pragmatic and more inclusive' policy towards Taiwan, suggesting direct air, sea and telecom links were now possible, which the imminent admission of both countries to the World Trade Organization would make useful. Already there are some links between the Taiwanese islands of Qemoy and Matsu with the mainland, for food, trade and people. In 2001 the Taiwanese invested some $2 billion in China, double the figure for the previous year, and a cumulative stake of some $40 billion, all arranged expensively through third-party countries. Taiwan's opposition Nationalist Party leader, Lien Chan, is soon expected to visit the mainland.

Nothing else has really changed. Chen infuriated China by visiting New York and seeing congressional leaders. China has continued to reiterate that Taiwan is part of the mainland and that it seeks a one-country-two-systems Hong-Kong-style reconciliation with Taiwan. Taiwan has not just rejected this out of hand – unsurprisingly, in view of the gradual whittling away of Hong Kong's freedoms by China – but has continued to develop its own democratic institutions in a way that threatens China's communist autocracy.

Taiwan represents not just a standing affront to the powerful Chinese armed forces' concept of national sovereignty. It is also a political threat to the whole communist structure, offering the emerging Chinese middle class a vision of much greater prosperity allied to political freedom. As such, senior Chinese view the threat of ideological contamination from Taiwan as increasing, not receding or static, and therefore requiring action. Any monitoring of Chinese rhetoric over Taiwan over the past five years reveals two things: it is unremitting and if anything increasing in stridency; and it views the one-country-two-systems offer as the final one on the table.

The message is clear. Pick up the offer or face the consequences. The issue is when, not if, those consequences will come. Taiwan has meanwhile shown it has no intention whatsoever of accepting the offer.

China's dictators are being held back not by fine humanitarian motives from launching their war, but by three brutal considerations of realpolitik. They are fearful of the impact an attack upon Taiwan could have upon their economy. American and Western economic retaliation would hit China, with its considerable surpluses in trade with the United States, far harder than the latter. And they are not at all sure that they can win. In addition Taiwan is the world's third biggest producer of information technology hardware, particularly silicon-based products, which give the world a huge vested interest in the country's economy. A humiliation in a war with Taiwan could precipitate the collapse of China's gerontocratic regime, which consists of a mix of ageing apparatchiks and powerful military men.

These considerations underline the latest moves in the war of nerves across the Taiwan Straits. There is currently no prospect of a successful Chinese invasion of Taiwan. China's army is in no shape to launch one, Taiwan's control of the air over the Taiwan Straits is absolute, and the population of Taiwan is so united against such a prospect that a massacre would ensue on the beaches if China's landing craft ever succeeded in reaching them. Taiwan's capacity for guerrilla warfare would be huge even if the Chinese secured the beaches. China's navy is a large but creaking coastal defence force. To compensate, China has bought two 8,000-ton Sovremenny-class destroyers from Russia, carrying Sunburn supersonic missiles. Two more are on order, in a bid to deter the United States from despatching aircraft carriers to Taiwan's side in any confrontation across the Straits.

This leaves the Chinese government with the bleak alternatives of 'missile terrorism' – launching missiles in sufficient quantities to do enormous damage to the country's infrastructure, terrorize the population and ruin the economy – or trying to wrest control of the air from Taiwan in the long term, thus giving an invasion a chance of success.

In response to the former threat, the Taiwanese army issued its 2000 National Defence Report, which warns of the danger from Chinese missiles, some 400 of which are now in place following the intimidatory launch of a couple of missiles close to the island four years ago. The report states that 'missiles are the most seriously threatening' form of mainland attack and goes on: 'together with the ground-attack cruise missiles now near completion, they can be employed for multiple-wave and multi-directional saturation attacks.'

The report marks a huge change of tactics by Taiwan in expectation of a possible Chinese attack. Although it pays lip service to the need to erect defences against the Chinese missiles – a few Patriot anti-missiles are in place around Taipei – and expresses some wan hopes of either participating in or acquiring some of the technology of the Americans' Missile Defence Project, which the United States is highly unlikely to concede for fear of offending China, the Taiwanese are now prioritizing an 'effective deterrent'.

According to the then Defence Minister Wu Shih-wen, 'this contains a principle to prevent war or conflict from extending to the island proper or territory so as to reduce casualties and property damage.' In other words, the threat of inflicting massive damage on the mainland in the event of a missile attack by the Chinese.

Chen has already told his countrymen to prepare to fight a 'decisive battle beyond its borders' – meaning the mainland. Some analysts believe this threat lacks credibility. Any such strike from Taiwan would be a pinprick to the immense Chinese mainland. But with several major population centres within range, including Shanghai, the threat is real enough. Would China's repressive political system survive the impact of major strikes on population centres in response to an ill-thought-out assault on Taiwan?

There is also a menacing vagueness about Taiwan's new doctrine of deterrence. In the last resort, China has the nuclear bomb and Taiwan has not. If major Chinese population centres came under attack, the temptation for China to use it would be considerable. But it may be that Taiwan, with its booming economy and highly developed technology, is further along the road to possessing its own nuclear weapons than anyone suspects.

The second and vital factor for the Taiwanese is the maintenance of air superiority. They have put in a bid for a new generation of fighter aircraft to replace their 60 ageing French-made Mirage 2000-5 fighters and already possess 150 advanced American-supplied F-16 fighters. Chen has publicly announced that Taiwan is looking to a new purchase of advanced fighters. The United States has agreed to sell Taiwan a $1.3 billion arms package including 200 AIN-120C medium-range air-to-air missiles, 71 Harpoon anti-ship missiles which can be fired from long distances and at night, and 146 self-propelled howitzers. The arms will be kept in America and Taiwanese pilots trained there to operate them, for use in an emergency. In addition, the United States is to provide some $5 billion worth of Kidd-class destroyers, 12 anti-submarine aircraft and 8 submarines.

This has infuriated the Chinese. Shen Dingli, a leading arms control specialist in Shanghai, says, 'China's public view of the United States has changed quite seriously since 1998. The US has been painted the threat to Asian-Pacific security. We've never said it so bluntly before. I think China is more clearly preparing for a major clash with the United States.' The authoritative armed forces publication *China Military Science* has written: 'A new arms race has started to develop. War is not far from us now.' Consequently, the United States now regard China as its single most serious security threat, and is determined to prevent its emergence as a major military power.

In 2001 China has sought to update its huge but creaking air force with the purchase of 40 advanced Sukhoi-30 fighters from Russia to bolster its 48-strong force of Sukhoi-27s, which it plans to quadruple over the next few years. It has also purchased five sophisticated Ilyushin A-50C early warning aircraft for $600 million. There can be little doubt that the United States would move (as indeed it is obliged to under the 1979 Taiwan Relations Act) to prevent Taiwan losing its air superiority over China, however fiercely the Chinese might bluster. That leaves the Chinese with the missile option, and senior Chinese military figures are anxious that it should be exercised before Taiwan is in a position to get its new doctrine of deterrence into place. The prospect of an actual shooting war (including missile and air strikes) between China and Taiwan has narrowed over the past years. The consequences for Taiwan's economy would be huge in the short run, and for China's economy initially limited. But failure in the long run could start a chain reaction that would bring down the regime.

Chinese–Japanese relations are, of course, much more balanced and much less likely to lead to any kind of conflict because both countries have been down that road before, and suffered accordingly, and because the result would be globally catastrophic. Japan, moreover, has huge investments in China, creating vested interests in both countries for peace. Yet the ancient suspicions remain intense. China's defence budget and armed forces, widely believed to be around three times what it acknowledges, approach Japan's in size, if not in terms of modern technology. Japan's constant lectures to North Korea over the violation of its territorial waters and occasional missile tests are also aimed at China.

Above all, the constant reiteration of Chinese concerns about Japan's refusal to acknowledge blame for such historical events as the invasion of China and the Rape of Nanking remain clear indicators of the limits to trust and co-operation between these two traditional rivals. The visit by the Japanese Prime Minister, Junichiro Koizumi, to the Yasukuni shrine for the Japanese war dead sparked indignation in China, only partially offset by an earlier conciliatory visit to Tokyo by China's most pragmatic leader, former Prime Minister Zhu Rongji.

Japan

In spite of Japan's disastrous experience during the Second World War, the suspicions of its Asian neighbours are not entirely unfounded. Japan has jealously continued to guard its sense of isolation and uniqueness, has reinstated many of the economic and human structures that existed before the Pacific War, is deeply reluctant to acknowledge its guilt for a war it considers a legitimate exercise in colonialism (and spearheading Asia in resisting European colonialism) and is running a 'self-defence force' which is one of the biggest military structures in the world.

Following its headlong rush to economic superpower status second only to the United States, Japan has spent the last decade languishing in the economic doldrums. But it will not stay that way for ever, and Koizumi's government has further ratcheted up nationalistic rhetoric on such things as reforming the anti-war clause in the constitution (which has not prevented the build-up in its armed forces). Obviously there is no Chinese–Japanese military confrontation in prospect, but the potential is there, should good-natured rivalry ever turn nasty.

Almost all commentary about the election of Japan's new-style Prime Minister, Junichiro Koizumi, missed the main point. Koizumi came in with a mandate for economic reform of the vaguest kind, and seems unlikely to deliver. Japan, says Koizumi, needs a stance 'that does not fear pain, does not flinch at the barters of vested interests, and is not bound by the experience of the past'. His actual proposals for economic change are so opaque, because Japan sees little reason to mend its ways. There is one exception. Koizumi's plan to make banks write off more than $100 billion of their loans is in trouble and will cost 200,000 people their jobs in a country where unemployment is still a matter of acute shame. The significance of Koizumi is political, not economic.

Koizumi won office through a system of primary elections which, for the first time, consulted 1.4 million members of the ruling Liberal Democratic Party and bypassed the old backroom method of electing the leader. Building on this, Koizumi is advocating the direct election of the Prime Minister, a proposal supported by the opposition Democratic Party. Koizumi's standing in the opinion polls, once sky-high, has fallen sharply. He is clearly seeking to set himself up as a presidential figure, not one beholden to the traditional factions of the LDP, and capable of giving Japan a decisive role in world affairs, as well as leadership.

The key point about Koizumi, though, is that, possibly out of opportunism rather than conviction, he is a nationalist, possibly even exceeding the views of former Prime Minister Yasuhiro Nakasone, and Shintaro Ishihara, the Mayor of Tokyo, both of whom have warmly welcomed his election, and more so even than the outgoing Yoshiro Mori, whose crass remarks about war guilt so offended other Asian nations. Koizumi has put revision of the controversial Article 9 of the Japanese constitution, imposed by Douglas MacArthur, at the top of his agenda. This 'forever renounces war as a sovereign right of the nation'. Koizumi's obsession with this issue is deeply unhealthy – and may be frustrated by his cabinet partner New Komeito, the pacifist Buddhist party, as well as by the three-quarters of the Japanese public that opposes revision of the constitution.

Koizumi further played to the nationalist gallery by visiting the Yakusuni shrine, and has suggested that Japan was a victim, not an aggressor in the Second World War. 'I can't understand why we should not do this just because of outside criticism,' says Koizumi. But both he and the Japanese government know perfectly well the sensibilities they are arousing. Both the Chinese and South Korean governments vigorously protested, and twenty South Koreans cut off their little fingers in a quasi-official demonstration. Koizumi also wants to make the emperor head of state, rather than a symbol, returning him to his pre-war status.

Japan's new junior high school textbooks dismiss atrocities such as the Rape of Nanking and justify Japanese aggression. Manga – popular comic books – glorify the Japanese army and suggest, for example, that Asian women 'volunteered' to become Japanese 'comfort women' rather than were raped. A prominent Japanese ambassador, Eijiro Noda, went so far recently as to describe America's relations with Japan as resembling those of the Soviet Union to a satellite state. As a prominent South Korean diplomat warns:

> For the Japanese, the 1990s were a lost decade . . . The continuing economic malaise deprived Japanese society of a sense of direction. Coupled with the rise of a post-war generation lacking any memory of war, it provided ultra-rightists with fertile ground for promoting chauvinism. It is troubling for Asians to see Japan caught in this ethno-centric autism.
>
> Nowadays, one can hardly find the other end of the political spectrum on such divisive issues within the LDP, which had previously embraced a wide political spectrum. The Japanese media is also engulfed by the same tide, as was demonstrated by the daily *Yomiuri Shimbum* having taken a rightist position on the textbook question . . . All in all, Japanese society is showing a tendency to tilt rapidly towards the right.

However modern Koizumi looks, with his shaggy locks, he represents a leap back in time. Nor should the United States delude itself that he is about to espouse their free-market methods.

There is something distinctly odd about most current reporting on Japan. The conventional global wisdom is that the country is a long-term political and economic basket-case. The country is trapped in a mire of ineffectual, revolving-door leadership, its outgoing prime minister one of the most buffoonish in recent memory, the economy defies years of attempts to start it, the government and banking sector teeter on the brink of collapse and Japan's inertia is likely to drag the world economy into a potential recessionary hole. All of this is more or less true, but such views reflect the concerns of outsiders about Japan. From Japan's own point of view, things are perhaps not quite so bad.

Take the negative image first. Consumption, allowing for inflation, has fallen by around 2.5 per cent in a year. Unemployment is at an unprecedented yearly high of 5 per cent. The former Finance Minister, the immensely respected Kiichi Miyazawa, recently declared that the nation's finances were in a 'catastrophic situation'. Government debt as a percentage of GDP is soon expected to reach 130 per cent.

Yoshiro Mori, the former Prime Minister, committed a succession of gaffes, most recently his refusal to abandon a game of golf on learning of the sinking of a Japanese trawler, the *Ehime Maru,* by an incompetently managed American submarine, which took nine lives – potentially the most damaging crisis in Japan's worsening relations with the United States. As he explained, 'I instructed government agencies to do their utmost to save human lives and asked the United States for its co-operation immediately after I reached the call. Then my secretary requested I stay there so as not to disrupt communications channels.' This was greeted with almost universal derision. Mori was the tenth prime minister to lose power in just over a decade. Yet frequent changes in leadership underscore the underlying continuity of Japanese politics, which is driven by the bureaucrats, not the politicians.

The disastrous state of the country's finances arise from the government's attempts to restart the economy through deficit spending. There is no more scope to reduce interest rates, which are already almost at zero. To outsiders, the answer lies in the introduction of free-market reforms to permit greater competition, laying off of workers and loosening of the cronyism between government, business and banks. But the Japanese have been resisting such changes for decades, which would strike at their very way of doing business.

Yet this is not how it appears in Japan at all. Any visitor to Japan is hard put to see any signs of anything other than affluence compared with most of the rest of the world. The Japanese earn more than Americans on average, pay only 12 per cent of their earnings in taxes (compared to 16 per cent in the United States and 20 per cent in Europe), and enjoy free healthcare and subsidized childcare. Virtually every household in Japan has a colour television and a microwave oven, nearly nine-tenths own a car, and nearly half a computer. Japanese workers average an hour a day less than Americans. Only a third as many Japanese have heart attacks as Americans, and most live longer. And an eighth of Japanese earnings go into savings, which stand at a staggering national total of $6.5 trillion.

Japanese manufacturing output is still $1,260 billion a year – a little more than that of the United States (although the value of the yen plays a part). While America's trade deficit has been around 4.5 per cent of GDP, Japan's average trade surplus has doubled in the past decade in spite of a 40 per cent increase in the value of the yen (which therefore presumably is still undervalued). Japan's net external assets have soared from $300 billion to more than $1,100 billion in more than a decade (almost exactly the value of America's net external liabilities).

What about the collapsed house of cards in which Japan's manufacturing and service industries depend on the banks which in turn are beholden to the collapsed property sector? With a fall of around four-fifths in property values from their peak a decade ago, the banks are technically left with bad loans of around 120 trillion yen. This sounds colossal, but it is a one-off, and assumes no recovery in the property market. Meanwhile the government has effectively agreed to underwrite the loans. The 1998 pledge allows for up to 60 trillion yen in state funds to help the banks: only around 20 trillion yen has actually been used. The government is insisting that most of the banks affected merge into four big groups as a condition of support: these are the Mitsubishi Tokyo Finance Group, Mizuho Financial Group, Sumitomo Mitsui Banking Corporation and United Financial of Japan Holdings.

This is an exact reflection of the process of consolidation of the manufacturing sector under the government's paternal eye after the Second World War. As the threat of massive insolvencies recedes, around 15 trillion of the fund will be kept aside only for emergencies. Thus the crisis has actually resulted in increased government control of the economy – a slap in the eye for lecturing American free-market proselytizers. Japan has never accepted Western concepts of deregulation and non-intervention, and pays only lip-service to them now. Rather, the country seems intent on reorganizing the existing system in preparation for a revival. Meanwhile, the external accounts look enormously healthy. Apart from the nationalist drift the country's political mess is superficial and barely affects the economy, which is slowly overcoming the problems of the last few years and could soon be poised for another global offensive.

The man to watch in Japan has more and more clearly become the governor of Tokyo Prefecture, Shintaro Ishihara. His support among nationalist groups has blossomed since the 'earthquake readiness drill' in central Tokyo in 2000, when some 7,000 troops were deployed around the capital, raising uneasy memories of the political climate before the Second World War. According to one critic, Atsuo Nakamura:

Ishihara wants to change the constitution and turn Japan into a big military country again. The other purpose is that Japan is in a very bad economic condition and politicians like this are trying to blame people of other nationalities for our troubles . . . The Japanese people are very nationalistic, and he wants to awaken this feeling to become more popular.

Ishihara himself aroused anger when he addressed troops in remarks which evoked the massacre of 7,000 Koreans after the 1923 earthquake:

> Third-country nationals who have entered Japan illegally have perpetrated heinous crimes. In the event of a major earthquake, riots could break out, and there is a limit to the police's ability to cope with such a situation alone.

Ishihara is both intelligent and charismatic, and is continually asserting himself as the reinventor of modern Japanese nationalism, a role he has taken over from former Prime Minister Yasuhiro Nakasone. Ishihara's celebrated book, *The Japan That Can Say No* (1989), claimed wildly that the arms race between the United States and the Soviet Union ended because both sides needed Japanese technology, which the latter threatened to withdraw, and suggested that the Japanese might sell Russia essential computer chips unless the Americans became more amenable to Japan. Ishihara secured the governorship of Tokyo with some 30 per cent of the vote, around 1.6 million, although he did not secure control of the town hall.

Since then, while denying that he is anti-American, he has launched a fierce attack on the American air-force base at Yokota in western Tokyo, which he wants returned to Japanese hands. He has also stirred the pot boiled up by the rape of a young girl by American servicemen in Okinawa in 1995. He is even more anti-Chinese, using the derogatory term 'Shina' to describe the country, casting doubt on the numbers involved in the Japanese massacre of the Chinese in Nanking in 1937, and describing the country, not inaccurately, as a 'communist dictatorship'. Ishihara has stated that 'American racism stems from pride in colonial supremacy', and that 'Japanese should not forget that Caucasians are prejudiced against orientals'. With the further incident involving the sinking of a Japanese trawler, the *Ehime Maru*, by an American submarine, the *Greeneville*, apparently steered by civilian guests, Ishihara's support was greatly strengthened. The remarks by the American commander of US marines in Okinawa that the Japanese were 'wimps' and 'nuts', and his reluctance to turn over an American marine accused of arson to Japanese custody have fanned these flames.

Ishihara's loyalty to the Liberal Democratic Party, which on these issues has moved steadily to the right, seems conditional. He has much enthusiastic support within the party, but has hinted that he may break away to form a nationalist party with his LDP ally, Kamei Shizuka.

Ishihara is an ardent advocate of the revision that would scrap the provision in the constitution permitting the setting up of armed forces and allow the country to embark on an unashamed military build-up and conduct offensive operations. Ishihara is not a man to be taken lightly by regional and Western foreign-policy worlds, because of the echoes his views increasingly arouse in much of the Japanese political establishment.

In my book *The Undefeated* (1994), I revealed that Japan has the materials and technology to build a massive nuclear force:

> its defence establishment has already considered the option, has no inhibitions about proceeding, and does not believe that this violates the constitution. Japan is to all intents a massive latent nuclear power. In the event of a crisis, several thousand fully armed nuclear warriors could spring full-grown from the soil in a relatively short space of time . . . the power of the atom has come to Japan again.

This has now been fully confirmed. Ichiro Ozawa, one of the country's most powerful opposition leaders, has declared that Chinese 'bullying could lead to Japan producing thousands of nuclear weapons at short notice'. Ishihara has long pressed for such a course. Because the Japanese view China's arms build-up and North Korean threats with growing alarm, and because after the end of the Cold War they no longer really believe American nuclear guarantees (which were aimed at Russia), Robyn Lim, professor of international relations at Nanzan University at Nagoya, claims that 'few doubt that Japan, given its technological prowess, could produce nuclear weapons and the means of delivering them in a relatively short time'. (Delivery systems would not technically violate Japan's 'defensive' constitution provided the weaponry was for deterrent, not aggressive purposes). Most tellingly of all, the country's most powerful official, chief cabinet secretary Yasuo Fakuda, a scion of two of the country's greatest political clans, Fukuda and Kishi, recently declared that 'depending upon the world situation, circumstances and public opinion could require Japan to possess nuclear weapons' – a clear shot across the bows for China and North Korea.

India and Pakistan

Another economic power increasingly prepared to project a nationalist and military dimension is India. Its principal territorial rival is China, and both are deeply wary of each other. But its attitude to Pakistan remains profoundly nationalistic and hostile, and the argument between the two over Kashmir continues to be one of the world's most dangerous flashpoints. It is often forgotten through all the rhetoric about Pakistani support for terrorism in Kashmir that India has refused to permit a referendum on self-determination for the territory (as had been promised since partition) for the good reason that an overwhelming majority of Kashmiris would opt to secede from India although probably not to join Pakistan, but for self-government. India's aggressiveness on the issue reflects the self-confidence of a newly rich, powerful and populous nation.

The vultures of war circling the disputed territory of Kashmir on India's northern border with Pakistan appear to have backed away a little: India is withdrawing troops at last from the border, after pulling back its warships in May from battle positions and lifting the ban on Pakistan's overflights of Indian territory. However, the situation remains tense after a serious terrorist attack on India's parliament. Medium- and short-range missiles are stationed on both sides of the border, capable of carrying nuclear weapons. India has armed forces of 1.2 million, 3,500 tanks and 750 combat aircraft, as well as some 90 nuclear weapons, compared with the 620,000-strong armed forces, 2,300 tanks, 350 aircraft and 30 nuclear warheads of Pakistan. America's sudden closeness to Pakistan following September 11 and the lifting of sanctions on that country caused flutters in New Delhi, which was already threatening to carry out 'hot pursuit' across the 'line of control' dividing Kashmir in response to a terrorist attack on the Srinagar State Assembly, which killed forty people. The head of the Indian army in the region, General Ril Nanauatty, declared that further provocation would trigger a conventional invasion of Kashmir 'not entirely dissimilar' to that in August 1965.

There are daily confrontations between Kashmiri demonstrators and India's occupying army of 500,000 to 800,000 men, often involving death and allegations of torture. There were some 300 guerrilla attacks and 100 guerrillas killed during the ceasefire. There are fears of a return to heavy fighting of the kind sparked in 1999 by the invasion of Pakistani-based insurgents down the Kargil Valley, which caused the Indians to retaliate with air attacks.

According to a National Intelligence Assessment drawn up by the CIA and other American agencies, the possibility of all-out war between India and Pakistan on the issue (two of the previous three such conflicts since partition were over Kashmir) is now fifty-fifty. 'The likelihood of a nuclear conflict goes up and down. It's less important to assign a probability to it than to warn senior officials that there is a serious threat here that demands immediate and focused attention and action,' said a senior American official in the region. Former President Clinton classified the region as 'the world's most dangerous'.

The impact of a nuclear exchange on India's burgeoning economy and on Pakistan's much weaker one barely bears thinking about; even a conventional war would set back the region's economic development for years. Tensions along the border have reached their most serious level in decades, but a conflict can still be averted. The Indians intransigently declare that they are only prepared to negotiate 'within the constitution' – which asserts India's control over Kashmir – and they have also ruled out any participation in the talks by Pakistan. Both these preconditions are unacceptable to the Hizbul Mujahideen, although if India had dropped its insistence on sovereignty, Hizbul (and its Pakistani backers) might have been willing to abandon the demand for formal Pakistani representation (the Pakistanis would continue to pull many of the strings in any such encounter), at least to begin with.

The complexities of Indian politics make it almost inevitable that no Indian government has the authority to make substantial concessions over Kashmir. India has never carried out its pledge to hold a referendum in Kashmir – which is unsurprising, as the overwhelming majority of Kashmiris are Muslims who seek independence from India. The Indians are justified in arguing that Pakistan has sought to exploit the issue for its own purposes. But such support is also only natural for the neighbouring Muslim state.

The harsh reality is that India has possession of much of the state, believes itself to be militarily the stronger power in the region, and has no intention of giving it up. Anything between 34,000 and 80,000 people have been killed in the dispute over the past decade. Frankly, this is unacceptable for a democratic and potentially important economy and burgeoning regional power which expects to be considered a senior member of the global community. India's economy has been growing by around 6 per cent a year during the past decade. This could reach 10 per cent a year, transforming the lives of its 1 billion people if much needed infrastructure improvements were implemented, particularly in the information technology sector, such as ending the state monopoly on Internet gateways and ending the sales tax on IT products. This dispute should have been solved long ago through Indian generosity.

The issue is how far Pakistan's military government is willing to test this reality – or whether it will be content merely to expose India's intransigence to the condemnation of world opinion. This is turn may depend on a Pakistani assessment of the relative military strengths of the two countries: Pakistani generals privately concede the superiority of Indian conventional forces.

A much more dangerous possible scenario is an accidental drift to war. Thus, if a major guerrilla offensive were to be countered by a massive Indian military thrust into Kashmir, the Pakistanis might feel they had no alternative but to support their allies and co-religionists. If India retaliated with its greater conventional forces, Pakistan could soon be left with little alternative but to threaten a nuclear attack. The Indians would be obliged to threaten nuclear counter-attack. The Indians say they are not afraid of Pakistani nuclear weapons, because they have a second-strike capability that would annihilate Pakistan. They do not believe Pakistan would dare launch a first strike, because it could not destroy all of India.

Yet Pakistan might feel it has no option. It is far from clear that classic deterrent theory would apply in a regional theatre. In an area where neither side even talks to the other on a regular basis, and the 1998 detonation of Indian and Pakistani nuclear tests one after another marks the crudest form of dialogue between the two, American nervousness about what could happen is understandable.

The United States and its Western allies have some leverage. Pakistan remains a close Western ally and General Musharraf could be persuaded to bring pressure to bear on the guerrillas not to renew their offensive and so provoke India. Pakistan's still-shaky military government, whose life has been hugely complicated in 2002 by the entry of Islamic parties into the parliamentary majority, may feel it has enough on its plate dealing with domestic crises and Afghanistan to engage in military adventures in Kashmir; conversely, the Kashmiri situation, in the view of some senior Pakistani officials, might provide the ideal diversion from troubles at home to rally the nation behind the armed forces.

The United States and its allies should also make clear to India that a major thrust into Kashmir would be condemned internationally and might invite commercial retaliation: the root cause of the dispute remains Indian intransigence. Any first threat or actual use of nuclear weapons should attract the most stringent possible sanctions and pariah status for the offender.

A complicating factor in the dispute has been the emergence of severe divisions within the Kashmiri separatist organizations. The Pakistani-based groups, of which Syed Salahuddin's Hizbul, based in Muzaffar-abad, is the most prominent, appear to be losing ground to local insurgents, who object to Pakistan's influence on the movement. The most militant of these is Jaish-a-Mohammed (Army of Mohammed), led by Maulana Masood Azhar, an Islamic religious leader with links to, and training support from, the Taleban in Afghanistan, which initially claimed responsibility for the Srinagar massacre. Two other smaller militant groups are the Harkatul Mujaheddin, linked to Osama bin Laden, and Lashkar-e-Taiba. Tensions are evident even within Hizbul itself with Salahuddin's deputy, Abdul Majid Dar, apparently leading a peace faction.

The Pakistani influence on the guerrillas remains considerable, but the country may prove unable to restrain a guerrilla offensive, inviting massive Indian army retaliation. The silver lining of this potential mushroom cloud is that the emergence of a stronger Kashmiri voice might one day persuade the Indians to recognize that a self-governing region would not merely be a Pakistani puppet.

The shape of a long-term settlement has always been clear: a pro-longed spell of Kashmiri self-rule under nominal Indian sovereignty; demilitarization of the region; and the prospect, at the end of ten years, of full independence if the terms of the agreement are respected by both sides. Successive governments in New Delhi have failed to display the strength or the statesmanship required to concede the possibility that the Kashmiris might one day be allowed to do as they wish.

Iraq

To the west, across the zone of turbulence in the newly independent southern states of the future Soviet Union, past Afghanistan to Iran and the Middle East and further, more primitive examples of nouveau-riche nationalism proliferate (indeed, it is here, at its very heartland, that Huntington's thesis breaks down altogether). For all the empty rhetoric about 'Arab nation' and Arab brotherhood, the region is a hodgepodge of competing, and often openly warring, nationalisms, based, in many cases, on very recently drawn up boundaries. Iran itself was a thrusting, nationalistic country under the Shah until the Islamic revolution.

The present focus of global attention is Iraq, which the United States has made clear is being considered for punitive, possibly overwhelming, military attack unless the current UN weapons inspections verify that it is not building weapons of mass destruction. American determination on this score should not be underestimated, as President Bush's 'axis of evil' speech made clear. Equally, the Americans say that no firm decision has been taken: the practicalities of removing Saddam Hussein are still formidable, however desirable the objective. If Iraq is on the verge of acquiring nuclear weapons, there will be no alternative. If an attempt is made, it will probably have to be with overwhelming force: the consequences of a botched attempt to remove him would be calamitous. If nuclear weapons are still a long way off, it may be better simply to await his demise, as happened with Nasser in Egypt. Attention should be given as to whether an alternative policy is possible. This was being actively considered by the United States before September 11.

Iraq under Saddam is an aggressive, intensely nationalistic state with no less an ambition than to re-establish itself as the leader of the Arab world – a position it held until Gamal Abdal-Nasser took over in Egypt in 1956. Declaring war on Iran, invading Kuwait, bullying Jordan, constantly threatening Syria, Iraq has been something between a version of Hitler's Germany and Russia's Stalin in its behaviour towards its Arab neighbours. However, it is certainly not an Islamic or even an Arab standard-bearer: its neighbours, so often victims of its aggression, hate it. Iraq's secular socialist regime intensely dislikes Islamic fundamentalism, although occasionally it suits it to pretend otherwise.

The sanctions in place against Iraq for a decade after the end of the 1991 Gulf War are perceptibly eroding. Both President Bush and General Colin Powell, the Secretary of State, have acknowledged that sanctions have so collapsed that 'they resemble Swiss cheese'. With the reopening of Saddam International Airport in August 2000, dozens of international aircraft have landed containing government and business delegations. Iraqi Airways have resumed regular domestic flights through Western-imposed no-fly zones to the southern city of Basra and the northern city of Mosul. A recent trade fair in Baghdad hosted businessmen from forty-five countries. The deputy leader of the Russian parliament recently led a delegation of fifty deputies to Baghdad. France's TotalFinaElf is spearheading a drive by oil companies to seek to penetrate Iraq in the Majnoon and Mahr Umar fields, with a potential 1 million barrels a day. Shell has been discussing development of the Ratawi oilfield in south Iraq, with a potential of 1 billion barrels. Smuggling into Iraq amounts to anything between $1 and $3 billion a year.

The Jordanians have refused to allow Lloyds of London inspectors to look at shipments destined for Iraq arriving at the Jordanian port of

Aqaba which opens up Iraq's traditional sanctions-busting lifeline. The Jordanian Prime Minister said recently, 'are sanctions eroding? Yes. We feel they are becoming ridiculous.' Jordan, of course, benefits from Iraq's supply of cut-price oil to the kingdom. Meanwhile, the Iraqi-Syrian pipeline has been reopened, carrying some 150,000 barrels of oil a day.

Iraq was for the first time in recent years invited to attend the Arab summit, which was primarily called to discuss the Palestinian problem. Saddam Hussein at that summit took advantage to beat his old rhetorical drum, urging other Arab countries to wage 'holy war' against Israel and fatuously mobilizing units along the Syrian border to come to that country's rescue, if attacked. The Syrians, just as worried about Iraqi aggression as Israeli, asked him to pull back, as did other countries. He did.

Similarly, his call for 'those rulers and kings who have sold out their souls' to the Israelis to be overthrown by their peoples, and his allegations that the Kuwaitis are tapping into Iraq's underground oil reserves, seem to be no more than bluster – for now. His subsequent suppression of oil exports in order to try and bully the UN into paying the proceeds for them directly to his government rather than spend the money on aid and food is another example of the old growling.

Current Iraqi oil exports run at some 2.3 million barrels a day (he earns a further $3 billion a year in under-the-counter sales, and has some $11 billion held by the UN in its withholding account for Iraq). Yet the sanctions regime is still in place upon a huge range of goods which might have a military use, as well as key sectors of the Iraqi economy. But the policy, while containing Iraq, has not achieved its aim of either toppling Saddam or forcing him to give up his aim of acquiring weapons of mass destruction. There are four key issues here:

Are sanctions, now eroding as discussed, effective? Contrary to widespread assumptions, the sanctions that were maintained and tightened against South Africa over a twenty-year period were highly and increasingly damaging and one of the key factors in the decision by the country's elite white minority to hand over power a decade ago. In particular, a boycott by South Africa's international creditors was particularly effective and marked a turning point.

But the situation in Iraq is very different. The country is not a pariah among its neighbours in the way South Africa was, merely a wayward, if feared, member of the Arab community. The sanctions are not explicitly directed, and certainly not conditional upon, the overthrow of Saddam Hussein's regime, – but on his renunciation of weapons of mass destruction; American support for the internal opposition in Iraq had, until September 11, fizzled out in recognition of its divisions and ineffectiveness.

Saddam is very far from being cut off from international lines of credit as South Africa was – its hiccuping resumption of oil exports, supposedly in exchange for humanitarian and food imports, provides an adequate financial lifeline, as does sanction-busting and contraband. Half sanctions, hypothecated sanctions or ratcheted sanctions are arguably only barely effective. In other words, Iraq is in no danger of financial strangulation.

But that is very far from saying that sanctions are having no effect. As has often been commented upon, levels of malnutrition, disease and poverty have soared among lower income groups. According to Unicef, some 500,000 children have died and 800,000 are malnourished as a result of sanctions over the past decade. Just as significant, for a country that once enjoyed a higher level of oil-generated prosperity than any developing country, middle-class living standards have been shattered, with 63 per cent of professionals now engaged in menial work. According to the UN, Iraqi imports are lower than those of many small Third World countries. Faced with austerity, rising crime and social disintegration, the government has resorted to harshly repressive measures.

Obviously, Saddam's immediate entourage are unaffected by this hardship: his extravagant building of palaces and government complexes is well documented. But will very serious hardship, particularly among the middle class, eventually stoke up discontent among the hierarchy, or even a popular uprising? Will he react to this and alter course?

The answer to the first question is easier than the second. Ferocious repression by the regime is almost certainly sufficient to counter any real threat; but the danger of disaffection perceived by Iraq's policy-makers may urge a more moderate course whether or not Saddam is listening. In other words, sanctions, which are by no means crippling to the nation but are devastating in their impact upon Iraqis from both the middle- and lower-income groups, have a limited but significant impact upon the calculations of the ruling elite. But there is no prospect of sanctions bringing about the fall of Saddam's regime – the stated objective of the United States; indeed, they have buttressed his personal position to the extent that he is able to blame most of the hardship endured by ordinary Iraqis upon the Western powers.

This impinges upon the second main consideration: is Saddam merely a 'rogue' player, as dangerous and unpredictable, and possibly mentally unstable, as Libya's Colonel Qaddafi? He is often caricatured as such, and deliberately plays up to the image. Or is he rational and predictable?

There is reason to believe there is method in Saddam's madness. His invasion of Iran, it can be argued (and was by the United States at the time), derived from the perception that his own regime was under threat from the Islamic revolution across the border; his invasion of Kuwait arose from genuine grievances against the Kuwaitis, abetted by the misreading of signals from Washington that the move would not be opposed: it is often forgotten how close Iraq and the United States were in the pre-Kuwait period, when Saddam was viewed as a buttress against much more dangerous Iran.

Indeed, his failure to follow up the invasion with a move into Saudi Arabia, as well as his decision not to use chemical or biological weapons in the Gulf War, his alarming but limited use of missiles against Israel, and his care not actually to go to war with the hated rival Baathists in Syria all fit the pattern. Saddam is utterly ruthless, sometimes impulsive, and always prepared to use force. But he is not insane. He is a Stalin, not a Hitler. When he has understood that his actions might endanger his rule or Iraq, he has not so far tended to overstep the boundaries.

The same is evident in his reaction to the West's no-flying zones in northern and southern Iraq, for which he has shown a healthy respect, occasionally locking on to American or British aircraft with his radar, but never actually shooting one down. Altogether some 320,000 sorties have been flown since the end of the Gulf War, and more than 300 Iraqis killed and 1,000 wounded in three years; Western aircraft strike once every three days on average.

They have certainly performed a vital role in protecting the Kurds in the north and the Shias in the south. But the Kurds have kept their peace, although Shia intentions are uncertain; and guarantees for these peoples short of air support may be possible. It follows, if this analysis of Saddam is correct – as a coldly cynical, psychopathic, murderous and calculating player susceptible to pressure and conscious of his own limitations, rather than a man who can run berserk at any time – that a more flexible approach is possible.

How is progress on sanctions conceivable without either side dropping an apparently essential principle or losing face? For the United States the key condition is that Iraq must permit inspection to ensure that it has abandoned all its nuclear, chemical, biological and missile-building programmes (this is not domineering: it sets the tone for other such arms-control programmes across the world). After two years without inspection, it is believed that Iraq has become capable of producing the lethal ricin at its Falluja chemical and biological factories. The inspections are now happening under threat of American invasion. A peaceful deal is still, just possible.

Essentially, both sides must come out of any deal with something to show: the Americans with a verifiable agreement that the Iraqis will not develop weapons of mass destruction or resort to genocide again against their own people; the Iraqis with an end to sanctions.

Ideally any agreement would involve non-aggression pacts with other states in the Gulf and the Arab world and mechanisms for settling disputes of the kind that led to Iraq's invasion of Kuwait in the first place. As for lifting the no-fly zone in northern and southern Iraq, that will depend on autonomy deals that satisfy the West that no further punitive action will be taken against the civilian populations there.

The final element is the future of Iraq. The country is emphatically not an oil-rich decadent. This is a populous, well-educated country with a sophisticated middle class and emancipated women which should vie with Egypt as the Arab world's natural leader – or would do if its policies had been more responsible. It also has potentially the biggest oil reserves outside Saudi Arabia. The country's infrastructure, industry and agriculture are on life-support at the moment.

All of this will change virtually overnight if a deal is done. Unlike other war-torn countries where a long period of investment is required before sources come on stream, or where foreign companies have to be coaxed in carefully for years, investors can rush in with the knowledge that substantial oil revenues will take little time to be generated. There is a great deal to be done after a decade of destruction and neglect. Iraq has proven reserves of 112 billion barrels – half the Saudi total – and potentially several times that.

For business, the country has huge potential; for long-suffering Iraqis, dazzling daylight awaits at the end of the tunnel. For Saddam, there is the opportunity (his lifespan may not be very long) to be genuinely respected by his people with the prospect that, like Egypt after Nasser, Iraq may become the peaceful, sophisticated regional leader it deserves to be.

There are many who blame the United States for an appalling mistake in not pursuing the Iraqi army back to Baghdad and overthrowing Saddam at the end of the Gulf War. The consequence has been truly horrific suffering for the Iraqi people over the following decade. But further mistakes do not make a correct policy. If Saddam does submit to inspections and disarmament, America will have won a great victory. Maybe even Saddam, older and a little wiser, has realized the error he made in invading Kuwait in the first place; certainly, for all his bluster, he has not actively imperilled world peace since then. But, to repeat, if he frustrates the inspections at this eleventh hour and seeks to retain chemical and biological weapons, or seems close to acquiring nuclear weapons, the West will have no alternative but to act.

Syria

Syria, Jordan and Egypt all utter platitudes about Arab solidarity and all pursue determinedly nationalist policies: Egypt signed a separate peace with Israel, which it was convenient for Jordan to follow two decades later. Syria still denounces both and refuses to sign.

Syria's condemnation of the September 11 attacks on America marks another milestone in its cautious emergence from the political shadows into the light. Although President Bashar al-Assad publicly berated visiting British Prime Minister Tony Blair for the war in Afghanistan and 'the killing of innocent civilians', he condemned terrorism. But as for such groups fighting Israel from Syrian soil, 'I personally differentiate between resistance and terrorism.' Even this is a step forward. The succession of Bashar al-Assad to his father's tightly controlled regime was widely derided as a minor changing of the guard: the diffident young man, propelled into the role of heir only by his older brother Basil's accidental death, seemed likely to be no more than a puppet of the coterie of elderly advisers who sustained Hafez al-Assad's throne for so many years, stifling both economic and political liberalization.

Bashar's recent anti-Semitic tirade, using the Pope's visit to Damascus as a platform, both startled and confirmed the view of many observers that he is no more than a clone of his secretive, anti-Israeli father. This is erroneous. Bashar's power base is still extremely weak, and in the absence of any retaliation against Israel's strikes against Syria in Lebanon, rhetoric may have seemed his only option. In addition, in order to carry forward the changes he seems to be embarking upon in Syrian society, wrapping himself in anti-Israeli nationalism may be the only way to carry his people. Yet so far he has not deviated from his father's extreme caution in engaging Israel militarily. The Golan Heights remain one of the world's most successful ceasefire lines, with scarcely any violations in years.

But Bashar has taken his own countrymen by surprise. In alliance with the new Prime Minister, Muhammed Mustafa Miro, he has enacted land reform laws permitting foreign investors to buy land; he has allowed greater repatriation of profits and capital, as well as relaxing foreign exchange laws and creating a single exchange rate; he has drafted a law to create a modern private banking system; and he has limited corporation tax to an across-the-board 25 per cent. Syria has also mended its fences with international financial institutions, in particular the World Bank. The country's stagnant and dominant state sector remains an albatross, but the government seems determined to tackle this to boost Syria's considerable potential in oil and gas, agriculture and tourism. Corruption in the public sector has been cracked down upon.

All of this is seismic for Syria. One of the most controlled countries in the Middle East also shows signs of political relaxation. Some 600 political prisoners have been released. The President of the Committee for the Defence of Human Rights, Aktham Naesa, has been freed, while a draft law allowing non-government publications is being enacted. An independent newspaper called the *Lamplighter*, satirizing the bureaucracy, has been allowed. Elections are being permitted within the Baath Party, and even a measure of political pluralism, in the shape of rival parties, is being encouraged. Committees for the Revival of Civil Society, committed to pluralism, have sprung up, urging full political freedoms. Bashar told security chiefs bluntly, 'You have no right to prevent it.'

Bashar's attitude to Israel has to be understood in the context of his watching his back from the inevitable opposition among hardliners, many of them military, that his reforms have aroused. The young Assad has clung to the main tenets of his father's foreign policy. Apart from making no concessions to Israel – although not reacting to the jabs of Ariel Sharon's government – there have been a series of strategic alliances which Bashar has sought: with Iran, as a deterrent to the nearer neighbour Iraq; with Saudi Arabia, Syria's chief paymaster; with Egypt, in strategic alliance against Israel; and with Syria's satellite Lebanon, albeit with a diminishing military presence. The foreign minister remains the veteran Farouk al-Shara.

A couple of changes of emphasis are detectable, among them a slight improvement in relations with Turkey, whose own strategic alliance with Israel has disgusted Syria in the past. The Turks are still seeking an end to Syria's claim over the Turkish province of Hatay, while the Syrians want a share of the headwaters of the Euphrates. Syria's relations with its old Baathist rivals in Iraq are also on the mend. Iraq's Deputy Prime Minister, Tariq Aziz, has called on Bashar no fewer than four times since his accession. With a new generation in charge of both Syria and Jordan, there must be hope that they will eventually appeal to a younger generation in Israel – now led by the septuagenarian Ariel Sharon – for a peace based on mutual self-respect in place of the historical grudges of their elders.

On a wider level the various Arab states display very little inclination to co-operate. The oil-rich Gulf states display a certain obligation to help their much more populous and impoverished neighbours – in particular Egypt, Jordan and the Palestinians – but brotherhood does not extend to any real sharing of wealth between an often tribally or colonially delineated chain of Arab countries.

South Africa

To the south the tension is between a series of ex-colonial African states – some of which have evolved a high level of national identity, and some disintegrationist tendencies (which will be returned to later). The Pan-African attempt to establish a national consciousness advocated by independence leaders such as Kwame Nkrumah seems as stillborn as ever. Although strides have been made towards democratic elections in many countries, the tradition remains shallow.

Only South Africa, as the one African country with a really developed industrial and urban base, and Nigeria, with its oil wealth, size and population, provide any kind of leadership for the continent, and the latter's experience of corruption and military rule has often disqualified it. As both countries acknowledge, the task of uniting Africa on any issue is pretty desperate. The recent joint action by both in spearheading Zimbabwe's suspension from the Commonwealth was a very rare episode of unity of purpose. Fortunately, and perhaps surprisingly, the divisions there do not frequently extend to actual conflict between states; but the ones within states – Rwanda, Congo, Ethiopia, Sudan, Somalia, Zimbabwe, Sierra Leone, Liberia – more than make up for this.

The softly-softly leadership of Nelson Mandela's successor, President Thabo Mbeki is coming under increasing fire from right, centre and left. On one side Mbeki has been assailed for his failure to speak out in public against President Robert Mugabe's recent rigged re-election and for his toleration of land occupations in Zimbabwe to the north. From all sides Mbeki has been criticized for his assertion that HIV does not cause Aids, which he regards as a slur on those who suffer from it (an estimated 4 million of South Africa's 44 million people). He has been blamed for denying anti-retroviral drugs to sufferers – on the grounds that these are expensive, not necessarily effective and merely put money in the hands of

Western pharmaceutical companies. He is being castigated by the left for his free-market economic policies. Of the two, Mbeki regards the latter as much the more dangerous.

In October 2000, Mbeki finally broke his silence on the issue of Zimbabwean land seizures. He declared without equivocation that 'this conflict is wrong. The occupation of the farms must stop. They are a violation of the law,' threatening to bring about the economic collapse of Zimbabwe, 'which would be a disaster for Zimbabwe, South Africa and the region.' He added:

> militant statements might get good headlines but are unlikely to solve the problem. Our challenge is to do what we can to contribute to stopping Zimbabwe's further decline. We have a battle on our hands to avoid a collapse there. Our principal task is not to criticize. We are trying to find solutions.

But there was an obligation to be constructive. If Zimbabwe collapsed 'we would have to absorb the shock'. Sanctions would bring life to 'a standstill . . . Zimbabweans would cross our borders and come to us.'

Mbeki in fact regards the land reform issue as political dynamite, being less concerned about Mugabe's sensitivities than to prevent an equivalent movement spilling across his borders and gaining ground in South Africa. This was reiterated recently by Mbeki's ally, President Obasanjo of Nigeria, who argued that 'I told Zimbabwe [that] it should strictly follow the law that has already been put in place.' But both countries are doing too little. Mugabe's blatantly rigged election in 2001, his torture and murder of opponents and his blatant violation of the law, have now been exacerbated by the drought sweeping the land, which his policies have largely induced. Western sanctions have been minor and ineffectual, and much tougher action is required. Mugabe says he will take over 3,000 to 4,500 white farms, virtually without compensation and has forced out the country's white supreme court justice.

White farmers are vital to South Africa's prosperity and, Mbeki argues, are not comparable to Zimbabwe's, the land in South Africa being of low fertility and subject to drought, which makes only large-scale cultivation possible; in any event 60 per cent of South Africa's black population is urban. Against that the enforced mass resettlement from tribal lands to the poorer homelands under apartheid gives millions of blacks today the right to reclaim former farms. Under the Restitution of Land Act passed by the ANC government in 1994, some 3.4 million blacks were given rights to compensation, most of which did not materialize. Mbeki believes the small-scale farming of the land desired by black radicals is simply uneconomic: the government points to the fact that nearly 2.5 million rural families occupy 13 per cent of its land but generate only 3 per cent of the country's income (mostly admittedly in the homelands with their poor soils). The government also claims that only around 700,000 hectares are available for distribution outside the homelands, and 1.2 million people want them.

There are fears that land-hungry blacks could take matters into their own hands. The radical Pan-African Congress is believed to be plotting illegal farm occupations and the country's 80,000 or so white farmers have stepped up security (around 600 have been killed since 1994, mostly by criminals). According to opinion polls, more than half of South Africa's blacks would support such seizures. Mugabe, far from being seen as a monster by many ordinary South Africans, is something of a hero. However, Mbeki recently received much-needed support in opposing the seizures from the 1.8 million-strong Congress of South African Trades Unions (Cosatu), which is often his sternest critic.

Cosatu is instead dismayed by Mbeki's markedly free-market economic policies. The President has been running South Africa largely through an inner circle of the government, led by Trevor Manuel, the Finance Minister, Alec Erwin, the Trade and Industry Minister, Jeff Radebe, the Public Enterprises Minister and Membathisi Mdladlana, Minister of Labour, as well as Defence Minister Patrick Lekota. ANC leaders complain that they are infrequently consulted, and Cosatu barely at all.

Mbeki has been arguing unequivocally that strikes discourage investment and that South Africa will have to adapt to new technology. He has declared: '[We] have to understand that there is nobody in the world who formed a secret committee to conspire to impose globalization on an unsuspecting humanity.'

He also stated:

We all know that there are opponents of the movement working within the movement who make the same claims as those made by our opponents, that as a movement we are not doing anything to address the interests of the people.

This was a reference to his perennial radical opponent, Winnie Madikizela-Mandela, Nelson Mandela's divorced wife, who has been attacking Mbeki's stance on Aids as well as travelling to Zimbabwe to encourage blacks to seize white lands. She seems so far, however, to have failed to stir up much support.

Reports that Mbeki's vanquished political rival, Cyril Ramaphosa, is likely to mount a challenge are wide of the mark. Ramaphosa, currently successfully ensconced in the private sector, has made clear that he does not diverge from the broad lines of Mbeki's economic policy. Even so, the capable and cultured President would be wise to develop more sensitive political antennae. If he continues to be seen as too aloof, pressure will emerge for a more politically charismatic and attractive figure, such as Ramaphosa, to guide South Africa on its chosen free-market course in, say, a couple of years' time. Against that the structure of the ANC is authoritarian, and Mbeki has most of the political levers in his hand.

The economic effects of the land seizures in Zimbabwe on South Africa's economy have been severe, denting both inward investment and the rand. But the government has kept its nerve, and Mbeki's decision to speak out publicly against the Zimbabwean occupation suggests that he is getting more confident he can maintain the position in South Africa. He has firmly stated that urbanized South Africa has no intention of following down the path taken by its more rural and less-developed northern neighbour, and prospects for the country remain bright if it can attract much-needed foreign investment. Mbeki has no intention of altering course, and the only alternative to him, Ramaphosa, is similarly realistic. South Africa is a viable economy that suffers from vastly exaggerated jitters generated elsewhere on the continent.

Elsewhere in Africa, only Namibia's 4,000 or so white farmers feel threatened – but the land is too poor for small-scale farming. In Kenya, land reform for the Kikuyu in small-scale farms at White Heights has proved hugely successful, while coffee, tea, sugar and sisal plantations, many of them white-owned, remain highly prosperous. The land has to be cultivated on a large scale, and the government has no intention of following the Mugabe route. In Malawi, southern farmers struggling to live on tiny smallholdings could present a threat – but any attempt to seize the large exporting tea plantations is likely to result in a sharp fall in living standards.

Latin America

A leap over to Latin America shows a continent uneasily poised between a series of petty nationalisms and a common cultural heritage that ought, in theory, to provide it with the incentive to unify in rivalry and co-operation with the colossus of the north, the United States. The region's often understated maturity has long prevented armed conflict between its countries, but the national identities have never been subordinated to their common Spanish or Portuguese colonial heritages, even if their armies no longer run their governments.

In 1926, that master of pithy plain speaking, President Calvin Coolidge, remarked contemptuously, 'It would seem that revolutions and natural disasters are the main products of Latin America.' In spite of the continent's heartening switch from crude military regimes to democratic ones in the last quarter of the twentieth century, it would seem that not all that much has changed. The region's embrace of free-market economics, under United States prodding, has resulted in bitter disappointment: growth has barely kept up with population increases during the last decade.

As a result, many Latin American countries now seem to be reverting to type. Argentina's economy has plummeted and a more nationalist Peronist regime seems likely to take charge in 2003. In Brazil a working-class social democrat, Luis Inacio da Silva (Lula) has been elected, pledged vaguely to greater social justice and a 'new economic model', succeeding the fairly successful free-market government of Fernando Enrique Cardoso; the Brazilian real plunged by a quarter in 2002. Another military populist, Lucio Gutierrez, has been elected president in Ecuador, following hard on the heels of Alejandro Toledo in Peru. A populist who has been in power for longer, Hugo Chavez in Venezuela has presided over sharp economic decline, and was almost toppled in a coup, suggesting the populist route offers little hope either. For the moment democracy continues to survive around the continent, although it may soon be under pressure.

The only way out may lie in greater co-operation across Latin America, in imitation of the North American and European models. Moderate populists like Lula and Chavez, as well as their free-market counterparts, should have no ideological objection to doing so, pursuing a 'pan-Americanist' solution first enunciated by Simón Bolívar, reinvented at the First Pan-American Conference held in Washington in 1889, and then with the foundation of the Charter of the Organisation of Inter-American States in 1948. Since then, little local groupings like Mercosur in the south, the Andean Pact in the north west and the Central American common market have evolved, in competition with the huge Brazilian economy and Mexico, linked to the United States through the North American Free Trade Area.

But taken together, the Latin Americans are a much more formidable grouping than they are separately. The Hispanic world, excluding Brazil, is now some 400 million strong and Spanish is on the way to becoming the world's second language. The Hispanic influence in the United States is colossal, and growing. Los Angeles is already the second biggest Spanish-speaking city in the world, after Mexico City and ahead of Madrid and Barcelona. The Hispanic population of the United States, at more than 30 million, now 12 per cent, is expected to reach a quarter of the population by 2050. Since 1990 the Hispanic community in the United States has grown by nearly 40 per cent compared to 9 per cent for the rest of the population. The commercial relationship is equally striking: Latin America, which absorbs 21 per cent of US exports, treads hot on the heels of the European Union with 22 per cent of US exports and Asia with 25 per cent. The US Department of Commerce expects Latin America to overtake the other two by 2010.

With Hispanics forming an increasingly powerful voting block within the United States and the region becoming America's most important trading partner, the way ahead lies clearly with a much more respectful partnership between the two regions than in the past, and one based on Latin American integration (including Brazil, which also has its own special trading links with Africa). Mexico has long subordinated its sense of national affirmation to such pragmatic co-operation. Brazil, although unlikely to do so, has always exercised its self-assertion as a trading power, rather than in pursuit of nationalist goals.

The different countries of Spanish America can still retain their nationhood while pursuing much more co-ordinated policies with each other, with Brazil and Mexico, and with the United States. Having eschewed nationalism, the only way forward for Latin America is regional co-operation and partnership with the United States in imitation of the European model, rather than the unproductive nationalist rivalries of Asia. Otherwise the continent, while unlikely to breed nouveau riche nationalist security challenges, could breed internal security ones – like the narco-guerrilla struggle in Colombia, which could yet spread into a more general one affecting Venezuela, Peru, Ecuador and Bolivia, – or even a resurgence of social disintegration and guerrilla activity of the kind that plagued Argentina and Uruguay in the 1970s.

Germany

Only in Europe, perhaps, is the era of nationalism beginning to pass. It is not coincidental that this was the continent where the nation state first evolved. Yet for all the hype about the European Union, the national dimension remains overpowering and defining. The Union, healthily, exists largely to maximize common influence where the individual countries prove unable to do so because they are too small in relation, in particular, to the United States, to the economic power of Japan or to the continental mass of Russia, but Germany continues to be Germany, Britain to be Britain, France to be France, Italy to be Italy and Spain to be Spain.

However, Germany, perhaps the archetype of old-fashioned nationalism is likely eventually to emerge as Europe's leader. The image provided by Germany over the past four years is highly misleading. Politically, the country had apparently been weakened by the traumatic adjustment from sixteen years of stability under Chancellor Helmut Kohl's CDU/CSU coalition to the SPD/Green coalition under Chancellor Gerhard Schröder. This was followed by three further political earthquakes: the departure of the main left-wing bulwark of the new government, Oskar Lafontaine; the scandal surrounding CDU campaign financing, which left the opposition party tainted and Kohl's reputation in tatters; and the succession of resignations and scandals affecting the government. The 2002 election saw a sharp recovery by the CDU/CSU coalition under Edmund Stoiber, which could conceivably regain power in a year or two. Schröder lacks a mandate to enact the necessary harsh economic measures and could conceivably be forced into a grand coalition with the opposition. Following a tax increase, Schröder's popularity has slumped.

Add to this the dismal performance of the Euro over the past two years, the slowing of the German economy to near stagnation largely as a result of the contraction in export markets following the American turndown, the Far Eastern and Russian economic crises and the continuing cost of reunification, reflected in the colossal public sector debt and the disappointing performance of the East German economy, and the prospects look bleak indeed. Unemployment, at just under 4 million, is still depressingly high, and government targets for a 2003 decline to 3.5 million look unlikely. Moreover, under union pressure, the reform of the pension system has been watered down.

Yet this surface gloom hides the fact that a significant long-term transformation of the economy is beginning to take place that if pressed forward could restore the country to its old status as the powerhouse of Europe – only this time a much larger one. Reunification, plus the Kohl government's decision to postpone major and badly needed economic reforms, have imposed huge burdens on the German economy over the past decade. When Schröder came to power it seemed likely, under Lafontaine's prodding, that these problems would be exacerbated.

Instead the Chancellor has taken advantage of his lieutenant's departure to take the first of the unpopular decisions needed to pull the economy out of the doldrums, and the effects are just beginning to work through. He has not gone far enough, and further bullet-biting will be necessary. In all events, there is no question of abandoning the German model of a social market economy, with a major degree of consensus having long existed between government, business and the unions, on worker participation, the cosy relationship between government, the banks and business, as well as on the generous welfare state. These are the anchors of Germany's post-war society, and will not be given up.

But there is an understanding on the part of all the players around the table that the awesome public sector debt must be curbed; that high unemployment benefits and above-inflation wage indexation are past luxuries; and that, with an ageing population, pension provision is simply too generous. This is not a matter of abandoning the social market economy; it is making it live within its means.

The departure of Lafontaine was an immediate consequence of this grasping of realities on Schröder's part, and he showed part of the necessary steel and ruthlessness to carry it through. The Chancellor's former political rival on the left, who now absurdly claims his enemy's 'Weimar' policies could lead to a new Hitler coming to power, shows no sign of constituting a threat to Schröder. The consequence of unpopular policies has, inevitably, been a sharp decline in the government's popular support and the narrow re-election of Schröder. The Chancellor's days may be limited, not by Lafontaine but by the challenge from the right which came so close to unseating him.

Nevertheless, the significance also of his break with the foreign policies of post-war Germany shold not be underrated. In first sending troops out of Europe to help with the Western intervention in Afghanistan, and then in breaking with Germany's slavish verbal support of American global policy by staking out his opposition to American intervention in Iraq, Schröder has made two highly significant departures from his predecessors. Germany will no longer be afraid to intervene abroad, nor to disagree with America.

The global political community has failed to take in the implications of an economically resurgent Germany, after years of underperforming. If it happens these would be profound, now that the post-war generation, with its far more limited sense of guilt about the country's Nazi past, is finally in power. It would affect Germany's relations with the United States, with the rest of the European Union, with Eastern Europe, and with the global economy as a whole. It bears remembering that the German economy is the world's third biggest, accounting for almost a third of Europe's GDP, that Germany is Britain's biggest trading partner in Europe and the fifth biggest trading partner of the United States.

The Euro's woes have provided an unexpected and much-needed boost to German exports, more than compensating for the oil price increase of 2001. International investment in Germany has recently boomed, particularly from Britain. However, government red tape remains a major problem, and does favour local producers who know their way through it. With both France and Germany likely to break the European Central Bank's tight budget limits, that particular corset imposed by Kohl is likely to be eased, and the Union may be able to resume its role in global economic expansion.

The long-term consequences of Germany's long-term structural reorganization are going to be enormous. President Chirac of France has talked of 'decoupling' to describe the loss of his country's former dominance. Within Europe the German economy will be increasingly dominant, with France becoming a junior partner in the Union from being in the driving seat for nearly half a century. Unless France engages the support of smaller EU countries – *nos petits cousins* – which is unlikely in view of its previous arrogance, or Britain becomes an effective counterweight in alliance either with smaller countries or France, within five to ten years the Union is likely to be German- rather than French-driven.

In turn, Germany's hitherto close but subordinate partnership with the United States will be affected – as has already happened over Iraq – with the Germans demanding a more equal bilateral role on global issues, including possible admission to the UN Security Council, and pursuing its Eastern European interests much more vigorously. Germany, rather than the United States, is likely to become the principal interlocutor with Russia.

Two improvements are likely to follow as the balance of power in Europe shifts from France towards Germany. The French penchant for bureaucratic dirigisme is likely to be diluted, although by no means abandoned, in favour of the more co-operative and decentralized approach favoured by Germany (already the issue of European over-regulation is becoming a major political issue in Germany). Second, the French government's pronounced anti-American bias is likely to be subordinated to German Atlanticism. This is in accord with the spirit of

British foreign policy, and argues for a much closer British relationship with Germany, its major trading partner.

The community's most powerful member would be a major ally in the drive to make Europe less bureaucratic and regulatory, and more open to the outside world, particularly the United States. Germany's response to the September 11 tragedy has been a mature and discreet reassertion of its right to play a part in international peacekeeping. Against this, nostalgic fears of German predominance in Europe dating back to the two world wars seem absurdly exaggerated. With the age of French EU dominance setting, and of German power dawning, a more balanced – and economically much more powerful – Union may come into being, abandoning federalist flights of fancy (which anyway will be more remote than ever as the EU expands to include even more members, many of them strongly nationalistic). In addition, German experience in the East should diminish the old knee-jerk bipolar relationship that still sometimes characterizes US–Russian relations.

Provided the German domination does not in turn become arrogant or hegemonic, but depends on the willing co-operation of its European allies, it may prove far more acceptable than the old French hauteur. Schröder has declared himself 'a German patriot who is proud of his country . . . particularly of the achievements of the people and the democratic culture'. Germany will emerge over the next decade as the dominant force within Europe, in place of France, and on the whole this will create a less centralizing, more equilibriated, more outward-looking and more powerful Union, and one which both the United States and Britain will find more acceptable.

In Eastern Europe the smaller countries newly enfranchised from Russian domination are likely to become more, rather than less, nationalist over the next half century, enjoying the heady experience of real independence for the first time after centuries of being crushed between the hammer of Germany and the sickle of Russia. In Western Europe armed conflict is, fortunately, definitely a thing of the past in a continent in which perhaps 20 million died in the course of the last war. In Eastern Europe, this is not yet certain, particularly in the Balkans (and here the conflicts are overwhelmingly within, rather than between, states) but the bigger European states and Russia should be able to prevent serious further fighting.

CHAPTER 10

THE THREATS TO STABILITY

The Proliferation Crisis

One threat closely connected with the newly nationalist states is the problem of weapons of mass destruction. There are nine nuclear powers in the world today: the United States, Russia, Britain, France, China, India, Pakistan, Israel and, just joining the club as its most repellent member, North Korea.

There are more than seven that I will define as 'latent' nuclear powers – countries which at short notice, such is their technological and industrial base and probable access to nuclear materials – could assemble a nuclear arsenal. Effectively, these can be regarded as nuclear powers too. They are Japan, Germany, Brazil, Argentina, South Africa (which has renounced the bomb it had already developed under the apartheid regime), Taiwan and South Korea. In a third category are three pariah countries seeking to acquire a nuclear capability, some of them quite close to doing so: Iran, Iraq and Libya.

That means there are sixteen countries to all intents and purposes in possession of nuclear weapons, and a further three striving for them. The age of nuclear proliferation has indeed arrived.

Mass destruction is, of course, not confined to nuclear weaponry. The three aspirants have long been seeking to acquire arsenals of chemical and biological weapons and, in Iraq's case, have actually used the former against the Kurds in the north of their country. All three are also attempting to acquire missile delivery systems. North Korea appears to be well advanced in this with Dong missiles capable of an

800-mile range; the Iranians have a few Shahab 3 missiles, while Iraq is seeking to develop missiles with a 1,800-mile range capable of hitting Europe.

In addition, the whole question of advanced weapons sales to potential combatants needs to be addressed. Landmines scattered in their millions across places like Cambodia and Afghanistan are slowly becoming a repellent form of warfare. But is the sale of all kinds of weapons to potential belligerents (usually justified on the grounds of 'if we don't, someone else will', 'maintaining the balance of power', or straightforward commerce and jobs in the vendor country) any more acceptable?

There are no instant solutions to these problems. Nuclear non-proliferation is a well-trodden path, as are chemical and biological weapons prevention, involving adherence to treaties, policing and painstaking inspection, and the prevention of technologies and materials reaching possible users. The attempt to ban landmines offers a route for controlling the sale of weaponry, sophisticated and unsophisticated. Obviously this is a long road, and one which is likely to be achievable only for a very few categories of arms in the near future. Moreover, the least sophisticated arms – ordinary guns and landmines – are the most widely used and easily produced even by the standard of today's awesome technology (as anyone who has witnessed Afghanistan's 'gun factories' – hammer-and-anvil backroom armouries – can attest). But it is worth embarking down the road.

The anti-proliferation cause has hardly been helped by the United States' unilateral withdrawal from the Test Ban Treaty, for all its faults. It is to be hoped that a substitute can quickly be put into its place. The great problem, of course, is enforcement. What is the point of an anti-proliferation or a biological or chemical weapons regime if the countries most likely to violate them and use such weapons in anger are the very ones least likely to adhere to such treaties? In this, the test case of Iraq is crucial. Earlier, I argued that American policy must be very carefully considered. But there should be no mistake that the principle at stake – the need to prevent the spread of such weapons – is of the utmost importance. North Korea has already poked a venemous head out of the bag. The 'bottom line' is that potentially dangerous and irresponsible Third World powers simply cannot be allowed to acquire such weaponry in a manner that might endanger millions of their neighbours.

Two issues instantly raise their heads: how? and how to determine what is an 'irresponsible' country? To deal with the second first, Third World countries have long complained of the 'nuclear club' being a rich man's gathering. By what principle of international equity are other countries to be barred from joining? There are two quick answers: nuclear weaponry, for all that it helped preserve global peace for so long through the balance of terror, is a danger for mankind and intrinsically undesirable. All countries should be working towards the eventual elimination of nuclear weapons as the world community eventually becomes responsible enough not to need them as a deterrent.

That moment has not yet arrived. It is therefore desirable that such weapons remain concentrated in as few hands – and as responsible ones – as possible. With the steady reduction in nuclear arsenals, the United States and Russia are leading the way. They and Britain have already destroyed their stocks of chemical and biological weapons. The argument that possession of nuclear weapons turns an irresponsible country into a responsible one is flawed. The world came perilously close to a nuclear exchange during the Cuban missile crisis (and also possibly the Berlin crisis of the same year) even with weapons in such 'responsible' hands as the United States and Soviet Union. It is desirable that as few countries as possible possess nuclear weaponry, and that those that do so work towards their elimination.

The problem of enforcement is trickier, and ultimately has to be resolved in a crude, rule-of-thumb fashion. It is quite simply unacceptable for nuclear weapons to fall into the hands of a 'rogue' regime and all available means should be employed, including war if necessary, to prevent this. In Iraq's case the ceasefire following the end of the Gulf War explicitly provided for the country's renunciation of weapons of mass destruction and international inspections to verify this. Up to now, sanctions have been used to try and secure compliance, with mixed results. Iraq is still trying to obtain nuclear weapons and probably has stockpiles of chemical and biological weapons. International pressure has probably succeeded in preventing it acquiring the former, or expanding and using the latter, at least since the 1991 Kurdish uprising.

This may not be enough. For practical reasons argued earlier, an invasion of Iraq today would be very difficult (although would be perfectly justifiable). But the Iraqis have been left in no doubt that the acquisition of nuclear weaponry and/or the expansion of its biological/chemical weapons programme to one capable of doing serious damage to a neighbouring country would be regarded as a *casus belli*. Whether this would involve overthrowing the regime or surgical strikes to eliminate the specific threat must be left open to conjecture: the Israelis did the global community a service by blowing up Iraq's Osirak reactor in 1981, almost certainly with American foreknowledge and connivance. Iraq simply cannot be permitted to obtain a nuclear capability.

The two most dangerous potential nuclear proliferators other than Iraq have been North Korea and Iran. In October 2002 North Korea shocked the world by announcing, when confronted with US intelligence data, that it was engaged in a clandestine nuclear weapons programme to produce weapons-grade material from highly enriched uranium; and that it had 'nullified' its 1994 agreement to freeze all nuclear weapons activity. The North Koreans also claimed they had 'more powerful things as well' – presumably a biological and chemical weapons capability.

This effectively demolished the 1994 nuclear agreement negotiated by former President Carter which avoided near-war at the time – Stealth bombers were sent to South Korea by President Clinton to deter a North Korean pre-emptive strike – and which offered the Koreans two proliferation-proof nuclear reactors. Although these have been started, they were subsequently abandoned. It was believed then that the Yongbyon reprocessing plant had already produced enough plutonium to manufacture two nuclear weapons. North Korea is now unfreezing the plant which could provide plutonium 'triggers' in a matter of months. Defense Secretary Donald Rumsfeld said he believed 'they have a small number of nuclear weapons'.

The initial American response was muted, and sanctions have not yet been imposed. The South Koreans, Japanese and Chinese all said they would continue talking to the regime, even though it has been exposed as a cheat on the earlier agreement. President Bush, in sharp contrast to his bellicose rhetoric about Iran, which is still years away from acquiring nuclear weapons, declared, 'I believe we can deal with this threat peacefully, particularly if we work together.'

Yet North Korea has a worse record than Iraq on mistreating its own people, pursuing policies which have directly led to mass starvation, has sponsored international terrorism, unlike Iraq recently, has test-fired missiles across the straits with Japan, has engaged in numerous international incidents with its neighbours and is a major exporter of missiles to other countries. In short, except in the field of outright armed aggression – Iraq's last venture was in 1990, while Korea's was in 1948 – it has a much worse record than Iraq.

The reason why President Bush is using kid gloves to deal with the piranha state is simple: North Korea is much more dangerous than Iraq. Any 'surgical' military strike to take out North Korean facilities would, it is feared, lead to artillery bombardment of Seoul just south of the border, costing thousands of lives, and all-out war which, according to one retired American commander, could lead to the deaths of 1 million people and some 10,000 Americans; South Korea is in effect a hostage.

Short of that, the North Koreans could use economic sanctions as a pretext to start converting the plutonium rods it already has, which are 'canned' under the 1994 agreement, to make several nuclear weapons. In addition, North Korean spokesmen have threatened to 'export missile and nuclear technology to the highest bidder. It's a capitalist practice.' If America tried to knock out Yongbyon, the North Koreans threaten to attack South Korea and Japan, possibly using the missiles they already have and the one or two bombs they may have. This straightforward blackmail puts Saddam Hussein in the junior league.

Currently America's only option seems to be to negotiate and offer North Korea inducements to abandon both programmes: these might include economic aid and normalization of relations. The North Koreans say all issues, including the nuclear one, are negotiable. The danger is that North Korea will continue to cheat. If indeed the North Koreans despite inducements continue to build up their nuclear arsenal, the United States might quite quickly have to decide whether to risk full-scale war in the peninsula on the grounds that Kim Jong-il's regime is too dangerous to be trusted with a significant nuclear arsenal.

At the very least, America will have privately to indicate that a nuclear attack on either South Korea or Japan would immediately invite nuclear retaliation from the United States, and hope the deterrent theory applies; otherwise the South Koreans and Japanese seem certain quickly to develop their own arsenal. The United States is of course perfectly justified in seeking to prevent Saddam Hussein getting to the same point, the logic being that traditional deterrent theory does not apply to the likes of Saddam or Kim. All of North Korea's neighbours believe that Kim is seeking a bargain: full recognition and aid in exchange for scrapping his bomb. This is blackmail, but better perhaps than all-out war. Kim's regime is doomed in the long run and unlikely to find imitators.

The Iranian proliferation danger is only a shade less dangerous than the North Korean and Iraqi problems. Iran's nuclear programme was initiated by the Shah with the help of the German company Siemens at a cost of $6 billion and has been revived by the mullahs. It is currently spearheaded by President Khatami's Vice-President, Gholamrez Agha-zadeh, a former oil minister. The main focus of concern has been the $800 million Bushehr nuclear reactor, a huge project for a country awash with oil, which was rebuilt with Russian help under President Yeltsin, and has reportedly also had the assistance of Abdul Qader Khan, the 'father' of Pakistan's nuclear bomb.

The WER-1000 light water reactor at Bushehr is a year from completion, and will take another year and a half to come on line. Iran's current nuclear programme is to build three more reactors at Bushehr and two at Akhvaz. Spent fuel from these reactors could be converted to weapons-grade plutonium and enriched fuel for weapons could be used with the technology at the Bushehr reactor. However, it is also believed that Iran may be concentrating its nuclear weapons effort at clandestine sites scattered around the country of which only one has been pinpointed with any certainty – Sharif University of Technology in Teheran. This leads to fears that once Bushehr is built and the technology acquired, the programme may be unstoppable, because it can be reproduced at the clandestine sites.

The CIA reckons it will take seven years for Iran to acquire its first nuclear weapons; the Israelis calculate five years. The Israelis have stated bluntly that 'everything must be done, including if necessary using force' to stop the programme, and the Americans believe that the Israelis are serious about staging a pre-emptive strike. The Americans have so far confined themselves to seeking to pressure the Russians to stop their help, which the latter have steadfastly refused to do.

Now they are being offered an extraordinary bribe by the United States: permission to become a major storer and reprocessor of radioactive materials from around the world (currently 90 per cent of this is done by the United States and much of the rest by Britain). With Russia's appalling record on storage and security of its own nuclear material, this has horrified environmental groups. It is clear there must be some better form of bribery. The Russians are also developing Iran's new Shahab 4 missile, which would have a range of 1,200 miles compared with the current Shahab 3's range of 800 miles, allowing it to reach as far as Greece. Meanwhile the Israeli threat is to be taken seriously, although some would argue that Iran is a slightly more responsible and pluralist society than North Korea or Iraq. This particular crisis is probably a couple of years off.

The prospect of both Iran and Iraq obtaining nuclear weapons does not bear thinking about: could countries which have already sacrificed a million of their people in a futile 1914-style trench war less than two decades ago really be trusted not to use them against each other or against a third party? Even to pose the question justifies the loss of life that may be necessary in an attempt to enforce the non-proliferation of weapons of mass destruction in these countries. In addition, any existing nuclear power which appears in danger of succumbing to the control of extremists – Pakistan is the most likely example today – must be liable to preventative action, as would a country which harbours terrorists feared to be seeking or acquiring such weaponry.

There remains the issue of 'latent' nuclear powers: countries whose technology and access to nuclear materials is at such a stage that within a short space of time, certainly within the duration of a conventional conflict, could assemble a credible nuclear arsenal. I have pointed to Japan, Germany, Brazil, Argentina, South Africa, Taiwan and South Korea. There is very little the world community can do about this – because such countries are not in violation of the Nuclear Non-Proliferation Treaty – beyond seeking to tighten the control against the supply of nuclear materials.

When countries like Iran and North Korea seek to acquire 'peaceful' nuclear technology, it is hard to deny them that right beyond enforcing the most stringent inspection regime to ensure that it really is for peaceful purposes (although why oil-rich Iran needs to go down the nuclear power route is not immediately obvious). The line in the sand, however, has to be the actual development of nuclear weapons themselves. Sadly, India, Pakistan and Israel all slipped through the net before it was closed (still incompletely) and the world is not a safer place as a result. South Africa's renunciation of nuclear weaponry is a deeply welcome gesture and a step towards a safer world.

There is a final line of defence. This author, at least, has watched with incredulity the chorus of disapproval that has greeted the American attempt to develop 'Missile Defence' – a space-based programme to intercept missile threats, in particular nuclear ones, across the globe. Obviously much of this reflects parochial concerns: the Russians fear that their strategic inferiority could become an absolute fact, the Chinese that the system may be used to deter an attack against Taiwan, the Europeans that the American shield would extend only to its continent, not the rest of the world, and so on. But these concerns can each be addressed.

There is also a more vague concern about the 'militarization of space'. But this instinctive, primal, Armageddon-like fear for many people is as logical as arguing against the 'militarization of the oceans'. Space-based defence seems inevitable as the technology improves, and it is far better that space be in the hands of a responsible power or powers than irresponsible ones. That issue aside, Missile Defence is the ultimate 'ban-the-bomb' system.

September 11, far from diminishing President Bush's determination to go ahead with Missile Defence (MD), on the grounds that determined terrorists can go under such systems, has strengthened the case. President Bush believes that if a handful of terrorists can inflict such horrors, imagine the consequences of a nuclear-armed rogue nation going unchecked.

Opposition to MD falls into two categories: first, technological:

1. It is a 'Maginot Line in space' – deceptively reassuring but incapable of providing complete protection.
2. It is unworkable – as the failure of some tests have shown.
3. It is expensive, costing, by some estimates, $80 billion even for limited deployment.
4. It could be overcome by multiple warheads – which the Chinese, for one, show signs of acquiring.

The political objections revolve around the concept that post-Cold War America is now primarily content with its immediate obsession of protecting the mainland itself against largely imaginary enemies. These objections can be summarized as follows:

1. By going ahead with a limited defensive shield, the United States is effectively decoupling itself from the defence of Western Europe or anywhere else in the world. The only clear long-range missile threat to the United States today comes from North Korea; by contrast, Iran, Iraq and conceivably Libya are closer to Russia and Western Europe, to which the United States may not extend the shield.
2. Deployment of MD would trigger another arms race. China would expand its currently limited arsenal of 20 long-range nuclear missiles to 200; its nervous neighbours India and Pakistan would soon follow, as maybe would Japan and Taiwan.
3. There are far more efficient ways of addressing the North Korean threat, which is anyway overblown. The country's economy is tottering, the regime is showing signs of megalomania, its nuclear prowess is overstated, and the cost of 'Son of Star Wars' almost equals the entire North Korean GDP.
4. Deployment would threaten Russia with an 'invulnerable' United States, and thus end the (albeit reduced) nuclear balance

based on each side's capability to annihilate the other. The Russians might be tempted to go for their own missile defence system, or to fit multiple warheads on their long-range missiles (as seems more likely now that President Putin has opted for strengthening the Soviet conventional army and cutting back its nuclear forces).

President Bush would be well advised to dismiss most of these concerns, apart from the technical. The recent failure of a test firing – because a ten-year-old circuit had failed – is no more a sign that the system is unworkable than innumerable glitches in America's space programme and other military programmes. The expense can probably be borne. The boost-phase system would permit co-operation with Russia, be regionally based and not violate the ABM system, and could be buttressed by 100 mid-course interceptors. Apart from satellite information, it would not be based in space.

The political objections are even shakier. By installing such a system, the United States is said to be selfishly protecting itself at the expense of Western Europe; yet there is scope for extending this protection to Western Europe, and the Americans have offered to share the technology with Britain. By not establishing the system at all, the Americans risk leaving the United States and Western Europe at the mercy of missile-equipped nuclear-armed Third World powers. Instead of carping, Britain, Germany and France would do well to involve themselves in the project.

China's overheated economy can ill afford a nuclear arms race with the United States. The country, which is heavily dependent on the United States for its exports, can surely not believe that the United States is planning a first strike; if America was so disposed, it would strike today while it has an immense preponderance of nuclear forces against China's puny arsenal.

The Chinese know that America has no such intention – although it might use MD to stop China intervening against its neighbours, such as Taiwan. The Chinese are already showing signs of realism. The influential arms control expert at Qinghua University, Li Bin, commented recently:

if the American intention is to use this system to defend against China, then I can't see any room for compromise. But if they really are just worried about the so-called rogue states and they aren't trying to undermine China's deterrents, then it may be possible in principle to reach agreement.

Of course, Son of Star Wars would be an overblown reaction to the threat posed by North Korea if that were the only one facing the international community. But it is in fact a pre-emptive deterrent to a whole host of North Koreas.

The idea that the Russians would re-engage in an arms race with the United States is equally unrealistic. The Russians were priced out of the arms race that was ruining their economy by the threat of 'Star Wars'. While they retain the capacity to knock out American cities, they have as little interest in doing so as the Americans have of seriously targeting Moscow and Leningrad. The ABM Treaty was born in another era of huge missile build-ups. President Putin may see mileage in pandering to countries like North Korea and China in opposing MD; he knows that Russia's security will not be affected, although the Americans would be wise to continue to offer shared technology and even participation in the project to the Russians. The Russians' recent proposal to move anti-missile interceptors to places to counter specific threats is almost certainly unworkable, although it bears studying. More significant was their implicit acceptance of the need for missile defence against rogue states: 'We are ready for a substantial dialogue with the United States,' Foreign Minister Igor Ivanov recently said.

The real problem is entirely another one, largely ignored in the current debate. Nuclear proliferation is a fact of life in the modern world. In place of superpower confrontation we have the prospect of a number of nuclear powers, most of them far less responsible than the United States or Russia. North Korea is only one of these. Although it secures congressional support to describe it as a threat, it is not primarily the United States that is in danger.

In Asia there is the very real possibility of nuclear confrontation between India and Pakistan. Nuclear-armed China is increasingly at odds with Japan. North Korea is targeting Japan. There is a possibility of a Chinese nuclear strike against Taiwan, which probably is developing nuclear weapons of its own. In the Middle East, Iran, Iraq and Libya are seeking to acquire a nuclear and missile capacity (while Israel already has both). There may be many more such nuclear pygmies.

Some of these countries are signatories of the Nuclear Non-Proliferation Treaty, which is a powerful weapon among the responsible members of the international community, and no weapon at all among the out-of-control ones. The United States is seeking, for a limited cost, to embark on the first stages of a system that might be able to deter nuclear weapons and the missiles to carry them, the technology for which is relatively accessible. The alternatives are to preach non-proliferation and hope for the best, or to pray that little local difficulties can be solved (as, for example, between India and Pakistan).

Yet a single miscalculation could leave millions dead. MD needs encouragement from America's allies, not schoolmasterly hand-wringing. Granted, it is probably the next generation that will have to face the consequences of post-Cold War Western inertia and sloth. They will not thank us for doing nothing about an awesome human problem so clearly discernible at the time.

The Soviet Union was eventually forced to reduce its nuclear arsenal because of the threat of a Star Wars arms race. The hard men in charge of potential mini-nuclear powers are unlikely to be deterred except by a stronger power which effectively neutralizes their nuclear capability. This is much more likely to be the much larger boost-phase system proposed by George W. Bush (and being considered by the Russians) than the modest one supported by the former President Clinton. The boost-phase system would shoot down missiles as they take off, when they are travelling relatively slowly, producing a huge amount of easily detectable energy, and have not sent out decoys or multiple warheads.

But a start has to be made. And if the threat itself pushes Third World nuclear powers into abandoning their ambitions and into the non-proliferation camp, so much the better; Son of Star Wars can be suspended, as the father was. What seems certain is that without any threat there is little reason for any of these countries to respond, and a million or two dead – not in San Francisco or New York, but in New Delhi, Karachi or Taipei – will become a real possibility. To repeat: the purpose of Son of Star Wars is to ban possession of the bomb by a dozen potential nuclear powers around the globe – and, as usual, it is the Third World that is most at risk.

As I have already argued, the world community simply cannot permit certain countries to develop nuclear weapons, and those that have them to use them. The clear, if unstated, last resort of the United States today against any power falling into one of those two categories is the threat to use its own force – including possibly a nuclear strike – against that country. This has already been exercised. In 1961 the United States threatened to use tactical nuclear weapons against the Russians during the Berlin crisis in an effort to contain the threat of an all-out nuclear exchange. In 1991 the United States threatened to use tactical nuclear weapons against Iraq in the event of the latter's using chemical or biological weapons against allied troops in the Gulf. This worked.

No one must be in doubt that to prevent, for example, a nuclear exchange in the Middle East, the United States would threaten to use each and every weapon at its disposal. There is thus already a crude, ad hoc deterrent in place on a case-by-case basis: the world policeman today will use every weapon in his armoury to prevent a much greater loss of life at the hands of international outlaws if he has to. President Bush has now made this explicit but how much better for a much more calibrated, less dangerous system to be put into place to deter potential missile attacks wherever they might occur across the globe.

One further issue needs to be addressed. If the line is to be drawn against any other country acquiring nuclear weapons or weapons of mass destruction, and if the nuclear club is to be believed in its commitment to renounce nuclear weapons and their delivery systems, and if Missile Defence is to gain the acceptance it deserves, then it is essential that all three objectives obtain the widest possible global consensus. This calls for the Nuclear Non-Proliferation Treaty to be expanded into a Global Nuclear Forum, in which the nuclear powers debate with the non-nuclear the framework for enforcement of non-proliferation regimes, guidelines for the peaceful use of nuclear energy, and spell out the steps they are taking to wind down their own arsenals of weapons of mass destruction, as well as accommodate the concerns of all countries about Missile Defence – which, after all, in its ideal form, will provide protection for all countries.

The 'nuclear club' will lose nothing by such consultation: any decisions they make will continue to be their own. Such a forum will no doubt sometimes degenerate into a Western-bashing talking-shop. But it will at least permit the overwhelming majority of countries currently shut out of the nuclear club to feel that they are part of the debate on the use of this extraordinary global resource (and threat), and draw the sting from the charge that this is merely a 'have-bombs' club seeking to exclude the have-nots.

The Rogue State

The issue of weapons of mass destruction is, of course, intricately linked with the sixth of the twelve major threats to post-Cold War world peace

– the 'rogue state' or, as President Clinton later modified it, 'state of concern'. My view is that this problem has been much exaggerated and that, as global economic development proceeds, is fast declining. The days of crazed dictators are on the wane, although not entirely past. In addition, a more conventional form of nationalism based on economic self-assurance, as already touched upon in the section on the newly rich nationalist states, seems more likely to pose a real threat tomorrow. But as it takes only one bull to wreck a china shop, the issue still needs addressing.

The first problem lies in defining a rogue state, as the United States found out. Is this merely a (invariably undemocratic) country which pursues an erratic and unpredictable foreign policy that might lead to conflict with its neighbours? Or are there clear tests of roguery? The three obvious ones are the use of unprovoked aggression as an instrument of foreign policy, state sponsorship of terrorism or permitting terrorist groups to operate from its soil, and a refusal to abide by international treaties and methods of settling disputes, such as, in particular, those prohibiting the development of weapons of mass destruction.

Extraordinarily few countries in fact fit into all, or even one, of these categories. And those that do are not often seen as rogue states. Take the usual suspects: is North Korea a rogue state? It has observed the terms of a ceasefire with South Korea which has survived for barely half a century with an astonishing minimum of violations. It has attacked no other country, although occasional flare-ups have occurred such as, for example, the seizure of South Korean vessels in North Korean territorial waters, the testing of a missile over Japan's territorial waters and, more recently (although the incident is still shrouded in mystery), the sinking of a North Korean patrol boat just outside Japanese waters by the Japanese. The North Koreans defended themselves on each of these occasions as having flouted no international agreements.

Yet the harsh regime in Pyongyang – with its comic father-son succession from Kim Il-sung, the 'Great Leader', to Kim Jong-il, the 'Dear Leader', who preside over a country where millions starve unnecessarily, public services have long ceased to work, the state is one great repressive machine of Orwellian-style newspeak, and a huge army is maintained on full alert – is one which would normally be classified as a rogue state. However, even on the issue of nuclear weaponry, Kim the younger has until now deftly avoided flouting international agreements such as the agreed framework of 1994, halting missile development tests and exports. By the standards mentioned it was not a rogue until 2002, when it admitted to cheating on the 1994 agreement.

Indeed, for a country that is small, isolated and has one of the ugliest political regimes on earth, North Korea has recently performed a quite extraordinarily successful courtship of no fewer than five global powers, playing each off against the others. Quite what any of them see in the nasty little brute – other than its promise to stop screaming imprecations at them after decades – remains a mystery. But North Korea cannot be gainsaid its diplomatic accomplishments of the past years.

Consider: the regime in North Korea presides over a police state of such ruthless and barbaric inefficiency that virtually the entire economy is seized up, except for defence-related industries and those providing luxuries for party bosses. Some 2 million of the country's 22 million population are living so close to starvation that, according to reliable reports, cannibalism and the eating of bark and shoes have been common.

According to Norbert Vollertsen, a German doctor who worked in the country until he was expelled in 2002, old beer bottles are used for intravenous drips.

There is no material for surgery, no money, no sanitation . . . You can't do anything when it's dark [because there is no lighting] and in winter patients are shivering on the operating table. Very few operations are in fact performed because alcohol is the only anaesthetic available.

While this appalling suffering continues, in a state where the slightest questioning of authority is answered by imprisonment, torture or death, the North Korean armed forces of 1.1 million continue to absorb some two-thirds of all government spending and more than half the country's GDP. American military analysts say that North Korea has staged a heightened number of military exercises recently, and that more than two-thirds of North Korean troops have moved to within 100 kilometres (60 miles) of the Demilitarized Zone separating North and South Korea.

According to one American intelligence assessment, the North has 'an offensive military capability designed to prosecute a short and violent war'. Most, if not all, of the Korean peninsula could be taken before American reinforcements arrived – which in fact was what happened at the beginning of the last Korean War. The current 37,000 American tripwire force in South Korea could not last long. The North is demanding the withdrawal of the US Second Infantry Division of some 15,000 troops defending the northern approaches to the South. In addition, suspicion remains over the extent of North Korea's effort to establish a nuclear weapons capability, and its export of missile technology to other countries, as well as its testing of missiles close to the Japanese mainland.

In spite of all this, the last American administration of President Bill Clinton fell over itself to establish a dialogue. It was seriously mooted that one of Clinton's last acts would be a historic visit to North Korea. What purpose this would have served, in the absence of clear agreements to abide by international norms, is unclear. Luckily, he was persuaded otherwise. Clinton's swansong visit to Vietnam was one to a country that currently presents no threats to its neighbours and is seeking albeit slowly to move towards Western-style economic freedoms. Neither is true of North Korea.

Mrs Madeleine Albright, the former Secretary of State, on her last visit to Pyongyang, gushed that the hereditary North Korean leader, Kim Jong-il, was a 'very good listener and a good interlocutor. He strikes me as very decisive and practical and serious.' Earlier, Kim's most prominent military chief and probably the real power in North Korea, Jo Myong Rok, had visited President Clinton in Washington for a forty-five-minute meeting which was described by the Americans as 'very positive'. While it is possible that he privately offered the Americans assurances on key issues that could make a Clinton visit possible, contrast all of this with the American refusal even to enter a dialogue with Cuba's Fidel Castro, who presides over a regime that presents no military threat to anyone, that is only half as repressive, militarized and inefficient as North Korea and that actively encourages overseas visitors: it is clear how successful Kim Jong-il has been in his charm offensive towards the United States. Prudently, the Bush administration put American policy towards North Korea on hold.

None of the three main issues between the two countries have been resolved yet. When it was discovered in 1993 that a North Korean reprocessing facility at Yongbyon had the potential to produce enough weapons-grade plutonium to equip ten nuclear warheads, the United States, South Korea and Japan all agreed to provide oil and technical advice so that the North Koreans could develop a peaceful nuclear capability, and the spent fuel rods at Yongbyon were encased – although the North Koreans had probably already produced enough to equip two nuclear warheads. However, it was believed that the North had another ten sites where plutonium was being produced, although the inspection permitted of one such site offered no evidence of this.

A second major issue has been the country's supplying of missile technology to third countries such as Iran and Iraq, as well as its own vigorous development of a missile capability. It is believed that North Korea offered a freeze on both recently, although not the destruction of the 100 or so missiles it possesses. North Korea has temporarily suspended its own test launchings, but is believed to be still working on a new generation of long-range missiles that could reach the United States. However, the United States seems ready to accede to a North Korean proposal that any reduction in its missile exports be compensated for by trade and aid packages that make up the shortfall. There seems to be no progress at all on the issue of reducing North Korea's huge armed forces, twice the size of the South's, or of the army's aggressive posture towards the South.

As if this dialogue with the United States, at the highest levels, and with no perceptible shift in posture, was not proof enough of the success of North Korea's diplomacy, the young dictator has found himself courted by all four of his other regional neighbours. The 'sunshine' visit by South Korea's President Kim Dae-jung, which earned him the Nobel Peace Prize, while triumphant in public relations terms (mostly for the North), also yielded no visible policy concession of any significance, other than a readiness to accept food aid previously regarded as an affront to the North's dignity, and the opportunity for a handful of North Koreans to visit their relatives in the South. Kim Dae-jung's popularity in the South sharply declined as a result of economic difficulties and bribery scandals and he has been succeeded by another moderate, Roh Moo Hyun.

Similarly, North Korea's often wary relationship with China seems recently to have been strengthened. Kim Jong-il recently played host to Russia's President Putin, to whom he floated the extraordinary idea of a cut in sales of weapons technology in exchange for America's providing piggyback rides of North Korea's satellites on its space missions – an idea as irrelevant to the gothic reality of North Korea's economy as the slowness of its development. In law enforcement terms it is also an interesting precedent: an offer to stop beating one's wife in exchange for a hefty bribe from the police.

Finally, North Korea has been making overtures to Japan, which was recently deeply alarmed by the North's missile tests in its coastal waters. There seems to be almost a race on to establish contacts with this repulsive 'hermit' kingdom. How impressed starving Koreans were with the lavish hospitality enjoyed by successive top-level delegations arriving in Pyongyang is not recorded.

There are wider consequences. If there were to be a reconciliation between the two Koreas, the rationale behind the American troops stationed in South Korea would disappear. As it is, a recent poll suggested that 78 per cent of South Koreans favour a gradual withdrawal of American troops, which in some areas are deeply unpopular. If the Americans there were brought home, there would be intense domestic pressure from both right and left for a recall of the American troops stationed in Japan, as there was a decade ago in the Philippines.

The consequences of an American troop withdrawal from East Asia have hardly been thought through, and could be catastrophic. They perform a far wider role than keeping the peace in Korea. Traditionally, both the Japanese and the Chinese have regarded the Korean peninsula as a bone of contention: the Chinese because they border upon Korea, the Japanese because of the narrowness of the straits between the two countries and the threat it poses to Japan's defence.

The Japanese are deeply concerned about the consequences of possible Korean unification. According to Terumasa Nakanishi, professor of international politics at Kyoto University:

> the closer the Koreans grow together the more the rationale for American forces will change, and if there is rapid movement it will have a major impact on Japan's security. Koreans tend to be very complacent and overly optimistic about China, and that worries the Japanese. The nightmare that Japanese have is that the peninsula will one day fall under the strategic sway of China. We have a fear of seeing the Chinese naval colours being flown in Pusan one day. To American eyes this may seem rather far-fetched, but this comes from a deep-rooted historical and cultural experience of the three nations in north east Asia.

Traditionally, Japan's attempts to maintain Korea as a buffer against China have extended to the point of war. The United States' presence and the division of the Koreas has kept the peace for half a century. An American withdrawal would provoke real tensions between the regional superpowers, China and Japan. Intriguingly, during their summit, according to Kim Dae-jung, Kim Jong-il told him that it was 'desirable' for American troops to remain on the Korean peninsula.

According to South Korea's former President:

I began the discussion by pointing out that American forces must stay even after unification for stability in North East Asia. The peninsula is surrounded by big countries, and if the American military presence were to be withdrawn, that would create a huge vacuum that would draw these big countries into a fight over hegemony. His exact response was, to my surprise, 'well, I read the South Korean newspapers, and I read your position on this issue. I said to myself, how similar [your] view was on this issue with mine' . . . he further went on to say, 'yes, we are surrounded by big powers – Russia, China and Japan and so therefore it is desirable that the American troops continue to stay.' In fact, he added that several years ago he sent a high-level envoy to deliver this position to the American side.

If this is true (and it seems so far-fetched that only the fact that it comes from the Nobel Prize-winning ex-President and has not been denied by the North Koreans makes it credible), it suggests that there is a real prospect of an uneasy détente between South and North akin to the relationship between West and East Germany after the former's policy of Ostpolitik – but not one that goes so far as to allow the two sides to stand down most of their armies, or the Americans to withdraw, and certainly no prospect of reunification.

This analysis suggests North Korea does not qualify as a rogue state on at least two of the three key tests. Burma, another regime of rhinoceros-hide insularity which has indulged in gross repression of its own people, has similarly violated no international treaties.

Iraq is perhaps the rogue state par excellence, with Saddam everyone's idea of what a rogue looks like. Yet what has he actually done to fit the definition? When he declared war on his neighbour Iran in the late 1970s, alleging an Iranian conspiracy to stir up trouble among Iraq's Shia community in the south, he was tacitly supported by the United States and most Western nations. He occupied Kuwait in 1990 after misinterpreting an ambiguous briefing by the American ambassador as a declaration of support for the enterprise, alleging that Kuwait had been stealing its oil – which may in fact have been true.

Since the end of the Gulf War he has largely abided by the terms of the ceasefire, occasionally provoking the Western aircraft that patrol the 'no-fly' zone – with one very important exception: apparently flouting the regime of inspection imposed to ensure that Saddam did not ever develop weapons of mass destruction. This exception alone allows Iraq to be classified as a rogue. But the real roguery (which does not count) is the regime's appalling treatment of its own people – the gassing of Kurds in the north, the massacre of Shias in the south, the amputations, political murders and tortures.

Milošević's Serbia? Although this had practised war and 'ethnic cleansing' against three of its neighbours – Croatia, Bosnia and Kosovo – technically this did not constitute aggression, as all three were part of the largely mythical Yugoslav confederation of which Milošević was the head.

Syria? Syria has behaved with impeccable restraint in observing decades of ceasefire along the Golan Heights with Israel, and arguably has brought peace to war-torn Lebanon. Its roguery is limited to permitting 'terrorists' to train on its territory – which Syria rejects with the argument that these are freedom fighters fighting for liberation against an occupying power (although as these groups target civilians as well as military men its argument cannot be sustained). Once again, the real roguery lies in the regime's repression of its own people, in particular the slaughter of thousands of members of the Muslim Brotherhood in 1982 – but that does not qualify.

Libya? Colonel Muammar Qaddafi's regime is as close to attaining the definition of a rogue one as any country on earth – possibly sponsoring the terrorism which caused the Lockerbie bombing, and in the past engaging in a host of activities beyond its borders, as well as seeking to develop weapons of mass destruction (with less success than Iran or Iraq) and repressing its own people. Has the 'rogue' definition helped? America's sole major air strike against the country proved controversial, and failed to topple the regime. Libya has appeared to calm down recently, but this may merely reflect the fact that Qaddafi is getting older.

Iran? After the 1980 embassy hostage crisis, when the staff of the US embassy in Teheran were held for a year, clearly a 'rogue' display, the Iranians have embarked on no overtly aggressive acts, although they have been responsible for helping to train, equip and fund Shia terrorist organizations on their territory, certainly 'rogue' behaviour. Again, it is the treatment of their own people – the executions, tortures and public stonings – that are unspeakable.

Zimbabwe? True, the country's increasingly 'roguish' leader, Robert Mugabe, has intervened in the continuing civil war in the Congo – but then so has Uganda and even possibly France. The real charge against him is the terrorism unleashed by his thugs on black opponents and white farmers alike.

Cuba? Fidel Castro has confined his defiance of the United States to his own island stronghold since the end of his African and Latin American adventures a decade and a half ago.

This brief tour d'horizon suggests that the term 'rogue state' is not a particularly helpful one. Far better to enforce action against states which are guilty of violating one of the other categories of global misbehaviour – for example, external aggression or the development of weapons of mass destruction.

Worse, because the definition overlooks the terrible things such states do to their own people – usually the worst kind of 'rogue' behaviour – it provides no real redress for millions and appears to show up the West as the worst kind of hypocrite – prepared to tolerate mass murder and suffering so long as this does not impinge on its own interests. This respect for the right of tyrants to wreak suffering on their own people is absurd, repellent, and long in need of revision. I would advocate ending the category altogether and replacing it with the concept of 'psychopath state' – one which behaves with intolerable cruelty and violates the rights of its own citizens and/or which threatens the citizens of other countries. I will return to this shortly.

The Disintegrationist State

If we have scrapped one type of global threat, the next is a comparatively new phenomenon – the collapsed, imploding or 'black hole' state – the country in which central authority has largely disintegrated in the face of local warlordism, ethnic groups, crime syndicates or terrorist groups. The list that springs to mind is growing: Lebanon (which, however, has almost recovered), Yugoslavia, Afghanistan, Yemen, Sudan, Somalia, Chechnya, Congo and Colombia.

Disintegrating states such as these provide all kinds of challenges to world peace: they can suck in outsiders to back rival factions in a civil war (Yugoslavia, Chechnya, Lebanon, Congo); they can export refugees, which may endanger the stability of neighbouring states (Afghanistan, Somalia and Colombia); they can become centres of international crime, which affects other countries and invites retaliation (Afghanistan, Chechnya and Colombia with their respective drugs trades); and they can provide terrorist havens outside the control of the host country itself (Afghanistan, Yemen, Sudan, Somalia, Chechnya and Colombia).

This sudden upsurge in disintegrationist states is, of course, one consequence of the relaxation of superpower control around the world and another indication, on a micro-scale, of the upsurge of ethnic nationalism. Some of the divisions within states are so deep as to provide no easy answers. But this mostly new problem calls for outsiders to limit the danger these black holes can pose for their own people and their neighbours.

Poverty, Overpopulation, the Environment and Crime

The eighth challenge to global peace in the post-Cold War era comes from an old harridan: global poverty, and her four handmaidens, mass migration, hunger, disease and debt. These problems have been analysed in depth for decades and will be looked at in Part III of this book. I will confine myself here to the observation that while poverty rarely leads directly to threats to world peace, arguments over scarce resources often do, as has happened in parts of Saharan and sub-Saharan Africa, particularly Congo. It is, of course, false to argue that poverty fuels ancient territorial disputes, or has given rise to international terrorism (terrorists are often drawn from among the more affluent); the poorest countries of the globe, in particular in sub-Saharan Africa, have so far provided only occasional soil for terrorist recruits.

Yet the image of the United States, and to a lesser extent its Western European allies, as exploitative capitalists living off the labour of the global poor, however unfair, certainly helps to stir the resentment felt towards rich countries. As such it is an issue that needs to be addressed for reasons of enlightened self-interest by those countries – quite apart from the overwhelming moral imperative to do so.

Global poverty remains the scourge of mankind; it is beyond the scope of this book to address the issue, save to make a few gross over-simplifications:

- There is no connection whatever between terrorism and international rogue behaviour and poverty. Most of the 'nine-eleven' hijackers came from Saudi Arabia, still one of the richest countries in the world, mostly from an educated background. The tension there is of master and servant; the bosses of al-Qaeda are from much better social origins than the footsoldiers. This is an old pattern: the Tupamaros, the Red Brigades, the Baader-Meinhof gang, most Palestinian terrorists, the Montoneros, etc., tended to derive from educated, middle-class, relatively prosperous households, although many of their followers might be 'proletarians'. Some of the poorest parts of Africa and Latin America have contributed few recruits.

- World inequality is increasing sharply. Between 1965 and 1990 the share of world income owned by the richest fifth is estimated to have risen from nearly 70 per cent to 83 per cent. In 1965 average income per head in the former was about thirty times higher than the poorest 20 per cent; by 1990 this had doubled. The top fifth account for some 85 per cent of global spending, the bottom fifth for 1.3 per cent. The 358 billionaires living in 1996 had combined assets larger than the GDP of countries containing nearly half of the world's population (today there are some 500 billionaires). More than three times as much of world output was concentrated in 1996 in countries containing 20 per cent of the world population, as for the other 80 per cent. Some 204 billion people have no access to sanitation and 1 billion have no access to clean drinking water. Some 250 million children have to work.

- Even so, the lives of those at the very bottom have improved considerably. In 1980 some 1.4 billion lived on $1 a day; this has now fallen to 1.2 billion. The proportion of the world's population living in absolute destitution has fallen from over 30 per cent to 20 per cent. Average life expectancy has doubled for all classes over the past hundred years and in the past thirty years by ten years. In 1970, according to FAO, just under 1 billion people were undernourished; this figure has fallen below 800 million in spite of a huge population increase. Food production has tripled in the developing world. Only a decade ago nearly nine-tenths of the world's rural population lacked proper drinking water; the figure is now 25 per cent. Adult illiteracy has been reduced by half and infant mortality by 40 per cent over the past thirty years.

- Most of these improvements have nothing to do with globalization. Nearly half the world's population is in China and India, mostly in the countryside. The economies of both have gradually opened up, mainly benefiting an urban minority. Changes in archaic rural practices have taken around a tenth of India's population out of poverty and more than 200 million people out of subsistence levels in China in two decades. In both countries demographics are beginning to turn the corner as well. The picture is nothing like as bleak as it was around 1980, when exploding populations suggested there would be a steep increase in those living in absolute poverty. The recurrent droughts and famines of China and India are largely things of the past, although alas this is not true of parts of Africa where in 2002 some 14 million people in Swaziland, Zimbabwe, Zambia, Mozambique, Malawi and Angola risk severe malnutrition or starvation. Health spending per person in Africa is $13 a year, life expectancy in Botswana and Malawi is 40 years, and Africa owes some $300 billion in foreign debt. While there is no room for complacency, there is much room for hope. But while poverty and ignorance certainly breed local trouble in many countries, there is no evidence whatever that they breed interstate or global violence.

There are libraries of books and studies dedicated to overpopulation. For the purposes of this book, two observations will be made. First, although often cited as a cause of war in the past, it is hard to think of any conflicts precipitated by overpopulation alone – unless Japan's attack on China or Hitler's demand for German 'Lebensraum' are included. Overpopulation has not been cited as a factor in conflicts involving such countries as India and China. Second, at the risk of a huge and controversial generalization, the evidence of recent years suggests that as countries emerge from starvation levels, which provide their own Malthusian system of population control, population growth accelerates, but as countries develop above that, it slows as more people practise birth control and do not feel the need to have large families to support them in old age. The problem is still colossal, but not entirely hopeless any more.

The tenth threat to post-Cold War peace is the environment. The environmental disputes that transcend borders, and hence cause immense anger between countries, are growing, and likely to continue to do so as more and more countries become industrialized. Chernobyl, the leakage of radiation in the Baltic, pollution of the Caspian Sea, oil spills and the anger caused by the Indonesian fires in 1997 are all examples.

More serious still is the global anger directed against the United States for failing to control the emission of greenhouse gases, and specifically for its gas-guzzling habit. Whatever view one takes of Kyoto, the abrogation of such treaties widely seen as being for the common good sends a hugely negative signal across the globe, and stains the United States' peacekeeping credentials.

The eleventh of the twelve plagues of the modern world is the globalization of crime. Crime has always had a significant global dimension in areas like piracy, contraband, money transfers between countries, fugitives from justice, the relocation of the Mafia from Sicily to the United States, and so on. But the area in which it actually represents a threat to peace is drugs, because the enormous rewards involved have the ability to bring whole countries under the sway of criminals, and to affect a society even as large as the United States, as well as other major developed countries.

Three Latin American countries have been so suborned by drugs as to come under the control of cocaine bosses at different stages – Paraguay under General Alfredo Stroessner, Bolivia under General García Meza (the 'Cocaine Coup') and Panama under General Manuel Noriega. The latter actually triggered an American invasion to depose him. Huge swathes of Colombia have come under the control of drug traffickers (and briefly under the presidency of Ernesto Samper, the government may also have been in their palm), as have parts of Peru and Mexico. In Asia the Taleban regime was for a time actually running the drug trade, while the 'golden triangle' of poppy-growing embraced a large area of Central Asia, cross-crossing three borders – Burma, Thailand and China.

The sheer power and scale of the drugs traffic was graphically illuminated on a visit I made to Colombia in 2001. John F. Kennedy famously left Lyndon Johnson with the seeds of large-scale American involvement in Vietnam. Apart from the Middle East, one of the most forehead-furrowing decisions President Bush faces is how to carry along his predecessor's slowly escalating record of American intervention against the heady mix of drugs traffickers, Marxist guerrillas and right-wing killers in Colombia, much nearer to home. The wrong choice could leave America floundering through as inextricable a mire as Vietnam.

Francis Ford Coppola's Vietnam epic, *Apocalypse Now*, has recently been re-released. Its admirers are familiar with the scud-scud-scudding of helicopter blades across the jungle canopy, the villagers fleeing in panic, the armed river-boat churning up sluggish waters, the innocent woman killed in panic firing, the wanton brutality of local warlords, the aircraft spraying napalm across virgin forest, the drug-dazed American GIs sucked deeper into a conflict they neither comprehend nor have the stomach for.

Today's Colombia is eerily reminiscent. The helicopters, a first wave of American-supplied ones, are already in the air. The villagers are fleeing war in their tens of thousands. American river navy Seals are training on the Amazon. Warlords in remote areas torture and chop up their opponents. Herbicides are being sprayed across the countryside in huge quantities. America is once again being sucked into a conflict it little understands. *Apocalypse Now* was based on Joseph Conrad's *Heart of Darkness*; yet Conrad also wrote *Nostromo*, a Latin American story of over-ambition and despair.

More than Conrad, Colombia is Gabriel García Márquez's land. The grand old man of Latin American literature and the creator of magic realism is seriously ill in Mexico. What can he think now of his beloved Colombia, a nightmare of black magic unreality, its capital, Bogotá, under siege, a country visibly disintegrating into a maelstrom of armed troops, drug traffickers, kidnappers, Marxist guerrillas and murderous vigilantes? García Márquez, in his luminously well-written homage to the dying Simón Bolívar, *The General in his Labyrinth*, puts the words into his hero's mouth: 'For us America is our own country, and it's all the same: hopeless . . . it's all gone to hell.'

Around half the countryside of this immense land is now controlled by insurgent forces. The mountainous, volcano-strewn south, the tropical, forested west and the alternately sodden and sunbaked flatlands to the east, the llanos, from which Bolívar led an army to seize Bogotá, are under the control of the Revolutionary Armed Forces of Colombia (FARC). The north is disputed between FARC and its rival, the more orthodox pro-Cuban National Liberation Army (ELN), as well as right-wing paramilitaries. Some 40,000 people have been killed in fighting over the past decade. Around 1 million have fled the countryside to the comparative safety of the cities. Huge tracts of the country are used to grow coca leaves (and smaller ones to grow heroin poppies). A new and fearsome criminal sub-industry has sprung up in recent years to finance the insurgents: kidnapping, of which 3,600 were officially recorded in 2001 although the true figure may be three times as big.

The country's laws are so respectful of personal rights that securing a conviction is well-nigh impossible: the conviction rate for murder is around 7 per cent, while two-fifths of killings are never investigated and arrests take place for only one in ten. Average murder sentences are only four and a half years. Small wonder that ruthless vigilantes are big business.

How does a country so disintegrate? A decade ago, Colombia was relatively ignored, suffering from many of the classic Latin American ailments: a weak central state; chronic corruption; and an alienated working class of both rural peasants and recent migrants to the cities (in addition to the traditional Liberal–Conservative rivalry – La Violencia, as it was dubbed, which claimed 300,000 lives in the 1950s), while Marxist guerrilla groups operated in the vast outback, at that time supported by the Cubans. La Violencia died down. Things got better. Working-class conditions improved, and electoral turnout rose to nearly 60 per cent.

Then, like a virulent form of cancer, drugs appeared, attacking all the old weaknesses. The process unfolded over two decades: first laboratories and refineries sprang up in the early 1980s to process the coca leaves grown in Peru and Bolivia (marijuana was also cultivated in the Caribbean province of Santa Marta). The Medellin cartel soon established a stranglehold over the trade. Pablo Escobar was the head of the few families that dominated the trade, leading a fabulously wealthy, sybaritic, murderous lifestyle.

I was in Bogotá at the cartel's height when its men fired a missile at the headquarters of the United States Drug Enforcement Administration in Bogotá, as well as nearly succeeding in blowing up an aeroplane over the centre of the capital, which would have resulted in horrific casualties. A multi-storey police headquarters was also reduced to a heap of rubble. Three presidential candidates were murdered by the cartel in a concerted attempt to destroy Colombia's democracy.

Yet the Medellin cartel was broken up, under ferocious prosecution by the DEA and the police, only for the rival Cali cartel to take its place. This was less ruthless, more corrupting, diversifying exports to Europe as well as the United States. Between them both cartels were incredibly effective, wresting distribution of cocaine from the Mafia in the United States. The drugs meanwhile suborned politics: the administration of President Ernesto Samper was treated as a pariah by the United States, secured support among the peasants, who made a good living from growing coca, and secured the protection of the dwindling bands of guerrillas who now gained a huge source of income to replace shrinking outside support from Cuba.

Then the cocaine industry entered a third phase. The coca was grown in Colombia. It was no longer under the control of small cartels, but of medium-sized businesses under provincial criminals, middle-class professionals and local warlords from either the guerrilla movements or the gangsters that used to protect the cartels, as well as local vigilantes acting to protect local landowners from cattle- and horse-rustlers. The latter two groups of disparate armed men became known as 'paras' – paramilitaries – loosely organized under the United Self-Defence Forces of Colombia.

As coca-growing has become more diffuse, it has spread: while many peasants have smallholdings of two or three acres, the FARC lord it over huge plantations. Some 42,000 square kilometres (16,000 square miles) are controlled by the guerrillas in the south, much of it coca-planted. Central control is loose, with the guerrillas organized along 'franchise' lines: provided the growers pay their dues to their protectors, they can get on with cultivation.

Coca farming has grown steadily, from around 110,000 acres in 1995 to around 340,000 in 2001. Much of the growth in Colombia is the result of coca producers relocating under pressure: as a result of President Alberto Fujimori's crackdown in Peru, coca cultivation there fell from 290,000 acres to around 85,000 last year, while Bolivia's coca plantations have shrunk from just over 120,000 acres to less than 40,000.

The drugs money has provided a huge shot in the arm to the flagging guerrilla movements: FARC's income from drugs and kidnapping is around $300 million a year, while the paramilitaries earn some $200 million a year. The drugs industry as a whole is worth around some $4 billion a year to Colombia (although some estimates put this much higher). The FARC continue to deny they are drug traffickers, but this is no longer seriously disputed.

In a dramatic arrest in 2001, a legendary Brazilian drugs baron who had been sheltered by the FARC, Luis Fernando da Costa, known as Fernandinho, was seized in an air strike by Colombian authorities. Alerted by reconnaissance planes, a Colombian fighter ordered a small aircraft apparently straying off its flight path to fly to an airbase. The plane disobeyed, landing at a small airstrip under fire; five men fled into the jungle.

Another light aircraft from Venezuela soon made for the airstrip to pick the men up. It was ordered to land at an airbase, and on disobeying was shot down. Some 300 soldiers were landed at the site of the first plane's landing, and Fernandinho and his four companions were tracked down.

Fernandinho's evidence to his captors was devastating: 'In Colombia not a kilo of cocaine moves without the FARC's authorization . . . FARC's leaders live like capitalist millionaires: good women, good food and good drink.' Fernandinho painted a detailed picture of how he bought cocaine from the FARC's entrepôt at Barrancominas in Guaviare province. Pilots were paid $25,000 a run to carry cocaine cargoes for which the FARC were paid $15,000 dollars ($500 a kilo or over $1,000 per pound). Every month some 18 to 20 tons of cocaine were lifted out, yielding an income of $10 million to $12 million a month to the FARC.

Fernandinho received $3,000 a kilo (or $6,500 per pound) at the other end, a mark-up of some 600 per cent. His destinations were Paraguay and Brazil. In Rio he was alleged by the police to have been in charge of the distribution of some 60 per cent of the cocaine. Much of the drug travelled from Brazil and Paraguay via a well-worn route through Surinam to Ghana and then Holland, where the street value of each kilo was $160,000 (about $350,000 per pound or $157 per ton).

Around half of the payments were made in arms, bought on the Paraguayan black market, or from Jordan via Peruvian sources. In a year Fernandinho says he provided FARC with more than 10,000 AK-47 rifles and 5,000 boxes of ammunition. Fernandinho was forced on the run by a Colombian army assault, Operation Black Cat, which seized the Barrancominas base, destroying some 150 processing plants and 50 crystallization installations. Fernandinho himself was wounded; he was captured in the attempt to airlift him out of Colombia, and has been speedily extradited to Brazil, where he had been serving a twelve-year sentence.

Drugs invigorated Colombia's flagging guerrillas with new life. FARC now has around 20,000 guerrillas, and the ELN has some 12,000, while the paras have around 13,000 men. The results are murderous: some 6,000 killed in 2000, double the number the previous year. Against this the traditionally underequipped armed forces number only 140,000 men and the police some 100,000, while the defence budget is under $3 billion.

The response of the Pastrana government to the challenge was, in the eyes of his many domestic critics, feeble. Although his transparent honesty ended the country's pariah status under the corrupt Samper government (the United States shot themselves in the foot by suspending aid to Colombia during his presidency, allowing the drugs culture to flourish), Pastrana attempted to end the war through negotiation, agreeing not to pursue the guerrillas into their 42,000-square kilometre (16,000-square mile) 'demilitarized zone' around San Vicente in the south. The President even flew into guerrilla territory to talk with Manuel Marulanda, FARC's clapped-out quasi-septuagenarian leader, who agreed to such bromides as visits by foreign diplomats.

But Pastrana seemed to have misjudged his opponents: flushed with money and weapons, they saw little reason to surrender; the objectives of this primarily peasant-based movement (Marulanda has never been to a big city) are partly Marxist, partly 'Bolivarian' and bent on 'doing away with the state'. As the only time FARC has ever participated in the democratic process, it won just 4 per cent of the vote, its prospects for achieving its aims politically are slight. Pastrana's objective was merely to 'reduce the intensity of the conflict' as a prelude to persuading the guerrillas to lay down arms. In September 2001 a senior State Department official voiced American concern that the demilitarized zone was being used to 'train terrorists, run prison camps, and traffic drugs' with no agreement in sight.

The dialogue between a government offering what it considered to be reasonable terms for a surrender and a guerrilla movement that thought it had the money and the weapons to overthrow the state at last was that of ships passing in the night. Conservatives accused Pastrana of merely giving breathing space to the FARC to recruit (mostly children and teenage boys kidnapped from their parents or orphaned), organize and arm. Pastrana defends himself by arguing that the guerrillas were indeed on the brink of laying down arms. Pastrana was succeeded as president in May 2002 by the hard-line President Alvaro Uribe.

The ceasefire has ended and parts of the demilitarized zone reoccupied, while the guerrillas have retired to regroup in the hills. The guerrillas may have acquired ground-to-air missiles (some believe they already have them) and an aerial offensive could be highly dangerous. Colombia can ill afford to lose helicopters: the country's entire force, until the American reinforcements came, was less than that of Leeds city police.

In one area, Pastrana's peace offensive may have paid dividends: the ELN's 12,000 guerrillas and their leader, Nicolas Rodriguez Bautista, have borne the brunt of paramilitary attacks and have been largely disowned by their Cuban backers, themselves starved of funds by their old Russian sponsors. The ELN could be ready to do a deal. The big hurdle is that the last time a substantial number of Colombia's guerrillas did so, around 1,000 (the 'reinsertados' – those who disarmed) were murdered by their old enemies within a few years. So far, though, no breakthrough has occurred.

The answer may be to integrate them into the armed forces and make them responsible for prosecuting the war against their old enemies – the paras. Pastrana agreed to European demands to prosecute the war against the paras with as much vigour as that against the guerrillas. The paras, under the loose control of the psychopathic Carlos Castaño, are turning into a major threat to public order, mushrooming in numbers and controlling large tracts of territory while running their own profitable drugs operation (although their kidnapping tends to be limited to 'educating' those who disagree with them, or killing them outright). In 2001 they were responsible for around half of all political killings – some 3,000 – many of them purely money- or revenge-motivated, and including many chainsaw massacres, literally chopping their enemies into pieces. One day they could pose as big a threat to the authority of the state (such as it is) as FARC.

It is this fearsome hodgepodge of national disintegration that poses the Bush administration with one of its key challenges: to rush in where angels fear to tread. So far the United States has been cautious. Having mistakenly allowed the problem to fester by cutting off the corrupt Samper administration, under Pastrana President Clinton came up with the ambitious Plan Colombia, in which both countries (and a few others) would provide some $1.3 billion on top of an existing $330 million in American aid.

Of this, $375 million is earmarked for 18 Blackhawk helicopters for raiding drug processing plants and fighting guerrillas, and 42 Huey helicopters for moving troops and equipment, to be joined later by 15 others. Three 450-man Colombian army brigades are to be trained by the Americans. In addition some $20 million is to be used for crop eradication as well as $68 million for P-3 radar aircraft to detect drug-carrying aircraft. Some $120 million is to go into human rights programmes and $80 million for crop substitution. An American airbase is being built at Manta in Ecuador, as well as airstrips on the islands of Aruba and Curacao. American trainers and pilots are strictly barred from combat missions – although it seems only a matter of time before an American perishes, whether a regular soldier training Colombians or one of the many American ex-servicemen now advising the Colombian army, either in a crash or shot down by guerrillas. The American effort in Colombia dwarfs those in Ecuador and Peru (around $80 million apiece) and Bolivia (around $160 million).

Even this low-profile approach has drawn fire. The main concern is the use of a herbicide, glyphosate, to eradicate coca plantations, which has been compared to American sprayings in Vietnam. Yet the resemblance to Agent Orange or napalm is far-fetched. This preparation, which is highly effective, leaving acres of withered crops, is in fact a commonly used over-the-counter weedkiller in the West whose trade name is Roundup. However, it affects ordinary crops as well as coca bushes, and there are concerns that it is going into the food chain through human consumption of such staples as barley and lettuces.

The governor of Putumayo province, Ivan Guerrero, favours crop substitution: 8,000 peasants from his province were forced to move by the destruction of their legitimate crops. There are claims that sickness and fever were common in areas sprayed as well as some instances of deformed babies. The government is offering grants of $1,000 to substitute legitimate crops for coca leaf, as well as guaranteed prices for the produce; spraying is suspended for the year during which this happens. Around a fifth of coca and poppy plantations in Colombia haven taken advantage of this.

The environmental cost of cultivating coca is vastly greater than that of eliminating it. Some 3–4 tons of herbicide per hectare must be used to prepare the ground to cultivate coca leaf, compared with the 2.7 gallons of glyphosate per hectare needed to kill the plant. Acids and alcohols flow freely into local drainage systems from the coca cultivation process, and huge swathes of vegetation are stripped from the hillsides when the coca growers move on, having exhausted the land. It is calculated that 3 hectares of woodland are destroyed to prepare 1 hectare of land for coca cultivation. Moreover, some 900,000 tons of toxic chemicals have been used in coca processing since 1985, mostly in remote areas, whose residues drain into the land.

Will the Americans go in deeper? Should they? The Afghan intervention and potential Iraqi war make this highly unlikely at present; there are limits as to how many wars the United States can fight at any one time. Yet, as with the September 11 attack, it is worth recalling that most of the United States' post-Cold War interventions have been under pressure from some domestic lobby or problem – from the threat to American oil supplies in the Gulf to the intervention in Haiti to peace-keeping in the Middle East and Northern Ireland (intervention in the Balkans was extraordinarily slow in coming and only in response to harrowing television coverage that finally galvanized public opinion). Colombia falls squarely into the bracket of huge domestic concern: drug abuse is close to the top of America's domestic policy agenda, and Colombia is cast as a villain corrupting America's youth.

Toss in the fact that its cocaine entrepreneurs are now synonymous with Marxist guerrillas of various hues and murderous right-wing paramilitaries, and the temptation for American intervention seems irresistible. Surely Colombia, a tottering and weak democracy, needs the firepower that only the world's megapower can bring to bear? Unlike in Vietnam, Colombia's guerrillas are not supported by any huge man-power reserve (North Vietnam) or superpower (the Soviet Union); they appear to be a little local difficulty. Or so they must seem to senior American military men.

Yet the Bush administration should resist the temptation to intervene, for a multiplicity of reasons. To begin with, intervention is highly unlikely to succeed, however many men it puts into the field. The Colombian army has been trying for decades without success; the American public would not stomach tens of thousands going in. The reason is simple. As one (pro-American) diplomat in Bogotá put it:

> superimpose a map of Vietnam on Colombia, and it is obvious that the latter is many times larger. Then look at the terrain, which is even worse than Vietnam: high forested sierra, tropical and sub-tropical vegetation, abysmal communications.

One could add that the country has porous borders – even longer than those of Vietnam. To the south there is the rugged mountain boundary with Ecuador and the tropical rainforest border with Peru; to the east the empty outlaw llanos – flatlands – of Venezuela, as well as highlands further north. These boundaries are virtually unpoliceable: drugs smug-glers, guerrillas and refugees cross at will: a determined American onslaught inside Colombia would merely nudge the problem across the frontiers, as happened in Vietnam with Laos and Cambodia; indeed, the offensives against the coca industry in Peru and Bolivia have already displaced the problem into Colombia.

Worse, more open American intervention would be deeply counter-productive. Opinion polls today suggest that most Colombians would welcome an American offensive to rid their country of the drugs-and-guerrillas scourge. This view is unlikely to last. Already in Colombia there is simmering resentment that a largely American habit (drugs abuse) should have so destabilized their society.

The hitherto declining guerrilla movements after the demise of Soviet communism would suddenly acquire a new infusion of support if they were seen to be fighting American 'imperialists' on their own territory. Even the paramilitaries could pose as selfless nationalists. Conservative Colombian politicians would find it hard to defend such a policy: 'Colombians must resolve their own problems,' says a senior political figure.

In all this, it is vital for the Americans to disentangle the drugs issue from the guerrilla issue, tempting as it is to see the two as inextricably linked. There has been no sudden surge of support for Marxists in Colombia, no imminent threat of a take-over: it is simply that drugs have given them the money to hold the country to ransom. The guerrillas are as far as ever from real power in Colombia. Almost all the metropolitan areas, where four-fifths of the people live, are outside their control: they are just richer and more effective than before. Communism is not the issue, drugs are. But an overt American intervention would polarize the country to the Marxists' benefit into a fight between poor Colombia and its bullying overmighty imperialist neighbour; students and peasants would flock to the revolutionary cause.

In fact, the United States, so careful about the 'body-bag' syndrome, so intent on avoiding casualties in the post-Vietnam era, seems hardly likely to step in with a major commitment of ground troops; the temptation is to go for all-out aerial assault, apparently successful in the Gulf War and the Balkans. This would be hopeless in the vastness of Colombia's thickly wooded mountains and tropical lowland vegetation. Only well-equipped ground troops, copying the guerrillas' own tactics, could keep them on the run; and the United States could not risk the casualties.

So back to a slower, more patient, less instant-results strategy: let the Colombians solve the problem for themselves. Most important, Colombian ground troops need training in anti-guerrilla tactics. The Colombian air force is also undermanned, undertrained and underequipped: the United States (and its allies in Europe, equally at risk from drugs) should help to supply and equip them on a much larger scale than Plan Colombia calls for. The current danger is that Colombia's inadequate armed forces will use the paramilitaries to do their dirty work for them – something that already occurs to a limited extent. Some officers have been suspended for their links to the paras. The same pattern has occurred in Central America's recent civil wars and Algeria's more recent one. Military aid must be made conditional on a rigorous prosecution of the war against the paras as well as the guerrillas – with a promise of amnesty and integration into Colombia's armed forces for those who surrender.

As for drugs, the opinion of ordinary Colombians – previously marked by mostly indifferent shrugs that this was the United States' problem – is now turning hostile to the scourge. In Bogotá, cocaine and heroin are now becoming serious problems; in the remote settlements where the crop is grown, local youths are increasingly resorting to cocaine, to their parents' disgust.

'Pastrana restored integrity and acceptance from the outside world to Colombia,' says a senior politician. 'The next administration will be one of real force in dealing with these problems. That is what is required – a strong leader. The Americans cannot solve our problems for us.' Uribe campaigned on such a platform. But there are allegations he has links with the paras. Once the cocaine crop starts to wither, so will the guerrillas, who have been decades-long losers anyway, reinvented by cocaine.

But the drugs problem for the West will not go away even if it is defeated in Colombia. It will simply move on to some other suitable sub-tropical country where growing conditions are ideal but which is beyond the rule of law – whether in Latin America, Africa or Asia. With increasing interception of Colombian supplies, for example, there are already signs that the Mexicans are becoming the dominant middlemen to the United States.

Huge strides have been made in particular through UN agreements providing for interdiction by air and at sea, and the investigation of bank accounts to prevent money laundering and to seize assets. But the problem remains the vastly lucrative market for cocaine and heroin, particularly in the United States. A new offensive targeted at education in the effects of drugs and rehabilitation for minor offenders seems to be the most promising way of dealing with the problem, to supplement draconian imprisonment policies which have led to the jailing of some 460,000 people in the United States in 2001 for drug offences – ten times as many as twenty years ago. John Walters, America's new drugs 'czar', should be experienced enough to see this.

With some $40 billion a year being spent on drugs programmes inside the United States, it is clearly important to increase the less than $2 billion being spent on external efforts to prevent the drugs coming in (less than the equivalent street value of 20 tons of cocaine). Moreover, the Americans point out that while US imports of Colombian cocaine remain stable at around 330 tons a year, the quantity flowing to Europe has doubled in five years to 220 tons (43 tons was seized in 1999) and the Europeans spend very little to fight it. The problem lies within the consuming countries, more than the producing ones. And this does not extend to getting the United States bogged down in a Colombian quagmire deeper than Vietnam.

The Globalization of Human Rights

So to the twelfth and final of the major post-Cold War sources of instability. Drugs, like so many of these threats, respect no borders and call for action across national boundaries. This should equally apply to crimes committed by governments within their own borders, and calls for a redefinition of sovereignty itself (the British Foreign Office, to its credit, has done some pioneering work on this definition).

If a tyrant murders and enslaves his own people, by what conception of justice, natural or otherwise, is this purely that country's concern? A crime against a person or millions of people is still a crime to the world outside. A murderer is a murderer whether he kills in his own country or someone else's, as indeed the law recognizes; and international law today increasingly goes after those alleged to have committed crimes against their own people except, ludicrously, when a mass murderer is still in power in which case he cannot be indicted and is free to go on killing.

But as far as the world community is concerned, it is and should be a matter of huge concern if people are being killed, tortured and repressed even by one of their own countrymen. What difference does his nationality make? Most tyrants have seized power by force and have no mandate to murder their own people (there was never a more mendacious saw – that 'people get the government they deserve'; as far as most tyrants are concerned, the people never had any say in the matter). In dealing with people's human rights, including the elementary right not to be murdered, there should be no such thing as boundaries or 'internal affairs'. Every death at the hands of a tyrant is a matter for all humanity, and shames humanity. This might be labelled the globalization of human rights.

As Professor Fred Halliday has rightly observed, there are only three dozen or so full-fledged democracies in the world: the rest all suffer from imperfections or human rights abuses of some kind; obviously there are practical limits to the action that can be taken against all but the worst violators. Countries evolving towards fuller democracy need to be encouraged through trade, contacts and incentives, as well as criticism. But there is still a great deal more work to be done on this elemental principle. Part III of this book will look at just how far most of the world has to progress towards anything resembling full democracy and freedom. But the world's major countries have at least to address the issue.

A human rights treaty, akin to the Non-Proliferation and Test Ban Treaties, needs to be set up under which countries practising an ascending scale of brutality towards their own people suffer an ascending scale of penalties. The United States Congress, which was responsible for human rights certification, has led the way; the UN has powers to declare a situation genocidal, but is vague about the penalties.

A human rights treaty, or consensus of the kind suggested, would set up an international inspectorate, with links both to the UN and to Amnesty International, establishing minimum acceptable criteria for the respect of human rights by governments. Those accused of gross violations – and they are only a small minority in today's world – could realistically be targeted. Thus there could be trade and banking sanctions against a dictatorship guilty of imprisonment, torture or the murder of significant numbers of people for political reasons.

For a country guilty of gross violations of human rights against its citizens or of genocide, the penalty should include possible external intervention on behalf of the citizens of that country. A government that declares war upon the people of its own country forfeits the right to rule within its borders, and invites others to declare war upon it on behalf of its people.

Countries that would certainly face action under the former, lesser category today would include Cuba, a diminishing number of African countries including Zimbabwe, as well as Syria, Iran, Saudi Arabia, Libya, Vietnam, China and North Korea. Only Iraq, North Korea and possibly Burma would qualify under the gross violation or genocide provisions for direct possible external intervention.

The key to such a treaty is that it must be multilateral. The United States human rights certification process suffers from the fact that no other country applies sanctions, so that there is a risk that trade rivals step in and fill the breach – which incenses Americans and makes them reluctant to apply sanctions. It may be argued that this is pure pie in the sky: that countries such as France would never sign up to such a treaty or apply sanctions themselves.

I believe, on the contrary, that public opinion in developed democratic countries can be mobilized to force governments to sign up to just such a convention and punitive measures. Time and again, public opinion has shown itself less willing to tolerate bloodstained tyrannies than governments are. There is nothing impractical about such an appeal to squeeze out the last of the world's really barbarous regimes and to try and improve standards among more routinely authoritarian ones.

To the old objections that sanctions don't work and that they hurt ordinary people, not the rulers, the answer must be to look at South Africa: for all the platitudes about sanctions not working, they did in the end (particularly the financial boycott of the country by the banks). Many black South Africans, and the organizations representing them, supported sanctions in spite of the hardship. Obviously sanctions wherever possible should be tailored towards the ruling elite – restricting sales of weaponry, luxury goods and so on (the elites are also particularly hit by boycotts of academic, sporting and cultural exchanges); but where it is clear that the fall of a regime would result in a substantial improvement in the well-being of ordinary people, most would be prepared to endure even further hardship to achieve it.

Massive humanitarian support to help those suffering under Saddam's repression or threatened by outright starvation under Kim Jong-il in North Korea is not only justified but imperative, provided this reaches the people for whom it was intended (and this can increasingly be verified). But the treatment of a human rights pariah as an equal and acceptable member of the international community cannot be condoned.

To repeat: an attack by a gang of armed men that have seized power in a country on its people is as much a violation of world peace as an armed attack by that country on another. This may flout time-honoured diplomatic practices, but they should have been flouted a long time ago.

CHAPTER 11

NATO AND THE NEW WORLD ORDER

So to how existing institutions fit in with the new post-Cold War international security structure, which should have been established within five years of the collapse of the old order, and have been in place for seven years already. The foregoing analysis has been intended to lay down the clear imperative to build this. It is an urgent and pressing global necessity if war between major emerging powers, further terrorist onslaughts, particularly in the developed world, the disruption of trade and travel and the spread of international crime are to be avoided. It is essential to preventing a fourth world war.

The first part of this book tried to show how, as the concerns of the Cold War have faded, terrorism, nationalism and lesser conflicts are now bubbling to the surface. With astonishing shortsightedness, the first reaction of Western governments (except France) to the diminution in tension in Central Europe was to throw away some of the armour that made it possible and slash military spending, none more so initially than the United States, which has already withdrawn fully two-thirds of its forces from Europe.

President Clinton declared that there was no region in the world more important to the United States than Asia: 'The time has come for Americans to join with Japan and others in the region to create a new Pacific Community.' Warren Christopher, Clinton's Secretary of State, declared bluntly that 'Western Europe is no longer the dominant area of the world.' Washington, he said, had decided to shed its 'Eurocentric attitude'. Yet Western Europe still accounts for 60 per cent of overseas profits of American firms, half their overseas investments, and 65 per cent of all foreign investment in America. In Britain the white paper Options for Change resulted in substantial defence cuts, some reversed.

In practice, while the enormous conventional forces drawn up in Central Europe were a deterrent but never likely to be used, force is likely to be much more necessary today to intervene in regional conflicts. Western security policy is a shambles: a kind of halfway house where Nato is still drawn up against an apparently non-existent enemy, but without the clear mandate to intervene where it should – in regional conflicts. No mission is prescribed for Nato beyond the old adage that an attack upon one is an attack upon all. The Nato intervention in Kosovo was ad hoc, and showed up huge planning deficiences. It is an alliance bereft of purpose and meaning.

No one is more responsible for this inertia than Nato's military establishments, which display an obsession with not taking casualties that amounts to a phobia. Yet military bureaucrats should consider that, while every consideration must be made for protecting the lives of the men under them, there can be little justification for maintaining large armed forces and the Nato structure itself, unless the threat of their deployment, which implies a willingness to accept casualties, is a real one. Most Western armies are volunteer, and most soldiers accept the risk as part of the job. A war machine that can never be used is much worse than no war machine at all, because it is hugely expensive to maintain.

It should be one of the most urgent tasks of post-Cold War security to decide what the Nato forces in Europe are for; otherwise they will slowly dribble away, leaving nothing but a series of competing national defence policies that at best would be ineffectual, and at worst in rivalry with each other. The end of the Cold War removes the really compelling sense of national danger and urgency that has kept the United States fully committed to Europe. If American forces there are run down any further from their current 70,000 troop strength, it is hard to see the United States returning to a continent where it was always historically difficult for administrations to commit their forces, and which many Americans now consider is less important than the Pacific and Middle Eastern theatres.

A first step at re-energizing the alliance has come with America's proposal to set up a Nato response force of some 21,000 men for rapid intervention in crises around the world. This would not compete with the 60,000-strong European defence force which would usually act as peacekeepers, but be an elite fighting force.

The crises over Bosnia and Kosovo underlined the problems. For the United States, Bosnia and Kosovo were minor civil wars in Europe, and therefore ultimately its responsibility. However, decades of dependence upon an American-led Nato has created a European inability to act separately in the military sphere. Thus, when America took no action, Western Europe was paralysed, lapsing into bitter squabbling about the desirability of action, followed by a manifest lack of co-ordination over what should be done.

Yet it was not to be expected that the Europeans would be able to agree on a common policy in a matter of months, after decades of being warned that any such development would result in an American with-drawal from Europe. American partnership in, and leadership of, a common Western system of collective security remain essential. Leader-ship does not mean passing the buck as soon as a challenge arises. It was particularly mistaken for America's Secretary of State first to announce America's intention of taking action on Bosnia, then to fly to Europe only to be dissuaded from doing so. Western European countries will not initiate major collective security action because they are too accustomed to the role of follower.

If America wants a global system of collective security to work, then it must take prime responsibility. Of course, if the Americans were indeed withdrawing into a period of isolationism or unilateralism, Europe would have no alternative but to try and assemble its own defence structure through the European Union. Differences of national interest and of perception make it unlikely that this will be effective for a long time to come.

Far better, though, for the United States to go on accepting the reality understood since Franklin Roosevelt – that in an increasingly smaller and interdependent world a continental global megapower has huge respon-sibilities. America cannot retreat from a world in which security is globalized: if it does, the challenge will be much worse when it has to re-enter. September 11 underlined this. America's challenge is to provide leadership once again, and to give Nato the purpose it now lacks.

There was nothing academic or remote about the new isolationism in the immediate aftermath of the Cold War and before September 11. It was outlined chillingly by American columnist William Pfaff as far back as June 1993:

Today there is no physical threat to the security of the United States. Such threat as exists is to the country's economic well-being and comes from allies, Japan and Western Europe.

There is no great idealistic motivation today for international involvement. American feelings are rightly but ephemerally engaged by human suffering in Somalia, Ethiopia or Bosnia, but these are affairs whose causes are indigenous and seemingly beyond the ability of others to much influence. There certainly is no great crusading answer to African misery and anarchy or to Balkan hatreds.

The Clinton administration maintains and manages the international obligations already in place, with a bias toward their reduction. Budget and risk-assessment both dictate the run-down of overseas bases and foreign commitments. The administration offers an increased emphasis on human rights and environmental issues as its contribution to foreign policy, but this usually yields when it meets practical obstacles, as in Mr Clinton's decision not to withdraw most-favored-nation trade status from China because of its rights abuses.

Unease was not stilled in May 1993, when a senior Clinton administration official, off the record, asserted that 'it is necessary to make the point that our economic interests are paramount' over America's traditional foreign policy interests. With limited resources, America must 'define the extent of its commitment and make a commitment commensurate with those realities. This may on occasion fall short of what some Americans and others would hope for.' The same official asked candidly if 'people are dying [in Bosnia] because the United States could do more if it wanted to? Yes.' But the stark truth, in his view, was that, 'We don't have the leverage, we don't have the influence, the inclination to use military force in dealing with "middleweight powers" after the end of the Cold War'.

These remarks were quickly disavowed by the State Department and the White House, but they clearly reflected a strong current of feeling there; this view showed an alarming reversion to the belief that intervention abroad is a luxury. In practice, every previous attempt by the United States to withdraw from the world has been rudely awakened; the longer-term costs to the United States have always been greater than American deterrence in advance. The rude awakening this time came on September 11. Is Nato the embryo of a new world security order? A quick look at the organization is called for.

There could be few more poignant signs of how the strategic map of Europe was changed than the decision in 1990 at Nato Headquarters

Allied Forces Central Europe in Brunssum, Holland, to drop the term 'Edge of the Battlefield' to describe the boundary between East and West Germany where eight Nato divisions were long drawn up to face an attack that, over four decades, never came. With the unification of East and West Germany, those forces were left facing a virtually non-existent army of around 150,000 men, which were reduced to just 50,000 and merged, without trace of its former self, into the West German armed forces.

'This process is from west to east,' one of Germany's most senior generals told me brutally at the time, as he described how retraining, re-equipment and re-education were annihilating the East German army's separate, goose-stepping identity. Prussia had been conquered by Schleswig-Holstein, Bremen, Hessen and Bayern, and Bismarck was turning in his grave. The Russian forces in East Germany became isolated garrisons, protected from the ire of ordinary East Germans and gradually thinned down until their evacuation. Under the terms of reunification, Nato forces as such could not be stationed in the old East Germany (although the German forces there were to all intents and purposes to be a Nato appendage). So whither those huge armies along the Rhine, all dressed up with no one to fight?

The activity at Nato headquarters in fact became frantic after 1990, as the Alliance sought to establish a role for itself. The Alliance's planners were refreshingly realistic. It was accepted that the threat from Russia in the new Europe was 'very remote indeed', and that the prospect of a surprise attack by Russian forces along the central front, after the conventional arms treaty had been signed in Paris on November 1990, was non-existent. The treaty, made possible by the Russians' astonishing decision to drop its remaining condition that limits be imposed on the number of sea-based aircraft, pushed much of the Russian armour necessary for an attack in Central Europe beyond the Urals; any build-up on the central front would violate the treaty and be instantly visible.

Should the Russians have reassembled their forces, they would have suffered from the disadvantage of having lost their buffer zone in Eastern Europe; the then Czechoslovakia redeployed its forces from the Nato front to face a possible threat in the east. Nato succeeded in imposing a limit on any country's forces allowed on foreign soil within Europe. The only country affected was Russia, and the implications were staggering. From a superiority of Warsaw Pact conventional forces of around two-to-one in 1989, the Russians, bereft of allies, accepted a ceiling of some seven armies between the Urals and their western borders, compared with combined Western and Eastern European forces of some fourteen armies.

The strategic equation in Central Europe was, in effect, stood on its head. Soon after, Ukraine secured its independence. Nato was enlarged in 1999 to include the Czech Republic, Poland and Hungary. In 2002 a further seven countries were invited to join – the three Baltic States, Slovakia, Slovenia, Romania and Bulgaria, bringing the total member-ship to twenty-six. Obviously, these bring virtually nothing to the Alliance's defensive might – except further to slow consultation. They underline that Nato has become a political alliance binding America with most of Europe. Nato's armed forces are 4.5 million strong, and its total defence spending more than $500 million. The only possibility of conflict seems to arise through a Russian re-invasion of one of its former satellites; that, too, is remote. The shadow of conventional war has been lifted from Europe.

A nuclear deterrent is being retained by Nato for two good reasons. First, the Russians are keeping a major stockpile of long-range missiles, as well as short-range missiles. Second, while the Alliance has scrapped its short-range nuclear artillery and not modernized its land-based missiles, it retains airborne weapons to reassure the Americans that their forces would never be left unprotected in Europe.

Now that the walls of Jericho have come tumbling down, it was only a matter of time before Western public opinion demanded not just a 'peace dividend', but the virtual dissolution of the Alliance (the Warsaw Pact being dead already). Nato planners rose to this challenge and are arguing persuasively that, while Nato must be drastically restructured, it would be dangerous to do away with the Alliance entirely. Nato knows, in effect, that it is fighting for its life; its arguments are by no means purely special pleading.

Why Nato? One not-very-good answer is that while the Russian threat has diminished radically, it has not disappeared. It will remain a for-midable nuclear power and the most effective conventional power on the Euro-Asian continent. Until democracy and stability are guaranteed there, the West would be unwise to drop its guard altogether.

More plausibly, Nato also discerned a new role for itself during the Gulf crisis as an ideal co-ordinator and staging post for the rapid projection of forces to world trouble-spots, in particular the Middle East and the possible flashpoints between the newly assertive national-ities of Eastern Europe. Troops and equipment were removed from the central front for deployment in the Gulf; crises such as that in Yugoslavia or, potentially, between Hungary and Romania, beckon. The experience of forty years of co-ordination will be invaluable in forging such an intervention force.

Nato also has two major political roles to play: it remains the only forum that directly engages America in Western Europe and inhibits a retreat across the Atlantic which, in almost any scenario, could be dangerous; and its continued existence is crucial to preventing what senior generals discreetly call the 'renationalization' of national armed forces – in particular Germany's, with all the dangers that that might imply.

The alternative to radical overhaul may be no less than the neutralization of Germany and its 370,000-strong armed forces, followed, probably, by the withdrawal of American troops from Europe. This would be a recipe for renewed instability. The very vigour with which Nato is responding to the need for complete overhaul suggests that the Atlantic Alliance is indeed worth preserving in a slimmed-down form to meet the challenges that are rearing their heads around the globe.

The American Nato commander during the Kosovo operation, General Wesley Clark, is in no doubt of the Alliance's continuing value:

> The machinery of Nato served as a powerful 'consensus engine' that enabled the allies to do what no single nation, not even the United States, could have done alone. The problems in the campaign were less a function of war by committee than a result of divisions within the US government. The real lesson of Kosovo is the importance of allies and the political clout they bring.
>
> Of course Nato has military problems. But why not fix them? Help Nato create a military-political decision-making architecture that can cope more easily with the stresses of target development and operational planning in modern warfare and that can field and command the kinds of high-tech elite forces that will win the campaigns of the 21st century.
>
> Full participation in US campaigns under the aegis of Nato will spur European military transformation more effectively than any number of studies, committees or harangues. At the same time, the United States should build on the values it shares with its closest allies in order to harvest their commitment in addressing the threat of al-Qaeda and in healing the trauma of failed states exploited by terrorist organisations.

Lord Robertson insists that Nato is still relevant, although François Heisbourg, the French strategist, has talked of 'the death of Nato'. The Alliance is slowly and collectively modernizing. Germany has taken the lead in acquiring strategic aircraft by leasing US-made Boeing C-17. Airlift capacity with the A400M Airbus is being developed. Spain is developing air-to-air refuelling, while the Dutch are pioneering precision-guided missiles. A huge new aerial radar surveillance system is to be set up.

More nonsense has been written on the subject of the creation of the supposed 'European army' than almost any recent subject in the past year. The decision to set up a European 'rapid reaction force', capable of deploying 60,000 troops, 72 combat aircraft and 18 warships, is none of the things it has been portrayed as by Euro-enthusiasts (particularly the French) and Euro-sceptics alike.

First, the force was conceived of not as a rival to the United States and Nato but at America's insistence. The United States enthusiastically welcomed the idea at first, because it believed that Europe had a responsibility for protecting its own backyard: the dangers of requiring leadership from the Americans in situations where the latter saw no vital national interest at stake, and were waiting for the Europeans to take the lead, were profoundly illustrated by the two-year delay before Western intervention in Serbia, a conflict which could probably have been stopped by a small force at the outset.

General Clark expressed it well:

We should make clear to the Europeans that we accept our responsibilities. We should state unequivocally that we will be there with Nato when they know there is a security challenge in Europe and the Europeans should make clear that Nato is a security and defence instrument of its first choice. Nato is not yet 'a relic of history'. Time is short, but it is not too late.

What former American Defense Secretary William Cohen made clear was that America does not welcome development of such a force *independent of Nato* – in other words, it should require authorization or planning from Nato's American-dominated command-and-control structure, Shape (see below). The force will be an adjunct of the Western alliance to take part in operations of which the Americans approve, but do not want to take part in themselves.

It is absurd for the French to posture about an independent force on purely practical grounds. The force will be too small for any but peacekeeping operations, and entirely lacks the necessary airlift, logistical and intelligence support which only the Americans can provide in strength. While Europe might one day be an economic challenger to the United States (although much more likely and constructively an economic partner), the idea that Europe could conduct military interventions without the approval or support of the United States, or even challenge it militarily, is so ludicrous as to cross the borders into Euromania or Europaranoia.

Second, the 'army', tiny as it is now proposed, is in fact not a new one which will take troops from Nato, but a shadow one, a command and co-operation structure to permit troops to be seconded from Nato in situations in which the Americans feel they have no obligation to intervene but approve of European action. It is nonsense to argue that this will weaken Nato: clearly on occasions in which the United States feels a responsibility to intervene, a Nato deployment will have priority. When the United States has no direct interests at stake and prefers the Europeans to do the job, the troops will be seconded to European command.

Where, after all, does anyone imagine these troops will be sent? Possibly to the Balkans, or to some flare-up in Eastern Europe, for example between Romania and Hungary, or possibly on humanitarian peacekeeping missions in Africa, for example Rwanda – with US approval. Obviously not to the Middle East (without the Americans) or to reconquer Europe's lost empires!

Third, any decision to send in these troops will be taken by national governments, as is today the case in Nato. Troops will not be eating British breakfasts, wurstel for lunch and foie gras for dinner (much as they might like to). There will be no supranational army command that overrides the authority of the nation states except the existing structure. Finally, the claim that co-operation between European armies is impossible or will quickly degenerate to the lowest common denominator is fantasy. The armies will be no more integrated than at present under Nato.

The American stance on all this could not have been spelt out more clearly. As the former American Secretary of Defense, William Cohen, originally put it: 'we agree with this goal, not grudgingly, not with resignation, but with wholehearted conviction: we recognise that the development of a foreign and security dimension to the EU is a natural, even inevitable, part of the process of European integration.'

General Joseph Ralston, the then Supreme Allied Commander in Europe, was much more explicit in a key, but little noticed, article in setting out how closely Shape, Nato's highest command structure, will be involved in the force. According to General Ralston, Shape has reinforced:

> the transparency and complementarity between the alliance and the European Union . . . As supreme commander, and therefore the strategic commander for Nato's operations in Bosnia and Kosovo, I already have direct experience of the high quality of Europe's armed forces.
>
> Many EU members, including non-Nato nations, have forces in the Balkans under the command of Shape. Others are part of Nato's partnership for peace programme, which is based at Shape. Multinational operations are a challenge, given the need to build and maintain a collective consensus while preserving operational effectiveness.
>
> Both the EU and Nato have recognised this and agree that Shape has a key role in the operational planning as a trusted and experienced source of military advice for the EU on the risks and resources required for any future EU operation. Shape's military and technical advice will help the EU and Nato to decide autonomously which organisation will take the lead.
>
> Nato / Shape experience in the Balkans has shown that many countries cannot deploy their forces quickly in crisis response operations. A key reason lies in the way many armed forces are still organised largely for national defence. This means that all too often key capabilities for deployment outside national territory – engineering, logistics and medical – are to be found in national reserve forces. As the only multinational headquarters which has direct experience of such operations, Shape was closely involved in the design of the [European Defence Initiative]. Experts from all Nato nations in Shape worked alongside experts from the EU throughout the summer and early autumn to provide technical advice.
>
> In the Balkans, too, Shape is working with European multinational formations to give them the vital operational experience they need if Europe is to act when the alliance as a whole is not engaged.

As Cohen later emphasized:

> There will be no EU caucus in Nato. If . . . they try or are too desirous of a separate operation in planning capability, separate and distinct from Nato itself, then that is going to weaken ties between the US and Nato and Nato and the EU. There should be a single planning operation, and not duplicative and redundant, because that will only weaken Nato itself.

He added:

> If there is openness, transparency and a non-competitive relationship [between Nato and the EU] the United States would remain committed. If there was an element of using the EU force structure in a way simply to set up a competing structure . . . then Nato could become a relic.

Without United States support, a European effort will be a damp squib.

Nothing could be clearer: the rapid reaction force is welcome to the United States as an arm of the alliance under the umbrella of Shape – that is with the Americans involved in approval, direction and planning – on missions where the Americans themselves do not wish to deploy troops. All this is obvious because without American approval and airlift support, no such deployment could take place anyway.

General Ralston's comments, in particular, underline one key point. The clumsiness of the intervention in Kosovo showed up really dangerous deficiencies in the Nato command structure, in particular the cumbersomeness of getting all members of Nato to agree to detailed operational decisions during the war, as well as overlaps and competition between the national forces. The Americans believe that Europe must streamline the effort to work effectively: the rapid reaction force would be a way of knocking European heads together.

Nevertheless, Nato remains the principal defence structure, and will have 'first refusal' of any military operation. Most likely, in any conceivable scenario, the European allies will be begging for American involvement and support, not spurning it, before taking any action of their own. Any member state such as Britain will be able to opt out of any joint operation if it does not see its own interests involved. No such operation is likely to go ahead in the face of opposition from the United States or other major member state.

In fact, the European force cannot be more than a mere flexible arm of Nato which permits action by the Europeans that the United States believes lies outside its own responsibilities and interests. This should, and has been, warmly welcomed on both sides of the Atlantic. The alternative – for the Europeans to continue to depend on America's taking the lead in peacekeeping – is simply no longer an option, given the current state of American thinking; for the Europeans to continue to abrogate their responsibilities would invite a major rift between them and the United States; for the Europeans to act autonomously would invite an even larger one, and potential American disengagement from Europe. The French, in particular, are deluding themselves if they seriously think otherwise.

What about the United Nations? This currently consists of a secretariat, headed by the Secretary-General, which runs a host of UN agencies; a kind of executive head, the UN Security Council, with five permanent members and a number of rotating members, which has the authority to legitimize UN peacekeeping and global interventionist actions; and the General Assembly, a kind of parliament, which is virtually powerless, but provides the only forum in which all the nations of the world can express their views.

It is a sadly flawed construct, almost as flawed as the League of Nations before it, but not quite so disastrous because no one placed any faith in it to resolve world problems from the beginning: the superpowers and their allies pursued their own agendas of conflict resolution largely outside the UN framework, which they merely used for legitimization and as a platform for their views.

UN agencies – the UN Development Programme, Unicef, Unesco, the UNHCR – do immensely good work. But the Security Council has been heavily manipulated by the major powers and the General Assembly has all too often sounded like a Third World megaphone for airing grievances against the West. In only one area does the UN have anything like moral authority – in authorizing armed intervention – and that is where Western powers primarily look to it as a kind of global grand chamberlain, giving its seal of approval and imprimatur. This role should not be belittled: any military action against an illegal act by a country must be legitimized by the world community or run the risk of itself being denounced as an act of piracy or global illegality.

It is tempting to believe that there are imaginative, original solutions to the awesome problems of the post-Cold War era. In fact, the answers are straightforward. Much more difficult is the process of acquiring the political will to implement them.

On terrorism and narcotics there is already a system of international co-operation, which has often scored major successes, but which needs to be deepened and given greater resources. On nuclear proliferation, the rudiments of a system of control are already in place, but a more explicit statement is needed on the consequences of the spread of such weapons to deter those that might be tempted to acquire them. The potential acquisition of nuclear weapons by a country outside the terms of the Non-Proliferation Treaty needs to be treated as a violation of the international order on a par with an act of aggression.

On the issue of global security in a world bereft of the disciplines of the Cold War, the position is a mess. Three elements would help to reorder it. First, the United States and its Nato colleagues have to spell out a new doctrine of when intervention is justified in a regional conflict. Second, it is essential that a structure of deterrence across potential conflict epi-centres be set up to make clear to potential aggressors before, rather than after, the consequences of their actions; this should be accompanied by an effective system of international arbitration, for which the UN might be suited. Third, the mechanisms of deterrence need to be put into place, and must command the widest international support possible, without in any way paralysing the intervention process itself, which must be rapid, effective and preferably American-led.

The first element can be dealt with quickly. The United States remains overwhelmingly the most effective military power in the West, and has no challenger for the job. The ad hoc interventions already practised by the Americans in alliance, for example, with Britain and France, have been entirely dominated by the former. No American ally can have anything but a marginal role to play in advising the United States when to intervene, because they bear the overwhelming brunt of the costs and the numbers.

However, consultation should be made as effective as possible. A world without a policeman would be awful to contemplate. Equally, the United States has every right to expect its allies to contribute, if not in men because of the constitutional restraints in Germany and Japan, then in money. For intervention to succeed, United States leadership is necessary for the foreseeable future.

Nor, in spite of domestic rhetoric, can the United States afford to abdicate from the world in view of the costs to itself, because of the world disorder which would follow. America initially attempted to shut itself off from global conflicts in 1914 and 1939 before being sucked in. As September 11 has shown, it cannot afford to do so even briefly now. The machinery for intervention remains that of American consultation with its allies through Nato, followed by an ad hoc alliance of those prepared to take part, without any need for the full alliance to concur, or any provision for veto or majority support. Military intervention cannot be decided by democratic vote in a large and cumbersome alliance. All for one and one for all was an appropriate doctrine when a Soviet threat endangered all of Western Europe. It is not appropriate for regional intervention where some countries may have major interests at stake and others none at all. Nevertheless, Nato, with its colossal experience of deterrence, remains much the best framework for intervention.

The second element, regional deterrence, is the most important of all: since 1948 much of the world operated under a system of global deterrence, which has served to keep international disputes in order. This system has now disappeared. Most areas of the world were governed by fear of superpower confrontation, or the withholding of client status. This no longer applies – hence the emergence of ancient nationalist and ethnic rivalries. It is clear, on humanitarian grounds alone, that this will have to be regulated by a structure of deterrence across most of the world's trouble-spots.

This seems hard, in some respects: the West, and the Americans in particular, can hardly afford to be involved in dozens of conflicts across the globe of no direct national interest to them. But in another respect it is easier: these conflicts are never likely to be on the global scale that deterrence in Europe required: most are tiresome, difficult and murderous little local confrontations. But the potential of the deterrent structure is to prevent them breaking out at all – and here Nato has shown the way. If potential local antagonists are impressed, well before the conflict, with the knowledge that aggression will immediately invite massive retaliation from outside, such conflicts are less likely to occur.

In most of the major American post-war interventions, misleading signals were sent as to whether action would be taken – and the consequence was a much bigger intervention than would probably have been necessary at the outset. This applied to Korea, Vietnam and the Gulf. If, however, defensive alliances were already in place, then the consequences of aggression would be apparent to potential perpetrators.

So, for example, if a formal defensive structure existed throughout the

Gulf which guaranteed the territorial integrity of all the states in the area, with an intense probability of Western intervention if it were violated, there would be much less likelihood of matters reaching this threshold. This would need to be buttressed by a proper arbitration mechanism, for which the United Nations, with its interminably legalistic approach, would seem perfectly adapted.

In the event of a dispute over oil, for example, a state could go to the UN and seek binding arbitration. In the event that this failed, and one country invaded another, the international community – America and its allies – would be obliged to intervene massively against the aggressor. But it is important that the UN, while performing a mediating role, should not have the sole power to authorize such intervention. This should be left to the military powers themselves, or the threat of intervention would not be credible. Further, in view of the undoubted limits on the projection of American military force, such deterrent alliances should be constructed on a regional basis.

It is possible to envisage a full security alliance of deterrent guarantees, based on the threat of Western intervention, in certain key areas: in the Gulf – in particular Saudi Arabia; in the Far East, again guaranteeing the territorial integrity of each nation there, which would be largely policed by the Americans, with minor European, Australian and New Zealand involvement; in the old Soviet empire, mainly left to the Russians, but with possible Western military units involved; and in Africa and Western Europe, with former European countries primarily responsible for their own former colonial territories, but with limited American and Soviet support.

Indignant criticism will no doubt bubble up at this juncture: such interventions would be impossible, because of the difficulty of identifying aggressor and victim, because of the impossibility of fighting several wars at once, because of the problems in securing domestic support for faraway wars, and so on. In addition, the real problem is that both America and Russia – never mind Europe – cannot see why they should get involved in other peoples' conflicts when their national interests are not directly at stake: a system of guarantees risks this occurring.

Yet this is defeatist thinking, and there is no other way in the long run. For nearly half a century the world was committed to mutual nuclear annihilation – something far worse than intervention in regional wars – and as a result no conflict occurred. There may have been an element of bluff in this: would a serious crisis or invasion of Western Europe really have triggered an overwhelming nuclear response by the United States? Neither side dared take the risk, so it did not happen. Similarly, some rogue state in the Third World might test the threat of massive Western intervention – but most would not take the risk.

If a deterrent structure is in place around the world, the chances of conflict are far reduced, even if occasionally the police force will have to be called out. A future Saddam or a Milošević is likely to think twice before attacking if he fears massive retaliation; yet when both launched wars of aggression, not only was no deterrent structure in place, they were given every indication that there would be no retaliation at all.

Regional deterrence and intervention may be a much easier task than global deterrence during the Cold War. General William Odom of the Hudson Institute prophetically argued in 1993 that the nature of American force projection would be altered unrecognizably as a result of developments in technology, in many ways making intervention overseas easier than in the past: aircraft have intercontinental ranges, ballistic missiles can strike against distant powers, and satellite and other means of surveillance allow American forces to 'spot' targets thousands of miles away. America can now contemplate long-distance war. The distant tactical operations centres which managed war close to the actual site of conflict can now operate on minute-by-minute directions from the National Military Control Centre at the Pentagon and the White House.

Naval warfare is changing radically: instead of the need to maintain a huge, expensive and vulnerable surface fleet, missiles can target enemy ships and submarines from land. Similarly, the old idea of a separate air force, charged with strategic bombing, may be obsolete. The impact of such bombing was always open to question. The Gulf War showed that co-ordination between ground forces and air attack was now necessary to the extent that the old distinction between the services – with its interminable arguments and costly duplication of resources – may now be actually harmful.

In fact the effectiveness of the massive aerial softening-up bombardment of Iraqi forces before the ground attack was launched in 1991 is open to question. The accompanying chart shows that the great majority of military equipment was destroyed during the ground offensive, not during the aerial bombardment.

Cumulative Destruction of Equipment in the Gulf War

Date	Tanks 4,550	APCs 2,880	Artillery 3,257
22 Jan	14	0	77
27 Jan	65	50	281
1 Feb	476	243	356
6 Feb	728	552	535
11 Feb	862	692	771
16 Feb	1,439	879	1,271
21 Feb	1,563	887	1,428
23 Feb	1,688	929	1,452
24 Feb	1,772	948	1,474
25 Feb	1,865 (41%)	992 (34%)	1,462 (45%)
26 Feb	2,040 (45%)	1,009 (35%)	1,505 (46%)
27 Feb	3,708 (81%)	1,450 (50%)	2,140 (66%)
1 Mar	3,847 (85%)	1,856 (64%)	2,917 (90%)

Source: US Department of Defense APC = Armored Personnel Carrier

Accuracy was sharply improved during the Kosovo War, but even so most of Serbia's armed forces escaped unscathed. In Afghanistan there was a further quantum leap in accuracy, but many al-Qaeda and Taleban forces escaped, as did most of their leaders.

Another lesson of the Gulf War is that the only country capable of large-scale military intervention around the globe is America, because of its clear lead in the unromantic field of logistics and force lift. Odom argued:

> At present, no country other than the United States has the means to provide adequate logistics for a major campaign far beyond its borders. This fact puts serious limits on where all armies except those of the United States and its allies can fight in the world. The logistics challenge lies not only in a state's capacity to provide supplies at great distances. It also includes capacity to produce certain kinds of weapons and equipment, to afford to stock them in adequate numbers, and to expand production of at least some of them, all in a fairly short time. Complexities in the production of new weapons raise serious questions about the adequacy of traditional approaches to surging production during a crisis or war. The World War II pattern has lost much of its validity for present industrial and technological realities.

The experience of the Gulf War revealed that the United States military had not prepared adequately for strategic lift to provide the necessary projection and supply of its forces. Iraq fortunately allowed the United States the time necessary to overcome its shortfall in strategic lift. The imperative conclusion is that strategic lift and logistics are fundamental elements of modern military power. They distinguish minor from major powers, and major powers can be reduced to minor status in some conflicts if they do not plan for sufficient strategic transports and stocks of matériel.

Odom argues that, despite this, America still has a long way to go in developing both air and sea lift capabilities. Another problem is that modern 'smart weapons' cannot be rolled off civilian production lines and hastily converted to military use in the event of general mobilization. Unless huge stocks of these sophisticated weapons are built up, a sustained war would quickly see the use of smart weapons tapering off into simpler, mass-produced, more old-fashioned weaponry. Indeed, after the successes in Afghanistan, the shortage of smart bombs made it impossible for a serious effort to be mounted in another country – for example, Iraq – for several months. America's technological edge might thus fade in the event of a long war: Odom believes that quality of weaponry is much more important than quantity – where in some categories it lagged behind the Soviet Union during the Cold War.

The requirements of modern weaponry also make the United States dependent on some foreign sources of technology, unless it pursues hugely costly policies of making itself self-sufficient in technology. The three countries essential to America's modern arms technology are Japan, Germany and South Korea. The United States thus will need access to at least one of these three in wartime.

In addition, America's space capabilities make its participation in any major allied military engagement absolutely essential. Odom writes:

Space-based systems played a greater role in the Gulf War than is generally appreciated. Both communications and intelligence means in space were critical determinants of the campaign. The global positioning system for ground navigation in the desert also depended on space components. The military uses of space in this regard promise to become more important. Although most of these capabilities were developed to deal with a NATO–Warsaw Pact conflict, they have proven very adaptable to small wars in the Third World. They give the United States and its allies advantages that are easy to underestimate.

Some of the new technologies, particularly for intelligence and space, cannot be fully exploited unilaterally by the United States.

Cooperation with allies, especially in providing ground stations, adds to their capacity. During the Cold War, some of these capabilities became a kind of 'public good' within US alliances. For the United States to enjoy them, they had to be shared with other states. This is likely to remain true in some respects for the indefinite future. It is not an exaggeration to say that modern technologies for warfare require coalitions of states for their most effective use. The implications of this are important, particularly for some second-level powers. Within coalitions including the United States, such powers enjoy much more military potential than would be possible outside such coalitions. Any plans for an independent European military coalition inevitably will mean a decline in the military potential NATO has given Western European states. A European coalition would lack the space capabilities, the en-route basing for force projection to distant regions, and other features. These technical realities are often ignored in policy debates about alternative military alliances in the post-Cold War era.

On the nuclear front, the collapse of the Soviet Union creates the possibility of virtually eliminating nuclear weapons carried by bombers, which are much easier to defend against than are those carried on ballistic missiles. The latter should be based in mobile launchers, not silos and, together with submarine-based missiles, would provide an adequate defence against a shrunken Russia or any other conceivable nuclear power. With Star Wars technology still in a much earlier state of development than generally realized, it is necessary to retain an adequate defensive structure against ballistic missiles.

Neither the United States, nor Russia, nor Western Europe can afford to let the present vacuum of responsibility after the collapse of the Cold War structures continue: a world of proliferating terrorism and regional wars that could even involve nuclear confrontation between other countries is otherwise in prospect, which would permit none of the big three the luxury of isolation. Security pacts, a mechanism of arbitration supervised by the UN, with the prospect of overwhelming deterrent force projection by the major powers, each taking prime responsibility for its own area of the world, are the long-term keys. This would authorize the developed world to intervene to prevent carnage in the developing world; otherwise the developed world will be shirking its responsibilities – and in an increasingly shrunken world, it can only get away with that for a short time. This is not the new colonialism; it is the new responsibility.

CHAPTER 12

THE NEW SECURITY ARCHITECTURE

The different strands and building blocks can now be brought together. If the analysis of the first part of this book is correct, the United States as dominant world superpower must engage more fully in the world in its own interests as well as that of the planet as a whole. The two building blocks it has at its disposal – Nato and the United Nations – are seriously flawed. At present, the UN provides legitimization for police action by the world community and brings together the whole global community in a debating forum, however ineffectual, while Nato provides a (today highly cumbersome) framework for taking international military action against a country which transgresses the world order.

It does not require a genius to see how these two functions – authorization and implementation – might be brought together into a new global framework, with both the authority to act and the ability to implement its decisions. To do this requires savage surgery on both organizations and, in Nato's case, probably even a change of name and formal dissolution of the alliance, retaining its core structures while allowing an entirely new structure to be built upon it. Specifically, the new order must be based on:

1. The reality that the underpinning of global security is the world's megapower, the United States. While some countries might be unwilling to acknowledge this publicly, it is the central truth of the global condition at the beginning of the twenty-first century: the United States is the cornerstone, the guarantor, the shield.

Others like Napoleon and Hitler have dreamt of such power: America is more powerful than any empire has ever been, and there is no discernible challenger. Napoleon's dream lasted just fifteen years, Hitler's 1,000-year Reich barely a decade. The United States has been the world's most powerful country for nearly sixty years, and its unchallenged master for more than a decade. Only its democratic, constitutional and benevolent nature and, sometimes, its indifference to the outside world, constrain it.

Possessed of the sole effective nuclear arsenal, a satellite surveillance system which will soon extend in detail to every corner of the world, armed forces that can arrive en masse to any world trouble-spot, the most technologically advanced aircraft, tanks and weaponry and a massive industrial base, America can do most of what it chooses; and the reality of American power will not go away, whatever the wishful thinking of others. If, in any global conflict, the Americans were to turn the full extent of their industrial might on an enemy, as in the Second World War but with an economy one hundred times as strong – heaven help its opponent.

While I would strongly argue that it is in America's interests to defuse global tensions, I have no doubt who would win in any showdown. The key lies in persuading the United States of the benefits of a particular course, not in believing that America can ever be overcome. Any global security structure must recognize this reality, and be thankful that the United States is such a benevolent megapower.

This established, the United States now has to take a hold on itself. It is no longer enough for the world's megapower to make foreign policy by the seat of its pants, in an ad hoc, occasional manner determined by which party is in power or the considerations of mid-term elections. Its own security, as well as that of the globe, is too important for that. President and Congress, Democrats and Republicans, politicians and public have a duty to resolve a new foreign policy consensus to fit the twenty-first century of the kind worked out at the end of the Second World War, and one which learns from the successes and mistakes of the following half century.

The neo-isolationism of the Clinton years and the erratic shoot-from-the-hip interventionism of the early Bush years (which is at least preferable) needs to be replaced with a more measured approach, involving at least three elements: a declaration of willingness to work in partnership with the rest of the world, preferably through representative regional groupings of nation states; a determination to extend and enforce international law throughout the globe; and a readiness to take the lead in backing up this new global outreach with force or the threat of force if necessary on a fair and systematic basis. In addition, the ideal of spreading democracy and freedom throughout the globe needs restating, while accepting that this cannot be done overnight. The first requirement of leadership is to treat other people as equals, even where this is obviously not the case, in an effort to secure their support and co-operation. This might be called the partnership concept.

The Clinton-era idea of America as an oasis of tranquillity in a troubled world with the luxury of looking after its own interests while watching war, strife and poverty from afar was brutally and definitively shattered on September 11. The concept of America as sheriff, doing its own thing against global bandits while cowardly bystanders watch, is so transparently childish that it is remarkable that it merits serious attention: even old-style sheriffs needed deputies and posses; anyway, who frames the laws? and who looks after the other side of town while the sheriff is away?

The idea of American empire, so favoured by neo-conservatives, is not just ridiculous but dangerous. It is not true: America has huge economic and latent military power but it does not occupy large parts of the globe (nor can it in the modern world; that is why the old European empires collapsed). It is also immoral: America has no right to dictate to the world on any issues save those of respect for legality, peace, human rights and democracy, which are universal. And it is heavily counterproductive, inviting other nations to assemble against it in the long run.

What is required is a much more modern concept – senior partner, chairman of the board, head of a grown-up family. The point is that the system and objectives of global law enforcement should be agreed by nine-tenths of the global community, and the actual enforcement should be accomplished by as many of these as possible, while acknowledging that megapower America will usually be at the head of the troop. The global Wild West or jungle of paranoid neo-conservative thinking in America, populated by rogue states, terrorists, criminals and law-breakers, is a myth: nine-tenths of the globe is peaceful, and 99.9 per cent of peoples would wish it to be so. They will respect America if it acts on their behalf as well as its own.

2. America's relationship with its allies in Europe and Japan. This may not seem obvious at a time of endless transatlantic bickering, as well as the distinctly tepid reception Washington has accorded European monetary union. There are even those who foresee Europe emerging as America's chief rival in the next century. Japan, too, has long been regarded with ambivalence by the Americans.

Certainly trade rivalry and competition for third markets will continue, and may intensify. And certainly there is backbiting from the Americans on the one hand about Europe's failure to contribute more to global security, coupled with intense criticism whenever Europe tries to take the initiative, and on the other from the Europeans about America's 'Wild West' diplomacy. But it is absurd to talk of hostility between the two when they have so much in common in dealing with the wider and far more serious global challenges beyond. Both are bound by a common democracy, a common heritage and a common economic system. Both share the same values of respect for the individual and interest in upholding global peace.

What is required is a much greater tolerance on both sides: a respect for America's economic vigour from the Europeans, and a respect for Europe's growing togetherness and efforts to find a voice in global affairs from the Americans. The European Union should not be seen as dangerous by the Americans: rather, it should be seen as a partner and ally. Seeking to fragment the Union and divide and rule Europe is no longer an option for the United States, and its most far-sighted foreignpolicy practitioners know it.

Far better for America's own national interests to be able to look to the European Union as a partner in exercising joint global responsibilities. If the Americans encourage Europe's foreign policy and global role, they will have less of a burden of policing the world and much greater influence with the Europeans. A long way down the line an 'Atlantic Union' between the United States and the European Union is, I believe, in prospect, creating a common market between Nafta and the EU – something only possible between equal economic partners. Similarly, the creation of the Euro is a force for currency stability, not rivalry with the dollar: co-operation between the two great currencies can only be good for global prosperity. If Russia eventually qualifies for EU entry, this axis of developed responsible powers will be strengthened.

The cultural, political and economic differences between the United States and Europe, and Japan, are somewhat wider, as are the divergences in strategic interests. Here again, though, it is in America's interest to retain mature Japan as its principal ally in an Asian region fraught with potential conflicts and competing economic interests between immature, newly emergent middle-sized powers. Not least, it is in America's interests to retain a special relationship with Japan to prevent the country ever re-adopting its former foreign policy course of national self-assertion.

The 'alliance of good' for global stability must thus be the United States, Europe and Japan, with Russia as a candidate member. For all its strength, America's burden as sole global megapower will become intolerable unless it is shared with its European and Asian partners.

3. A 'northern alliance' not seen as exclusionary or hostile towards the four-fifths of humanity outside it. However difficult this may be to sell to Congress or special lobbies, the United States, in its own interests, must seek to reach across the abyss of distrust that separates it and its northern allies from the non-European-descended nations of the world. America is uniquely well placed for this: for in addition to being a European nation, it is an African nation, a Latino nation, an Asian nation and a Middle Eastern nation. Precisely because of its overwhelming power it cannot afford to attract the mistrust of the rest of the world: its efforts to win friends should be redoubled. There are many ways to do this. America and its northern allies should reach out to Islam with its more than 1 billion followers, engaging moderate Islamic countries in a dialogue alternately on their territory and on United States territory at least once a year.

Regional leaders such as Brazil, Mexico, South Africa, Nigeria, Egypt, Saudi Arabia (and one day Iran and Iraq), India, China, Indonesia, South Korea, Taiwan and Australia should also be engaged in a continuous dialogue, as should regional economic and security groupings. A much higher level of better-targeted economic aid needs to be assembled in a 'development offensive' to widen the still all-too-narrow oases of economic development in the Third World. However much this goes against the grain, the United States must re-engage – while seeking to reform – the UN, as this is still the main forum for consultation between the developed and developing world.

4. UN reflection of the reality of the world today, not as it was half a century ago. Ideally the Security Council would be chaired by the US as a single global superpower, although politically this is probably impossible. What is not impossible is a Security Council that reflects the real division of power in the world – in fact one made up of the second tier of world powers after the United States, specifically Japan, Germany, France, Britain, Italy and Canada (G7) as well as Russia, China, Brazil, Egypt, South Africa, India and Australia (regional leaders). The principle of rotating membership for other countries on the Security Council should be retained.

The principle of the veto would ideally be abolished, although this may prove to be politically impossible, in which case the five countries that are its permanent members (the United States, Russia, Britain, France and China) should retain it. Otherwise a simple majority of the permanent members should suffice to authorize international intervention. In this fourteen-man directorate it will be seen that the Western countries have a majority, but then so do smaller countries outside the Nato area; in addition, there would be five non-white members, compared with just one at present.

Internationally, any military action would ideally be authorized by the widest possible consensus. All four recent major military interventions – the Gulf, Bosnia, Kosovo and Afghanistan – would have secured overwhelming support from such a council (probably unanimous in the last two instances). The chances of the United States and its allies failing to secure a majority for intervention in a case they deem appropriate would be very remote.

5. Nato should be renamed the Alliance for Peace (AP). This would be divided into two components: its core countries; and its member states. Core countries would today consist of the United States, Canada, Britain, France, Germany, Italy and Spain. Russia and Turkey might also be allowed to join. Global military intervention would require the consent of the core countries. Each of these would assemble a substantial force of volunteers from their own armies (say 20,000 each) to form a Peace Army for secondment to UN-authorized interventions as and when the necessity arises. These forces would be the elites of their own armies and remain based in the mother countries as part of their structures until called upon for intervention, but exercised to prepare them for joining an AP command. Additional regional forces could be used depending on the extent of the emergency.

The ordinary, non-core membership of the new Nato, the Alliance for Peace, would be extended, and include countries from across the world. The conditions for membership would be a willingness to participate; subscription to the major international organizations and peace treaties (e.g. the Non-Proliferation Treaty); and constitutional democratic government respecting the rule of law and the rights of its citizens. Ordinary AP members could provide volunteer forces, in particular on a regional basis, for the Peace Army if they so wished; but they would not have the say to authorize intervention (other than to refuse to join in a particular intervention).

By limiting the Peace Army to just six or possibly seven or eight core countries, the new organization would be much more operationally effective than the cumbersome existing alliance, and would obviate the clumsy need for the United States to get its allies on board, which manifested itself after September 11 (of course only as many members of even the core group as were necessary – in practice the US would decide – need actually take part).

By widening its membership to all supporters of international order across the world, the AP would have far greater legitimacy than Nato currently enjoys as just a rich man's club. By establishing the concept of (usually) all-volunteer forces as well as internationalism, armed intervention would be possible with much less of the morbid obsession that domestic media and publics have for 'body bags' – the fear of casualties incurred in foreign wars. By placing authorization for the use of Peace Army forces under the control of the expanded UN Security Council, such interventions would no longer be the actions of one nation acting alone or with one or more of its allies, but authorized by a UN council acting in the name of the whole global community.

It is important to emphasize that the new structure would not – could not – preclude acts by a country in defence of its own interests. The purpose of the structure would be to provide global legitimization for justified interventions around the globe, and the means to bring participants in such interventions together in an effective common structure. But if, for example, the United States chose to act alone to enforce an action which it saw as essential to its security (as it did in Panama or Grenada, for example) or if Britain did so (as, for example, occurred in the Falklands), provided that this was legitimized, there would be nothing to stop either country.

6. The new structure would work in conjunction with a series of local security alliances, with the aim of engaging the most powerful countries in each region. These would embrace South and Central America; North Africa; sub-Saharan Africa; Central Europe; the Middle East; South West Asia including the former Soviet republics; the subcontinent; South East Asia and Australasia; and East Asia. Such security alliances would provide for an early warning mechanism to determine the onset of approaching crises, and a mandatory arbitration procedure to resolve disputes between member states.

Those refusing to take part – possibly because they fear a judgement against them – would lose the advantages of membership, in other words they would not be consulted on regional issues, and even on those affecting their own security. The United States and other core AP members with direct interests in the area concerned would also be members of the regional security alliance and might, although not necessarily, take part in arbitration, policing or intervention. Typically, any intervention decided upon by the Security Council would seek the support of the regional security alliance members and their participation (where this was not a matter of local sensitivity) in the intervention force.

7. A key component of the new global security structure would be the early warning system for impending regional crises. Member states and UN missions would have a duty to report potentially threatening situations or build-ups in their regions to a secretariat answering closely to the Security Council, so that these could be brought to international arbitration. This is intended to avert future Bosnias and Rwandas before they happen (not that the international community was unaware of these looming situations, but there was no statutory duty to offer any response). Countries refusing to co-operate or accept the results of arbitration would run the risk of UN-sponsored global intervention against them.

While such intervention would not of course be automatic – rigidity is as dangerous as it is unworkable in international systems – and each instance would be decided on a case-by-case basis by the Security Council, taking into account its feasibility, the seriousness of the violation, the likely duration of the commitment, etc. – the normal course of action would be effective military intervention authorized by the world community. This step-by-step and predictable approach to potential global flashpoints is in marked contrast to the current state of uncertainty surrounding each international dispute. Equally, situations like the current absence of a dialogue between India and Pakistan over Kashmir, or between China and Taiwan, would become things of the past; these would have to be discussed at regional forums and, if tension escalated, arbitrated upon; again, a state that refused to talk or abide by arbitration would put itself in the wrong.

This seven-point charter would bring together the current jumble of unilateral American-led military enforcement, multilateral bodies, the UN and Nato, into a single global architecture, with clearly defined procedures and roles for all countries, as well as realistic provision for mediation and enforcement. To the immense majority of countries outside the immediate 'loop' of the United States and its closest allies, it would bring huge reassurance; the United States would address their immediate concerns directly in partnership in the context of their own regional security organizations; military interventions would take place as and when authorized by the UN through the enlarged Security Council, which would include a regional head, and would be debated by the General Assembly; and every country that qualified would have the right to be a member of the Peace Alliance, the military alliance and implementing branch of the UN.

There will be those in the United States who argue, why bother with additional structures and bureaucracy? The reply must be that if the current unilateralism of American global policy is allowed to continue, the country will find itself not just alone in a sea of enemies but witness to flare-ups across the world that will be very costly to stop, disrupting its trade, inflicting serious damage on its interests abroad and resulting in September 11-style strikes.

Obviously America would survive such attacks and inconveniences, but why undergo them at all? Friendlessness is not an option in an increasingly integrated world. The danger for America is not isolationism – that is impossible today, and the consequences of such a policy are brutally evident even as far back as 1941 – but isolation. The world will respect a global system which it has shaped and which it feels it is part of, however much it might object to individual decisions; but it will increasingly contest an order which is enforced arbitrarily and unpredictably by a self-appointed sheriff who it believes is often acting merely in his own interests.

A framework for a new global order, the flattering offer of partnership by the United States to all countries that respect that order, co-operation in regional security organizations, consultation and friendship – these are the hallmarks of the global leadership that America finds itself the first country in history ever to be in a position to practise, an awesome responsibility. They are also the hallmarks of the democratic, open, multi-ethnic society that is the United States.

Unilateralism, the imposition of solutions, lack of consultation, capriciousness, naked self-interest, defensiveness in its dealings with friends, and edgy aggressiveness in its dealings with adversaries – these are the characteristics of an arrogant imperial power certain of its military muscle but unable to persuade others of the righteousness of its cause. The megapower would certainly prevail, but as a global imperialist. This would be profoundly unworthy of a great nation founded on the three ideals of liberty, the rule of law and a fair deal for all, and unworthy of a people characterized by generosity and friendship. In the very long run such an approach is doomed, as empires have been throughout their history – as no country knows better than the United States, conceived in opposition to empire. If it treats the rest of the world as potential enemies they will become so in reality, and eventually coalitions will form that will challenge America. It is ever so.

Instead, in the position of global dominance without competition that the United States finds itself in today, it has a unique opportunity to fashion an entirely new role for itself, one unprecedented in human history: that of benevolent head of the family of nations, settling disputes through negotiation and conciliation rather than force, commanding the affection and respect such a role deserves, and with an indefinite tenure at the head of the table for as long as both survive.

The United States has frittered away the past decade celebrating its new status as uncontested world megapower (just as it took six years of chaos after independence for America to formulate a constitution). The next ten years should be spent putting into place the relationship that will allow it to enjoy benevolent dominance for decades to come – or it will find itself to be a continent surrounded by a hostile, anarchic and possibly war-torn world which it will not be allowed to ignore (the lesson of September 11). America's best use of megapowerdom is to share it.

Disengagement is not an option; but the United States can choose to engage the world on its terms while it yet enjoys considerable global goodwill (although this is gradually ebbing) and to shape the international agenda; or it will have to engage when events are largely beyond its control, at times and places of its enemies' choosing. The choice is between the United States against the world or a United States with the world, in which America accords the same respect to other countries that it does to its own citizens drawn from so many other lands. That, truly, would be a worthy goal.

PART III

THE NEW STATE AND THE NEW ECONOMY

CHAPTER 13

THE NEW COMMUNISTS?

A decade after the fall of communism, and well over a century since its birth, is a new spectre stalking the world? Birmingham 1998, Seattle 1999, the City of London 1999, Prague 2000, Genoa 2001, New York 2002, Porto Alegre 2002, Barcelona 2002, Florence 2002. The World Social Forum, Jubilee 2000, Reclaim the Streets, Stop the City, Attac, Corporate Social Responsibility, the Black Bloc – the venues and the names are spreading, with varying objectives and degrees of militancy. With the ignominious collapse of communism (anti-capitalism) in the early 1990s, a 'new Bolshevism' seems to be springing up in its place, as fissured as the groups immediately preceding the Russian Revolution but universal under the banner of 'anti-globalization'. Even the crassly repressive tactics in places like Seattle, Genoa and Barcelona are reminiscent of the repression of the Bolsheviks before the First World War.

When in 1994 I predicted the birth of 'a new communism . . . born of today's capitalist failings' and spoke of 'the globalization of capitalism as presenting greater challenges still', I little suspected it would happen so soon. Like communism, anti-globalization feeds on the injustices of a rapidly changing world. Like communism, it has the potential to grow exponentially. Like communism, it is diffuse in its objectives, crassly ill-targeted, largely negative and destructive, and has the potential to inflict great damage. Like communism, though, governments, international organizations and corporations ignore it at their peril. For they have the power to stop it in its tracks not through crude repression but by returning to their democratic roots, acting with greater sensitivity towards ordinary people across the world, and displaying a greater sense of responsibility.

What is globalization? In 1994 I wrote that this was the most potent, potentially beneficial and potentially dangerous phenomenon of the post-Cold War world. Since then, a huge anti-globalization movement has sprung up which seems almost as ignorant of what it is fighting as the capitalists are ignorant of the system they favour. The answer is that while it certainly exists, it is a much more limited and partial phenomenon than either adversary believes.

Globalization has, of course, been facilitated by the quantum leap in communications across the globe – from air-travel to fibre-optic telecommunications to the Internet. In 1960 a three-minute, 3,000-mile telephone call cost $50; today it costs some 50 cents, while the Internet is free. This has favoured huge movements of capital across the globe – the essence of globalization. The flows have been expressed in four principal ways: the exponential growth in world trade; the spread of multinational operations beginning in the 1960s and 1970s; the spread of international bank lending during the 1980s; and the flow of speculative currency, equity and futures transactions during the 1990s. But the growth of these flows has actually been a much more partial and inefficient phenomenon than either its supporters or critics allow, and its impact has been both beneficial and destructive.

A quick glance at 'globalization' reveals that it is nothing of the kind. It is in fact provincial: the global activities of a relatively small number of companies and markets based in three dominant areas – North America, Europe and Japan – upon a limited number of countries such as the Asian 'tigers' or enclaves of larger countries like China or India who offer access to plentiful labour, a relatively well-educated workforce, large markets or cheap raw materials. In this respect it could be clumsily called 'enclavization', 'entrepôtism' or even economic colonialism rather than globalization, because it affects such a restricted part of the globe.

A glance at the so-called boom in trade confirms this: while the volume of trade has grown enormously, trade as a percentage of the GDPs of the three dominant blocs has, if anything, diminished, rising between 1982 and 1992 from 19 per cent to 22 per cent in the United States, but falling from 28 per cent to 17 per cent in Japan and 23 per cent to 19 per cent in the European Union. Fully 40 per cent of all cross-border trade is between subsidiaries of the same multinationals. Foreign direct investment has not mushroomed to compensate: three-quarters of such investment has instead taken place between the three blocs. A further 14 per cent has flowed to the handful of favoured countries and regions plus the coastal provinces of China. Some nine-tenths is thus limited to the developed world and its economic satellites, which have only a quarter of the world's population.

The multinationals sell the overwhelming majority of their products to their home countries (some three-quarters in the case of Japan and Germany, and two-thirds in the case of the United States and Britain). More than 90 per cent of Japan's multinational assets are in Japan, 60 per cent of Britain's in Britain, and 70 per cent of America's in the United States. Multinationals were responsible for around two-fifths of total world output in 1990, but only 7 per cent of this went abroad. As Paul Hurst writes, 'these are not footloose capitalists but are rooted in a major market in one of the three most prosperous regions of the globe.'

With regard to the financial markets, while in 1995 some $1.2 trillion was traded daily across the world, about double the daily GDP of all the OECD countries put together, while total trading in financial derivatives in 1994 was around $20 trillion – greater than the combined GDPs of North America, Western Europe and Japan – these are highly misleading figures. As Hurst points out:

> The huge volumes traded daily on the financial markets and the huge positions built up in the derivatives markets appear to dwarf and dominate the real economy, but one must remember of what these vast sums are actually composed. The main players are financial institutions that utilise the assets which they can raise in national markets for financial products, and their ability to borrow on the strength of these assets, repeatedly to 'churn' large sums through the various international financial markets. Their traders either earn small profit margins by exploiting small and temporary imperfections between the different world market centres, or establish positions on future market movements, suitably hedged to minimise risk (if they are careful). When a given cycle of trading ends, the borrowed sums are met by market outcomes if trading has been successful, and assets are redeployed. Typically the percentage return on such vast sums is quite modest, although the profits from repeated churning can be large in total.
>
> Institutions have to use these earnings to meet their obligations to depositors, to pensioners and to life policy holders. International trading thus recycles a substantial portion of its output back into the domestic financial system.

If globalization is as limited as this suggests, a number of significant conclusions can be drawn which go against today's conventional wisdom.

The first is that 'globalization' affects relatively few countries. Thus the left-wing outcry that the world is being taken over by a handful of multinationals is wide of the mark: most of the world is largely untouched. The problem with globalization is that there is not enough of it: most countries neither suffer nor benefit from the phenomenon: they go on as before. A glance at most of Africa, Latin America and the interior of Asia confirms this. Because globalization has not spread widely enough, and it's unlikely to do so under the control of a small number of companies which prefer the markets they know best, a 'Marshall Plan' is required with multilateral institutions co-ordinating and directing private sector investment into countries which undertake the necessary structural reforms. The World Bank already does this on a small scale in conjunction with the IMF. It needs to be done on a much bigger scale, and more flexibly.

Second, developed-country trade unionist and protectionist bleats about investment going abroad to cheap-labour competitors are similarly unfounded: most of the investment stays at home.

Third, free-market economists are equally mistaken when they assert that globalization is spreading competition and entrepreneurship across the world. When taken together with the growing concentration of multinationals through mergers – cross-border takeovers ran at 6,000 for a value of $230 billion in 1995 – economic power is being concentrated in fewer hands as a result of globalization in relatively few countries.

Fourth, the host countries of the major multinationals – only three if the European Union is treated as a single block – still possess immense powers of regulation, particularly if they co-operate.

Fifth, capital flows, although huge and increasing, are not necessarily ungovernable.

Finally, a related point, *pace* Bobbit, the state has not contracted in the face of these changes, rather it has changed, or even expanded – in particular by becoming 'global' itself – by co-operating through multilateral institutions. For example, the World Trade Organization charter binds its members to its statutes, and a WTO ruling against a member state is compulsory unless unanimously opposed by all member states – a tougher system of control than even that exercised by the EU. With companies competing to attract foreign investment, a nations independence to pursue different economic strategies, to levy higher taxation or to provide greater welfare states has been seriously eroded, but their regulatory power at a transnational level in co-operation with others has increased. Since 1945 more than a hundred regulatory international organizations have been established: the OECD, the Bank of International Settlements, the WTO, the International Organization of Securities Commissions and the Paris Club are all examples, along with international players such as the IMF and the World Bank. Regional groupings include the EU, Efta, Nafta, Asean, Apec, the Andean Pact, Mercosur and the Central American Common Market.

In one key area the state is being radically transformed by 'globalization'. While its power may even be expanding, as is the undirected power of financial markets, the democratic constraints upon the state are shrinking fast. Whatever electorates decide, governments increasingly make decisions at a supranational level through agreements with other governments, supranational bodies, or by appealing to the marketplace. Britain's New Labour government, which has pursued rigorously orthodox and free-market economic policies, is a case in point.

Back to the original triangle that lies at the heart of government and society. Powerful organizations are getting more powerful and are increasingly operating across borders. The state is probably getting more powerful and similarly transcending borders. The ordinary mass of individuals from whom it derives its legitimacy are losing their ability to restrain and influence the state. A yawning democratic gap is opening up.

This is a profoundly dangerous development, a historical regression, which explains much of the cynicism, apathy and non-participation of ordinary citizens who feel, with good reason, that whatever party they vote for will follow much the same policies tailored to the global economic environment. It also explains why many citizens are now looking to international action or protests to make their voices heard. A demonstration at Westminster is not much use if the real power is in Washington or Davos or Geneva. Moreover, because most international organizations are unelected or indirectly chosen, the street rather than the ballot box appears a better place to protest their decisions. Only through making these organizations more accountable to governments, and business more accountable to shareholders, can this dangerous trend be reversed. The next few chapters will look at the forms of political organization of the state today. Those in this part will look at the economic forces that are eroding democratic choice. Part IV will suggest how these problems can best be confronted.

CHAPTER 14

THE STRONG,
THE WEAK AND THE STATE

One of the great achievements trumpeted alongside the collapse of communism was the triumph of capitalism and of free-market economics. The Soviet Union was seen to have imploded under the weight of a lumbering system of bureaucratic central planning, unresponsive to the needs of the market and repressive of the spirit of free enterprise that is so central to human nature.

In many respects this was true. But its converse, that Western capitalism had forged a super-efficient free-market system, was not. Within months of the fall of the Berlin Wall, the global champion of free-market economics, Mrs Thatcher, had been driven out of office. George Bush, a more lukewarm exponent of the doctrines of his predecessor, Ronald Reagan, was to be ejected from office within two years by a Democrat with much more interventionist ideas.

Under President Clinton, the West went down the Japanese *keiretsu* (cartel) route. In October 1993, the White House announced 'a historic new partnership aimed at strengthening US competitiveness for developing technologies for a new generation of vehicles'. The research and development divisions of General Motors, Ford and Chrysler were placed effectively under the supervision of Mary Good, under-secretary of commerce for technology. In addition, President Clinton bailed out the shipbuilding industry to the tune of some $6 billion in loan guarantees. Shipbuilding was to enjoy a substantial export subsidy – another leaf out of Japan's book. President George W. Bush's administration has continued these policies.

In France, free-market economics had never operated under the Mitterrand presidency; even with the victory of the right in the 1993 election, these were modified by the country's tradition of central planning and opposition to free trade which soon continued under Prime Minister Pierre Jospin. Even in Germany, a degree of planning remained a key to economic success, which, by the late 1990s, was faltering under the monetarist restraints of the Bundesbank. Chancellor Gerhard Schröder returned to this tradition. In Italy and Spain, state intervention continued to play a key role even upon right-of-centre governments. The first flush of free-market experimentation in Poland and one or two other Eastern European countries was quickly reined in by political realities – notably the impact upon ordinary people; the same happened in the Soviet Union in 1994.

In China, Japan and the Asian economies, competition was accompanied by continued massive state direction and a consciousness of the need to disarm discontent through lifetime employment, safety nets, protected agricultural prices, hidden unemployment and other artefacts. While the extreme form of bureaucratic centralization represented by the Soviet Union had certainly collapsed, it seemed that free markets and free enterprise had anything but unequivocally triumphed.

What had happened, then, in Eastern Europe? What revolution had occurred if not an assertion of democratic free-market values? George Kennan, architect of the policy of post-war Soviet containment, argued vigorously in March 1993 against the idea that communism had been 'defeated' by capitalism. In fact, what had happened was more fundamental – a triumph of the self, of the human yearning for self-expression from within those countries. It had been an assertion of independence by a rising middle class, and a crushed working class, against the suffocating weight and conformity of communism, a situation that occurs rarely in history when a system becomes too heavy, unresponsive and blatantly corrupt. The direction of popular feeling was neither necessarily free market, nor democratic, although initially it flowed in those directions. It was nationalistic, ethnic, sectarian, individualist, anti-big.

Soviet communism had long derived its sole legitimacy as an expression of nationalism. Thus, the Eastern European upheaval was directed by suppressed nations against the colonialism of the Soviet Union; within Russia, instead, the pressure for change, while strong, was less than that among its subject peoples. The wave of revolt in Eastern Europe was not so much pro-capitalist as anti-authoritarian, the authority of the remote, absolute state represented by Soviet communism, the kind of elemental force that has spawned furious change throughout history – from the English Civil War, to the French, American and Iranian revolutions.

It can be argued that the collapse of Soviet communism was achieved as a result of a decision imposed from above by President Gorbachev. It does not detract from his historical achievement to assert that he was brought in to defuse what the Soviet leadership already saw were irresistible pressures building up within the system. The eruption of popular anti-communist sentiment in Eastern Europe and the Soviet Union, once the iron hand of repression was relaxed, showed how close both were to a revolutionary condition. Exactly the same assertion of the self would explode against any system that had become too remote and authoritarian for its own good – including other types of political regime, and even the institution of capitalism itself.

The root tension within any social structure is that between self-expression and authority. Contrary to some philosophies, it bears asserting at the outset that both are necessary and, provided they do not get out of hand, beneficial. To go back to the very roots of political theory, there are three elemental bases of any political system: individuals, strong individuals and the state (society, government).

A few political philosophers have held that in a perfect society, all individuals can be entirely self-regulating, acting with full responsibility, in particular, so as not to impinge upon the freedom of others to do the same. To most political philosophers, and just about anyone with any experience of life, this may be an ideal to be worked towards, but it can be no more than that. In Hobbes's pessimistic 'state of nature', life was nasty, brutish and could be a short one for ordinary people, who were preyed upon by the strong (Hobbes, like other conservative political philosophers, believed that human nature could not be improved, and did not accept the notion of progress). Whether because, as in some countries, the state became dominant in each society, or whether because, as in others, the weak looked to a benevolent leader to control the excesses of the strong, the central authority came into being.

This was looked upon as the defender of the weak against the predations of the strong – a role it did not always fulfil, often becoming chief predator itself. The triangle is true, of course, of much lesser social organisms than the nation state – anything from a school to a village to a military unit. The ordinary pupils, villagers and soldiers look to the teacher, village headmen and officers to protect them from the biggest and strongest among them. Similarly, in any modern society, people count on the police to protect them from criminals.

All this seems blindingly obvious. Yet it has to be stated to advance beyond the model of free-market libertarianism which was recently fashionable in America and in Britain. For them the model contains only two elements: the individual and the state. In this scheme of things, the state is a tyrant and usurper of the freedom of the individual. Any society in which state power is minimal is a better society. This neglects the point that in the state of nature – where there is no state – the strong tyrannize the weak. There is no freedom for the majority where there is no central authority governing in the name of society as a whole. Indeed, the state derives its traditional legitimacy, in Anglo-Saxon political theory at least, as guarantor of the rights and freedoms of the individual.

Of course, in an enormous number of cases around the world, this has not worked out in practice. In the real world, the state has shown an all-too-frequent propensity to accumulate power and sometimes work in alliance with the powerful interests it is supposed to be protecting the people from. Over time constitutional safeguards evolved in the best political systems to prevent this happening, hedging about the power of the state and guaranteeing personal freedoms. Over time, too, legitimacy based upon force has not been enough – although even in a democratic state this is an important component. In countries where the power of the middle class or even of the working class is such as to threaten the state, the latter has had to secure their consent to government – usually through elections.

But none of this alters the fact that the state, the central authority, came into being, and derives its legitimacy, from the notion that it exists to protect the rights of the individual from his stronger peers. The state is different from other powerful individuals to the extent that it should enjoy the contractual legitimacy and consent of the people. There is no freedom in the state of nature, the society without the state, because the strong – the warlords, the barons, the big industrialists, the monopoly unions – predominate. In many cases people live in fear of a state which has encroached on individual freedom, but removal of the state as a political entity would result in much less freedom for the individual as the strong bully the weak again.

All parts of the trinity – the individual, the strong individual or interest and the state – are necessary and inevitable. In the ideal society a balance is achieved: the individual is protected, but does not inhibit the strong from acting as the driving force of society; the strong are not permitted by the state to push others about, but their energies are channelled on behalf of society as a whole; and the state is permitted to regulate the strong for the good of society, but not to dominate either them or the weak. There is an equilateral triangle. Conversely, if the equation gets out of balance, instability results. If the state becomes too powerful, an explosion of the self may follow. If the strong overpower the weak, the latter may call for a stronger state. If ordinary people become too self-assertive, there may be a demand for tougher rule from the centre or the strong.

A brief excursion into the basis of political theory is necessary in order to understand the crucial notion of consent. Thomas Hobbes was in every sense the father of modern political philosophy. Before him, the main philosophical and theoretical justification for exercising authority and the power of the state had been religious, best exemplified by the doctrine of the divine right of kings, that God had empowered some to have authority over the rest. This legitimized the exercise of power through family dynasty and brute force. Hobbes, between 1640 and 1651, pioneered three immense leaps in political thinking.

He argued that the source of the state's authority was man, or more specifically his nature, not God (this had the welcome effect of divorcing the Church from responsibility for political affairs, a development which many enlightened clerics welcomed). The reason why state authority was necessary was because in the state of nature the selfishness of men would compete so fiercely that it was in the self-interest of all that order be imposed.

From this he then deduced, most controversially, that the state must have quasi-omnipotent powers. He was widely denounced as the prophet of absolutism for this observation. But, in fact, by rooting the source of the state's authority as deriving from the needs of ordinary people for order and security, he was the forerunner of those who argued that the state only existed to serve the people. For if it failed in its task of keeping order and protecting their interests and, above all, their lives, it forfeited its right to exist.

This presaged the idea of many subsequent political philosophers that there is a social contract between rulers and ruled. The former ruled on the understanding that they delivered good government to the people and if they failed to do so, they forfeited the right to rule. This was a revolutionary idea at a time when the right to rule had been considered God-given, and the ruled had an obligation to obey. The new idea of contract became the foundation of liberal democracy, for it was father to the view that government required legitimacy through the consent of the governed.

Although Hobbes could never have imagined it, he was the father of the Western democratic tradition. For Hobbes, the need for state authority arises from the horrors of the state of nature, where man's passions govern everything in competition with other men (he did not condemn passion – rather, he argued, as future economists were later to argue, that self-interest creates wealth, that the passions are the origin of just action).

As Perez Zagorin writes:

> The state of nature is the hypothetical alternative to the common-wealth and sovereignty. It is a condition, therefore, in which human beings in pursuit of their ends are subject to no power or authority beside what they can casually impose upon one another . . .
>
> A situation is displayed to us of unending and oppressive fear. There is no property, for nothing is anyone's with certainty, nor any arts, letters, sciences, or the comforts of life. An unremitting war of all against all takes place, and every man goes in terror of his life. In such circumstances, the notions of justice and injustice have no place, every man having a right to everything, because everything is, in a literal sense, as much his as it is anyone else's.
>
> The first foundation of natural right is this, that every man, 'as much as in him lies, endeavours to protect his life and members'. Because man's absolute priority is self-preservation, which is not guaranteed in the state of nature, he is prepared to hand over authority to the state, which can guarantee him his life through enforcing the law on those who might threaten it.

Zagorin conclusively exposes the contradiction in Hobbes's theory, and how in fact his theory of absolutism limits the ruler contractually and through natural law:

> However it may have originated, government rests on contract – this is all Hobbes is concerned to argue. Contract, therefore, is a postulate of reason, and need never have occurred as a distinct event. The emphasis here upon the contractual foundation of government is not inconsistent with Hobbes's general position, as has sometimes been erroneously contended. It is, on the contrary,

a strict deduction from his previous assertions. His theme has been
that men make and maintain government as the rational expression
of their right to preserve themselves. Government, in consequence,
must always presuppose consent; and the hypothesis which corre-
sponds to consent is that of a covenant. For this reason, Hobbes
insists upon the covenant in despotic and institutive government
alike; it is the correlate to his belief that the political order is
unthinkable except as something in which men voluntarily acquiesce to secure life and contentment . . .

But the power of the sovereign is, in practice, limited: no man,
says Hobbes, 'is bound to obey a command which frustrates the end
for which . . . sovereignty was ordained.' The sovereign, he argues,
'has . . . no other bounds, but such as are set out by the . . . Law of
Nature . . . All punishments of innocent subjects are against the law
of nature . . . to equity as being a precept of the law of nature, a
sovereign is as much subject as any of the meanest of his people';
sovereigns 'may in diverse ways transgress against the . . . laws of
nature, as by cruelty, iniquity, contumely and other like vices.'

Zagorin concludes that there was a deep cleavage running through
Hobbes's thought:

This cleavage is nothing trivial. It lies, rather, at the very heart of his
political philosophy, and arises from the conflict between two
fundamentally opposed tendencies: the stress on natural right,
and the desire to validate any government as such. The former is
liberalism, the latter absolutism. Between the two, it is the stress on
natural right which is unquestionably stronger, for it is that concept
on which his theory rests. Even against his will, therefore, Hobbes
has forged a revolutionary weapon. If he defended absolutism, it
was only on the grounds that absolutism is in the general interest;
and should this be denied, as his own thought gives us a basis for
doing, absolutism disappears, and in its place is substituted the
liberal system for which the philosopher's nineteenth-century uti-
litarian disciples contended.

It is, then, quite accurate to call Hobbes 'a radical in the service of
reaction', and to hold that his ideas contain 'the germs of the
constitutionalism he combated'; indeed, I should say they contain
more than the germs. He has affirmed that men, in virtue of their
humanity and apart from every social circumstance, possess a

natural right which it is the commonwealth's duty to fulfill. This right involves more than a claim to bare preservation; it is a right also, as we have seen, to 'contentment', to 'commodious living', even to 'happiness', for government is instituted so that men may, as far as their human condition permits, 'live delightfully'. This being the case, we are irresistibly brought to conclude that men will be rationally and morally justified when they reject a commonwealth in which the fulfillment of their right has become an impossibility.

Thomas Locke later built this up by arguing that government had an obligation above that of preserving the lives of its subjects to protect and respect individual rights, in particular that of private property. George Sabine pointed out that Locke interpreted natural law 'as a claim to innate, indefeasible rights inherent in each individual. Of such rights that of private property is the typical case. Consequently his theory was by implication as agnostic as that of Hobbes. Both government and society exist to preserve the individual's rights, and the indefeasibility of such rights is a limitation upon the authority of both.'

Other English political thinkers were to elaborate these beginnings into a full theory of personal rights and liberties. John Stuart Mill was to argue that all individuals possessed absolute rights which they partially submitted to the community in which they lived, and the object of the community was the pursuit of the greatest happiness for the greatest number. The American constitution went one further and enshrined 'life, liberty and the pursuit of happiness' as self-evident rights which the state was bound to respect. The key points about the Anglo-American tradition of political philosophy were, first, its emphasis on individual rights independent of any bestowed by the state, from which the latter derived its authority, and which it could not violate, and its absolute acceptance of the need for a state to guarantee those rights. The two are completely interdependent – without the state there can be no respect for rights in the state of nature; without respect for those rights, the state has no purpose, no legitimacy, and deserves to be overthrown.

It can be seen that, over several hundred years, the principal bone of contention for political philosophers in Britain was not whether the state had a right to exist – that was taken for granted, in fact during hundreds of years of monarchy could not even be questioned – but the balance between the state and individual rights. In some continental countries, notably Germany, political theorists held that all rights derived from the state, a view that was to be terribly warped by the doctrines of communism and national socialism last century. The argument about the balance between the state and individual rights was then quite naturally to evolve into the wider subject of how the state should observe those rights and represent the individuals it had to protect, which then led on to the question of extending the franchise and establishing modern democratic institutions.

However, towards the end of the eighteenth century, parallel to this steady development, there came into being a different line of thought which, while responding to the economic advances of the time, represented a throwback to the political thought of the Dark Ages in its advocacy of the interests of the new 'strong' – confident capitalists. This was the new economic thinking, which was to exercise an enormous and disproportionate importance in the twentieth century, dazzling in its mathematics, but short on insight as to how human beings actually work. The prime purpose of the new economics were twofold: to justify and legitimize the new inequalities of wealth and domination by owner and manager over worker under private enterprise; and rigorously to resist 'wasteful' regulation and intervention by the state.

The first of these two objectives of the new economics was not too difficult to achieve. Inequality had been a part of the human condition for recorded time, and the capitalist could argue that he was at least contributing to the common wealth by his enterprise. The second involved much more specious arguments, as a large part of early state interference took place to regulate the appalling exploitation and conditions of the Industrial Revolution, and another large part existed to prevent small businesses being trampled underfoot by larger monopolistic competitors.

When Marxism emerged as a monstrous child of capitalism, using the pseudo-scientific, anti-individualistic theories of Kant and Hegel to justify its doctrines of state absolutism, the economists that were the intellectual handmaidens of capitalism were quick to elaborate their own equally repellent mirror image. This view proclaimed that the state had no place in economics, that absolute freedom for the market was as perfect a mechanism for creating a prosperous and well-ordered society as Marxists argued that absolute state control of the market was.

For Marx, there was 'dialectical materialism', historical inevitability, a completely 'scientific' view of history, which obeyed laws just as physics or chemistry did. For the free marketeers there was the mathematical precision of the market mechanism, working smoothly and ingeniously to ensure that the equation balanced perfectly in the end, whatever appearances and the consequences in the real world outside might suggest. Both theories had in common that they were formulated in academic, intellectual hothouses, far from the coalface of politics and business – although elements of both were to make ample use of such theories.

Marxism was a crude child of the new scientific age, whose philosophical insights were a throwback to sixteenth-century political absolutism. The new advocates of laissez-faire went back still further in political insight, to the Dark Ages, the barons and the Wars of the Roses. Both ran counter to the evolution of all political thinking since the time of St Thomas Aquinas (and, arguably, Aristotle).

The new doctrines wrought havoc with the cosy British political system of the time – broadly divided between a party representing town (the Whigs) and country (the Tories). The latter clung to the more structured and paternalist order of the countryside, and enjoyed a deferential vote among the new industrial working classes. The Whigs instead attempted to do all things for all men: to straddle both the new tough-minded capitalist anti-state interests and the cause of social reform and workers' rights. It was notable that while many of the great reformers of the nineteenth century were Whigs (later Liberals), those who put most of the reforms into practice were Tories (later Conservatives).

The Liberals broke spectacularly apart in the early twentieth century, as a result of Lloyd George's unequivocal espousal of the workers: the capitalist component migrated to the Conservatives, its social reformist and worker components to the Labour Party, leaving the Liberals a sorry rump. In the past decade, the Conservative Party has shown signs of being taken over by its ex-Whig, stridently capitalist component with its passionately anti-interventionist message, which threatens to be divisive and to endanger the party's unique cross-class appeal.

The thrust of the argument of the major new economists, in particular Hayek and Friedman, partially elaborated in antipathy to the absolutist state theories of the communist world was, in essence, that the state which governs least is best. Virtually any interference with the marketplace creates inefficiencies and distorts it. The government's job is simply to remove any distortions in the way of the free functioning of the market. Governments have no obligation to alleviate the effects of recession, to stimulate economies out of slowdowns, to impose curbs on wages, to regulate or subsidize business.

In practice this ideological stance was far too severe: governments remained necessary to protect society from the worst effects of the market, which was as much a 'state of nature' as anything envisaged by Hobbes in the political sphere. Certainly this ideological assault had a major effect in cutting back on the fat of bloated government bureaucracies; but in its crudeness, it lost sight of the need to make government more accountable.

Indeed in some respects it developed a momentum as authoritarian as that of the communist systems it so disliked. The new orthodox economists frequently suggested that the market needed no regulation from the state. Instead economics should be left as an autonomous, independent 'state of nature' of its own – as if economic priorities are not usually determined by political choices. Many new economists argued that the democratic state itself, with its politicians currying public favour in elections, was an interference in the marketplace and was best set aside by benevolent military regimes, independent central banks, and 'technocratic' economic managers. Thus was 1,000 years of political evolution from feudal warlordism to liberal democracy to be swept away by the new 'expert' economists.

The contradiction was that many of those same economists were the most ardent advocates of political freedom in the communist bloc. Indeed, political freedom was often identified with economic freedom as being indivisible. This was to boomerang when political freedom began to clash with the tenets of the absolutist free market. In the end, its advocates were grudgingly forced to accept that, in a democratic society, politics represent the preferences and aspirations of society, are dominant and are here to stay. The free market, far from being a new ideal of society, has to accept subordinate status to politics, and is in no sense autonomous and independent. Society cannot, and must not, return to the state of nature in the huge sphere of economic activity, as that represents the model of society in which there is least freedom of all, the tyranny of the strong over the weak; so political philosophers over the centuries have long concluded.

This excursion into basic political theory is necessary to emphasize the point that central authority is not in itself bad. Indeed, it is essential, except in a society of perfect human beings. Many wielders of central power are corrupt or despotic, as Lord Acton believed; many are conscientious people grappling with enormous responsibilities. For any country or institution to work, you cannot do without it. Excess freedom from it may be freedom only for the gunmen, the robber barons, the big industrialists, or the monopolistic unions to tyrannize and trample upon the freedoms of the rest of us.

While authority is thus a necessity, self-expression is also an absolutely fundamental human force – arguably the most fundamental. From a very young age the smallest child seeks to express himself, to do what he wants to do without help – even if it is not right. It is not normal for the human animal to do what he is told, even if this is in his own interests and he is unable to see them. It may be necessary for him to be forced to do certain things when he cannot be convinced by reason – hence the existence of a legal system at all.

But the reverse side of the coin to the assertion that authority is necessary – to run a country, company, military unit, village, school, family – is that those in authority who ignore this hankering after individualism, even lust for self-expression and personal freedom, do so at their peril. It can topple authority in an explosion of popular feeling – with, as in most revolutions, usually unsatisfactory results for all concerned, governors and governed. Such an upheaval was the recent one in Eastern Europe, although, unusually, it has generated more freedom than repression, more order than chaos (with some exceptions, perhaps where authority had become so fundamentally corrupt (Romania) or ethnic tensions had been suppressed for too long (Yugoslavia)).

The key point about communism was not that it was based on a specific economic-political credo which another – capitalism – triumphed over. It is that pure authoritarianism had gained control of the credo, utterly detaching itself from ordinary people's yearning for self-expression. Exactly the same could happen to any political or economic system, socialist, capitalist or otherwise, that neglects the need for self-expression. In fact, any glance at the political systems that have grown up around the world shows that all other forms – dictatorships, military regimes, even sometimes excessively bureaucratic democracies – have sometimes lost the consent of the governed. Capitalism as an economic system could similarly fail.

The striking thing about the development of contemporary capitalism is the extent to which its organization, particularly in very large companies, increasingly resembles that of the communist regimes it so detested: the systems have shown marked signs of converging, even if there are important differences. This is not so surprising. Capitalism, like any other structure of authority, works through hierarchy, just as communism and feudalism did. Methods of control are usually much the same; the hierarchical-bureaucratic structure of communism (which itself was rooted in traditional ruling structures rather than Marxism) was its governing force – along with Russian nationalism, which at least gave the system some legitimacy in the eyes of the people. The increasingly hierarchical-bureaucratic structure of capitalism could just as easily prise it away from its roots – the need to sell competitive products in the market.

CHAPTER 15

FATHER AND SON

B ut in an even more important way, capitalism itself does not represent the pluralist opposition to communism that it thought it did. The key to understanding the rise and fall of world communism is to realize that it was essentially a child of capitalism: a deformed and parricidal one, to be sure. But communism sprang from capitalism in three key ways: it was, most obviously, a reaction against the working conditions imposed by capitalism; its stormtroopers were – or were supposed to be – the sullen proletariat of the capitalist system, the urban workforce; and its system of organization, while radically different in its nominal responsibility (to the workforce, not the owners) and centralization (to the state, not individual companies) was based in most other ways on the capitalist organizational structure which, in turn, probably had military origins.

In this, as in so much else, Marx got it wrong. He believed that the key to a worker state was ownership of the means of production. In fact ownership, even by his time, was becoming increasingly irrelevant to the control of industry. It was the powerful managers, with a new structure of hierarchy beneath them, who really began to run the businesses; this soon was to be true of enterprises in communist states. Worker control was never a serious Marxist option, except in some sections of the extreme left, and is probably unachievable. But the structure of communist enterprises, although generally much larger and differing from capitalism in some key respects, as we shall see, was modelled on that of capitalist enterprises. Hierarchical management delegating key responsibilities to lower levels of specialized officials ultimately supervising the workforce – bureaucracy, to put it baldly – was an invention of capitalism, not communism.

Max Weber, the father of the study of modern organizations, normally a subject of extreme aridity, expressed this precisely, and also despaired about it:

> Today it is primarily the capitalist market economy which demands the official business of the administration be discharged precisely, unambiguously, continuously and with as much speed as possible. Normally the very large modern capitalist enterprises are themselves unequalled modes of strict bureaucratic organization. Business management throughout rests on increasing precision, steadiness and, above all, the speed of operations . . . Bureaucratization offers above all the optimum possibility for carrying through the principle of specializing administrative functions according to purely objective considerations. Individual performances are allocated to functionaries who have specialized training and who by practice learn more and more. The 'objective' discharge of business primarily means a discharge of business according to calculable rules and without regard for persons.

Although capitalism has evolved somewhat more flexibly than he outlines, many capitalist enterprises still recognizably answer to his description. He lamented:

> Already now, rational calculation is manifested at every stage. By it the performance of each individual worker is mathematically measured, each man becomes a little cog in the machine and, aware of this, his one preoccupation is whether he can become a bigger cog . . . it is horrible to think that the world could one day be filled with these little cogs, little men clinging to little jobs, and striving towards bigger ones . . . this passion for bureaucracy is enough to drive one to despair.

Any brief historical study of the rise and fall of communism must begin with a look at the system that gave birth to the changeling. Capitalism first evolved with the provision of capital to set up industry. This might be called the age of the owner-entrepreneur in late eighteenth-century Britain. It took place during the mid- to late nineteenth century everywhere else in the developed world (and the process is still under way in developing countries).

As firms expanded, contractual relationships became the norm: workers performed specific tasks for a specific rate, according to contract, and were not employees of the firm. Worker specialization followed, through the introduction of new industrial processes and production lines, as well as an expansion in the size of firms, which required supervisors. Thus the professional manager came into being, at around the same time as the growth of capital markets, in which ownership became divorced from day-to-day management. Middle management – men with the job of telling others what to do, instead of actually producing something themselves – flourished.

Today there is the 'post-Fordist' – that is 'post-assembly-line' – revolution, which is only just beginning and promises to transform the traditional methods, in which the huge vertical structures of capitalism, its bureaucracy and segregated workforces become increasingly unnecessary while information technology and automation make them obsolescent, paradoxically concentrating control in fewer and fewer hands. Of these, the first four preceded or accompanied the spread of Marxism, and directly influenced it.

A glance at Britain's Industrial Revolution starts with capitalism in its first two 'pure' phases, those understood by Adam Smith. The tough, risk-taking owner-entrepreneur is there with his workers. In this early stage the problem was to find capital: in Britain the Agrarian Revolution both displaced workers from their traditional lands by creating cultivation on a much larger scale, and yielded the kind of profits that could be invested in the new industries. (Other countries like France, Germany and Japan, arriving at industrialization later, used the state to channel capital to industrial enterprise.)

The industrial historian R. Edwards describes the first British phase:

A single entrepreneur, usually flanked by a small coterie of foremen and managers, ruled the firm. These bosses exercised power personally, intervening in the labour process often to exhort workers, bully and threaten them, reward good performance, hire and fire on the spot, favour loyal workers and generally act as despots, benevolent or otherwise. They had a direct stake in translating labour power into labour, and they combined both incentives and sanctions in an idiosyncratic and unsystematic mix. There was little structure to the way power was exercised, and workers were often treated arbitrarily. Since workforces were small and the boss was both close and powerful, workers had limited success when they tried to oppose his rule.

Josiah Wedgwood was justly hailed as the epitome of the entrepreneurial class, catering for a new mass market. The historian G. M. Trevelyan wrote:

> Wedgwood, in his Staffordshire works, catered for all classes with his pottery and jasper ware, creating a big market both at home and abroad . . . He experimented ceaselessly with new scientific methods, new moulds and new designs. He was indefatigable in promoting canals and turnpikes to reduce his costs of transport and percentage of breakages, and connect his remote Staffordshire potteries, built far inland, with his raw material of China clay in Cornwall and with the overseas markets he hoped to exploit.
>
> Between 1760 and 1790 he succeeded in filling not only England but Europe and America with his goods. During this period, pewter went out of general use and was succeeded by earthenware plates and vessels, so that eating and drinking became more hygienic and more delicate. In the next generation, men no longer spoke of 'common pewter' but of 'common Wedgwood'. Thus a radical paper writes satirically of 'lords and ladies' as the 'china trinkets of the nation, very superior to the common Wedgwood pottery of the mass of the people'.

In the United States and in Japan, the same phases occurred later. But in Britain in the middle of the nineteenth century, there occurred the third great phase, the specialization of labour. This replaced the subcontracting system which was a feature of early capitalism where enterprises paid people at home to produce goods which a relatively small entrepreneur sold to a bigger one, for a specified contract price. 'Internal contracting' began to decline towards the end of the nineteenth century, being replaced by the more formal system of large companies directly employing large numbers of workers in specialized, usually dreary, tasks made possible by the new technology.

This did three things to capitalist organization. It resulted in the creation of middle management, people whose job was to tell others what to do. Then there evolved the modern bureaucratic structure of the large enterprise based, probably, on that other large organization of the time, the army. People had to do as they were told, middle management had to defer to senior management. A hierarchy evolved.

And it soon became clear that management was much more powerful than the owners of the enterprise who, when they were interested at all, were at one remove from its actual running. The bigger a firm became, the less likely it was to be owned by a single man or family; as it expanded it would require more capital, raised from others alongside the original shareholding. The original owners would be less likely to exert real control over the tentacles of the business. The age of the professional manager had arrived.

Thus, almost simultaneously in the large firm, a large industrial workforce was created, doing largely repetitive work, in accordance with the primitive machinery of the time, and a bureaucracy of only indirectly responsible management with power hierarchies all of their own. As stock markets expanded, the relationship between ownership of an enterprise and its control grew more remote still. Meanwhile, the ethos of capitalism, as preached by men like Ricardo and Malthus, was that the workers were responsible for their own poverty, and should be paid the minimum for the maximum work. The conditions of Britain's Industrial Revolution, which were later to be repeated during the industrialization of virtually every other major nation, were created.

However, in the Britain of Robert Owen and others, an awareness developed of the terrifying conditions which resulted – particularly when it was observed that the fall in the death rate between 1780 and 1810, which was considerable thanks to medical advances, suddenly stopped still over the next forty years because of the unspeakable conditions in the slums.

G. M. Trevelyan sums up the conditions of the time:

Throughout the 'forties nothing was done to control the slum landlords and jerry-builders, who, according to the prevalent *laissez-faire* philosophy, were engaged from motives of self-interest in forwarding the general happiness. These pioneers of 'progress' saved space by crowding families into single rooms or thrusting them underground into cellars, and saved money by the use of cheap and insufficient building materials, and by providing no drains – or, worse still, by providing drains that oozed into the water supply. In London, Lord Shaftesbury discovered a room with a family in each of its four corners, and a room with a cesspool immediately below its boarded floor. We may even regard it as fortunate that cholera ensued, first in the year of the Reform Bill and then in 1848, because the sensational character of this novel visitation scared society into the tardy beginnings of sanitary self-defence.

Edwin Chadwick, Secretary to the Poor Law Commissioners, argued that:

The prisons were formerly distinguished for their filth and bad ventilation; but the descriptions given by Howard of the worst prisons he visited in England (which he states were among the worst he had seen in Europe) were exceeded in every wynd in Edinburgh and Glasgow inspected by Dr Arnott and myself. More filth, worse physical suffering and moral disorder than Howard describes are to be found amongst the cellar populations of the working people of Liverpool, Manchester and Leeds and in large portions of the metropolis.

As a result of his report, the Public Health Bill of 1848 was passed, a first step towards the social legislation in Britain towards the end of the nineteenth century. These scenes of squalor are today repeated across the world, from São Paulo to Shanghai. The combination of intense misery, which some suggested was less bad than poverty in the countryside (which at least had the virtue of being less unsanitary and often subject to some kind of paternalism), the inhumanity of the new employers and the creation of a large urban population was to provide the fodder for the left – the trade union movement, communist egalitarian revolutions, and the socialist creed of state intervention.

In the circumstances of contemporary capitalism, this was highly understandable; only in Britain, with its tradition of social reform, and the United States, with its pioneering frontier spirit – if you didn't like your lot, you moved elsewhere – was serious unrest avoided. In America revolution reared its head with the Depression, and the 'bonus march' on Washington – only through Roosevelt's skill in defusing social unrest through Keynesian economics was capitalism saved. Elsewhere in Europe and Russia, in the throes of early industrialization, strikes, demonstrations, left-wing attempts to seize power and fascist reactions became common.

Communism, that most appalling authoritarian blight on humanity, was thus a direct descendant of capitalism. Communism, a reaction against the excesses of capitalism, was used by a series of intellectuals and power-seekers taking advantage of the blind rage of the working class to seize power. Communism became an authoritarian system modelled on bureaucratic capitalism but with none of the latter's accountability and efficiency.

The next major development in capitalism – which towards the end of this century has become all the more management-led – is computerization, which threatens the whole tottering system of hierarchy, control and empires of subordinates. 'Post-Fordism', as this is called in the jargon, will do away with thousands of jobs and will concentrate power ever more into the hands of a small management clique. This is being bitterly resisted by many lower level power wielders, whose domination of their own workers gives them prestige; but it is inevitable. A further recent development is that through the introduction of stock options, bonuses and other mechanisms, senior management has acquired the ability to secure great wealth through maximizing share prices, which makes the managerial elite still more remote from the concerns of those beneath them.

This subject will not be addressed in this book, because it is a challenge beyond, and less immediate than, the danger of global economic and political anarchy in the post-Cold War period. But it is of immense long-term importance, because it will divorce wealth and employment in a socially dangerous way, and because it will lead to further concentrations in the balance of wealth and power which could create a backlash.

Meanwhile, the advent of communism in the early twentieth century can only be understood in terms of the conditions created by capitalism, just as potential social and political disaster in the twenty-first century will have to be explained in terms of the globalization of modern capitalism and its failures. Communism inflicted untold misery on the world, but arose directly from the failings of the crude capitalist system that preceded it.

Capitalism was and is the most productive system the world has ever known – harnessing human energy and self-interest to create wealth. But it is up to public policy-makers to channel its crude and vibrant energy in a direction that benefits the whole of society, or at least does not create a revolutionary backlash. Currently global capitalism is reaching a critical mass of irresponsibility and remoteness that could incubate another horrific anti-capitalist changeling early in the millennium. It is in this way that communism, a crude, sub-intellectual theory of no great worth or scholarship, had a huge and fertile breeding ground of discontent to exploit that ignited revolutions, plunged whole regions into war, killed millions and put into place the most tyrannical and repressive regimes the world has ever known.

CHAPTER 16

THE SIX STRUCTURES

The collapse of communism in the Soviet Union and Eastern Europe lifted the hand of authoritarian conformity from a large swathe of mankind and, with some justification, led to exultant claims that the world was entering a new era of liberal democracy. Freedom, it seemed, was infectious, breaking out all over: in Latin America during the preceding decade, a gaggle of military governments had given way to elected civilian ones; in the Philippines, the dictator Ferdinand Marcos was toppled while traditionally military-run countries like Thailand, South Korea and Taiwan made tentative steps towards democracy. Even in Africa, a traditional one-party system – that of Zambia – held an election that resulted in the peaceful ejection from office of one of the continent's senior statesmen, Kenneth Kaunda (much to his credit). In South Africa, the remarkable political maturity of two leaders, Nelson Mandela and F. W. de Klerk, permitted the holding of a relatively violence-free election in 1994, and an astonishingly smooth transfer of power to the black majority – so far – over a potential racial powder keg. Indonesia's President Suharto and Serbia's Milōsević are the latest to fall. Kenya's one-party domination has now been overturned.

Democracy had become fashionable; but huge parts of the world remained under authoritarian rule, and the triumph of the ballot box could hardly be taken for granted. What had gone, with the collapse of communism, was the specious claim that an unelected, authoritarian system of government can impose itself on the people because it represents their – or more specifically the workers' – best interests, and that a government which claims to rule in the name of equality has no need for popular consent expressed through elections, as it can be taken for granted that it represents the will of the people. This was the monstrous lie, the self-deception that was cruelly exposed by the popular revolts in Eastern Europe.

To many free-market ideologues, the collapse of the Soviet Union and of its empire in Eastern Europe represented the triumph of freedom in its purest sense. People had refused to endure the weight of totalitarianism any longer; and, individually, they broke away to express themselves through an unfettered free market. The power of the central state was everywhere on the run. In fact, this was far too simple a view.

The collapse of the Soviet Union represented the destruction of the absolutist anti-democratic totalitarian model of state control. It did not mark the defeat of the state as such. The role of the state around the world continued to be immense, both in democratic and authoritarian societies. No purely 'free' country exists anywhere – that is, without a powerful central government. Even in international relations, over the past forty years, the rule of law has made a major entrance, governing international agreements and treaties, regulating the extensive contracts between nations, and even the ways in which wars are fought, and seeking to order the relations between states. Only in one field, that of global economics, was any attempt made to assert that this was outside the realm of international regulation and supervision.

Given the power of the state in virtually every country around the world, a power that needs constant checking to ensure that individual rights are not violated, but which nevertheless is here to stay, the issue becomes not one of rolling the state back – except from some economic activities which it should never have strayed into – but one of authority: from what does its legitimacy derive?

The following chapters will look at the six modern sources of state authority: dynasty; imperialism; force; rule by elite or the establishment (aristocracy or oligarchy in the past); confucianist authoritarianism; and liberal democracy. It will conclude that only the last, because it is founded on the consent of the governed, an unwritten contract between ruler and ruled, and a system of rights and the rule of law, has true legitimacy and will prevail in the long run.

As the world slowly adjusts itself to that fact, political explosions and dangerous security crises are likely to occur, contributing mightily to the instability of the post-colonial world. Alongside emergent nationalism, the efforts of doomed authoritarian systems to stay atop the bubbling magma of the demand for popular rights is likely to produce ever more violent upheavals. If liberal democracy seems likely to triumph in the end, appalling security crises, as despotisms struggle to retain their hold, are likely along the way. This part also seeks to identify some of the potential flashpoints and fault lines. Again, the probability here is that unresponsive systems are probably doomed, not that state authority as such is. As long as the state remains powerful – and it will for the foreseeable future – the important thing is for it to become representative, responsive, accountable and respectful of personal rights, not to seek to roll back its authority in favour of forces which are none of these things.

CHAPTER 17

THE KINGS MUST DIE

The legitimacy endowed by family rule lingers on in only a few backwaters. With the exception of a handful of small, tightly knit communities, such as Tonga, and the constitutional monarchies of Western Europe, where kings and queens represent continuity and tradition without power, only in the Middle East are there monarchs that rule as well as reign. To understand why, and to judge their prospects of survival, one must look briefly at the peculiar history of the region.

But first a glance at why the legitimization of family dynasty has failed elsewhere. It is, probably, the world's oldest form of government, and certainly the one that has survived the longest. Without offering too many hostages to social history, in the most primitive societies, the notions of family, paternal authority, and a hierarchical ordering of class seem to have been one of the earliest forms of human organization. While other forms certainly existed in ancient times – Greek 'democracy', Roman rule by consuls, then emperors – hereditary monarchy seems to have retained enormous appeal across the centuries, sustained by not quite believable theories about the 'divine right of kings', yet sometimes in vigorous opposition to the Church.

How was this achieved? Regal behaviour, fine clothes and dazzling displays of pomp were only part of the explanation, because they do not sustain monarchy today. In largely rural societies, the three most important sources of power were ownership of the land; the ability to raise armies – which was partly related to ownership of the land, through enlistment of those who worked upon it; and the dispensation of patronage and favours, including landed estates.

In early societies, the most important landowner of all – although rarely achieving a monopoly – was the king. Where land ownership and wealth were the most important factors in royal power, it was natural that the traditional means of passing them on, inheritance, should apply too to royal power. Hereditary rule was a natural extension of the hereditary right to property.

Yet when one of the three sources of royal power came under challenge, the Crown's authority was diminished, as it was if there was any challenge to the monarch on grounds of heredity, by, say, another claimant, or because of the Crown's failure to produce an heir. Thus if coalitions of large landowners could be assembled against a king or queen, along with the men they could raise in arms, the monarch's powers of patronage would count for little (although a victorious king could create a new class of supporters by stripping his opponents of their lands and distributing them to his supporters).

With the evolution of a middle class, in the shape of yeomen (independent) farmers and merchants, for example in England in the sixteenth century, the king, from being *primus inter pares* among the landowning class, based his claim to rule on his desire to represent the wider interests of his countrymen, both in regard to overseas threats and to the selfish interests of his fellow landowners. This worked for a while; indeed it represented the final brilliant fling of royal power, the absolutist dazzle of the renaissance prince.

With the seventeenth century in England, and a little later elsewhere, came the realization by the new middle class that they were the backbone of the nation, the new source of power, and when vain and inept rulers like James I, Charles I and James II tried to rule without consent, the gentry rose in opposition. By the end of the seventeenth century in England – again a little later in most countries – real royal power was a thing of the past (as was rule by the big landowners), although the façade was preserved. The middle classes ruled – because they were more numerous, independent and wealthy as a class. As their size grew, so the political system became more complex, reasserting itself through the limited vote, the extended vote and, eventually, as the pressures from women and the working classes made themselves felt, universal suffrage.

Royalty by now was a mere spectator, enjoying its privileges only on sufferance from the middle classes. The monarchs that clung to absolute power in the face of this inevitable social change tended to get overthrown – with greater violence the longer they clung – as in France or Russia. Huge though royal landholdings might still be, the middle class as a whole now controlled infinitely more wealth, the previously loyal royal army increasingly owed its allegiance to the nation rather than a particular king, and patronage was now largely exercised by the government in office, not the king.

So why has absolute monarchy defied the laws of political gravity in the Middle East? The answer is twofold: the sheer poverty and primitivism of the region, until this century; and oil, an enormous and peculiar form of extreme wealth. It is hard to underestimate that poverty in the past. More arid than any region except Saharan Africa, the bulk of the Middle East afforded a living only to hardy nomads moving from oasis to oasis. Permanent settlement was possible only in three principal areas: the fertile Palestinian coastland; the Yemeni upland; and relatively fertile and irrigated northern Iraq and some parts of Syria and Lebanon.

Unsurprisingly, these were the most developed and populous regions, rich in architecture and civilization. Perhaps because of the relentless pressures of their existence, the Arabs and the Jews, both an extremely talented people, had created great civilizations in Jerusalem, Sanaa, Babylon, Damascus – and the fount of three of the world's greatest religions: Judaism, the oldest; Christianity, with the widest following; and Islam, with perhaps the greatest appeal for the world's poorest people (unsurprisingly, as it was born in the sparsest and most impoverished land of all, the Arabian peninsula).

The power of the Middle East's religions, alongside the vastly sophisticated civilizations they spawned in ancient times, has to be set against the desperate struggle for existence in pitiless terrain of most of the region's inhabitants. Between the overcrowded cities with their tilted tower blocks with several storeys in the feudal uplands of Yemen and the placid greenery of northern Iraq overlooked by Alpine-style mountains lies a vast sea of sand where small, hardy groups of Bedouin swirled about, romantic in appearance but to the few settled peoples of the Middle East, the lowest of the low, without property or land and condemned to wander, as nomads. While undoubtedly attractive in the mould of other wanderers – gypsies, cowboys, the tribes of central Asia – Bedouin social organization was as primitive as could be imagined: familial, clannish, the organization of primitive man throughout the ages – only the sophistication of Islam as a religion leavened it.

By the beginning of the last century there was little to suggest that this forsaken, inhospitable corner of the world was ever going to escape hardship or ignorance. Most of it was under the control of the vastly corrupt and centralized Ottoman Empire. While a world war was being fought in Europe, the Turkish grip was relaxed as Britain gave its support to the Arab revolt and installed the most prestigious Arab family, the Hashemites, direct descendants of the Prophet, to rule Iraq and Jordan. The Arabs' natural leaders were installed in place of the Turkish imperialists; they were, above all, a family dynasty, representing the prime source of social allegiance of the region. In Saudi Arabia, a new and powerful tribe, the al-Saud, installed itself in control of that peninsula, ousting the Hashemites. The primitiveness of the region was underlined by the way the British carved up the new countries with lines on a map.

Within years, a revolution had occurred: oil, the fuel of modern industry, had been discovered in large and unbelievably readily exploitable amounts under the poorest parts of Arabia: Saudi Arabia, the Gulf states, southern Iraq and, on the Mediterranean, Libya. The derided nomadic peasant warriors of Saudi Arabia, capable only of living in tents, were suddenly, vastly, the richest people in the Middle East. They were cultivated by the Americans, who were relentlessly determined to chase the British out of Arabia. Within a few decades, with the quad-rupling of oil prices in the early 1970s, followed by their doubling at the end of the decade, the Arabs' wealth was, quite literally, mind-boggling.

Meanwhile, the traditionally rich, civilized, developed parts of Arabia – Egypt, Palestine, Yemen and northern Iraq – were reduced to the status of poor relations. Populated, sophisticated and hard-working, they were blocked from sharing in the wealth of the desert by the frozen colonial boundaries, and were reduced to the status of supplicants. Perhaps no greater irony has ever existed in modern history: Egypt, cradle of modern civilization; Yemen, certainly home to the loveliest Arab architecture; Syria, cradling one of the most beautiful cities in the Middle East, Damascus; Palestine – shorn by the creation of Israel of its richest lands, but actually containing the most developed of the Arab peoples – were reduced to begging for alms from the nomads they had despised for millennia.

For their part, the nomads and the scruffy trading statelets of the Gulf responded to the oil bonanza in the time-honoured way of any humble man winning the pools. They went wild. Gin palaces were erected by a people that lacked any architectural tradition of their own around the shores of the Gulf, creations not of ancient Arab but of the flashiest British interior designers.

The Saudis, busy demolishing what was left of the old city of Riyadh and erecting dreary, Dallas-like skyscrapers in its place, built one of the world's largest airport terminals at Jeddah shimmeringly, and not entirely ineffectually, based on the design of the sole architectural inspiration the Bedouin could call their own, the tent. Kuwait, built upon perhaps the most torrid and bleakly sunbaked part of the Gulf, a combination of mudflats and scrub desert with a climate dominated by overheated sandstorms, founded a large, featureless skyscraper city, with a network of motorway rings, as extensive as those around a large Western capital, that dwarfed the few cars that used them.

Unsurprisingly, given their wealth, the inhabitants fled their over-heated, bogus cities for older, more attractive ones – London, Paris or Rome – for months at a time. In the Arab societies that had contact with the real world, uninsulated by the oil wealth, tumultuous change resulted. The French mandate in Syria and Lebanon was finally forced out in 1946. Iraq's monarchy was toppled in 1958. Egypt's bloated and corrupt King Farouk had already gone. Libya's elderly and unworldly King Idris followed in 1969.

Appalling as most of the successor regimes were, they followed the general rule that absolute monarchy in a modern, complex, pluralist world is a thing of the past. Monarchy lingered only in the Gulf and in two largely desert kingdoms: Morocco and Jordan. Kings Hassan and Hussein owed their survival to skilful diplomacy and political shrewd-ness, the support of a feudal and loyal praetorian guard, and the essentially desert and underdeveloped nature of their countries. Now Kings Mohammed and Abdullah represent a younger generation.

Gulf royalty owes its survival largely to money. Unlike the ownership of land – the traditional fount of royal power in Europe, later overtaken by merchant and industrial wealth, thus undermining the monarchies – the oil is entirely owned by the state, which meant the royal families concerned: any benefit from it is enjoyed by those families, and by no one else. Any who seek wealth or patronage have to go to those families.

The populations of the oil-rich states are necessarily tiny: the nomads had been few, the territory vast. Citizenship of states no one could ever wish to migrate to but for their wealth has been hard to come by: as the Gulf states grew oil-rich, the destitute from places like Pakistan and Bangladesh were conscripted by their own misery to do the menial work. The lowest Kuwaitis employ such servants, and expect to retire at forty on generous welfare payments. There are huge amounts of money to be dispensed to very few people. Revolutions are usually made by the economically desperate. There are none of the latter in the oil states; provided they conform, they are treated very well. But after the initial euphoria and shock of wealth wears off, there are signs that the ambitious are beginning to assemble.

The keys to the survival of the Gulf monarchies are also their probable long-term undoing: the control of oil revenues and the wielding of huge powers of patronage and a degree of ownership that no medieval monarch could aspire to: no British king, for example, ever controlled three-fifths of his country's income, as Saudi Arabia's Prince Abdullah does. The small populations involved represent another means of control: even a people of 17 million scattered across Saudi Arabia cannot be bought; but it is easier to try to do so than with a population of 50 million. In fact, of course, total control is impossible even over a few hundred thousand; in the desert societies of the Gulf, there is little evidence that the rulers enjoy popular esteem.

The current generation may be rendered docile by their rags-to-riches rise to wealth. But now a new generation has grown up which sees little reason to accept archaic systems of government and the near-monopolist control of the main source of wealth. Unless the oil states adapt, the danger is that change will be violent, extremist and sudden. Oil, previous poverty and small populations have pickled the monarchy in aspic in the Gulf, in a way which has not occurred elsewhere; but this will not necessarily last.

A glance around the Gulf confirms this: every Arab country on its fringes that lacks oil possesses the rudiments of a modern economy and has lost its monarchy, usually violently; only the desert kingdom of Jordan, with its scant economy, survives by the skin of its teeth. Instead the Gulf is dominated by one large monarchy, Saudi Arabia, and a host of lesser princedoms. The region provides the potential for the globe's biggest security crisis early this century.

Of these, the kingdom of Saudi Arabia bears the nearest resemblance to a modern society, possessing two major cities – Riyadh and Jeddah – and substantial industry and infrastructure made possible by the oil price rises of the 1970s. Saudi Arabia is ruled through a complex system of control based upon patronage, repression, Islam and tribal links. The patronage is lavishly distributed by the state, which is wholly identified with the al-Saud ruling dynasty (the name of the country enshrines this). It is immense, in the form of a generous welfare state, lavish state support for private industry, a large bureaucracy and special assistance for such groups as the Bedouin.

Repression is of a fairly standard kind: there is no free press, broadcasting or political activity, ostensibly in the name of religion; independent political movements or meetings are suppressed, while Islamic police are used for surveillance, to enforce personal morality, and to administer punishments. The strict enforcement of Islamic law gives the authorities *carte blanche* to police every aspect of Saudi life: the dual police forces are further buttressed by the existence of two armies, the regular army and the National Guard. The point of having two is to prevent one seizing power, as happened in Iraq in 1958.

The desolation shrieks in the wind at the traveller as his car follows the tarmac strip across miles of dull red rock, through miles of travelling sand, loosely rippled across the rock and then into the monotonous dunescape of the deep sand. The emptiness stretches, beyond his sight, for hundreds of miles in every direction. The desert is empty by day beneath a dusty yellow horizon fading into merciless bluish glare, and by night beneath a star-studded, crystal-clear blackness. The Saudis tell you that when it clouds over and rains, it pours. You have only their word for it.

It is one of the world's greatest wildernesses, a sand continent the size of India, the pasture around the occasional oasis too sparse to persuade the Bedouin trekking interminably from the overpopulated Yemeni mountains of the south-west towards northern Arabia, to settle. In the desert, humanity was stripped to the essentials. Arabia's heartland was the preserve of a hardy few, driving flocks of sheep and goats from one patch of grass to another, eating camel's flesh and lamb's butter. Scarcity dictated ferocity: they had to be tough fighters, able to hold their own against other tribes. Religion dictated cleanliness: when they came to water, they had to wash before they drank.

The strict rules of Islam grappled with the anarchic sides of their nature. Islam alone united a people bereft of a written culture. Then, early this century, the al-Saud, a tough clan from the village of Riyadh in the centre of the country, successfully bribed, browbeat and battled the other tribes into submission in alliance with Wahhabi religious warriors under the al-Sheikh clan. The head of the tribe, Ibn Saud, little knew that his wasteland contained the world's largest reserve of black gold. When his successors learnt that, life did not change much at first for the Bedouin.

It has now. Today, emerging out of the emptiness at night to reach the ancient capital of the al-Saud, the Arabian traveller suddenly comes upon a sea of light, an urban sprawl some forty kilometres (25 miles) across, a grid of giant three-lane highways and flyovers down which Park Avenue Buicks coast line abreast. The city boasts two enormous airports, its skyline bristles with slim, austere minarets, plump watertowers and busy yellow cranes.

Creating a city of millions of people at the heart of a desert seems mad. Its location is purely symbolic, as the capital of the al-Saud tribe and the geographical heart of a country which has been unified for little more than half a century. No matter that crops must be fertilized and irrigated at enormous cost to grow at all around Riyadh, no matter that most of the city's needs must be brought 900 kilometres (500 miles) from Jeddah (the Saudi development plan even provides for the 'air transport of cows'). Never mind the cost of digging for water for the city. With the rest of the world picking up the bill, the Saudis could afford their Xanadu.

Is the capital of oil, lacking all life support but money, doomed one day to be reclaimed by the desert, as Brazil's rubber capital, Manaus, was reclaimed by the jungle in the last century? Will puzzled archaeologists of the future pore over the ruins of the Marriott and the Intercontinental Hotel as they do the sand-immured cities of south Afghanistan and Iran?

It depends. It depends on whether the Saudis destroy the market for the oil they possess in such abundance; on whether intelligent men in the governing class realize in time that an anachronistic system of government, even a cleverly run one, cannot survive for ever; and on whether the standards of international self-restraint that have allowed a very few people to squeeze the rich and poor of the world will long endure when the people doing the squeezing show such lack of self-restraint.

'The very rich,' Scott Fitzgerald once observed, 'are different from you and me.' 'Yes,' replied Ernest Hemingway, 'they have more money.' The Saudis have been very rich. In 1992, Saudi Arabia's GDP was around $200 billion – about one-ninth as much as Britain, a country which has been developed for a long time with three times as many people, or about two-and-a-half times as much as Egypt, an Arab country with three times as many people.

The Saudis are different. The fact that they have been very rich for so short a time makes them more so (in 1970 they had only $600 million in the bank). They have passed from rags to riches without having to strive and lack the rough edges of men who have to work for their fortunes. They have tried to carry the simplicity of their former pastoral poverty over to their new lifestyle. The plain white ankle-length Arab tunic is as egalitarian a dress as Mao uniforms were once in China. Seniority in

Saudi Arabia is denoted only by the silver and gold borders of their black shoulder capes.

The two-storey royal palaces are curiously low-key. I once visited a successful Saudi multi-millionaire's home which was striking for the simplicity of its stark Moorish style. There is a sense of *noblesse oblige* in the way Saudi offices are open to all comers, whether they have appointments or not – with the result that those that do have them can be kept waiting for hours.

The Saudis are soft-spoken, shy almost, utterly different from their excitable northern Arab brothers. As Bedouins, they used not to push themselves very hard; as millionaires they do not need to. No demand on their hospitality (once it has been extended) is too outrageous, a legacy of the days when you shared or somebody went without.

Yet their unhurried approach to life can also be maddening. The defensive distance they affect comes dangerously close to arrogance and their offices, manned by male secretaries, work with awesome incompetence. They are as sensitive as lilies about what is said about them, but compel observers to speculate by keeping the facts from them, and can be secretive and ambiguous in their pronouncements.

The secretiveness, the ambiguity, the commitment to a way of life no longer relevant to their material circumstances are defence mechanisms. Because the old way of life was so stark and empty, the void is being filled by Dullsville, USA. Underneath, in private, Saudis talk, live and behave like the American oilmen they have come to know so well. As video sets, peanut butter and Pepsi-Cola threaten to become the Saudi way of life, so they cling all the more desperately to the two closely interwoven roots they have always possessed: the family and Islam.

The family was the social unit of the desert: and now that money has come tumbling down from above, dispensed as patronage by heads of family, its authority has, if anything, been strengthened. The family abides by the strict rules of Islam: the mother has no life outside it, apart from her women friends. In the most liberal Saudi household, she may receive male guests, but will then withdraw. But she gets money – and so independence and power – as of right. And she gets her own back on this sexual apartheid by wielding absolute power over her children until their late teens, by which time she has probably wrested control of her husband from his mother as well. Then the father rules his sons through the purse strings of a family business partnership.

Islam is both a way of life and the chosen instrument of the government's political control. Ever since the Iranian revolution of 1978–9, the

Saudi government has been congratulating itself on the foresight it showed in never relaxing its hand-in-glove alliance with the country's puritan Wahhabi clerics. The alliance was founded in 1744, with the marriage of an early al-Saud to a daughter of Islam's Savonarola, Abdul Wahhab. His strict interpretation of the Prophet's teachings has put Saudi Arabia in a straitjacket since the al-Saud united the kingdom.

After the austere King Faisal was assassinated in 1975 by a disaffected minor member of his clan, the ruling clique, led by the shrewd but self-indulgent Crown Prince Fahd, marginally eased the iron rules of Islam. But Shia disturbances in the country's oil-producing eastern region and the seizure by Muslim fanatics of the Grand Mosque at Mecca in 1979 showed that there was no room for further relaxation. The disturbances have not recurred, largely thanks to a discreet infusion of money into the affected areas; and the Grand Mosque incident has passed into history as a 'Saudi Jonestown' – a group of suicidal zealots drawn largely from a disgruntled western tribe following a self-appointed imam. Their profaning of the holy places outraged most Saudis.

The Koran provides handy weapons of political control. The censor, it is explained, is a guardian of Islam, not of the nation's rulers. Yet his pen strikes as vigorously at political grumbles as exposed calves. Stick-wielding religious policemen patrolling the streets are a constant reminder of the presence of authority. Publicly administered floggings and executions are as effective in deterring political as well as ordinary crime.

Cinemas are banned as potentially corrupting, but in reality it is because the Saudis do not like crowds to gather. Potentially more corrupting private video sets are allowed. Strict Islam, with its catalogue of 'thou-shalt-nots', is a big brother forever tapping on the shoulders of ordinary Saudis. As the then minister of justice, Sheikh Ibrahim al-Sheikh (a descendant of Abdul Wahhab), once remarked to me: 'Public security dominates the whole place.'

Saudi law is at least punctiliously observed in the traditional way. There is less of the extra-legal brutality – the midnight disappearances, the summary trials, the torture – that are common to most countries which have undergone revolutions in the region. The minister of justice, a grave, reflective man, insisted that even the king is subject to the law. The forms of punishment, while horrifying to Western eyes, are at least publicly admitted (and administered). They can be defended on the grounds that they belong to Saudi Arabia's feudal age, which abruptly ended only two decades ago.

The principle behind the law is simple: Saudi Arabia used to be a country of tribal blood feuds. The House of Saud took the enforcement of the law out of the hands of individuals and placed it into the hands of the state. The state must be seen to administer retribution to keep its citizens from taking the law back into their own hands. Now, said Sheikh al-Sheikh, 'there is less crime here than in any other nation'. This is almost certainly true.

Chopping off heads and hands concentrates the minds. In an age when officially sanctioned non-legal killings in many Third World countries can be counted in their hundreds, Western indignation about punishments in Saudi Arabia is overdone. About a dozen people are executed a year. The method is usually beheading, though the execution is sometimes carried out by a firing squad, or by the method the murderer used against his victims or, in certain cases of adultery, by stoning.

Legal process is a sham, with torture, forced confessions and phoney trials standard procedures. Capital punishment is administered only when a killing has been premeditated and the killer has confessed. He has a right of appeal: the supreme council of the judiciary, a body of between ten and fifteen Islamic scholars, must give their approval. The king must give his. The sentence can be commuted in cases of mental disorder or if the family of the victim exercises its prerogative to waive punishment.

As for wayward princesses, only one person has been stoned for adultery during the past twenty years. And no wonder: the Saudi delegation at a human rights dialogue with European jurists some years ago defined the Koranic circumstances in which stoning applies as being:

> Only when the culprit, prior to his delict, had contracted a legal marriage and if four witnesses known for their righteousness and their integrity were present at the accomplishment of the sexual act in a manner which would exclude the possibility of doubt: it would not have been sufficient, namely, that they had seen the accused completely naked and stuck together.

After all, the Saudi jurists pointed out:

> If the act was accomplished in the presence of four witnesses, the judgment is that public order has been seriously offended . . . It is always improper for the sexual act to take place in public . . . We suppose that if such a thing had happened in the street of a capital of a civilized country, passers-by would have taken it upon themselves to lynch the perpetrators.

Whereat Mr Sean MacBride, heading the European delegation, was moved to reply: 'It is here, in this Muslim country, that human rights should be proclaimed, nowhere else.'

Just as the king is subject to the law, so is he subject to his people. This delightful fiction is based on the hallowed institution of the *majlis*, when any subject, high or low, can present his (but not her) request in written form to the king, shake hands, and maybe have a word or two. The petition may range from a grievance to a personal request for money from the king to finance, for instance, a prostate operation abroad – because no government subsidy exists for the purpose. Something will usually be done. The *majlis* is brandished by Saudis as evidence of democracy. The fact that there are thousands of princes is flourished as evidence that the government is in contact with the people.

Both claims are nonsense. But it is true that power in Saudi Arabia is oligarchical, and does not hang on one man, as it did in Iran. The power structure is hard to get to grips with because, like so much about the country, it is unfinished. Even sections of the frontier remain to be inked in. The country's provinces were formalized only during the past forty-five years. In 1924 Ibn Saud promised the country a constitution and a middle-class consultative council, a *majlis al-shura*, as an 'intermediary between the people and me'. No constitution has emerged, and the council was set up only in the 1990s.

The governance of Saudi Arabia remains improvised, and those seeking to understand it could do worse than read Mario Puzo's *The Godfather*, for an idea of how a large clan with money and force at its disposal operates in the modern world. Ibn Saud had forty-five sons by twenty-two different women. The clan has a dramatic advantage over the Shah's one-man rule: it provides a pool of potential rulers, as well as a means for replacing them. The disadvantage is that power struggles take place within the clan. But these have not been murderous because the House of Saud knows that divided it falls.

In 1967, for example, the fun-loving and decadent King Saud, who had duly succeeded Ibn Saud in 1953, was shoved aside by his brothers in favour of his austere younger brother, Faisal. When the latter was assassinated in 1975, the next brother, Prince Mohammed, who had no wish to be king, stood aside. The most obvious contenders for the succession were Prince Fahd, a pro-American moderate, and Prince Abdullah, a defender of the old ways. The family compromised and chose their elder brother, King Khaled, a gentle man of unimpeachable reputation but without intellectual force.

Tall, imposing and with the quickest intelligence among the sons of Ibn Saud, the then-Prince Fahd's defects were sudden bouts of indolence, a playboy reputation; and a liking for the resort of Marbella in Spain. As King Khaled's health deteriorated, he withdrew into a largely ceremonial role. And as Prince Fahd increasingly concerned himself with affairs of state, so Prince Abdullah's power steadily declined even before Khaled's death.

Prince Abdullah controlled a formidable force – the 40,000-strong National Guard, consisting largely of Bedouins. But Prince Fahd's main ally was the defence minister, Prince Sultan, who headed the 35,000-strong army. Prince Sultan expected to slide easily into the job of crown prince when, on Khaled's death in 1982, Fahd became king. But Prince Sultan lacked the tact and grasp of his elder brother, and the other princes tried to block him. More than a decade later Fahd was incapacitated by a stroke and Abdullah took over in tandem with Sultan.

Power is money and money is power in Saudi Arabia: just over two-fifths of the national income comes from oil revenue, which goes directly to the government, providing around 75 per cent of its income. The oil money that is not saved in foreign banks is filtered through the budget to ordinary Saudis. About 12 per cent of this goes in social expenditure, the bulk on development. Tenders are the government's to give to its friends.

'Corruption', say critics in the West at once about this sort of thing. What would be called corruption in the West is not so much an unattractive feature of the Saudi economy as the way it works. Government by family sees nothing wrong in business by connection. Patronage is the way the princes get rich; it is also, much more than coercion, the main source of the government's authority.

Money is fast centralizing a country which a couple of decades ago consisted of pretty well independent tribes, studded far apart, bargaining with the al-Saud for favours and freedoms. Regional tribal disaffection is a more pressing concern for the al-Saud than Western notions of democracy. The al-Saud are enormously skilful in keeping the tribes happy while pulling the country together. Air services and roads linking population centres are snaking across the desert. An industrial port has been built at Yanbu on the Red Sea coast, linked by cross-country pipeline to the eastern province in order to dilute the concentration of industry there.

The princes have been trying to improve local government. Tribal disaffection played a major part in the seizure of the Grand Mosque at

Mecca in 1979. Early the following year, the government took the rare step of replacing four emirs, or provincial governors, including the governor of Mecca. The emirs of the fourteen provinces are the central government's proconsuls, responsible for keeping the tribes happy. Seven of the fourteen are brothers of the king; five are members of the aristocratic Sudairi tribe, to which the al-Saud are related by marriage; and two belong to the Ilawi tribes of the northern provinces. The emirs are trying to patch up relations with the tribes, which have been unsettled by the way unregulated local branch offices of the ministries have galloped over local sensibilities.

Sensitivity to tribal feeling was, until recently, about as far as the al-Saud family seemed ready to go in sharing power. Under pressure from the United States, in 1980 Prince Fahd dug up the old idea of a *majlis al-shura* – a body of representatives drawn from the rising middle class to advise the king. The proposal was shunted off to a committee headed by the minister of the interior, Prince Naif, who passed it to a subcommittee to draft a formal proposal. Nothing more was heard until 1993, when the idea came under consideration again.

The government's Islamic veil is slipping. In practice, many middle-class, middle-aged Saudis drink – although in private, usually with non-Saudis, and never in front of elderly Saudis. Saudi children devour Western films in high-technology 'family rooms' while the torrent of religion on local television stays firmly switched off. The sight of Saudis taking to their prayer mats five times a day is impressive; but the great majority do not pray regularly. Teenage girls have been caught dressed as boys at the driving wheel (women are not allowed to drive at all).

Cars of the religious police prowl around girls' schools to discourage leering males. The authorities decreed that any youth caught molesting a schoolgirl would be publicly flogged on the spot. When supermarkets close for twenty minutes' prayer women are turned out on to the streets, and offer irresistible targets for frustrated youths in their cars. The police now compel women to go home and return if they want to resume shopping. The Saudi attempt to shut out the moral lassitude, that usually goes with freedom endowed by wealth and technology, is being slowly battered down. Draconian rules are easier to observe when life is spartan.

The erosion of pure Islamic values does not directly threaten the government: those who want to indulge themselves tend to be apolitical and go abroad. But it is eroding the system's moral authority. And moral authority – the Saudis are the guardians of Islam's holy places – is the underpinning this archaic monarchy requires in a world where, as young Saudis must have noticed abroad, emperors have no clothes.

Many Saudis believe that the royal family is breaking the rules it asks them to live by. As the rules are increasingly flouted by those with money, the rules will grow less respected by their subjects. When an eighteenth-century ruling class wrapped in a cloak of moral righteousness loses respect, it becomes vulnerable.

In Saudi Arabia, the forces which could exploit that vulnerability are, in ascending order of probability:

- The 'street'. The uprising in Iran was staged by an alliance of anti-Shah mobs which dared his soldiers to fire; they wouldn't. Saudi Arabia lacks such a street, not just because its laws of assembly are harsh. There are too few Saudis too widely dispersed to stage a credible uprising. An uprising in Jeddah would not necessarily provoke one in Riyadh, much less in Dhahran, near the oil.
- Foreign workers (of which there are up to 7 million) are expelled at the first sign of trouble. But a flotsam of Yemenis and largely African ex-pilgrims who live in the western provinces, many without a job or the hope of one, might one day make up a street mob, particularly in the port of Jeddah.
- The middle class. In money terms, most older Saudis can probably now call themselves middle class. But few are educated. Their children are educated, and it is a moot point whether they will in turn be corrupted or end up denouncing the pervasive corruption and the power structure. Both, probably.
- Islamic fundamentalists – the most visibly troublesome opponents of the regime today.

Only a handful of men from the non-royal classes – Sheikh Hisham Nazer and Sheikh Ahmed Yamani, the former Oil Ministers, and Sheikh Aba al-Khail, the former Finance Minister – have penetrated the exclusive circle at the top. For them, the rewards of loyalty to the system were stupendous. But there was room for these men. Yamani, who resigned in 1986, has distanced himself from the regime and may become a focus for moderate opposition. How is a whole generation of educated, ambitious young Saudis going to feel about a system where hosts of idle young princes get preferential treatment? There may be tens of thousands of princes – a huge parasitic class.

The princes suspect everyone. Yet one of their critics within the system

has assured me: 'There is no organized movement.' The regime's technocrats are trying to create a middle class based on the private sector, to act
as a buttress against revolution, and perhaps one day to take over from
the princes. Yamani would make a plausible moderate national leader.

If the princes could see a little way ahead, they might see the advantage
of permitting some embryonic political institutions to emerge. Change
might otherwise come in the form of a coup. Acutely aware of the
danger, the Saudis pay their soldiers directors' salaries and lavish money
on military equipment that can hardly be absorbed.

Senior commanders, some of them princes, are none the less gaining in
independent influence. A cause that could lead to mutterings among the
ranks would be Saudi acquiescence in a Middle East peace that looked
like a sell-out to Israel. The princes have thus been careful to move no
faster than the Palestine Liberation Organization itself, although they
took a risk in acquiescing in the 1993 PLO-Israeli agreement.

Nationalism is strong in the armed forces. Saudi Arabia is largely
managed by foreigners and relies on American protection. There are
grumbles about the depletion of oil reserves. Junior officers may embrace
some form of Islamic fundamentalism or even socialism, like Colonel
Qaddafi's in Libya.

With their moral authority waning, the princes are increasingly
dependent on the army. In the end, one clever military man – even a
prince – could overthrow the system on an ideological pretext. A
conspiracy uncovered in 1969 resulted in the execution of a number
of officers in thoroughly un-Islamic secrecy. The main deterrent to a
would-be Qaddafi is not, however, the executioner's axe, but the fact
that America would try not to allow the wrong sort of coup to happen.
Saudi Arabia has become a kind of American protectorate.

The eyes of Saudi Arabia's Foreign Minister, Prince Saud al-Faisal,
flicker nervously this way and that; he moistens his lips frequently.
His face has the arch look of his father, King Faisal, but is more
conventionally handsome. He is the only prince with a senior political
post to represent the fifty-year-olds beneath the older, reigning sons of
Ibn Saud. He is the likeliest of their generation to be king one day. Highly
American-educated though he is, he says, 'Saudi Arabia is non-aligned.'

This statement belongs to the category of other Saudi official pronouncements. In fact, America's relationship to Saudi Arabia is that of
father to a growing and increasingly rebellious son. The Saudis can get
away with a lot, but the Americans ultimately provide the protection.

America took in Saudi Arabia when it was a ragged desert waif from declining imperial Britain. The American success in obtaining the kingdom's first oil concession against British competition in 1933 marked the passing of the torch. America, which offered Saudi Arabia lend-lease aid in the 1940s, became the kingdom's main trading partner and provider of its slight military might.

Today, the bonds are still close. American companies, the Ralph Parsons Company and Bechtel, are building Saudi Arabia's new industries. There are around 400 American companies and 45,000 American citizens in Saudi Arabia. Some 16,000 Saudis are studying in America. The United States geological survey charts the country's mineral resources, its Military Training Mission trains the army, air force and navy. The Americans are modernizing the Saudi National Guard and their corps of engineers manages contracts worth billions for the ministry of defence and the National Guard. Even before the Gulf War there were around 4,000 Americans engaged on military programmes there.

The Gulf War, and the huge American presence in Saudi Arabia, although kept at a distance from most of the population, has brought Islamic feeling against the monarchy to boiling point. As early as May 1993 six prominent Islamic clerics from Nejd, in the centre of the country, who set up an embryonic political party, were formally summoned and attacked by Prince Salman, governor of Riyadh. He said formation of the group was unlawful and un-Islamic, and threatened to issue an edict to declare this formally. The committee had reported that: 'The present Saudi model of Islam is not a good model. It is like the last days of the Ottoman empire, a degenerative state. The government should rule accordingly to the Sunnah, by consultation, with elections, and ensuring that everyone's rights are protected.'

The previous December, King Fahd had claimed that 'foreign currents' were behind a campaign to destabilize Saudi Arabia – a barely concealed reference to Islamic fundamentalists in Iran and Sudan. The King lambasted subversive tapes containing outspoken attacks on Saudi policies, including the regime's alleged corruption, nepotism, business practices and its co-operation with the United States during the Gulf War.

Earlier, seven of the seventeen clerics on the Supreme Authority of Senior Scholars, Saudi Arabia's highest religious body, were dismissed for failing to sign a denunciation of a memorandum drawn up by 107 Islamic fundamentalist clerics calling for a much tighter approach to religion in the kingdom. Fahd's increasingly tough response to the fundamentalists indicates the danger the regime felt it was under. In the summer of 1994, 110 Islamic fundamentalists were arrested for 'spreading sedition'. The government threatened to 'hit strongly anyone who seeks to disrupt security'. Simultaneously, by setting up a long-promised *majlis al-shura* of sixty members, Fahd has sought at last to co-opt the more enlightened Saudi middle class in the struggle against the fundamentalists. This body has no power to criticize the higher policies of government – but petitions it with local grievances. 'We are trying not to rock the boat,' said one member. 'We don't want the council dissolved.' There is an enormous tension in the Saudis' attempt to improve the living standards of the population by adopting Western technology and its efforts to resist the Westernizing influences that could spark a militant Islamic uprising.

So far, in spite of the inherently unstable nature of Saudi rule, the royal family has quite subtly maintained the precarious balance. There may be sense, too, in their refusal to consider even a small measure of popular representation: once the principle is conceded, the absurdity of rule by hereditary princes would be exposed. However, the land cannot be kept in the past for ever. Sooner or later pressure for change in a society divided between Islamic traditionalists and younger modernizers will surface. The al-Saud dynasty seems likely to become the target for popular discontent.

The ultimate prop of Saudi rule is the West. The United States has shown little historical fondness for hereditary monarchs: but its fear of the country falling into the hands of militant Islam or Arab radicals is so great that it has passionately supported the al-Saud – although the Americans sensibly have contacts with the moderate middle-class groups they ought to be supporting. After September 11 the atmosphere has distinctly soured, with important, although not yet decisive, lobbies in Washington arguing that the al-Saud and their Islamic fundamentalist allies are expendable. The stakes in Saudi Arabia are immense: the Gulf War took place primarily to protect Saudi Arabia, which President Bush feared would be the target for invasion in the first few days after the Iraqi occupation of Kuwait.

Saudi Arabia is not just the Gulf's 'swing' oil producer, capable of providing as much as all of the rest put together and thus – as has frequently happened – moderating oil price swings throughout the market. It also sits astride overwhelmingly the largest potential oil reserves in the world. As only a handful of oil-bearing areas around the peninsula have been properly explored, its proclaimed oil reserves are probably only a fraction of the real total. Aramco's estimate in 1980 was that Saudi Arabia had proven reserves of 114 billion barrels and probable reserves of 178 billion barrels. Sheikh Yamani, the former oil minister, has calculated that proven reserves are more likely to be 180 billion barrels, and as for probable reserves: 'Fasten your seat belts; you would be amazed.' In 1981, he claimed that Saudi Arabia had at least twice as much oil as generally thought.

Aramco itself has developed only two of its six concession areas. Saudi Arabia has forty-seven oilfields, but only fifteen are in production. Rock dome formations suggest that oil is present in many unexplored parts of Saudi Arabia. The country's probable reserves would not be exhausted until 2025 even if Saudi Arabia produced at maximum capacity.

If Saudi Arabia has as much oil as Sheikh Yamani thinks – 350 billion barrels? – reserves will last until around 2070. It costs Saudi Arabia about $1 a barrel to tap the oil, but it is sold at anything up to $30 a barrel, a mark-up of up to 3,000 per cent. Saudi Arabia used to justify this by pointing out that it was running out of oil. And now? The prize is immense. The prospect of Saudi Arabia falling into extremist hands is, in the opinion of most Americans, unacceptable.

This provides for a very major potential crisis this century, where the Americans might have to avail themselves of airbases expressly designed to take their aircraft to step in on the side of an anachronistic feudal monarchy to suppress an uprising. It is a huge irony that the most republican of nations should be prepared to prop up the al-Saud, but it is nevertheless true. The danger is that the ruling family, with its narrow base of support, might be unsustainable in the face of an uprising, and the Americans would get sucked into the kind of fighting they have sought to avoid since Vietnam. A civic insurrection against an unpopular government would result, with all the commitment of ground troops and casualties this would entail. All the same, in view of the stakes, it is hard to see what choice they have.

The only – slender – way out of this dilemma would be for America to encourage the moderate modernizers in the country, prompting them to forge a viable alternative should Saudi rule finally collapse under the weight of its own bloated corruption – and there are signs that the House of Saud enjoys as little popular support as the Shah of Iran did. Certainly the cultivation of a moderate alternative to the al-Saud seems advisable, or the United States risks being tainted with the Saudi hatred for their own ruling dynasty, and going down with the sinking ship. The Saudi conundrum has the makings of a major international crisis and military conflict drawing in the West – one second to none over the next two or three decades.

The other sheikhdoms around the Gulf are much smaller in size, wealth and oil reserves, and vary in the good sense of their rulers. Oman's Sultan Qaboos, with the smallest oil reserves in the Gulf, is commensurately more moderate and sensible in his rule. He presides over a sparsely populated country of some 500,000 people, mostly concentrated in smallish oasis settlements not too seriously disrupted by accelerated oil-fuelled development. Unlike the Saudis, who won most of their territory by comparatively recent conquest, his ruling family are of long-standing in the territory and enjoy genuine support among the largely homogeneous tribesmen in its rural settlements.

Qaboos used British support between 1965 and 1975 to stave off radical Yemeni attacks in the west of his country, and this proved sufficient. It is hard to detect any substantial opposition to his rule, which co-opts the small middle class of Oman. The combination of a tribal base, a small country, a traditional society, plus a commonsense approach to government, realistic development goals and a fairly light repressive hand, is healthy. Islam is less strict than elsewhere in the Gulf, partly because of Oman's racial connections with India. The country is more outward-looking towards the nations of the Indian Ocean than the inward-looking countries inside the foetid Gulf waterway.

The discreet British connection will help to ensure that the Omani dynasty will be one of the longest surviving in the region, as long as agreement can be reached about a suitable heir – as Qaboos has no children. If the Omanis prove flexible in modernizing their government, the dynasty could re-emerge one day as a constitutional government. The only visible threat today is the old Iranian attempt to destabilize the government, born of Oman's strategic position in the approaches to the Gulf.

Iranian subversion is much more evident in Dubai, and to a lesser extent in Abu Dhabi and the other United Arab Emirates: the presence of a considerable minority of Shias, coupled with a transient trading population of Iranians, has led the rotating emirs of this oil-rich corner to be carefully Islamic, as well as their being the most pro-Iranian of the Arab Gulf States. Oil prosperity has disrupted the traditional life of the emirates much more visibly than in, say, Oman. In addition there are tensions between the rival emirs of the UAE and their tribesmen, as well as with Saudi Arabia, such as the traditional dispute for possession of the

Buraimi Oasis. The small population (300,000) and the comparatively great shower of oil wealth has permitted the rulers to buy off their populations – for the moment; but it would be naïve to believe that these dynasties will last long into the twenty-first century.

Moving further up the Gulf is probably the politically frailest of the Gulf States, Bahrain, run by the al-Khalifa dynasty. Bahrain contains a large Shia population which is well-organized and unafraid of making itself felt and many observers there believe the regime would fall if given a serious push by the Iranians; it also has its share of Arab socialists. Relatively rich, highly urbanized, the al-Khalifas for the moment survive off the tolerance of their peoples, rather than through repression; their island status has reinforced their hold. The new young king has announced the formation of a parliament freely elected by 'men and women'.

Bahrain's island status has been compromised recently with the construction of a causeway to Saudi Arabia, which makes Bahrain the foremost destination for Saudis, as well as people as far away as Kuwait, a popular destination for a weekend of excessive behaviour. The spectacle of young male Saudis in long white robes wildly drunk, as only those unused to alcohol can be, in the bars of Bahrain, is not for those with weak stomachs. Bahrain is one of the most cosmopolitan, even diverting places in the Gulf; it is also one of its weak links, as is nearby Qatar.

The last of the feudal princedoms is Kuwait, recently the subject of invasion by Iraq. The Kuwaitis are perhaps the region's most arrogant and inhospitable people – which is saying something, if Saudi Arabia is included in the comparison. With its searing sands bleached by pitiless sunshine in off-white skies, the city of Kuwait is as characterless a collection of modern skyscrapers surrounded by underused beltways as can be seen anywhere in the world; the romance of Arabia is entirely absent from this Detroit-on-sand.

Kuwait, a major trading port for the northern Gulf powers, Iraq and Iran, was historically the first to shower its small population with oil revenues. The vast majority of Kuwaitis live a *rentier* existence off the interest from their wealth (the Koran's ban on interest has long since been circumvented). Men retire at forty with lavish welfare provisions, and live off the work of stateless foreigners – who comprised a majority of the population before the Iraqi invasion. As much as half the population spends several months abroad each year.

Faced with a comparatively well-off and educated people, the ruling al-Sabah dynasty was the first Gulf princedom to concede a kind of consultative assembly elected by male Kuwaitis, which was quickly rescinded when it took too independent a view. After fierce criticism of the al-Sabahs' behaviour during the Gulf War – first out when the Iraqis invaded, last back in after the Iraqi defeat would be a not unfair description – and under American pressure, the ruling dynasty has conceded another assembly, one in which the opposition secured over-whelming victory despite the rules being stacked against them.

It remains to be seen how far this gesture of the al-Sabahs will extend – or whether they have the power again to close it down. If they try, the al-Sabahs might find themselves the first Gulf dynasty to have to back down in the face of democratic pressure. Although there were elements of militant Islam and radicalism in the new assembly, the majority elected were the well-heeled bourgeoisie of Kuwait, somewhat contradicting the oft-stated contention that Arabs are unfit for democracy, too backward, ill-educated and immature for such Western nostrums, inevitably a prey to extremism.

The emir is elderly, vacillating and has a short attention span for work, which hardly commends him to his people. Paradoxically, Kuwait may be the state best fitted for an experiment in constitutional government. A constitutional success in Kuwait could quickly prove an example for the other city states of the Gulf and lead to pressure for an opening in Saudi Arabia – which is one reason why King Fahd would be the first to back the al-Sabahs in any confrontation with their parliament.

Thus the picturesque medieval emirs of the Gulf linger on, with their camel races and falconry and tents within palaces, exuding nostalgia for a nomadic Bedouin past of poverty that does not quite ring true beside their obvious enjoyment of the best things money can buy, an anachron-ism in the twenty-first century, preserved for now, but not for ever, by oil wealth. It is impossible to predict when the deluge will come, but come it will; and when it does, it seems likely to be violent and fast, blowing the whole collection away almost simultaneously, not so much like dom-inoes as like the elegant pieces on the chessboard in *Alice in Wonderland*, this time toppling the whole white-skirted collection of emirs, beglerbegs, sultans and kings.

It is just possible that the Gulf states will reform themselves sagely and in time; but it may be too late – an opening could self-fulfillingly release pent-up hatreds that are the fuel of extremism – and anyway the monarchs show no signs of sagacity. The Gulf's rulers are the exception that proves that the end of dynastic rule has arrived.

Dynasty has attempted a comeback in recent years. Some modern rulers have tried to found new dynasties imitating the systems they have often usurped themselves. Almost invariably, these attempts have failed. In Iran, Reza Pahlavi, a sergeant who took over the country in 1921, handed the 'peacock throne', ludicrously revived from Iran's imperial past, on to his son, the Shah, who with the nouveau riche naïvety of the second generation enthroned himself in astonishing ostentation while modernizing his country in an accelerated manner with a fine disdain for all its traditional power centres and constituencies.

He succeeded in uniting Islamic fundamentalists, the middle classes, radicals, the bazaar merchant class and large sections of the urban population against him. Even the army would not rally to his banner at the end. He was toppled in 1979, in a revolution that began bloodlessly and soon developed its own gruesome momentum.

In China, Deng Xiaoping long harboured ambitions for his son to succeed him; but the latter, a victim of repression during Deng's political eclipse, was patently not up to the job. In Singapore, Lee Kuan Yew carefully paved the way for his son to succeed, but internal resistance among Lee's own lieutenants may yet block him. In North Korea, Kim Il-sung's son, Kim Jong-il, precariously succeeded his father in 1994.

In India, Nehru's daughter, Indira Gandhi, created a second generation of rule through her iron will which also, after her assassination, carried her son Rajiv to the top, until his own murder. Sympathy and support for the Gandhi dynasty is still so considerable that if a suitable candidate could be found – Rajiv's widow, for the moment, demurring – it could yet rule again. In Pakistan, Benazir Bhutto's first spell in office proved a disappointment in the wake of her damagingly populist father, the executed Zulfikar Ali Bhutto; but she has acquired the toughness (excessively so, her mother would say) and staying power to make what looks like a more mature comeback. In Syria, the diffident Bashar Assad has succeeded to his father's rule, prompting fears that one of Saddam Hussein's detested sons, Uday or Qusay, may try the same. But they have too many enemies. President Mubarak of Egypt is said to be grooming his son.

Even in republican America, there was a brief flirtation with dynasty – not that of the distant Roosevelt cousins, both equally talented in different ways, but first with the Kennedys, who boasted one supremely talented politician, Jack, one tough-minded but skilful political fixer, Robert, and a rather weaker third brother, Ted. Yet the failure of the latter to stage a serious presidential bid underlined the fact that the two elder brothers were, unusually, both hard enough to make it to the top. Much more successful has been the Bush dynasty, which has succeeded in putting the tough-minded George W. into the presidency in place, after an interlude, of his somewhat lacklustre father, the single-term George. George W's brother, Jeb, the governor of Florida, is also highly talented.

The failure of modern dynastic rule – except in the Indian subcontinent – stems only in part from the fact that this no longer commands the popular legitimacy that it did in the past: it also arises from the propensity of modern societies to permit only those strong and able enough to get to the top. Dynasty does not guarantee that one strong leader will be succeeded by another; the Achilles heel of the hereditary system is that it does not necessarily yield an heir who is up to the job, or even necessarily wants it; and if he has not had to fight for it, he is not usually tough enough.

In spite of its glamour and glitter, dynastic rule seems likely to linger on in only a few of the world's backwaters. Sadly, because of their lack of receptiveness to popular pressure, their myopia and their repression, it seems likely that Arabia's monarchies will one day be replaced not by constitutional democratic rule, but in bloody revolutions by radicals and fundamentalists.

CHAPTER 18

THE LAST EMPIRES

It is perhaps the world's most beautiful place, a remote upland plateau the size of a small continent, fringed by the highest mountains on earth, inhabited by 6 million people belonging to an ancient race and culture inspired by a gentle Buddhism that, for hundreds of years, was its very government. It has one of the most spectacular capitals in the world, Lhasa, with the cascading multi-tiered Potala Palace as its centrepiece, and some magnificent monasteries as its adornments.

Yet it is a place of sorrow, oppression and fear, ravaged by one of the most vicious colonialist regimes the world has ever known, for more than forty years a massive concentration camp and charnel house. It is Tibet, occupied by China in 1951. Unlike other colonial occupations or acts of international aggression, it is hard to see this one being reversed: the Chinese have brought in 8 million of their own people, and now outnumber the Tibetans.

The purpose of the Chinese colonization has been simple in the extreme: to seize a huge swathe of territory extending to India. The conduct of the occupation has been as ruthless as any in history. It began gently, with Tibet's spiritual leader, the Dalai Lama, being received by Mao in Peking. The picture changed when the eastern part of the country rose up against the Chinese in the late 1950s and was ruthlessly put down. In March 1959 the Dalai Lama fled, fearing arrest. The Chinese reacted by killing thousands of his loyal monks and supporters, and arresting thousands more.

A social revolution began: landowners were arrested, expropriated or executed and the survivors turned into 'blackhats', a kind of underclass deprived of all rights. The Tibetan provinces of Amdo and Kham were absorbed into China. The province of U-Tsang, the size of France and Germany combined, was renamed the Tibetan Autonomous Region, but was similarly controlled by the Chinese, who used the schools to indoctrinate their language and propaganda into the people. The Chinese also seized Tibetan harvests in the early 1960s, causing mass starvation.

This terrifying regime could hardly get worse: but it did with the Cultural Revolution in 1966: a frenzy of slaughter and pillage ensued. Perhaps a million people died, some 300,000 in fighting, some 400,000 dying of starvation and some 300,000 being executed or dying in captivity; relative to the population, this was the most savage horror the world had seen before the killing fields of Cambodia in the late 1970s – but it attracted much less attention. The 3,000 monasteries and nunneries strung across this ancient and spectacular land, which had housed some 100,000 clergy, were destroyed, leaving just eight, and a clerical population of some 1,000. This was an act of cultural genocide without precedent.

Only with Mao's death in 1978 did the terror abate. Hu Yaobang, his reformist successor, came to Lhasa and admitted that 'mistakes' had been made: some of the monasteries were restored and some 10,000 monks and nuns returned. The collective farms were broken up and political repression slightly eased. In 1987, after the Dalai Lama, gathering international support, presented a 'peace plan' to the American Congress, demonstrations broke out in Lhasa. They were suppressed, with at least 200 Tibetan deaths and thousands of arrests, and were instrumental in Hu's downfall in China. Many protesters were sentenced to long periods in prison and many were tortured with electric shocks.

In 1992 the Chinese made plain their utterly ruthless approach: 'The central government will not make the slightest concession on the fundamental issue of maintaining the motherland's unification. Any activist sabotaging stability and unity in Tibet will be cracked down on relentlessly.' It is an irony of history that the world's last major surviving example of colonialism is one of the most horrific ever experienced. One of the toughest recent Chinese proconsuls in Tibet was Hu Jintao, China's new leader.

The second great source of modern state authority has been colonialism, the imposition of rule by one state over another based on military superiority. Today, with the collapse of the Soviet empire, this is nearly extinct. There are a number of small enclaves under 'colonial' rule, where the inhabitants themselves are reluctant to lose the protection of their foreign masters. For Britain, these are Montserrat, Anguilla, Bermuda, the British Antarctic Territory, the British Indian Ocean Territory, the British Virgin Islands, the Caymans, the Falklands, Gibraltar, the Pitcairn Group, the St Helena Group, the Turks and Caicos, South Georgia and the South Sandwich Islands. For France, these are French Antarctica, French Polynesia, Guadaloupe, Guiana, Martinique, Mayott, New Caledonia, Réunion, St Pierre and Miquelon, Wallis and Fortune. For Holland, these are the Antilles and Aruba; for Spain, these are Ceuta and Melilla; and for Denmark, Greenland. All of these might be described as 'voluntary colonies'. The French dependencies have some 2 million people, the British, just 150,000.

Russia stands accused of colonialism in the enclaves in which it has lingered – particularly Chechnya – sometimes on the pretext of preventing civil war; in others its re-engagement is actively sought by one side or another – for example in Georgia and Nagorno-Karabakh. It is possible to argue that Kurdistan is an enclave occupied by several colonial powers, although the Kurds have never had a state. Some African tribal minorities argue that they are colonial pockets of the majority. Yet so far Eritrea's justified dash for independence has not multiplied across the continent. Indonesia certainly made a colony of East Timor until its recent fightback. By far the biggest and most obscene is the continuing Chinese domination of Tibet.

But the contrast between the world now and that at the beginning of the century is truly awesome. Then, the British Empire dominated one-quarter of the world's population, occupying a quarter of its territory, including much of Africa, a large swathe of the Middle East, the Indian subcontinent, relatively large parts of Asia through trading proxies, and it had major commercial interests in Mexico and Argentina. France dominated a large swathe of North Africa and the Middle East. Germany had its African possessions. Italy had minor colonies, while Belgium had the Congo. The Portuguese Empire in Africa and its enclaves in Asia were considerable. The United States had a number of proxy colonies in Latin America and the Philippines. The Austro-Hungarian Empire extended into the Balkans, the Russian empire into Asia.

Imperialism was the norm at the beginning of the century; today it is treated as a joke, an utterly repudiated notion, almost vanished for good. This is not the place for a major survey of traditional imperialism, as opposed to economic imperialism (which continues and will be discussed later) because it is so rare a source of contemporary state authority and will almost certainly be a spent force for the future. But it is worth glancing at some of the trends that caused such a complete transformation of the map of the globe.

The key point about colonialism is that it was a more complex phenomenon than appears from the virtuous stereotype at the beginning of this century and the hostile one at the end. There were at least four strands to classic colonialism. First, chronologically, there was economic colonialism: the expansion of trade between more and less developed societies leading to the use of force by the former to secure their interests, particularly when the 'natives' were viewed as little more than savages and pagans.

Second, there was the religious motive, which was equally important in the Europe of the sixteenth and seventeenth centuries, viewed as a mission to proselytize Christianity around the world. While the first kind had been motivated exclusively by commercial greed and self-interest, the latter, although often even crueller in its consequences, was partly idealistic and led to the kind of missionary idealism that characterized the last stages of colonialism and was in many ways its best feature.

Third, there was – as with Clive's conquest of India in the eighteenth century – the belated imposition of rule by the colonial state to protect its interests and to regulate the countries involved, and even to protect the inhabitants from predatory commercialism.

Finally, there was competitive and often defensive empire-building pure and simple, as the industrial nations rushed to seize areas of the world, to pre-empt their trading rivals and secure their commercial interests there.

Colonialism was made possible by one simple fact: the superiority of European arms over those of the peoples they subdued. It was reversed largely for one reason: as those colonized acquired arms, in particular small arms that could be diffused among whole populations, it became impossibly expensive for the occupying powers, both financially and in terms of lives, to maintain adequate protection for their enclaves there.

As one colonial war after another erupted into bloodshed, the major imperial powers understood they had no alternative but to leave, covering their tracks in clouds of idealistic and hypocritical rhetoric. Another major factor in the collapse of the European empires was the opposition to them of both the United States (with huge global interests of its own) and the Soviet Union (itself an empire), the one providing fierce criticism, the other offering arms and assistance to anti-colonial movements.

Was there ever any legitimacy other than force to be attached to the imposition of rule by one people upon another? There was certainly a legacy of modernization, infrastructure and education that colonial society indelibly left upon the more backward colonized societies. There were certainly a great many involved in the colonial administrations, as well as their political masters back home, that saw their mission as a civilizing one and harboured high ideals of protecting the inhabitants from naked commercial interests.

Yet the assertion of political independence by the subject peoples, even while often directly contrary to their own economic interests, was an entirely elemental expression of the self. Without a monopoly of military force, minority colonial administrations could not survive. The empires that lasted longest were those most ruthless in flexing military might and prepared to suffer the highest casualties – Portugal, the Soviet Union and China. With modern weaponry now diffuse and guerrilla techniques well understood, no colonial regime could survive today without virtually genocidal ruthlessness.

Traditional colonialism, while virtually extinct, was replaced by two more subtle forms: economic domination by external business interests which frequently benefited from the absence of skilled colonial administrators to check them, as well as from the distance of concerned opinion in the home country, and, latterly, a growing realization on the part of the governments of developed countries that their political expulsion from the colonies did not enable them to abdicate responsibility for the less developed countries, and that they had a role in volunteering assistance to their former subjects.

The exceptions to the end of formal colonialism are East Timor and Tibet. East Timor has its own special corner in the graveyard of recent colonial atrocities. On 7 December 1975, after Portugal had abruptly departed from its former colony, Indonesian troops entered the capital, Dili. The single faint radio report received in Darwin, 300 miles away, was Nanking-like in its horror: 'The soldiers are killing indiscriminately. Women and children are being shot in the streets. We are all going to be killed. I repeat we are all going to be killed . . . This is an appeal for international help. This is an SOS. We appeal to the Australian people. Please help us.' Later the Bishop of Dili, Costa Lopez, reported that: 'The soldiers who landed started killing everyone they could find. There were many dead bodies in the street – all we could see were the soldiers killing, killing, killing.'

Some 200,000 people, approximately a third of the population, were slaughtered in the next few years, in a wholesale colonial annexation based on terrorizing the population. By 1994 a tiny, 400-strong guerrilla movement, with widespread popular sympathy, formed the only challenge to the Indonesian yoke. The peace of the graveyard, and of the concentration camp, reigned until the recent Australian-led intervention designed to secure self-government.

As for Tibet, why does this huge area and population of 6 million people continue to endure a colonial yoke shrugged off throughout the rest of the world? The major factor, undoubtedly, is China's determination: for strategic reasons, China regards Tibet as critical to projecting its power into central Asia and as a buffer state against any threat from India. Thus the Chinese have been prepared to devote a huge commitment to the region, in terms of oppressive military force and millions of settlers.

Human rights and casualties are of no great concern to the Chinese; nor have the traditionally pacific Tibetan people managed to halt the systematic destruction of Tibet's national identity. There is no sign of any lessening in China's determination to hang on to Tibet. Given Tibetan traditional nonviolence (although an increasing number of the Dalai Lama's followers are advocating armed action), and the size and ruthlessness of the Chinese force in Tibet, it may be the one major colonial enclave that, tragically, endures. But this exception stands out from the collapse of virtually every other major colonial experience. Classic colonialism, if it ever enjoyed legitimacy other than through force, does not now and is consigned to the past. The diffusion of arms to less developed countries makes it highly unlikely that it will ever be revived.

CHAPTER 19

RULE BY THE JACKBOOT

Military rule is a truly grim, depressing experience. Take Argentina's ordeal. In September 1973, Argentines of all classes flooded the Plaza de Mayo, in front of the presidential Pink House, parading uproariously down the avenue, which is overlooked by the parliament house. They were celebrating the return to power of Juan Domingo Perón, eighteen years to the month after they had poured into the streets to celebrate the tyrant's overthrow. At the age of seventy-seven, after nearly two decades of comfortable exile in Madrid, Argentina's former dictator had won a staggering 62 per cent of the popular vote.

The middle classes voted for him because they thought he was a bulwark against revolution. The working classes, whose view of Perón had grown rosier through glasses clouded by years of army rule, remembered him as the man who gave them some sense of dignity. The far right supported him as the world's last authentic fascist, apprenticed in the 1930s on a military mission to Mussolini's Rome. The Marxists thought of him as a gaga old man of whom they could take advantage.

Because the army had barred Perón from taking part in the elections the previous March, a left-wing stand-in, Héctor Campora, was elected president. Campora promptly freed every Argentine jailbird, political or otherwise, and invited Perón back. El Lider, as Perón was called, insisted that new elections be held and picked as his vice-presidential running mate his wife, Isabelita, a dancer with some of the looks and none of the political savvy of his second wife, the legendary Evita.

In March 1976, laconically and with a week's advance notice, Argentina's army reluctantly took power over a Hogarthian bedlam of a country. Annual inflation was 600 per cent. Isabelita Perón, who had succeeded her husband to the presidency on his death in 1974, was on the verge of a nervous breakdown, being attended by Svengali-like courtiers including José Lopez Rega, an astrologer. Politicians and union leaders had left by plane, their suitcases stuffed with looted cash. Once-tranquil Buenos Aires suburbs were reverberating to the sound of explosions and gunfire as extremist groups battled it out. The day after the army took over, many absentee civil servants reported for the first time in months to their ministries for fear of losing their jobs. Fistfights broke out between those claiming the same desks.

In September 1979, General Luciano Menendez, the commander of the Third Army stationed in Córdoba, called a press conference to demand the resignation of the army commander, General Roberto Viola. General Menendez was angry about the government's decision to release from house arrest Jacobo Timerman, the former editor of the newspaper *La Opinion*. Although allegedly linked with far-left terrorists, Timerman was never formally charged with any crime after his 1977 arrest. He was tortured and, after an international outcry, placed under house arrest. In September 1978, he was put on an airplane to Israel after receiving members of the Inter-American Commission on Human Rights, who were appalled by his story. His book, *Prisoner Without a Name, Cell Without a Number*, was to bring the horror of Argentina to world notice. General Menendez was outraged by the government's 'weakness in releasing Timerman'.

Menendez was immediately relieved of his command – but not before he had set out for Jesus María, a small town in the hills, to rally his forces for a march on Córdoba. Asked by General Viola over the telephone what he was up to, General Menendez replied, 'routine manoeuvres'. These manoeuvres included assembling a force of 750 military engineers and anti-aircraft gunners, who marched, Quixote-style, on the 15,000-strong Viola garrison in Córdoba. When his contingent was surrounded, General Menendez was persuaded to come to his senses and surrender.

He was then forced to fly to Buenos Aires and apologize in person to General Viola in order to restore the respect due to that officer. For openly attempting to overthrow the government by force, General Menendez was sentenced (in a country where editors under suspicion were tortured) to sixty days of dignified confinement. This bizarre story of an armed rebellion, of the military feathers it ruffled, and of the magnanimity extended to the barons but not the serfs, was straight out of the Middle Ages – or perhaps Bolivia.

But Argentina is neither Bolivia nor the Middle Ages. Argentina is potentially modern and wealthy. It is the world's eighth largest country with only 38 million people to share its riches. It has a mild climate and its humid pampas are considered one of the world's five richest agri-cultural areas. In addition, the Patagonian plateau is ideal for sheep grazing and Argentina is the world's second-largest beef exporter. The nation could be one of the largest grain producers if it cultivated its pampas, and it is its fourth-largest wine producer. Four-fifths of Argen-tinians live in cities, and nine-tenths of them can read. Argentina is self-sufficient in its production of oil and has huge natural gas deposits, boundless hydroelectric potential and enormous coal reserves that it does not exploit. Its hills are rich in copper, molybdenum, gold, silver, lead, zinc, barium and uranium, with very little of it mined.

The popular gibe (among Brazilians) is that God lavished natural wealth on Argentina, but other countries complained. So God gave it Argentinians, to redress the balance. This is unfair. But they have made a mess of their politics, and that, more than anything else, stopped Argentina from becoming a paradise on earth.

The juntas that ran Argentina between 1976 and 1982 were unfairly criticized as the source of Argentina's ills. In fact, Perón's uniquely unpleasant legacy of nationalism, populism and military might have been the source. The subsequent juntas were certainly responsible for acting with the utmost brutality, waging a savage war against the opposition that revolted the conscience of the civilized world. The report on the fate of the disappeared, *Never Again*, compiled by the democratic government of President Raul Alfonsin, makes appalling reading. There is a nauseating voyeurism about books on torture; yet the issue cannot be avoided. This excerpt from *Never Again* will suffice:

M de M was abducted in Buenos Aires. She was taken for a long distance in a pick-up truck. Judging by the sound of crickets and other details, they took her somewhere in the country. It was like a camp, a provisional set-up, with canvas sheeting and tents every-where. They left her in a sort of room where she felt terrified and started to scream. Thus alerted, her captors put her into a tank full of water. Her breasts were hurting a lot, as she was breast-feeding at the time . . .

Then they bound her hands and feet with wires and passed

electric current through them. She began to have convulsions. They said that was the breaking in she needed in order to confess. Then they stripped her and raped her.

She asked to go to the toilet. They took her naked along an open gallery full of soldiers. She remembers that they all laughed. She also recalls them taking a group of people and putting them into a helicopter; they were thrown out at the end of a rope, and each time they were raised again they were questioned . . .

Teresa Cecilia Meschiati was abducted in the town of Cordoba: 'Immediately after my arrival at La Perla, I was taken to the torture room or intensive therapy room. They stripped me and tied my feet and hands with ropes to the bars of a bed, so that I was hanging from them. They attached a wire to one of the toes of my right foot. Torture was applied gradually by means of electric prods of two different intensities: one of 125 volts which caused involuntary muscle movements all over my body. They applied this to my face, eyes, mouth, arms, vagina and anus; and another of 220 volts called *la margarita* (the daisy) which left deep ulcerations which I still have and which caused a violent contraction, as if all my limbs were being torn off at once, especially in the kidneys, legs, groin and sides of the body. They also put a wet rag on my chest to increase the intensity of the shock.

'I tried to kill myself by drinking the foul water in the tub which was meant for another kind of torture called *submarino*, but I did not succeed.'

Yet military rule is the third major source of legitimacy for the modern state. Given the large number of countries that have recently undergone the experience of military rule – an area of the map also almost as large as that once covered by colonialism, also founded on the rule of force – this is a much neglected phenomenon.

A decade ago, the overwhelming majority of countries in Latin America were ruled by soldiers; some African countries still suffer a similar experience. It is arguable that some Middle Eastern countries are basically military regimes: Egypt, Iraq, Syria. Military rule even made its appearance in the former Eastern bloc – in Poland. The role of the armed forces in China has been considerable, and in some countries like South Korea, Thailand and Taiwan, often dominant. Some of this marching-boot empire has since crumbled, particularly in Latin America.

But military rule remains a real possibility in all of these countries and many others, even including Russia, and begs a large number of questions. Is military rule ever justified or legitimized other than through force? What ideas do military rulers subscribe to, if any, other than repression of the opposition? Why, given the armed forces' monopoly of coercion, are they so often pushed out of office? And is the case of some extreme free-marketeers, that authoritarian rule is actually beneficial when a country is undergoing accelerated economic development, ever justified?

It is worth briefly examining four controversial examples, although there are many others. In Chile in 1973 a Marxist president elected on a minority three-way vote attempted to push through radical social reform. Social disorder and inflation had occurred as a result, and the country seemed on the brink of chaos. When the army moved in, it had the support not just of the right but of Chile's traditional centrist political party, the Christian Democrats and, almost certainly, the majority of the population. What then happened was that the army stayed in power for a decade and a half, under a tough-minded general, Augusto Pinochet. But this does not invalidate the army's original decision to seize power in conditions of near-chaos in 1973.

Similarly, in Argentina soldiers staged a coup against the blatantly corrupt government of Isabelita Perón, which had presided over economic collapse, hyper-inflation and terrorism on such a scale that it threatened to turn into a civil war. The appalling repression and incompetence of the military regime subsequently could not detract from the fact that Argentina would have degenerated into anarchy if the army had not intervened at the time. Once the fire was out, it is terrible to discover that one's belongings have been soaked by the firemen's hoses; but they could have been destroyed much more comprehensively by the conflagration otherwise.

A third example is Pakistan in 1977. The economy was in tatters, with major ethnic violence also threatening under President Bhutto's regime. Virtually every informed Pakistani heaved a sigh of relief when General Zia ul-Haq staged his military coup. They were to become less certain when he pursued his vendetta against Bhutto to the point of hanging him, and clung firmly to power thereafter (he bore a strong resemblance to Pinochet in his political cunning, ruthlessness, refusal to budge and limited intelligence). But few at the time believed the military intervention was anything but inevitable to forestall chaos. This legitimized Zia's seizure of power. Another corrupt civilian government followed, before another, much more intelligent military figure, General Pervez Musharraf, seized power.

A fourth example is that of Poland in 1981. General Jaruzelski's takeover was prompted by fears of a Soviet invasion to suppress the country's Solidarity trade union movement and the political and social turmoil accompanying it, which directly challenged communist control of the country. The military authorities concluded that it was preferable for Poles themselves to put their house in order, and moved in to crush Solidarity.

While obviously repressive, the coup could be justified as an attempt to avert the much greater bloodshed and humiliation of a Soviet invasion; moreover, the armed forces moved quickly also to dismantle Poland's incompetent and hated communist leadership, so that the country was arguably closer to shrugging off the totalitarian yoke than it had been before. As ever, the Polish military leadership overstayed any welcome it had enjoyed and Jaruzelski was forced to compromise with a newly resurgent Solidarity in 1989, resulting in the first anti-communist government in the Eastern bloc at a time when the Soviet Union was too weak to intervene.

Thus a common feature of military regimes is that successful seizures of power usually take place only if the climate is right – if establishment and, sometimes, even public opinion, believes that a military government would be preferable to chaos or – as in Poland's case – foreign invasion. Sadly, few military men understand that this support constitutes a mandate in just the same way as an election provides one, and that it can be lost by a bad or incompetent military regime. Shielded from political reality and public opinion, military regimes frequently delude themselves that they retain a mandate when in fact the failure of opposition to make itself felt arises purely out of fear.

Another key characteristic of military regimes is the relegation of all political opponents to the status of enemies. Military training is necessarily carried out in black and white terms. There is your own side, and there is the enemy. Against the enemy, who will try to kill you, anything is permissible. The list of techniques practised by the military to eliminate or suppress opposition is well known: the elimination of political opponents either openly (Bhutto was show-tried and hanged, Allende probably killed in the bombed-out wreck of his palace, while thousands of his supporters were massacred in Santiago's main football stadium) or, as in Argentina, Guatemala and El Salvador, through 'disappearance'. In these countries people have been kidnapped off the streets, in unmarked Ford Falcon cars, and never seen again, victims of army-appointed death squads; imprisonment; routine torture, more to terrorize the opposition than to elicit information; the exile and expulsion of opponents; control of the press and public assembly; and the propagandist creation of a mythical 'enemy'; in Latin America, as elsewhere, this was usually international communism.

In fact, most countries have had minority communist movements, which were the most effective clandestine political operators under military regimes; a number, particularly Argentina and Uruguay and, more recently, Peru, all suffered from terrorism or, in Central America, guerrilla threats. Yet in many countries the communist label was used to suppress all political dissidence, from the centre-right to the extreme left.

Although military regimes tend to see even mild critics as enemies, they are not immune from the need for a source of political legitimization, indeed for civilian allies. The inability of generals to run a complex modern economy and state usually causes them to look for partners on the extreme right with simplistic solutions of their own which appeal to simple military minds: in recent times this has included enthusiasm for the Chicago School of monetarist economics preached by Milton Friedman.

However, there is a problem with this solution: the armed forces themselves are a major state institution, consuming, in Latin America's case, a large share of the national wealth. In countries like Argentina and Brazil, moreover, they also traditionally ran a fair-sized chunk of the nations' industries – Fabricaciones Militares in Argentina, Petrobras, the petroleum giant, in Brazil. So free-market solutions to their country's often chaotic economic problems on seizing power must stop short of cutting back on this huge area of state activity; more often than not it is substantially expanded.

The result has been a curious tension between the free-market technicians brought in to run the economy and their military masters which, while usually yielding short-term economic improvements, has resulted in further economic problems in the long term. In some countries, the social classes from which the army was drawn prompted it to behave in a populist, free-spending fashion, even espousing socialism: this was the case for a time in Peru and Ecuador and, also, briefly, in Bolivia.

A further characteristic of military regimes is their vigorous political infighting: while trying to give the impression that they are the unified servants of the nation, in fact, like any human institution, they are often deeply divided politically and corrupted from within. The most obvious division is between the rival services; it is also the easiest to resolve, because the army is almost always the most powerful.

In Buenos Aires on one occasion, the navy tried to press its claim by shelling army positions from the sea; but the army won. In Chile, General Pinochet ignominiously dismissed the air force commander, who had been critical of his dictatorship – and any air force men who might have defended him were quickly convinced by the size of the army units in the streets.

But other divisions are more complex – between rival personalities and generals, between central government and military governors with their local garrisons, between junior officers and senior officers. Some military regimes are characterized by ruthless hierarchy under a single all-powerful figure. Examples of the latter are Chile's Pinochet and Spain's General Franco.

Other armies are characterized by bitter political infighting, resolved only through rotating presidents. In Argentina, Generals Videla, Viola, Galtieri and Bignami followed each other in quick succession, while the frustrated naval chief, Admiral Massera, set himself up as a kind of internal opposition to them. He lacked much popular conviction, as he had presided over the most brutal of the intelligence services.

In Brazil, the problem was solved by institutionalizing change – presidential terms were limited: Generals Castelo Branco, Medici, Geisel and Figueiredo each had a fixed term of office. In Portugal, junior officers disgruntled with the country's colonial ventures succeeded in overthrowing their chiefs in the 1974 coup. If armies are not much good at politics, politics are not much good for armies.

A final feature of most military regimes is that, unlike Cromwell, they do not know when to go. Most such regimes would enjoy considerable popularity if, once they have stepped in to restore order for a year or two, they then would return to the barracks, placing themselves in reserve to intervene again if things go wrong. They would also retain their self-respect. Instead, after the initial emergency is overcome, there seems always to be a continuing peril to be dealt with, subversion to be resisted, the economy to be rescued, and so on. Military rulers deny vehemently that they also enjoy the perks and prestige of running countries and making money out of major industries; but they do.

Because of the climate of repression, it generally takes a fairly long time for opposition to organize itself so strongly that an army has to retreat from office, but it usually does eventually. Intriguingly, appearances to the contrary notwithstanding, armies are not simply brutal repressive machines; they are affected by the general climate of hostility to them, although thick skins take time to penetrate.

In Argentina, it took the unsuccessful and ludicrously misguided Falklands campaign to topple the army. In Brazil, it took the international debt crisis, run up by the military regime and invalidating its claim to responsible economic management as opposed to civilian profligacy and corruption. In Chile, it took a plebiscite into which General Pinochet was unwittingly lured, vainly believing he did indeed enjoy popular support. In Central America it took the loss of American support for the caudillos. In Spain – one of the longest lived of all – it took the death of General Franco, and in Pakistan, that of General Zia (almost certainly assassinated). In Thailand it took the killing of scores of demonstrators in Bangkok, and in Poland, the resurgence of Solidarity and the virtual paralysis of the country when there was no longer any prospect of Soviet invasion. Very few military regimes have voluntarily relinquished power.

This leads to a further characteristic of military rule: when armies leave, they have usually achieved little; as a political and economic crisis generally clears them out of office, the country is often in the same state of chaos that they used to justify their initial intervention. Moreover, the crudeness of their policies often ensures that their civilian supporters are as unpopular as they. Genuine political parties in most countries, being necessarily organized from the bottom upwards, have deep roots that a few years of military rule cannot pull up.

In Argentina, on the army's departure, the Peronists and the Radicals re-emerged; in Chile the Christian Democrats came out into the sunlight smiling; in Turkey, the same Mr Demirel and Mr Elevit that were deposed all those years ago were the main beneficiaries; in Pakistan, it was Mr Bhutto's daughter, commanding the same old Pakistan People's Party.

If there is a moral in all this, it is that military rule is best avoided; indeed frequent military interventions give politicians the excuse to behave irresponsibly in office, while the going is good, in the knowledge that the armed forces will pick up the pieces. Of course, there are occasions when military intervention is justified, even inevitable, or preferable to the alternative. In one respect military government succeeded without qualification, although brutally: the war against terrorism in Argentina and Uruguay was undeniably won. But no one should harbour any illusions about the nastiness, incompetence and transient nature of most military regimes. Putting soldiers in to run a country is like placing a security guard in charge of a flight control tower.

Military-backed rule is now confined to a handful of African countries and Pakistan. As will be seen, the return to barracks was one of the great victories for democracy and individual expression in the 1980s. But it is far too soon to conclude that the soldiers will remain confined there. Already, in Latin America, they have threatened to break out in coup attempts in Venezuela and Guatemala.

In Russia, and in the Ukraine and Romania as well, military rule remains a much discussed option in the event of social and economic disintegration. The same is true of Africa's civilian governments. In Asia, although the army's influence has been sharply reduced in South Korea, Thailand, the Philippines and even Malaysia, it remains considerable and could re-emerge in an emergency. The countries that have already had a spell of brutal, incompetent military governments are on the whole less enthusiastic about it today and have more of an incentive for avoiding the mistakes that led to the experience than those that have not, like Russia.

CHAPTER 20

GOVERNMENT BY ELITE

C airo, on the face of it, seems to be a city that cannot possibly work: it can take hours to get from the airport downtown, through one of the ugliest and biggest sprawls of industrial suburbs on the globe, and its inadequate road network is entirely choked by traffic. The centre of the city is another mess, with the exception of some superb examples of Islamic architecture and a picturesque old quarter. The place reeks of pollution, with pedestrians fighting cars for street space. The only peace to be found, away from the clamour of car horns and shouts, is by the banks of the languid, slow-moving Nile.

The government of Egypt seems to work – or not work – along the same chaotic lines: beneath the Sphinx-like imperturbability of the forever slightly smiling President Mubarak, a coalition of interests jostles as best it can for a share in power. No elite is dominant amid the chaos. This is typical of the fourth major source of authority for the modern state, which might loosely be called rule by the establishment. In a host of post-colonial states, in particular, a curious hybrid of powers yields a kind of collective authority usually led by a respected, but not all-powerful figurehead. In many cases this has replaced the glow of charismatic leadership that immediately followed the triumph of libera-tion movements and the end of the colonial era. This is particularly the case in much of Africa, and in parts of the Arab world.

The main components of this establishment are part of the senior bureaucracy, the armed forces, the political establishment of the (usually) single political party that is permitted to run in the elections that legitimize the system, senior business leaders and, sometimes, government-sponsored trade unions. The system was first and most successfully pioneered in Mexico, where that contradiction in terms, the Institutional Revolutionary Party, for long continued to wield a largely autocratic power while the rest of the continent moved on to a functioning multi-party system.

The PRI evolved its leadership through careful consultation and competition between elites; it permitted opposition, but through patronage, strong-arm tactics, fraud, corruption and the denial of resources, never permitted its rivals to win. The PRI changed president every six years, so personal dictatorship was avoided and the regime never appeared stultified. However, in 2000 the party was at last forced out in fair elections by the opposition leader, Vicente Fox. Mexico has joined the democratic mainstream of Latin America.

In Egypt, the charismatic leadership first of Nasser, then of Sadat, has been replaced by the bumbling amiability of Hosni Mubarak, an air force officer whom no one pretends is more than *primus inter pares* in the government, which contains representatives of all the elites. In Algeria, President Houari Boumedienne's leadership was replaced by faceless soldiers and party apparatchiks.

In those African countries which have not slid over to military rule – Uganda and Kenya, for example – the leaders President Museveni and Daniel arap Moi were not one-man rulers but pragmatists presiding over establishment coalitions of the dominant interests and tribes. Of two other historic figures in post-independence Africa one, Hastings Banda in Malawi, lost control of his country and the other, Kenneth Kaunda of Zambia, was ejected in a democratic election. Moi has now lost power. Only Zimbabwe's Robert Mugabe has become a traditional dictator.

Two other countries with a similar alliance of ruling party, armed forces and bureaucracy bear mentioning, although these are slightly different: Iraq and Syria. They each bear the panoply of a single-party socialist state, which to a degree they practise. They each use the armed forces and security services ruthlessly to crush dissent in a manner unthinkable in gentler 'establishment' states like Egypt or Mexico.

They are each personal dictatorships, where the decisions of the ruler – the al-Assads in Syria, Saddam Hussein in Iraq – primarily determine state policy. Both are incredibly tough-minded products of the different varieties of Baathist socialism and both rule through guile and terror – the immediate elimination of political threats, as has invariably happened to scores of challengers in Iraq. It may be too much to hope that Assad and Saddam will eventually be replaced by a gentler, more consensus style of leadership; but it is not impossible. Young Bashar Assad is a cautious reformist.

Finally, a hybrid all of its own. Iran's regime is cited as a unique form of rule today – a theocracy. It is very unusual in that the clergy have an enormous influence within the government. But, following the end of Ayatollah Khomeini's charismatic leadership, the clergy has been on the defensive, with Ayatollah Khomeini fighting a rearguard action against the growing forces for moderation.

Establishment consensus systems derive popular acquiescence primarily through responsiveness and acute political antennae: as rule by an elite, rather than through democratic election, it could easily become unpopular and too remote. But the political front organization exists both to provide the illusion of popular rule, by winning rigged elections, and more importantly, to reflect genuine grievances among ordinary people, so that these can be defused.

The difference with, say, the Communist Party of the Soviet Union is that for a long time this projected itself as the party of the elite, local party officials telling others what to do with dire consequences if they didn't – as during Stalin's rule. A more efficient one-party system acts as a channel to connect the rulers with what people are thinking. In addition, the consensus nature of such rule, through taking into account the various interests that make up the modern state, does make for at least a fairly cautious government – even if sometimes a paralyzed and over-bureaucratic one.

Finally, while the repressive apparatus is always present, it is used as a last resort, rather than a first one. These systems are neither in place through the naked use of force or fear, as military regimes are, or through the exercise of one-man, charismatic personal dictatorship, but through the medium of consensus-building and acceptance among the elites.

They are largely a transitional phenomenon, partly owing to their staggering corruption. As states undergo rapid industrialization, it is highly probable that a gradually larger and more literate political class, and a slightly more prosperous workforce, will seek their own vehicles of political expression to represent their interests, and that it will prove impossible to contain such pressure within the single political party. In Egypt and Algeria, there is a very real fear that any move towards greater political pluralism will result in a victory for Islamic fundamentalists; so it might, because the fundamentalists are benefiting from being the only effective opponents of the regime.

However, it is far from clear that increasingly harsh repression of the fundamentalists is the answer. Rather the ruling elites should cast about for ways of organizing credible parties that could win free elections and rally the interests that would be threatened if the fundamentalists took over. It is a very real dilemma. Zambia has shown that one-party establishment systems can be transformed into functioning multi-party systems, although the Islamic element is lacking there. In countries with substantial middle classes like Egypt it should be possible for Islamic zealots to be beaten at the ballot box, or at least marginalized within wider and more moderate Islamic movements; that – rather than their survival in power – should be the priority of ruling elites in developing countries with regimes of this sort.

CHAPTER 21

THE NEW AUTHORITARIANS

The Diet building in Tokyo – Japan's parliament – is a colossal edifice in neo-Gothic mausoleum style, dominating Nagatacho district and close to the tranquillity of the moat which surrounds the Imperial Palace. It sits astride the oasis of public buildings and parkland in Central Tokyo, surrounded by the giant sprawl of the city, with its huge variety of jumbled and colourful high-rises, the glitter of the Ginza shopping district, the pleasant hillside two-storey residential areas, the ostentatious vulgarity of Shinjuku. Across this diverse and dazzling city march millions of salarymen in identical dark suits and white shirts, a giant army of conformity.

The Diet, in its modern baroque bulk, is theoretically the seat of government and power in modern Japan. In practice, it ranks third in the pecking order, behind the enormously powerful bureaucracy and big business, and ahead of the armed forces, astride the ordered hierarchy of society. The system can best be described as Confucianist authoritarianism. Its inventor is Japan, and a number of other Asian countries are following in its footsteps. They include, massively, China, as well as Taiwan, Malaysia and Singapore. In some aspects the system resembles that of the establishment one-party state. But it differs in that it has a philosophical underpinning, is much more formalized and happily coexists with a private enterprise economy.

Japan has evolved into a uniquely sophisticated political system. The main players in the 'iron triangle' of Japanese politics, as recently defined by a mildly reformist former prime minister, Morihiro Hosokawa, are the bureaucracy, the political system it controls and the business interests that penetrate both.

The political system, which ought to be the pinnacle of any society, is the weakest of the three: routinely electing the Liberal Democratic Party for nearly five decades from 1955, the politicians act as a vote-buying façade to permit the bureaucrats to get on with the job of running Japan: the analogy is with management running a business, while the politicians act as rather marginal shareholders on the outside. Not only do senior bureaucrats not take any notice of their supposed political masters; in some cases they do not even know their names. As political impotence becomes obvious, so politics degenerates into little more than a grubby game of faction-fighting and vote-buying. At the same time Japan's powerful business interests are engaged in the job of buying both politicians and bureaucrats. A further partner is the armed forces, greatly weakened after the Pacific War, but still a growing force in its own right.

Underpinning the power play at the top is a deference society, built on a remarkable system of indoctrination through the family, schools and business. An individual is taught that he exists only in relation to society and has no rights of his own, just a huge burden of debts to others which must be repaid on his journey through life. Schooling relentlessly curbs independence and original thought, placing a premium on the acquisition of vast numbers of facts and statistics through sheer hard work. The new arrival in a major company goes through a relentless process of indoctrination, chanting company slogans and performing menial work that is reminiscent of early military training.

The system produces an immensely ordered, hard-working, law-abiding, conformist society where self-expression and independent thought are only acquired through seniority. In economic structure, the state plays a large role in underpinning and 'guiding' businesses, which nevertheless compete furiously with each other as giant cartels and on which a huge substructure of Japanese business depends.

The system resembles nothing so much as a kind of competitive utopian communism – only it works. In practice, the Japanese model is probably something unique: no people that had not been taught Confucianism and Shintoism for centuries, and had only just emerged from international isolation and immense agrarian overpopulation and backwardness, could probably be made to adopt a system of such rigorous personal submission to the state.

But is the Japanese model at least a local Asian model? Mohammed Mahathir, Malaysia's intolerant and authoritarian Islamic prime minister, certainly believes so, and has expressed that opinion. He says bluntly: 'We should not be the slave of democracy; in Malaysia we accept democracy but we must not be too extreme. Unlimited freedom is dangerous.' Singapore's Lee Kuan Yew, always disposed to press censorship, rigorous central planning and political control, also agrees. But it is the colossus of China itself that seems to be the chief convert to the Japanese model.

It is now no longer possible to consider China a communist country. The country was designated in March 1993 as a 'socialist market economy' operating 'a political economy on the basis of socialist public ownership'. Deng Xiaoping, China's dominant leader for a decade, was once described by Mao as knowing 'nothing about Marxism-Leninism'. Deng certainly fulfilled his promise, being responsible for forcing the Chinese economy to accept hundreds of thousands of small businesses. He also accepted a fledgling private education system and permitted the rampant private investment that is already transforming the skyline of Shanghai, as well as in the large hinterland of Hong Kong, which is growing at one of the fastest rates in the world. The state retains control of key major heavy industries; but its share of the economy is already little more than those of Western Europe's mixed economies.

A senior Chinese economist said privately in 1993, 'Socialism is ridiculous. Our only hope is peaceful evolution. Otherwise we die.' Deng argued, 'the essence of socialism is to liberate and expand the productive forces.' Deng's pragmatic successor, Jiang Zemin, has welcomed capitalists into the Communist Party. The state now accounts only for around a third of economic output in China, with farming and retailing now quasi-private, although subject to government contracts. In 1991, state companies accounted for 53 per cent of industrial output, against some 36 per cent for collectives and 11 per cent for private business. Ten years later, the Communist Party formally welcomed businessmen, previously derided as 'capitalist running dogs', into its ranks.

The transformation is enormously exciting – and exceedingly dangerous. The main opposition to the attempt to open up China's economy comes from the peasants who were the bulk of Mao's own communist movement and the backbone of the Cultural Revolution, when reformists were purged in huge numbers. The peasantry is restless again, chafing at urban corruption, inflation and widening disparities of wealth, and could strike back. Rural strength is still overwhelming in population terms and within the Communist Party which reflects the rural-urban split quite faithfully.

An eighty-six-page report written for the Chinese Academy of Sciences held out the possibility of disintegration after Deng's passing from the scene. The report claimed: 'It is possible that a situation like post-Tito Yugoslavia will emerge. In ten years, at the soonest, and at the latest between ten and twenty years, the country will move from economic collapse to political breakup, ending with its disintegration.' China's central government currently negotiates the amount of tax it raises from the provinces. Another lurch backwards would destroy China's over-heated economy and create a xenophobic and suspicious nation.

Yet if the experiment survives, an extraordinary hybrid will have been created: a state that permits a huge share of the nation's wealth to sit in private hands, yet retains the political repression of a communist regime. There can be little doubt that China's political gulag is awesomely greater than almost everywhere else, now that the Eastern bloc and Latin America have largely made the conversion to democracy. Stagger-ing numbers of political prisoners and forced labour camps remain in existence: China has some 2,000 labour camps with a total population of 10 million. Number Thirteen Labour Reform Detachment, known as Tang-ge-ma farm, has some 20,000 inmates and is seventy kilometres (45 miles) wide, sited in Qinghai province, on the edge of the Gobi desert.

The Tiananmen Square massacre was as brutal a display of repression as anything seen in Chile, Burma or Thailand, rendered all the more shocking because it was unnecessary: the demonstrations there that had surfaced during the Gorbachev visit had dwindled considerably in size. The repression has now slightly eased, in response to adverse overseas publicity. Both Deng and Jiang permitted economic liberalism to evolve alongside the authoritarian, repressive aspects of communism.

The contrast with Russia could not be more obvious: as Russia liberalized politically, it found it difficult to do so economically without imposing enormous suffering upon the people. In retrospect it seems that China's Marxist-Leninist uprising was not that at all: it was a crude peasant revolt which invoked communist nostrums to begin with, succeeded in improving the living standards of the peasants at enormous cost, and shook the communist doctrines off when their failure became apparent. Stalinism in Russia was the very reverse – the brutal extinction of the peasant class and their power.

In Russia there was a much greater commitment to the ideology and it was much longer-lasting – seven decades as opposed to four. But the reliance on authoritarianism in China was also commensurately greater. In Russia there was a colossal authoritarian tradition, but also a democratic bourgeois Westernized one, backed up by a large and growing middle class which has now, to a large extent, taken control.

In China the middle class is small, the peasant and urban classes huge, the army extremely powerful in an almost Latin American way, and there is no democratic tradition at all. The danger is of accelerated economic growth whose accentuation of the differences between city and country creates the potential for social explosion. The Chinese view the Soviet experiment with contempt, as that of a politically weak regime trying to liberalize economically and stumbling in the process. But a politically insensitive regime like China's, trying to do the same thing economically, seems much more likely to hit the buffers.

The Chinese have thus largely adopted the Japanese model of Confucianist authoritarianism. They have liberated hundreds of thousands of small businesses, which provide the momentum for the country's remarkable spurt of economic growth. The big state industries remain under careful tutelage, however – rather in the manner of Japan's *keiretsu*. The three-quarters of China's 1.2 billion population that live in the countryside have benefited from the trickle-down of these new urban riches: the World Bank reckons that the number of Chinese living at subsistence levels in 'absolute poverty' has fallen from 220 million in 1980 to 80 million in 2000 – a staggering improvement.

Nevertheless it is in the countryside that the most active resentment at the corruption and inequalities ushered in by the economic boom can be registered. The peasants form the backbone of Communist Party support and its bosses – still labelled 'village warlords' – the bulk of the party leaders. The tension between town and country will determine China's future. It was these backwoodsmen who insisted that the pro-democracy movement in Beijing be crushed, they who bolstered Deng in his decision that order must be maintained at all costs; the urban intelligentsia demanding a political opening is, by contrast, relatively small.

Thus China has unconsciously emulated Japan's example of economic growth alongside a repressive political system (China's is much more openly repressive than Japan's). This might seem to contradict the widely held view that economic liberalism inevitably brings political pluralism in its wake; but it accords with the view, fashionable in much of the developing world during the 1970s, that political authoritarianism is a necessary accompaniment to rapid economic growth: the view that democratic politicians are too demagogic and corrupt to implement the right economic policies. In this, the Chinese actually considered themselves superior to the Russians: in their view, the latter made the mistake of permitting too much political liberalization and too little economic freedom. It remains to be seen which will prove to be right.

Is Confucianist authoritarianism an ideal system in itself, or merely a transitional model for countries undergoing accelerated development? There is much to suggest the latter. In spite of the rigorous mental conditioning in Japan, there are growing calls for more accountability. There is a growing recognition that Japan's economic miracle has been at the expense of the workforce and the consumer. There are demands for a more creative educational system. These should not be exaggerated: Japan's political, social and corporate culture remains intensely authoritarian and conformist; but it is possible that in a couple of generations, a more relaxed and affluent Japan will move gradually towards greater accountability.

In China there are those who see the booming coastal provinces adopting more pluralist systems; yet the enormous power of the peasantry remains a drag on political development. The greatest danger is that if China moves too fast towards free markets and democracy, a backlash could develop in some of the remoter provinces which could halt both political and economic development. Global finance, acting on its herd instinct to pour money into China, seems as blind as ever to the political dangers in this unpredictable country. If Confucianist authoritarianism is a largely transitional system, the transition in both China and Japan seems likely to be very long.

CHAPTER 22

GOVERNMENT BY TALKING SHOP

The sixth and fastest spreading political system is liberal democracy. A glance at the past two decades shows that it has been making converts at a truly awesome speed. Its cradle, Western Europe, harboured three dictatorships, Spain, Portugal and Greece in 1973 – all three are now democratic. In Eastern Europe, there were twelve communist autocracies, if the Ukraine and the Baltic Republics are each counted as a separate state, and only one democratic one, Austria. Now all have converted to democracy.

In the Middle East, a democratic desert for so long, Israel has been joined by democratic Turkey, while Yemen, Jordan, Kuwait and Bahrain are inching towards democracy and even the Palestine Liberation Organization is internally pluralist, if not exactly democratic. In the subcontinent, long-democratic India and Sri Lanka (although riven by sectarian strife) were briefly joined by Pakistan. In the Far East, South Korea, Taiwan, Thailand and Hong Kong have made strides towards full democracy. The huge sprawl of the Soviet Union is now at least half democratic.

In Latin America there were just three democratic states in the subcontinent: Venezuela, Colombia and Costa Rica in 1976. Now there are seventeen, and only one authoritarian system – Cuba. On a very rough count, 3 billion of the world's 6 billion people now live under governments which they have helped to elect, compared with proportionately half that number twenty years ago.

What is liberal democracy? How can it be distinguished from a system like Egypt's whose political leaders claim is representative in a different way? What is its special appeal? The first thing to understand about democracy is that it is a relative term. There is no full democracy anywhere in the world. On the assumption that human nature is imperfect it is probably unachievable.

Full democracy – full freedom – would mean that every individual was fully involved in every decision concerning his or herself. In an ideal, perfect world we would all agree what was in our own interests while not impinging on the interests of others. There would be no need for a parliament, indeed for a state, because we would all agree all the time what was right – a kind of utopian Marxism; indeed, authoritarianism believes it has found the answers on behalf of the people – but, of course, being managed by human beings is wrong much of the time. This of course is a dream. Democrats, acknowledging human imperfection, believe in the free interplay of argument and ideas.

In fact, we need a state to arbitrate between us and to represent us in the outside world. Modern liberal democracy provides a rather imperfect way of controlling that state: we elect representatives every few years, to make the state accountable to us.

A trip to the oldest liberal democracy in the world, Britain's parliament at Westminster, shows just how imperfect this mechanism can be. The ordinary voter, arriving there to meet his Member of Parliament, will be taken to the central lobby, which is rather like a great railway station, where hundreds can assemble and lobby their MP. The MP will promise to raise a constituent's grievance with civil servants or local authorities, and sometimes gets matters put right.

Turning to the left under the great Gothic ceilings of Pugin and Barry, the visiting constituent will be led along a corridor to a smaller, even busier lobby, where MPs have the right to buttonhole ministers and lobby on behalf of constituents. Through the swing doors, they can enter parliament itself: there MPs can express their points of view in speeches in debates, put down parliamentary questions to ministers designed to elicit information or make a critical point and, once a week, ask questions of the mightiest figure in the land, the prime minister.

In practice, the 600-odd MPs lack the resources and opportunities to monitor the actions of tens of thousands of civil servants: they can only scratch the surface of the bureaucracy and only the most energetic ministers leave a stamp on their departments.

In theory MPs vote on every piece of legislation brought before them in the best interests of their constituents. In the many votes on any one sitting day, the MPs will do exactly as their party whips tell them to, and vote many times on matters they know nothing about, because the government wants to get the legislation through. Only occasionally, on a matter of purely constituency interest or on a matter where their conscience troubles them will they disobey those instructions. The electorate – watching their representative go through the 'aye' or 'no' lobby at a fast trot, registering his presence, the main job of MPs – may feel this is something of a charade.

How representative is the mother of parliaments? The answer is that the people's will can make itself felt directly just once every few years, and indirectly in a number of ways. The population has the choice – and it is limited to that – to throw out a government they dislike. This is a considerable right, to be able to do so peacefully, without bloodshed or confrontation with an unelected government. In addition, through writing to an MP, and through the unions, professional associations, employers' associations and pressure groups, the voters can hope to influence political issues.

This should not be viewed as a minor right: MPs are acutely sensitive to their constituents, when they can reconcile their demands with the general injunction to follow the party line. However, their power to influence the bureaucracy, while not insubstantial, is not all that large.

What are the main ingredients of liberal democracy – given that it is still very limited? The essentials would seem to include the existence of one or more major parties, and the possibility of ejecting the government from office. It is true that in a number of countries one-party rule has been the norm, even though people are free to vote for other parties – Italy and Japan being the obvious examples. But this does qualify their democracy – Italy's to a lesser extent, because the Christian Democrats up to 1994 had always had to share power with others, Japan to a greater because, until 1993, it seemed virtually impossible to eject the Liberal Democrats from office (and the circumstances of 1993 were a revolt within the ruling party, not an opposition victory).

But in the United States, Britain, France, Germany, Canada, Australia, Sweden, Norway, Spain, Italy today and Portugal it is possible to throw the rascals out. In each of these countries this has happened in recent history at least once. The right of voters to change their government is perhaps the most fundamental qualification for democracy.

Elections must be free and fair: balloting must be secret, there must be safeguards against intimidation, counting should be scrupulously conducted, freedom of assembly must be guaranteed and party financing must be as even-handed as possible.

Another characteristic is freedom of the press. This is immensely important. There is a danger, even in a developed democracy, of the press being controlled only by a single interest – usually that of big business – because money has the power to acquire newspapers; as soon as choice is stifled, so a country slides towards the one-party option. The same, obviously, is true of broadcasting but the safeguards are usually much clearer there.

Obviously political freedom is essential, in the sense that anyone can express an opinion or organize a party without fear of being arrested, or of indirect retaliation. There is also the need for a whole set of guarantees of individual rights backed up by an independent judiciary. People's personal freedom must be protected from the tyranny of the majority: this means that the police should have no right to enter people's homes without warrants, of detention without trial, of interrogation without lawyers. In a large number of new areas, usually related to worthy popular causes such as health, road safety, the need to protect against crime or to define people as financial or insurance risks, worrying inroads are being made into individual liberties even in countries like Britain (even the press cannot be absolved). The state has to make the case for encroaching on the freedom of the individual, rather than the individual for defending himself against state authority because, by definition, the state is infinitely more powerful.

Finally, the apparatus of the state, the civil service, should be independent, prepared to serve whatever political master is elected, and at all times prevented from supporting or lending its political offices to supporting a particular political party. These six features are a bare minimum. The democratic ideal is always moving, and needs to develop. Greater decentralization, referenda, different types of electoral system, the possibility of a popular say in targeting taxation, greater participation in choosing political candidates, primaries – all of these are ways of deepening democracy; but the six factors discussed are the least necessary for a country to consider itself a democracy.

To turn to the second question: why is democracy so appealing, why is it spreading? Obviously everyone likes to have a say in their own government, the way they are ruled. Far better to have a government chosen by yourself in some degree than one imposed from above. Yet this was far from being a universal view even in relatively recent times: it was argued that democracy would lead to demagoguery, corruption, populism, the simplification of issues, the tyranny of the majority, the breakdown of authority, extremism. Autocrats throughout the century have argued that rule by the educated, the elite, is better than votes for all. Patrick Kennon's *The Twilight of Democracy*, arguing that 'only highly trained, anonymous technocrats' can be trusted to run modern countries, shows that the ancient line of thinking is far from dead.

The fact remains, though, that as a people become better educated and more prosperous they demand nothing less than a say in their own government, and democracy is the system that provides it. Moreover, there seems to be a kind of natural democratic equilibrium: when a system has a large enough middle class and a working class that is reasonably prosperous and not too oppressed, it is remarkable how sensibly people vote.

In a very few cases, populists have won power: Hitler was elected by popular vote – albeit by a third of the people; the ineffectiveness of his opponents allowed him to win absolute power. For the most part, almost every dictator, populist or extremist politician has won power through non-democratic means. Democratic choices have almost invariably been more moderate, stable, less nationalistic and belligerent, less ideological.

To return to the old triangle of powers: democracy provides a means by which ordinary people can peacefully check the power of the modern state – which is a huge and unchanging fact of life. If ordinary people lack the visible power, the rulers can behave as they will and an explosion of the self can quite quickly follow – as has happened in so many countries, from Iran to Poland. In much of the world democracy is necessary to guarantee social peace, not because it is an ideal system.

Elites never give away their power unless they have to: the more intelligent do so because they realize this is the means to guarantee their continuity and social stability. The more sophisticated a society, the more important democracy is as a means of reconciling different interests peacefully, and of securing the acquiescence of the governed to government which, *pace* free-market minimalists, is an absolutely central feature of modern life.

The trend towards democracy will continue even in places where it meets with much suspicion, as a challenge to a paternal system of rule, like China and Japan. It is fast becoming the minimum necessary to secure the acquiescence of those at the bottom to a society which necessarily has to be ruled from the top. Democracy is essential in part to defuse the assertion of the self, something which autocrats have long failed to understand.

But the whole happy picture of a world moving inexorably towards democracy out of enlightened self-interest after the collapse of communism is being grossly and terribly distorted by the possibility that elected governments no longer have the power to decide their own nations' destinies – a subject which we will now consider. It is not much use having the vote if the people you vote for are merely playthings for much larger, unelected, impersonal, directionless forces.

CHAPTER 23

THE NEW FINANCIAL TSUNAMIS

They emerge from seemingly peaceful waters, first as ripples, then as small waves disguising the huge size and energy beneath. By the time they reach shore they can be dozens of feet high, sweeping all before them. They are the new financial tsunamis – huge capital tidal waves which destroy the economic policies of sovereign governments in moments. Sometimes these undulations seem beneficial, flooding a previously capital-starved country, but when they flood out just as quickly they can leave devastation behind. Bank-lending ravaged Africa, Eastern Europe and Latin America in the 1980s. Currency and equity floods hit Britain and France, Mexico, Russia and East Asia during the 1990s. Argentina has been the first casualty of the new millennium.

Let us look at some examples. On 16 September 1992, the managers of one of the major economies in Europe, Britain's, led by one of the most technically competent finance ministers in history, Norman Lamont, awoke to what seemed a routine day. The economy looked in pretty good shape. Inflation was low and falling. A policy of rigorous financial orthodoxy and perhaps needlessly prolonged recession continued, but there were slight signs of economic movement in spite of still high real interest rates, running well ahead of inflation.

On other counts, Britain was performing well: its wage costs had been held down without industrial trouble. Industry was leaner and fitter than it had been for years. The budget deficit was under control, although social security costs were beginning to spiral. Direct taxation was low, following the orthodoxy of 'supply-side' economic theorists. The prudence of Lamont could not but be applauded by the international banking community, the OECD and the other central banks, as well as the IMF. Britain even had Walter Mittyish hopes of replacing its rival, Germany, as Europe's major reserve currency because of its reputation for single-mindedness and responsibility.

Above all, a general election had just taken place which the Conservative Party had won for the fourth time running – a post-war record. This confirmed the country's new political stability: the sick man of Europe was no more: strikes, absenteeism, trade union militancy, nationalization threats, constant changes of government – these were things of the past. The people had just spoken, and had plumped for caution.

There had long been mutterings that the pound was over-valued: that it had entered the Exchange Rate Mechanism of the European Monetary System at too high a level – it is said that the Prime Minister, Margaret Thatcher, had insisted upon this, overriding her chancellor, John Major, as the price of adhering to a system she deeply opposed. Whether she was acting for reasons of national pride, or because she knew the level was unsustainable, and was likely to bring discredit on the system itself, can only be surmised. For all that, the impact of British membership of the ERM, at a time when German interest rates were high in order to stifle domestic inflation, was a highly disciplinary one for the British economy.

Within a few minutes of the exchanges opening on 16 September, pandemonium had broken out. A massive wave of selling of sterling had begun and seemed to gather momentum every minute. Panic set in: the market was going to force sterling to devalue: thus, whoever started it – and the initial selling of sterling may have been quite small – other major funds had to join the rush in order to secure their position. To stay in sterling when it was about to be devalued would have left their investors with billions of pounds' worth of losses. The lament of the speculator – that while many do it for profit, others do it to avoid losses – is thus half true.

That this movement had nothing whatever to do with normal economics was beside the point. That Britain's economy was working, highly competitively, unaffected by trade union militancy and with a newly elected Conservative government counted for nothing beside the simple fear of devaluation that dominated the financial markets.

'You cannot buck the market' was the common refrain of the free-market economists which held sway through most of the 1980s; another such refrain was that the market is always right. If your economy is healthy and free enterprise oriented, you will be rewarded; if not, you will be in trouble. Britain's healthy, only a little too rigidly policed economy in 1992 was smashed by a wave of speculation followed by a wave of panic selling that had nothing to do with the country's fundamental economic health. You couldn't buck the market because of its sheer size – a straightforward truism.

Only a few days earlier a massive European safety barrier had been arranged for sterling; when the tide first rose past danger levels, Lamont attempted to erect hasty defences, raising interest rates first by 2 per cent and then by a further 2 per cent. If this policy had succeeded, Britain's fragile economic recovery would have been completely crushed. But the tidal wave was so great – some $700 billion – that it swept all before it.

Britain withdrew from the ERM, floating the pound to permit it to bob back to a natural level in the wake of the wave, rather than let it be anchored and swamped altogether. This was announced by Lamont at 7.45 in the evening. An economic hurricane had struck, leaving devastation in its wake.

All of this might seem merely a parable on the futility of fixed exchange rates. But it was also a cautionary tale about the new power of international speculation, the so-called 'market'. It was simultaneously repeated with the Italian lira, the Irish pound and the Swedish krona, and later with the Spanish peseta and the French franc – which had to be shored up with immense difficulty by the apparent villain of the piece, the deutschmark. Not only were national central bank reserves proved wholly inadequate as a defence against speculation; so were such European funds as existed to prevent currencies being overwhelmed in this way.

There was a predictable chorus of outrage on the iniquities of the ERM, which was partially justified. But currencies outside the ERM would have been even more vulnerable: in fact the lesson was precisely the reverse of the one proclaimed by the Eurosceptics: only a single currency, fully implemented, would have had the strength to withstand such a wave.

Yet the real issue was different: it was the power of international money, the sheer size of the flows, and the caprices that governed those flows. Some $300 billion cross the currency dealing rooms of the City on an average day. 'Hot money' similarly flows in and out of bond and equity markets across the globe, with seriously destabilizing effects – as was evident in Latin America in January 1995. In 1991, the financial derivatives market, a kind of gamble on future money, currency and stock market prices, alone saw transactions of no less than $7 trillion; this rose to $12 trillion in 1994. The collapse in February 1994 of Baring Brothers, the City's oldest merchant bank, as a result of investment on the derivative market by just one Singapore-based employee showed the urgent need for proper regulation of these markets.

The franc crisis of 1993 saw Germany, France, Belgium, Denmark, Holland, Spain and Portugal spend some $17 billion between them – a drop in the ocean – to support the franc, the Dutch kroner, the Belgian franc, the Spanish peseta and the Portuguese escudo. France, Belgium, Denmark and Portugal all had well-managed economies following orthodox policies. The analogy was again with the sea. Even large, well-steered ships like the British economy could be engulfed by currency movements as big as any previously experienced in the world.

What were the consequences for the British economy of this storm? What was the origin of this massive flow? Did it respond to economic logic? Did 'the market' – like Nanny – know best?

The answer to this last question has already been touched upon. The market 'knew' that the pound was overvalued. It probably was; many economists could not see the sense in keeping sterling at a rate of exchange that only served to make British exports dearer and imports cheaper; even if this is slightly inflationary, it always makes more sense for a currency to be undervalued rather than overvalued, as there is nowhere to go but up and it improves competitive advantage.

In orthodox economic terms, the pound was at a perfectly acceptable level, justified by reduced interest rates and the health of the British economy. However, the market's guess proved self-fulfilling: if enough currency dealers can be persuaded that the pound will be devalued, a run will start, and logical economics can take a running jump. The pound will be devalued solely because enough people fear that it will. The market decides, but not for reasons other than its own overwhelming size, certainly not for orthodox economic reasons, as traditional free-marketeers would have it.

The Times journalist Anatole Kaletsky brilliantly dissected the underlying irrationality of the markets in September 1994 when he pointed out that American investors at the time were panicking at the failure of interest rates to affect inflation over a two- to three-month period, when orthodox economics showed there was a time lag of two to three years between the two; that the market's latest fad was in believing that interest rates and inflation would automatically rise in line with economic growth – whereas inflation has usually tended to fall until the last two years of the growth cycle. Finally, he believed the market, correctly this time, also panics not because it fears a rise in inflation, but because it assumes central banks will raise interest rates because they fear a rise in inflation – thus compounding the errors of the central banks and making them self-fulfilling.

> It is for this reason that bond markets invariably fall when central banks tighten monetary policy despite the supposed improvement in anti-inflationary credibility that is supposed to follow such responsible moves. That is why long-term interest rates, as well as 'inflationary expectations' are higher today in Britain than they were before Mr George (the Governor of the Bank of England) made his 'pre-emptive' strike against inflation. And that is why it is often possible to go on making money in the financial markets by being stupid. As Keynes said, 'the successful speculator does not try to be clever, he merely tries to anticipate the stupidity of the market as a whole'.

To return to the second question: the origin remains obscure: it is now realized that major currency dealers like George Soros made as much as $1 billion by selling pounds early enough, and he seems to have accepted some of the status of 'lead' speculator; there were others, and there will be many more. At the time of the sterling crisis, there was speculation, particularly in Europe, that the Americans, and possibly the Japanese, were involved in a 'plot' to destroy the ERM, in order to weaken the whole process of European integration, viewed as hostile to their interests.

In February 1993, the German Chancellor, Helmut Kohl, alleged that unnamed forces were seeking to 'torpedo' the principle of a single European currency through market speculation. After the attack on the franc in August 1993, Karl Lamers, foreign policy spokesman for the Christian Democrats, suggested that the assault on the franc had been planned in 'government offices'. Kohl's aides privately suggested that the British government had encouraged the City and Wall Street to attack the franc.

Even the Belgian foreign minister, Willy Claes, suggested that the crisis had been the result of an 'Anglo-Saxon' plot to keep Europe divided and 'condemned to play a secondary role in the great economic debate'. Prime Minister of France Eduard Balladur denounced 'unjustified speculative movements and major upheaval in the financial markets' and called for measures to prevent rapid currency falls. However, a report by the Bank for International Settlements said that Europeans were responsible for nine-tenths of the funds crossing currency markets in the franc crisis.

The Americans pointed to their relatively small share of the speculative wave. However, as already argued, it does not take a huge sum to start the wave; once the perception of an imminent devaluation is under way, the currency traders have an obligation to their customers to join in on a massive scale. The possibility of American or Japanese 'triggers' cannot be discounted, a point which will be returned to: traditionally, neither country has shown much restraint in seeking competitive economic advantage.

As far as domestic economic policy was concerned, the impact on Britain, at least, was entirely to knock off course the policies on which the general election had just been won, and to substitute others – as it happens, rather good ones: a steady reduction in interest rates and a competitive upsurge stemming from the low rate of sterling – which got the sluggish British economy moving and even partly reduced inflation further. Yet these policies were the reverse of the ones thought sensible by central bankers and orthodox free-market theorists. The market had in fact stood orthodoxy on its head. In the process it had also comprehensively thwarted the will of the British people just expressed at a general election for the government to continue following prudent policies.

If the international currency market does not behave in an orthodox free-market manner, if it does not reward the virtuous and punish the spendthrift, what in fact does determine its sudden outbursts of pique and turbulence? The world has now experienced well over a decade of increasingly massive currency flows, and it is possible to draw some conclusions about the market's behaviour. Certainly economic virtue counts pretty low on the list of reasons for staying with a currency, even if the central banks, the IMF and the OECD set such a store by this.

The market is a dedicated follower of fashion. In a world always uncertain precisely which mix of economic policies is the right one – if there were a right one, everyone would pursue it – certain things are fashionable at certain times. In the 1970s rigid orthodoxy, corseted by stern monetary targets, was indeed fashionable: currency traders would buy currencies that conformed to certain orthodox prescriptions – low public borrowing, low inflation, low taxes, high interest rates, etc.

By the late 1970s and early 1980s, petro-currencies were all the rage.

Britain suffered one of the stiffest doses of deflation in its history in the early 1980s, the consequence of a soaring pound caused by currency inflows, attracted by its North Sea oil wealth: British products became enormously difficult to sell abroad at inflated prices, bankrupting thousands of otherwise perfectly solvent companies.

Stephen Dorrell, now a Conservative backbencher, published a devastatingly effective pamphlet at the time entitled *North Sea Oil: Black Gold or Black Death?* which argued this passionately; but he was running against the prevailing orthodoxy, later abandoned by Mrs Thatcher, that on no account must the government interfere in exchange rate policy. Towards the mid-1980s, interest rates seemed to be all that the market was interested in: money flowed to countries with the highest rates, whatever the actual economic health of the economies behind those currencies.

The first to take advantage of this on a grand scale was the United States in the mid-1980s, which by any orthodox economic analysis was in dire straits, with a massive and growing budget deficit, caused by a sharp, ideologically motivated reduction in taxes coupled with no corresponding decrease in spending – in fact a huge increase in defence outlays – as well as a huge trade deficit. In order to fuel the budget deficit, American real interest rates were raised to unprecedented levels, attracting vast currency inflows. America was able to get away with this because of its sheer size: if a medium-sized economy had practised such policies, it would have been accused of profligacy and a run on the currency would have ended in devaluation (although high interest rates might have stemmed this, leading to domestic recession).

Then, in Germany in the 1990s high interest rates set in order to control the inflation unleashed by the huge costs of German reunification resulted in a rush towards that currency. In both cases, the effect was highly negative and deflationary on weaker currencies which, in order to maintain themselves, had to raise their own interest rates and stifle domestic economic growth. The answer for those currencies would have been to devalue, and undermine the American and German bullies; but that is where national pride steps in.

The speculation against European currencies that started with 'Black Wednesday' has been of a more anarchic sort. There was not much wrong with British interest rates or economic policy, save that it was too cautious, but the currency was probably overvalued; the lira was more obviously fragile, with Italy's chronic budget deficit and political instability; but the currency was, if anything, undervalued. The franc, which soon came under intense pressure, was probably at about the right rate and should have been boosted by the return of a conservative government. Thus Britain, Italy, Ireland, Sweden, Portugal and France were each successively forced into devaluations.

The President of the European Commission, Jacques Delors, suggested that 'the time has come to study ways of limiting short-term money movements . . . Money movements are complex, but we should have an international agreement to enable us to establish the rules of the game.' Given the size of the flows, this seemed a tall order: the difficulty of differentiating between speculative and legitimate patterns of international financial movement seemed almost insuperable. Still, the issue of what was behind these huge, seemingly random flows was being addressed for the first time.

In immediate European terms, the danger inherent in the collapse of the ERM was not that each country would go its own way – a suicidal course – but that its revival in the shape of a common currency, after a decent interval, by the core EEC currencies, particularly the mark and the franc, but not including perfidious sterling, would transform Europe into a fast- and a slow-lane community, with the latter denied the kind of currency support that the fast would enjoy, becoming liable to be picked off at the currency market's whim.

George Soros, the currency speculator, is engagingly candid about the benefits of monetary union: 'In my opinion, freely floating exchange rates would destroy the Common Market because in this climate floating exchange rates are cumulatively destabilizing. The more they fluctuate, the greater the relative importance of speculation. Speculation tends to be trend-following and the excesses it produces can be self-validating . . . Since all exchange rate systems are flawed, it is best not to have one at all, but to have a common currency. The fact that it would put speculators like me out of business is one of its merits.'

Yet the central issue was more fundamental even than that: the size of international financial flows had successively demolished one country's economic policy after another in a seemingly capricious way. Thus, in a crucial area of economic policy, national governments even of large industrialized countries like Britain and France had lost much of their power. Around the world there might be greater democracy than ever before: voters might feel they had the ability to influence events. Yet in practice the economic policies of the governments they elected could be altered at a moment's notice by huge, impersonal, apparently directionless and illogical forces, colossal currency transactions and speculators.

Of course, the process had been under way for some time, with the growth of the offshore Eurodollar market, effectively setting up a reserve currency that escaped national financial regulation, and with the acceleration of the speed and extent of currency trading made possible by modern technology. Taken together with the liberalization of capital and financial markets, all of which resulted in the creation of a massive backwash of capital that could move within moments around the financial and equity markets of the world, this was scant consolation for the nations so affected.

'Black Wednesday' was the most dramatic example yet of the new phenomenon – the globalization of capitalism – which is changing the shape of the world and which, in fact, is fast eroding the authority of nations, and the ability of ordinary people, through the votes cast in new and old democratic entities, to influence their own destinies. It is not much use being allowed to choose your representatives and government if, in fact, they are powerless.

There are those who argue that this is desirable – that voters are poor judges of economic choices. But this has been the argument of authoritarians and autocrats throughout the ages, and runs counter to all political evolution and the spread of liberal democracy around the world. The new economic elitism has not been the subject of proper debate in the Western democracies and is both wrong – people are better judges of their own interests than experts and markets – and profoundly dangerous, threatening to ignite popular anger.

Exactly the same phenomenon of globalization is taking place in a whole variety of other areas. The flow of international bank lending was the crisis of the 1980s, just as the flow of speculative currency and equity transactions was that of the 1990s. The spread of the multinationals was the crisis of the 1960s and 1970s. In addition to these three, trade flows have become vastly more complex and less subject to control by individual countries. Both the latter phenomena have important implications for the shrinking of national sovereignty. Each of these three further features of the globalization of capitalism must now be taken in turn.

CHAPTER 24

BLACK HOLE

The international banking crisis of the late 1970s and most of the 1980s was perhaps the most foreseeable, irresponsible and destructive economic whirlwind to hit the global economy in modern times. It was foreseeable in that anyone on the ground could tell what was happening as early as the late 1970s; it was irresponsible in that those who should have known better – principally the commercial banks, but also central banks, governments and international financial regulators – turned a blind eye not just to the catastrophic effects upon the countries concerned, but also to the interests of their own countries and banking customers. It was destructive in the impact not just upon the economies of the countries concerned, but also upon the major banks involved – although there at least catastrophe was avoided amid much self-congratulation, even if just a little foresight would have averted the danger in the first place.

I hope readers will forgive my inserting a personal note, not because I was anything but a minor observer of these events, but just to show how myopic and callous the attitude of the 'experts' in charge of the banking system was at the time. I travelled to Brazil in May 1980, before there seemed any threat of an international debt crisis, and was horrified by what I found. I reported at the time in *The Economist* that:

> Foreign bankers should pay close attention to the thinking on the subject of the foreign debt that is taking place among the moderate opposition leaders who may be brought into a government of national unity before 1982, or may have a majority in parliament

afterwards. Senator Tancredo Neves (later Brazil's first democratic president in two decades) insists that 'Brazil has always paid its debts and always will.'

Yet another senior opposition leader, who preferred not to be named because of the sensitiveness of the subject, told your correspondent that he believes the government should go to the country's creditors and point out to them that the country is now borrowing not to finance its development, which would make Brazil an acceptable credit risk, but merely to service its debt. The government, he says, should then point to the political dangers of exacting impossible sacrifices from Brazil in order to pay for its foreign debt, and should ask for the terms of repayment to be substantially extended and the rates of interest to be sharply reduced.

The most vivid political danger, for a government that appears to be inflicting further hardship on Brazilians already living on the breadline in order to service the foreign debt, is that it provides a ready platform for that most traditional of Brazilian political animals, the populist nationalist. No one has yet emerged from the opposition's ranks to urge Brazil to tear up its debts and expel the exploiting multinationals.

So far the main nationalist drumbeats have come from within the army, where the right-wing officer in charge of recruitment, General Andrada Serpa, was fired for attacking the 'savage capitalism' of the multinationals. The present army chief of staff, General Ernani Ayrosa, is thought to share much the same view. It is the fear that some such figure will stage a coup that is keeping the opposition so quiet at the moment.

Brazil is no Jamaica, Peru or even Turkey. The very size of its foreign debt gives it a form of muscle. Mr Delfim Netto (Brazil's economic supremo) knows that western bankers have so much to lose should anything go seriously wrong with Brazil politically that they must put up the money in the end. For if Brazil were to default on its foreign debt, there are few effective sanctions that could be brought to bear. Mr Delfim Netto insists that nothing could be further from his thoughts than the idea that overborrowed developing countries should ask their creditors to write off part of their debt.

If pressure from the nationalists in the army or in the opposition threatens to topple the government, Mr Delfim Netto may (next year?) have to go to Brazil's creditors (or the International

Monetary Fund?) with a penitent smile and point out that, unless they soften the terms of the debt, a fire-breathing nationalist may end up in his place. Either way, the international banking system should start girding its loins for the possibility that it may never again see some of the money it has splashed out to Brazil.

This, written well in advance of the debt crisis, created a furore, with the vice-president of one of the biggest American banks exposed in Latin America flying out from New York specially to protest to my editor in London that 'irresponsible' speculation of this kind was not only inaccurate but – a directly contradictory argument – damaging to the stability of the international banking system (surely if there was no danger, my article could do no harm?). Three years later I predicted in *The Economist*, reiterating the tentative sentence at the end of my Brazil article, that 'most of the loans [to Latin America] are now irrecoverably lost'. The debts could never be repaid anything like in full, and the banks' main effort over the next few years would consist in attempting to find a suitable and respectable cover to mask their retreat and write off a large part of the money.

The Mexican debt crisis quickly followed, and a decade of financial turmoil ensued in which the banks, eventually recognizing that most of the loans were lost, tried to stage as dignified and ingenious a retreat as possible, selling debt at a discount, swapping debt for equity, renegotiating the debt on less and less favourable terms to themselves, always maintaining the fiction that they were hanging tough with the irresponsible borrowing nations, that the international banking system was working smoothly, that this was merely a 'technical' problem – a fiction exposed later by the huge losses of the banks themselves.

The retreat was something of a success, in that the write-offs were accepted gradually and without the collapse of any major part of the world banking system. Its main sequence was: an attempt by a major debtor to renegotiate its debt; then, after talking tough, insistence by the commercial banks that the IMF enforce a harsh austerity programme, which would improve things in the short run, but provide no long-term answer; and finally, conditional on that programme and accompanied by a great deal of lecturing by the irresponsible banks on the irresponsibility of the Third World, a write-off in real terms of part of the debt which was usually insufficient to prevent the same crisis recurring a few years later. There would be congratulations all around in international banking circles, huge losses for their shareholders and customers, and appalling suffering among the peoples of the under-developed borrowing countries.

A brief look at the origins of the crisis is in order, as it was the biggest and most spectacular demonstration to date of the insouciance with which global capitalism could treat not just nations, but whole continents.

The cast is the same, although the backdrop varies in the little scenes of human anguish being played out along the 3,000-mile length of Latin America. The toddlers are invariably barefooted with grubby faces, chubby yet undernourished, bearing earnest, puzzled expressions as they wipe their hands on cloth shorts or crinkly paper-thin skirts. The teenagers, their eyes burning with spare energy, hang around in the doorways of the local bars, poolrooms and fast-tortillas-and-beans joints, without the money to play, drink or eat.

The resigned, slack-shouldered men, middle-aged at twenty-five, chat in groups, at a loss what else to do, missing their work more even than the pay. The old women, plump and short, swathed in peasant black or in shapeless blouses and slacks, caw ceaselessly at each other. The teenage girls are usually indoors, helping their mothers make the most of the little they have: interminably washing clothes, because there are too few for washing to be allowed to pile up.

The just-above-the-breadline poverty looks much the same in the *cerros* (hills) surrounding Mexico City, where terrace upon terrace of no-cost housing made of cardboard, hardboard, old planks and rusty iron sheeting gaze sad-eyed over low-cost, rapidly deteriorating municipal units on the edge of town.

Much the same in Lima, where the poorest 40 per cent of the population is crammed into dusty, mud-brick slums. They appear to contain fair-sized houses until you peer into a doorway and realize it gives on to a miniature cobbled street with a single drain down the middle, overlooked by two rows of single-roomed houses, resembling nothing so much as pigsties in design. Much the same in Santiago, where to the south of the city, camouflaged by trees and brush, lie acre upon acre of tatty, jerrybuilt shacks in which, perhaps, 15 per cent of the population live.

The situation is similar in Rio de Janeiro, where conditions in the picturesque and precarious *favelas* that cling to the rocky hillsides compare favourably only with those on the bleak government-built housing blocks to the west of the city, where drainage, refuse and repair facilities were things of a fleeting past. And much the same in the stilt slums of Guayaquil, where a slip can be fatal for a three-year-old child negotiating the catwalks above putrid sewer-marshes that offer the only available building sites for families without money.

Latin America's bottom third are by no means the poorest of the third world's poor; they are better fed, housed and clothed than their counterparts in Africa or on the Indian subcontinent. But they were offered the hope of something better, and have seen that hope recede into the distance over the past two decades. That, probably, is worse than if they had never been offered any hope at all. It is no consolation that these people are the victims not, as they often believe they are, of *los ricos, las multinacionales* or *los gringos* but a world economic mega-accident which no one of those categories quite seems to know what to do about.

It should be no consolation for the West, either, that Latin America's once modern industrial structure is becoming obsolescent as investment declines; Latin America's political institutions are being undermined, possibly to the point of revolution; and the result of growing political unpredictability there could be seriously to weaken the West's financial structure.

External debt first piled up in Latin America in order to cope with the yawning balance-of-payments surpluses caused by the first oil price shock. Brazil's rose from $10 billion in 1973 to $47 billion by 1979; Argentina's from $3.5 billion to $11 billion; Colombia's from $2.7 billion to $5.5 billion; Peru's from $2.4 billion to $8 billion; Chile's, more modestly, from $3.4 billion to $5.5 billion. Even petro-plutocratic Mexico and Venezuela fed at the same trough. Mexico's external debt rose from $7.2 billion to $37 billion; Venezuela's from $2 billion to $10 billion. The debt increases, said the planners, were comfortably in line with world inflation and nothing to worry about.

They probably weren't – until the second oil price shock of 1979–80, which did three things to Latin America. It punctured the self-confidence of the non-oil-producing Latin American economies by imposing an almost intolerable strain on their balance of payments. Simultaneously, because the immediate response of the developed world to the second oil shock was medium to massive deflation, world money markets were saturated with petrodollars in search of a home. Latin America's third problem was that, owing to depressed demand in the developed countries, the bottom fell out of the markets for the commodities that the continent produced.

The response of the non-oil-producing Latin American countries was to borrow to cover their growing trade deficits. The response of the oil-producing countries was to borrow because the money was there for the asking and, what the hell, they had oil, the best of securities, to borrow against anyhow. By the end of 1982, the Latin American debt total stood at around $300 billion, with Brazil owing some $90 billion, Mexico $80 billion, Argentina $38 billion, Venezuela $32 billion, Chile $22 billion and Peru $10 billion.

This much is history. The response of the international banks and, behind them, the central banks of the developed world was to send for the local sheriff, the International Monetary Fund, to tell that saloonful of free-spending Latinos to sober up. The trouble was that at least five of those countries – Brazil, Mexico, Venezuela, Chile and Peru – found it extremely hard to service their debts and afford the imports that they needed to fuel economic growth. Economic recovery in America and some parts of Europe was a help; but recovery alone was not sufficient to deal with the scale of Latin America's debts.

Enforcing laws against borrowers is hard. Any bank offering a loan usually wants to be sure that the debtor will put the money where it will yield a return that will pay off the interest and eventually the debt; and that it has a security that the bank can grab in case something goes wrong. In lending to sovereign countries there is no such security, except a country's concern to preserve its creditworthiness (banks can lay their hands on a country's financial assets only when much of these are held abroad, as was the case with Iran in 1979).

Creditworthiness is a limited asset: there can come a moment when the cost of borrowing can outweigh a country's wish to be able to go on borrowing more. So a lot depends on the bankers' sense in lending money where there is some prospect of real return denominated in dollars, not in local currency. That means that borrowed money needs to be invested to boost exports or to save on imports. In the crazy world of 1980–81, where sober-suited bankers were chasing scapegrace adventurers in Latin America, there was never any prospect of a return on much of the debt. The money went:

- On new government spending. Brazil's hard-pressed government, wincing from the grumbles provoked by the country's 1979–80 recession, sighed with relief when it gained access to new foreign borrowing just in time for a pre-election year. The minimum wages of those the Brazilian government had most to fear from, the employed urban working class, could be promptly underwritten. The financing was there to polish off a host of projects, ranging from the São Paulo underground to the Itaipu hydroelectric scheme.

The Mexicans, themselves in a pre-phoney-election year, poured money into construction (up 12 per cent in 1980–81), mining (up 10 per cent) and electricity generation (up 10 per cent). Even battered Mexican manufacturing registered 6 per cent growth. In Chile, General Pinochet eased his spartan economic disciplines to give workers real wage increases of 14 per cent, and splashed out $700 million on improving Santiago's underground.

- On pure speculation. The worst examples of this were in Argentina and Chile, where a plethora of *financieras* – barely regulated financial holding companies – were set up to channel money largely into booming property markets. It was possible at one time for a more or less penniless *financiera* to borrow $1 million to buy a property in downtown Santiago and sell it for $2 million after a few months. That was all right for some, but when the boom came to a stop a lot of people found themselves stuck with properties they had borrowed to pay for at grossly inflated prices.

    Quarter-occupied luxury hotels and office blocks are the lingering monuments to the loan boom. Most Latin American countries enjoyed a short-lived construction boom: total value added by construction in Latin America jumped by some $8 billion between 1978 and 1981. In Argentina and Chile, many of the *financieras* and property companies went down with a resounding crash in 1981–82.

- Straight out again. Many Latin American countries had no exchange controls; where they existed, they could be evaded fairly easily. Western bankers reckon that maybe as much as $100 billion was recycled back in 1981–82 from Latin America to the United States and Western Europe. Mexicans were reckoned to hold some $40 billion in assets abroad, Venezuelans some $18 billion. At least $12 billion left Brazil in 1981. Even in an economy as small as Chile's the capital flight in 1981 was around $1 billion.

Most of the loans were irrecoverably lost, but did it make much sense for the bankers to try to stretch the Latin American economies on the rack to recover their losses?

In one sense, of course, it did. The IMF's arrival on the scene brought a healthy dose of sound financial sense to economies whose direction was for long dictated by local politics. The IMF's three main macroeconomic prescriptions for the Latin American countries were admirable. They were: a reduction in government budget deficits; limits to money supply growth in order to bring inflation down; and a policy of currency depreciation to achieve balance-of-trade improvements without contributing too much to inflation.

Yet if the IMF viewed its role as being that of restoring the Latin American economy to solvency, or seeing that the interest on the Latin American debt got paid anything like on time, or that the debt was repaid in full at all, it was condemned to frustration. The hope of some Western bankers, that the Latin American economies, taken in hand, could take advantage of a United States recovery to climb back to solvency, was a forlorn one.

There was a limit to the extent the Latin American economies could be squeezed. The Brazilians, for example, throttled domestic demand; imposed virtually prohibitive tariff barriers on imports (running a considerable risk of retaliation); and cut oil consumption (by guzzling alcohol and raising petrol taxes) substantially to some 795,000 barrels a day in 1982. A battery of incentives was installed to promote exports. Yet Brazil achieved only a modest trade surplus.

The Mexicans and the Venezuelans had more fat to cut; but their real oil revenues plummeted as the OPEC price cracked. The Argentinians had the biggest scope for a balance-of-payments turnaround. The country's ability to switch a huge deficit into surplus overnight merely by consuming less meat and grain and exporting more of both abroad was displayed in the mid-1970s, when a $1.3 billion current account deficit in 1975 was transformed to a $1.3 billion surplus two years later.

The Chilean economy, after seven years' hard labour and one year's respite, was squeezed hard again, but only yielded the very narrowest of trade surpluses. The Peruvians, after a prolonged spell under IMF tutelage between 1976 and 1978, did convert a $1 billion current account deficit into a $600 million surplus, but the improvement was short-lived and secured only at a huge social cost.

A revival of the economy of the United States would certainly boost raw material prices. It would provide new markets for Latin American goods only if the Americans lowered their non-tariff drawbridges against most Latin American products. Mexican textile manufacturers moaned that their slimmed-down, export-oriented businesses were denied access to American markets until approval of the NAFTA package in 1993. The Latin American scrabble to boost exports and reduce imports contributed to a sharp contraction in trade between Latin American countries.

Latin Americans pruned their public spending, under IMF pressure. But the pruning came largely from investment budgets, not current spending. Indeed, current spending rose in most Latin American countries, as governments tried to keep their restless people in a minimum of food and work. The state was no longer, however, fulfilling its traditional role as the locomotive of investment and modernization.

The private sector, starved of profits by the slump in manufacturing, was in no shape to take on that role. Borrowing from abroad for new investment in industry and capital projects, rather than for rolling over old debts, virtually dried up. Even in conditions of global recovery would more international money be available for private sector and project financing? Not necessarily: Latin American countries, with their dubious credit ratings, would have to compete with a revival in demand for credit from American and European and, now, Eastern European borrowers. The one part of the Latin American economy that ought to be most encouraged – private-sector manufacturing – suffered worst from the slump in export markets and in domestic demand.

The main burden on most countries' balance of payments was the cost of servicing the debt itself – even now that American interest rates were fairly low. Moreover, the problem, in the words of one Brazilian economist, 'does not have a mathematical solution'. Whatever, in fact, happens to interest rates or to Latin American trade, the debt is now so huge that it devours all improvement, requiring a still bigger improvement the following year. 'The debt is a black hole growing larger on the money it absorbs,' remarks another Brazilian economist, with a little poetic licence.

From being the main symptom of the Latin American malaise, the debt became the malaise itself, as a look at some case histories shows.

The Mexican economy, after speeding rather dangerously along the *autopista* of growth during the 1970s, spun wildly out of control in 1980–82, and crashed. The two main causes of Mexico's economic mishap were a huge increase in public spending after 1978 by the government of President Jose Lopez Portillo; and his decision to keep the peso overvalued in order to dampen down the inflationary effect of all this spending. The result was large trade deficits.

Borrowing soared to pay for the government spending and the trade deficits. By 1981, the public-sector debt had reached $53 billion, a 56 per cent increase on the year before. Short-term borrowing as a percentage of the Mexican public debt rose that year from 4 per cent to 20 per cent.

Only when the flow of borrowing began to dry up did the government take belated action. In February 1982, the peso was devalued by 40 per cent. The government promptly wiped out much of the benefit of the devaluation by raising wages by the same amount. In April the government drew up a seventeen-point emergency programme, which it then failed to implement. Public spending, which was supposed to come down from 14.5 per cent of GDP in 1981 to 11.5 per cent in 1982, instead went up to 16.5 per cent. In June, Mexico obtained a syndicated loan of $2.5 billion with considerable difficulty.

In August, the government was forced to devalue further: a rate of fifty pesos to the dollar was decreed for the payment of external debt (otherwise the domestic cost of servicing Mexico's dollar borrowings, 91 per cent of the total, would have multiplied), while the rate for most other transactions was allowed to float down, eventually, to 150 pesos a dollar. The United States rushed to the rescue, providing more than $3 billion in loans, while the Mexicans announced that they would start talking to the IMF about a restructuring of the country's debt following a three-month moratorium on all payments.

In September, the retiring President Lopez Portillo delivered a parting blow: he nationalized private banks and imposed exchange controls banning the import or export of currency. The loony intention behind the second measure was to trap private capital from leaving Mexico, while being able to keep interest rates low. But capital continued to soak out of Mexico, while domestic savings collapsed because of the negative real interest rates.

In November Mexico's treasury minister, Jesus Silva Herzog, announced that Mexico had signed a letter of intent with the IMF allowing it to draw on credit of some $3.9 billion. This opened the way for a postponement in repayment of some $20 billion in debt falling due in 1982 and 1983, and to a $5 billion commercial bank credit, which was tied down the following March.

Under the IMF letter, the Mexican government agreed to slash the public sector deficit from 16.5 per cent of GDP to 8.5 per cent in 1983 to 5.5 per cent in 1985 and to 3.5 per cent in 1985. The Mexican government agreed to phase out the country's by now triple exchange rate system and to allow interest rates to rise to realistic levels. The Mexicans promised to achieve a trade surplus of some $8 billion–$10 billion and to get inflation down from nearly 100 per cent to less than 70 per cent.

The Mexican economic and social landscape meanwhile looked as though a hurricane had swept through it. Hundreds of firms went bankrupt every month. Private investment declined some 15 per cent in 1982. Unemployment jumped from 8 per cent to around 13 per cent in the space of a few months, in an economy in which under-employment anyway probably stood at around 45 per cent. This, in a country where a motor mechanic earning $12 a month was considered employed.

Real industrial wages, hitherto the Alamo of the trade union wing of Mexico's ruling Institutional Revolutionary Party, fell fast. Mexico's economy stagnated, in a country whose population was growing by some 3 per cent a year. After a decade in which growth rates averaged some 9 per cent a year, ordinary people got a shock. Yet by the end of 1983, Mexico owed some $87 billion and was paying nearly $12 billion in interest.

Unless American recovery was spectacular, sustained, import-led (two-thirds of Mexico's trade each way is with the United States) and succeeded in driving up the price of oil again, there was no obvious respite in sight. At the end of 1984, the $20 billion in postponed loan repayment fell due, along with a pile of medium-term debt.

Consider a more cautious borrower: Brazil. Many of the problems of South America's giant arose from the increase in the price of oil. Brazil's borrowing grew much more slowly and responsibly than Mexico's, to around $90 billion in 1983. Much of the cash that was not compensating for the trade deficit was going into projects with some economic justification. The Brazilians also went through a dose of IMF-type deflation in 1979–80, before the temporary reprieve of 1981 and the disaster year of 1982.

'I am worried that Brazil has not taken the decision to postpone payment of a large part of its debt, but is surviving from month to month,' said one of the architects of Mexico's debt renegotiation. It was in Brazil that the difficulty of escaping the debt trap became clearest. The relatively modest growth in the Brazilian debt by $10 billion in 1980–81 took place firstly to service the existing debt, and secondly to finance a small pre-election boom. This brought the debt up to more than $80 billion, according to the IMF, or $90 billion, according to most Brazilians.

The world credit drought drove Brazil to the IMF. In February, the fund agreed to lend Brazil $5.4 billion, opening the way for commercial bank lending of $4.4 billion and a postponement of debt repayment of

$4.7 billion. Brazil also managed to get $9 billion in short-term debt rolled over.

The interest picture was bad enough; the repayment profile for Brazil's medium- and long-term debt was awful. On IMF calculations, debt repayment rose from $7.2 billion in 1983 quite sharply through to $15.9 billion in 1987. Thus, by 1987, Brazil had to shell out some $26.4 billion on service payments on its medium- and long-term debt alone – and that was only on the lowest possible projections of likely future borrowing.

Only by squeezing living standards savagely was the target hit. In 1981 Brazil's GDP fell by around 3.5 per cent. In 1982 it stagnated; in 1983 it fell by as much as 3 per cent. With Brazil's population growing by around 2.2 per cent a year, this amounted to an effective fall of GDP per capita of about 12 per cent in three years.

Unemployment was reckoned to have shot up among the industrial labour force from around 11 per cent in the mid-1970s to around 20 per cent (about 1 million of São Paulo's 4-million-strong workforce were without jobs). Under-employment was around 30 to 35 per cent. There were no social security payments to the jobless. Fearing labour trouble, the Brazilian government protected the purchasing power of the lowest paid while cutting back on salaries for skilled workers and the middle classes.

Impoverished Brazilians without jobs trekked back to the countryside, where they found that any prospect of a job was gone, thanks to some long overdue improvements in Brazil's agricultural efficiency. Brazil's industry meanwhile rusted; productive investment plummeted, while capital goods imports into Brazil fell by 16 per cent in 1981 and a further 10 per cent in 1982.

Argentina is a country much too rich for its own good. The country goes on wild spending sprees, ends up in a dosshouse, is set up in business again, and almost immediately returns to its bad habits.

The much-abused military government that took power in 1976 did in fact do a good job, to begin with, of clearing up the mess left by Mrs Isabelita Perón's mayhem of a government. By 1979 the government had turned a whopping trade deficit into a whopping surplus, had reduced inflation from a towering 600 per cent to around 50 per cent a year, and had cut the state sector deficit from around 17 per cent of GDP to 3 per cent. However, the then Economics Minister, Mr José Alfredo Martinez de Hoz, was told by the army not to squeeze as hard as he would have wished to, and to begin raising public spending again.

By 1980, things started to go badly wrong. The armed forces were becoming increasingly unpopular and tried to buy back appeal by inflating. The country joined in the general Latin American borrowing boom, its foreign debt rising from $11 billion in 1979 to $39 billion by 1982. The government spending, and the new money, caused inflation to rise again: the government tried to hold this by revaluing the peso, thus reducing import prices. The trade deficit grew.

Argentina's soldiers belatedly tried to do something about it all by squeezing the economy savagely in 1982. GDP fell by an unheard-of 5 per cent, causing unemployment to rise from its level of 3 per cent in 1978 to 13 per cent. Real incomes fell by around 20 per cent. Demonstrations against the military government became more frequent, as the trade unions and political parties became bolder. The junta tried to distract the attention of Argentinians from the mess by invading the Falklands in April 1982, but lost the war there and added the heavy cost of the military campaign to public spending.

Argentina trudged to the IMF after the Falklands débâcle, reaching agreement on a letter of intent in November. In January 1983, a $2.2 billion IMF loan was arranged in principle, payment of some $12 billion in short-term debt postponed, and the commercial banks agreed to provide $1.5 billion. The Argentinians agreed to cut their budget deficit from 14 per cent of GDP to 8 per cent in 1983 and 5 per cent in 1984. Targets were also set for a continuing improvement in the balance of payments, which had already improved in 1982. After a long period of suffering under President Alfonsin, Argentina's economy began to grow again under President Menem. Unfortunately this period, while initially promising, with a bonfire of government meddling and agencies, ended in a corrupt looting of the National Treasury, as so often before. The system imploded under the successor government of Fernando de la Rua, creating a deflationary black hole which has quartered Argentina's wealth in two years.

If Latin American countries had followed more sensible economic policies, would they have got into the quagmire of debt? This question can best be answered by looking at two medium-sized Latin American countries, Chile and Peru, which each pursued free-market economic policies during the late 1970s. Chile, under the stern eye of President Pinochet, provided laboratory conditions for a prolonged experiment by Mr Milton Friedman's disciples. Peru, which floundered into an economic bog in the mid-1970s, followed policies thereafter largely dictated by the IMF itself.

Chile at first became another economic disaster. The 'Chicago boys' went grey watching their achievements – a decline in inflation from 600 per cent under Salvador Allende's left-wing government to around 33 per cent in 1979, GDP growing by around 5 per cent a year, having fallen 12 per cent in 1975 – slowly wasting away. The Chicago boys were to some extent prisoners of their own ideology. In their dedication to the free market, they would not regulate the flow of private-sector borrowing from abroad, even though public-sector borrowing stayed at relatively sensible levels.

By 1983, the foreign debt had soared to $22 billion, most of it private. The inflow of foreign capital in a small economy jerked inflation up to around 50 per cent. The money washing in allowed Chileans to buy a multitude of imports across the country's newly lowered (to 10 per cent or so) tariff walls. The number of imported cars, for example, jumped by 700 per cent in 1980. Traditionally protected domestic industries went bust, but a boom in the construction industry kept their workers off the streets.

The reckoning came the following year; the tidal wave of foreign capital subsided; a lot of Chilean intermediaries between foreign lenders and local borrowers went bankrupt; and the price of copper, Chile's main export, tumbled. Real wages fell by 16 per cent. The construction industry collapsed, tossing workers out. Unemployment rose to 21 per cent, and the number of those on *empleo minimo* – the $20 a month minimum wage – rose to around 13 per cent of the population.

Chile's plight was all the worse because, in 1979, the government pegged the exchange rate, partly out of fear of adding to the domestic burden of servicing the foreign debt, 44 per cent of which was dollar-denominated. For ministers who believed in free markets, their attachment to a fixed exchange rate was bizarre – and damaging. Imports flooded in, exporters were demoralized, and Chileans took advantage of the relative lack of exchange controls to pile up their savings abroad. The current account deficit, and the debt to finance it, both soared.

After the dismissal of Chile's arch-monetarist, Mr Sergio de Castro, in 1982, President Pinochet went through three cabinets in search of a return to the economic calm of 1979. It was a salutary lesson for bankers that even a country with fixed monetary targets and a government budget surplus of around 5 per cent of GDP in 1980 could not survive the borrowing wave of 1980–81.

By 1982, as the Chilean government was forced to step in to rescue private companies, it was running a modest budget deficit of 4 per cent of

GDP. In January 1983, the Chileans secured a $550 million IMF loan, on condition they reduced the budget deficit to less than 2 per cent of GDP this year. With targets missed, international reserves plummeting and the country lurching from crisis to crisis, the IMF loan did not automatically open the way to new credits.

If Chile's undoing was sad, Peru's was tragic. After an economic spree under left-wing generals in 1968–77, Peru went through two years under IMF supervision, during which it slashed its public sector deficit to 1.2 per cent of GDP and secured a current account surplus of more than $600 million, although it failed to get inflation below 67 per cent. When a democratic government took over in 1980, these orthodox economic policies were continued. Peru's tariff walls were even lowered, from an average of 155 per cent to 35 per cent. Despite these policies, a balance-of-payments deficit, caused by the plunging price of copper, drove the country to the IMF in 1982.

Peru got $740 million from the IMF. In 1987 they went back and, with the IMF's blessing, secured $2 billion in loans rolled over and $880 million in new commercial bank loans at over-the-odds interest rates. The condition for the loans was that Peru slashed several tolerably sensible investment projects by $1 billion ($700 million to be spent on jet fighter aircraft was, of course, politically untouchable) and that they squeezed the economy further to get imports down (imports had already fallen by 25 per cent in 1982).

The debt crisis began in Latin America, and the biggest loans were made there. By 1991 Brazil's debt had risen to $116 billion, Mexico's to $102 billion, Argentina's to $64 billion, Venezuela's to $34 billion, Peru's to $21 billion and Chile's had fallen to $18 billion.

But even more intractable and wretched, if possible, was the plight of African countries with little industry, primarily dependent on low-priced commodity exports. Between 1973 and 1983 Africa's debt increased at 22 per cent a year to a total debt of at least $80 billion, and possibly as much as $150 billion. The debt-service ratio – that is the proportion of interest and payments on the debt as a percentage of exports – exceeded 50 per cent, and in some countries 100 per cent; if those nations tried to meet their obligations, they would have to hand over their total export income and import nothing!

The former UN Secretary General, Boutros Boutros Ghali, said that 'external debt is a millstone around the neck of Africa . . . easing the continent's debt burden must be a priority for the international community'. In Latin America foreign debt amounted to 37 per cent of GNP in 1993. In Africa, foreign debt was more than 100 per cent of GNP on average. Mozambique's debt was 400 per cent of GNP. Only a fraction of scheduled debt is paid in sub-Saharan Africa, so the debt steadily increased to $183 billion in 1993.

Meanwhile, crucially, because of the debt hanging over them and the fear of default, no one would lend any of those countries any new money: new lending to Africa fell by nearly half between 1980 and 1983. This was a consequence of the banks' refusal to accept a once-for-all write-off, which would have lifted the dangers of default by those countries, and made it possible to lend to them again, much more modestly and sensibly. But the banks needed their face-savers, their fig-leaves, their covers for retreat so as not to offend their depositors, now having to pay up for the banks' initial mistakes. The result was financial famine in Africa, as in Latin America, with a desperate shortage of new money even for very viable projects.

The IMF, as in Latin America, imposed its heavy-footed regime: trade surpluses, balanced budgets and inflation targets had to be met before IMF lending would be granted – which was pretty expensive, but was supposed to catalyse much larger amounts of bank lending and debt rescheduling. These programmes, while deepening the suffering of the very poorest in underdeveloped Africa, permitted the banks to maintain the pretence that repayments were being made and staved off financial disaster. Britain's then chancellor, Nigel Lawson, imaginatively proposed forgiving a number of African countries their debts to developed country governments in the mid-1980s; but the banks showed no such magnanimity with the larger commercial debt.

By 1985 debt service payments for Africa were around $10–$11 billion; a staggering amount for a desperately impoverished continent. The IMF, which applied its usual prescriptions, proved a mixed blessing. Between 1979 and 1983 IMF lending to Africa tripled. By 1985, payments to the IMF were between a half and three-quarters of debt service paid. A confidential report by one of the World Bank's senior economists at the time concluded bleakly and succinctly:

Official debt renegotiation takes place at the Paris Club. This is the name given to an *ad hoc* group of western creditor governments which meets in Paris. However, the Paris Club mechanism has not been effective in easing Africa's debt difficulties. The relief provided has been too little and too costly. The procedures are designed to keep the debtors on a short leash. This is accomplished by placing strict limits on the definition of the debt eligible for relief and by providing relief on a small part of the debt. This has resulted in repeated reschedulings and an increased debt burden. The rescheduling of debt at the Paris Club has also not had a catalytic effect in mobilizing additional aid, nor has it helped to restore short-term trade financing arrangements.

A country like Kenya, whose politics and economics are relatively stable, showed a decline in real wages of around a fifth between 1981 and 1983 and an increase in stunted children under five through malnutrition from 24 per cent to 28 per cent, reversing the gains of previous years, during the period of IMF tutelage. In Kenya, as in most African countries, the price of basic commodity exports was far more important to their economies than their domestic policies, however good or bad these might be. President Nyerere of Tanzania put it rather plaintively in 1986:

> This year the rains in Tanzania were quite good. The peasants in our major cotton growing regions have more than doubled their crop compared with that of last year. We are desperately short of foreign exchange with which to buy essential imports, and cotton is one of our major exports; we were therefore pleased about this big output increase. But the price of cotton dropped from sixty-eight cents to thirty-four cents a pound on a single day in July this year. The result for our economy – and the income of the peasants – is similar to that of a natural disaster: half our crop, and therefore of our income, is lost. Our peasants – and our nation – have made the effort, but the country is not earning a single extra cent in foreign exchange.

By then, too, around 60 per cent of the country's foreign export earnings were being devoured by debt service.

Zaire's debt by the mid-1980s had risen to some $6 billion, in spite of the Mobutu regime's total corruption and bankruptcy. Susan George, in her book *A Fate Worse Than Debt*, eloquently outlined some of the projects that contributed to the debt:

> The ONAFITEX (national textile enterprise) in 1973 purchased thirty ultra-modern cotton-treating plants in the USA for $7.5

million. The Zairian delegation that made the deal got $450,000 worth of commissions. None of the plants has ever functioned. One was set up at Gandijika, but the high-tech electronic control system was omitted, so nothing worked. The rest of the material has been lost, stolen, dispersed or has deteriorated, so that no complete plant now has a prayer of getting built.

Immediately after the runway at the Kisangani airport had been completely repaired and lengthened, a second runway was undertaken (the airport serves five flights a day maximum) at a cost equal to a year's income for the region. A worker in Kisangani would need several months' wages just to pay a taxi to the airport; but, once there, he could put his bags on an automatic conveyor belt and enjoy air-conditioned comfort. Total cost: $36 million.

The twenty-two-storey tower of the Kinshasha International Trade Centre is virtually deserted. You wouldn't want to work there either – there are no windows, and the air-conditioning, supplied by a French firm, broke down a month after the supplier's guarantee lapsed.

The TV-communications complex for the 'Voice of Zaire' (Cité de la Voix du Zaire), at $110 million, was a really good buy – surely far better than paying 165,000 primary school teachers for five years, which is another thing one could have done with that amount of money. In December 1980 the system was declared completed. The French manufacturer announced that Zaire was now 'one of the first countries in the world to possess its own domestic satellite communications network'. In any event, the fancy infrastructure for La Voix du Zaire broke down almost immediately. There is rarely any retransmission towards the interior of the country because the relay stations seldom work. Anyway, most Zairians live, as Kwitny points out, 'a day or more's hard travel from the nearest electricity. Most have never seen a telephone. So they don't need the ultrasophisticated communications system'. But foreign enterprises do.

Foreign enterprises, in this case American, are also deeply involved in the Inga-Shaba power project. The total cost of the project is over $1 billion, Belgian sources say (Kwitny says $1.5 billion) or about twenty per cent of Zaire's foreign debt. Zairian researchers note that the country could pay 290,000 Zairian teachers or nurses for twenty years with that kind of money.

Any serious energy policy for Zaire would have chosen to exploit the huge local reserves of hydro-electric power and build a series of small dams.

The Inga-Shaba power line is supposed to furnish electricity to a copper refinery and an iron and steel complex. The Maluku steel plant has never operated at more than ten per cent of its capacity; the 'steel' it produces is of poor quality and costs three or four times as much as imported steel. It employs 1,000 people instead of the 10,000 promised. The copper refinery has not, so far, produced a single pound of copper. What the project is *not* supposed to do is to furnish power for any of the Zairian villages along its 1,100-mile stretch. In fact, 'an engineering technique was intentionally employed making it difficult or impossible for any electricity to be siphoned from the line before it gets to Shaba.'

The Third World debt crisis, both in Africa and Latin America, came to global attention when Mexico declared its moratorium in August 1982, and a banking collapse was narrowly avoided after a frantic negotiation. As the decade proceeded, it was reckoned that, by 1985, there was a net transfer of some $26 billion a year from the poorer parts of the world to the richer, reversing the pattern of decades. Investment in Latin America as a whole fell by a third between 1980 and 1985, a case of the developing world becoming the undeveloping world. Latin America lost some $22 billion, sub-Saharan Africa some $2 billion, and Asia, for its economy a more modest $2 billion.

In 1985 American Treasury Secretary James Baker launched the 'Baker initiative', which proposed reducing the value of the dollar, partly in order to diminish the size of the debt, which was largely dollar-denominated, to encourage growth policies for the fifteen largest debtors, to provide another $29 billion in extra financing and to try to encourage private banks to adopt a more positive approach to rescheduling. The plan at least recognized the size of the problem for the countries concerned: but very little new finance in fact followed for countries like Brazil.

An influential and devastating report by the influential British Parliamentary Group on Overseas Development, under the chairmanship of two heavyweights, Bowen Wells and Jim Lester, concluded sombrely:

First, that in 1987, the Third World's debt problem seems no closer to resolution than it did in 1982 (when the crisis broke) or in 1984 (when the major international institutions predicted an upturn).

Since 1983, in fact, developing countries' net capital transfers have turned negative. They are, moreover, now paying more interest than principal repayments. Net bank lending to most lesser-developed countries has stopped, the expected spontaneous revival of lending has not materialized, and the 'Baker Plan' and the innovations of the late-1986 Mexico deal have not altered that overall pattern. Adjustment and retrenchment have not of themselves brought a return to creditworthiness.

Second, that so long as the debt burden cripples the performance of so many developing countries, it stifles the growth potential of the world economy – in particular world trade growth, but also the market for credit. Thus, economic and social costs are borne by us all in an apparent endeavour to satisfy some creditors' financial requirements. Senator Bradley told us how US exports to Latin America had fallen by twenty-five per cent between 1981 and 1985; over the same period, the World Bank calculates Latin American and Caribbean imports from all countries have fallen by forty per cent.

With a little foresight by the banks, usually shown in the excessive prudence with which they treat ordinary borrowers, the crisis and suffering need not have happened at all. It had been a global economic mega-accident for which the careless driver surely had greater responsibility than the beggar that had stepped into his headlights.

What conclusions are to be drawn from the debt crisis? They are pretty bleak. Allowing for normal human error, they involved probably the worst, most unnecessary hardship to affect the largest swathe of humanity for the longest time in modern economic history: droughts, famines, natural disasters and so on, although beginning to be avoidable by man's efforts, are part of the natural order of things. The debt crisis was entirely artificial from beginning to end; it affected an enormous number of people, and was entirely avoidable.

Not that many people actually died as a result of the debt crisis, although some did: but hundreds of millions were kept on a marginal existence, many dying prematurely of malnutrition, disease and poverty, while for hundreds of millions the progress of the previous three decades was dashed because of a technical, global macroeconomic problem. There had been no precedent for it, except for the mistakes that led to the Great Depression – and the recovery from that was much quicker; the depression in the developing world has been deeper than that of the 1930s for the industrialized nations.

The economic betterment of the Third World has been replaced by its deterioration – particularly in the poorest part. Much of the developing world has become the undeveloping world. A decade of progress has already been lost, and another threatens to be. The poorest are getting poorer for no reason other than sheer short-sightedness, not malevolence, or even greed. The world of career managers meeting specific lending targets in order to ascend to their next job was not equipped with the long-term vision to ask whether the lending itself was safe; repayment would be somebody else's headache.

What kind of development, how to feed people in resource-starved countries when there is a surplus of food in developed countries, how to wean countries away from dependency on aid without leaving them to starve, does foreign aid inherently lead to dependency? – these are all complex and genuine issues. The foreign debt problem, which has been on a much bigger scale and far more damaging in the long run, allows no such ambiguity: it is the product of stupidity, and has created untold suffering. It is the greatest and most terrible consequence of the unchecked, unregulated globalization of capitalism.

It is necessary to point the finger of blame, to avoid further such catastrophe. One element was a chance one, for which no one could have allowed: the oil price increase which first sucked liquidity out of the Third World and then, through the recycling of petrodollars in the form of loans through the international banking system, put it back in a massively expensive form. From then on, three parties shared the blame: the governments and central banks that encouraged the commercial banks to lend for fear of a liquidity crisis in the Third World (a good motive, at least); the commercial banks themselves; and the borrowing governments.

To take each in turn: usually sensible Western governments and central banks actually encouraged the commercial banks to put up the loans; there was much self-congratulation at the time about the recycling of petrodollars. Banks later quite justifiably say they were summoned to meetings with central bankers at which they were virtually ordered to play their part in rescuing the Third World.

The borrowing governments must also accept a major share of the blame: it was possible to watch with fascination as, for example, Brazil's Finance Minister, Delfim Netto, would turn up in London for yet another round to borrow millions of dollars for projects that were entirely mythical – they went into balance of payments support – to keep the country operating for another few months. No one in Brazil pretended that anything else was happening.

As it turned out, the money could not have been used more irresponsibly: for speculative ventures, amassing large fortunes, capital flight and so on. The bankers exercised no control, splashing out to crooks in corrupt developing countries with no questions asked in a manner they would never have dreamt of with sober clients in their own countries; the banks positively chased customers with money.

The bulk of the blame must rest with those that lent the money, the banks. It was always something of a fantasy to believe that 'sovereign' lending was copper-bottomed: a nation cannot be any more responsible than an individual, although it does invariably borrow much more. The United States in the late nineteenth century had funded part of its industrial development through defaulting on loans from British banks. Many of the projects for the Third World loans were transparently bogus. In many cases bankers competed with each other to lend, arriving in Latin America with their surplus funds, literally begging local governments and investors to take their money. The purpose was to dump their surplus liquidity, which the bankers' own governments feared would create inflation back home. There was no altruism in this: bank profits depended on their being able to get the money off their hands and into loans.

Proper examination of the projects into which the lending was going was not carried out. None was volunteered by the lenders. In Venezuela, I learnt of a famous German company which, in collaboration with the bankers, sold obsolescent plant to a country which had little experience of its own in the field, which paid for the deal with money put up by the West German bankers. In this case the banks were conniving in a loan they knew to be bad in order to do a favour to one of their domestic industries! There were many other examples of this kind of thing: the banks displayed knavery, as well as naïvety, in their lending.

Responsibility was never to be attached to individuals: provided managers met or exceeded their lending targets, they were promoted; other executives were in charge when the bills came in and the banks proved unable to recover their debts. The success of the banks during the lending rush of the late 1970s was judged by the number of loans they had made, not by whether they were likely to be repaid: short-term results were everything.

One of the most depressing aspects of the affair was that the men who made the decisions rarely had to pay for them. Those most intimately involved in the lending, such as Walter Wriston, chairman of Citibank, had retired before the problem became too acute. The overall perspective was lacking even at the top, as banks were judged by monthly, quarterly and annual results. How big is the spread? How much return do we get on a loan? This was the perspective of the bankers, while on the borrowers' side, a little more or less in interest rates was neither here nor there provided the money could be obtained and then used for whatever short-term purpose the borrower intended – sometimes just rushed out of the country to buy property abroad.

This non-responsibility has been one of the key and depressing features not just of banking but of major corporations. There was no intentional effort to wreck the economies of the industrialized Third World. It stemmed from huge mistakes made by people incapable of any overarching judgement. It does not take a genius to work out that if money is put into ill-managed countries to fund a mass of bogus projects, a crisis will result. Once the false premise was accepted – that there is no risk in sovereign lending – the banks were begging takers to borrow their money.

Dollops of righteous indignation have been heaped upon the corruption and economic mismanagement of debtor nations: yet all these things were plain enough before the lending rush began: it was the bankers' job to ensure that the credit risk was an acceptable one, not the borrowers' responsibility to restrain themselves when money was being offered with no conditions attached. Who is to blame: the crook, accepting the money, or the sober-suited banker, with the suitcase full of money that ultimately belongs to his depositors, who is offering it to the crook?

When the enormity of the crisis became apparent, and the banks realized they would not get much of their money back, they were forced to resort to ever more imaginative ways of writing off their losses and squeezing money to pay for these out of their depositors. British bank debt paid in 1991, largely as a result of the debt crisis, was staggering. Bank profits, for example, fell by a third to £533 million, after bad debt provision of some £1.75 billion. The main high street banks set aside more than $6 billion for bad debts in 1991. In the late 1980s some $9 billion had to be written off the Third World debt by Britain alone, with the result that 20,000 jobs were lost at Barclays, Lloyds and Nat West in 1991, many as a result of closing small provincial banks which had no responsibility in the matter, helping to prolong the recession.

Nat West's chairman, Lord Alexander, commented primly that 'there were undoubtedly some departures from the principles of sound banking', while Barclays' Sir John Quinton, even more nauseatingly, argued that many of the losses, 'even with hindsight', were made 'according to good banking principles'. The then deputy governor of the Bank of England, Eddie George, remarked that 'both now tend to blame the authorities for allowing, or even encouraging, the party to get out of hand, though I seem to remember they rather enjoyed it at the time'.

It is worth asking whether the British banks' desperate drive for business and increased credit in the mid-1980s was not prompted by the need to offset their losses on Third World debt. In addition, the huge expansion of personal credit, based on the security offered by soaring property values that created the inflationary boom of the period, helped to yield the funds to write off Third World debt; in turn this boom had to be dampened down by the prolonged recession of the late 1980s.

High interest rates, coupled with a continuing sharp expansion of credit were an unusual feature of that crisis, but one of great assistance to banks strapped for cash. High interest rates, wheeled in invariably as the orthodox solution to inflation, themselves in the short run help inflation, not just because they increase production costs for businesses and customers, but because they increase returns to the banks on a vast number of ordinary deposit accounts, on which no interest is paid at all.

This increased liquidity helped to write off Third World debt, and also increased the incentive for banks to extend credit further, even at a time of high interest rates and, later, recession. Customers were still being offered credit and services at a time when interest rates were so high it seemed unlikely that they would be able to pay them back. On a smaller scale (although in the United States quite a large scale) the banks' hard-line drive to lend caused similar problems in the developed countries during the 1980s to those of the developing countries in the 1970s.

If you thought the problem was solved, or that lenders learned from their mistakes, look at Argentina in the 1990s. The country was advised by the IMF to peg the peso at $1 to end its chronic hyperinflation. This was administered by an inflexible currency board. Things went well enough between 1991 and 1995, but as deflation loomed thanks to overvaluation, Argentina was forced to add fiscal restraint to monetary controls, thus deepening the depression – even though its budget deficit was small.

Because Argentina followed the banks' advice, they poured money into it even as the economy sank further. When the debt reached $140 billion, Argentina was forced to default and, at last, permitted to devalue.

The country is now an economic ground zero. The currency has lost more than two-thirds of its value in six months. Per capita annual income has collapsed from around $9,000 to less than $3,000. Unemployment has risen to 22 per cent and bank accounts are still largely frozen. The banks' advice was wrong, and they continued to throw good money after bad while maintaining the same advice – two cardinal mistakes. In 1998, on a lesser scale, they had similarly propped up two overvalued currencies, Russia's and Brazil's, on faulty IMF advice. A pattern has been established. As Philip Bowring has written:

> The capital market forces that brought recent US corporate debt disasters such as Global Crossing and Enron are the same ones that earlier provided absurdly easy money both to Asian corporations and the government of Argentina. In turn, similar forces provided a flow of debt capital into the United States, whether into corporations or to finance a consumer and housing price boom . . . The world now presents an unhappy picture – half is suffering from capital overindulgence. The other half is starved of capital and also hurting because globalisation has made corporate tax avoidance easier through transfer pricing and use of offshore tax shelters.

As far as international capital and country risk is concerned, it is fair to say that the market is almost always wrong.

CHAPTER 25

LAND OF THE GIANTS

The globalization of capitalism represented by the coming of the multinationals was, in its time, the subject of much alarm, now largely ridiculed. A famous tract by the French politician Jean-Jacques Servan-Schreiber, *Le Défi Américain* (the American Challenge), portrayed a Europe threatened with take-over from American multinationals acting in their country's interests.

Subsequently, the threat seemed overblown. American multinationals like IBM and Ford were careful to act in a reasonably responsible way to avoid antagonizing host countries: they were seen as bringing work to Europe, providing a boost to local economies and conferring the benefits of technology on the host country. In fact, governments and local authorities began to compete with each other to attract major foreign companies. In exchange the multinationals acquired access to European markets and the benefit, in some countries like Spain, of a cheaper workforce.

In addition, as time passed, the Europeans joined in the game themselves, with major companies like Volkswagen and Fiat investing heavily in, for example, Latin America. The British, for their part, engaged in an astonishing transatlantic assault on American assets, buying them at a rate that left Britain only just behind the United States and Japan in terms of global foreign investment. No one in America viewed this British acquisition of assets as a threat.

The tale of foreign investment, it seemed, had a happy ending. In the Third World there continued to be protests at the way the multinationals exploited cheap labour and raw materials, as well as the dangerous influence they wielded over local governments. But by and large, foreign investment, and the role of the multinationals, is perceived to be positive – and infinitely more so than the alternative method of capital export – debt. As between the extreme advocates and detractors of foreign investment, Britain's Norman Macrae and Tony Benn, the former seems decisively to have won.

The picture is indeed rosier than many people feared was at first the case. But this should not obscure certain real consequences of multinational control, size and foreign ownership. In the first phase this has been creative and beneficial: indeed local branches of the multinationals have been given substantial authority by their parent companies, and their boards and chief executives were often recruited from the host country: this was true, for example, of IBM UK and Rupert Murdoch's media conglomerate, News International; they thus became truly multinational, not American companies based in Britain – although ultimate control rested with the parent company.

The problems arise not in times of expansion, but in times of difficulty. Failure in one country may lead to retrenchment or a change in the role of the multinational in another country which is not justified by conditions there or local performance. Volkswagen's retrenchment in Spain in 1993, with the possible loss of 10,000 jobs at its Seat factory in Barcelona, has been caused by the company's global problems, as well as local ones. IBM's massive worldwide losses in the early 1990s have led to pressures for cutbacks at its efficient British offshoot, IBM UK. News International's risky borrowings at the end of the 1980s had to be financed by the profits of such profitable outlets as its British newspapers, the *Sunday Times* and the *Sun*, even though these should have been using the fruits of their success to finance their own further growth. When plants close, because of difficulties in overseas parent companies, this leads to justifiable anger locally.

In addition, there is the hard-to-define issue of the political influence of the multinationals. A major employer, anywhere, has a great deal of clout with local authorities and governments which are eager to retain investment and jobs. If that employer is an overseas one, local authorities, government and the unions will be anxious to keep it happy; as with the issue of currency flows, the right of ordinary people to share in their own destiny will be curtailed. A local authority may be elected that believes strongly in environmental control. That authority may, however, have to tailor its views to the interests of an environmentally unfriendly foreign-owned multinational.

Multinationals pick and choose locations for investment according to what they believe to be the economic and political stability of the country concerned, the benefits offered and so on: this is entirely understandable. But it is a buyer's market for them: countries have to tailor their policies to retain them. It is not uncommon for multinationals to pull out of a particular country because they disapprove of the political or industrial relations conditions there and to relocate elsewhere. Again, this is not unreasonable: but it does represent a diminution in the power of the nation state, and therefore of popular choice. A nation could regulate and control its own industries in the past; it must negotiate and even yield to the multinationals if it wishes to keep them.

A further development has been the growth of predatory international take-overs. One company, for example, buys another to suppress a competitor in the international marketplace, or simply to strip it of its assets. On a national level these actions are usually subject to regulation; on an international level, they are much more difficult to police. Who can prove the real intentions of the predator? It has to be said that these practices, for the most part emanating from America, have sometimes had very negative competitive effects: far from representing the glories of free trade, the intention has been speculative, to get rich quick. Viable industries have been pillaged with sometimes openly monopolistic and anti-competitive motives. The former British President of the Board of Trade Michael Heseltine has eloquently outlined the dangers:

> We are in a game of snakes and ladders – or, rather, in hundreds of simultaneous games – in which our competitors' rules allow them (but not us) to climb up the snakes, while we (but not they) find that the ladders mostly lead downwards.
>
> This is nowhere truer than in the arena of takeovers and mergers, where the habits of investors have left British companies riper for plucking than any others in Europe. Our European colleagues do not have a history of takeover battles fought by distant share-holders; they tend to talk through the advantages, take a longer-term view and negotiate in the interests of the company. They see the British advocacy of the unfettered market as focused on the short term, exploiting today at the expense of tomorrow. This is a view shared by capitalist Japan; although companies are more freely available, the sheer scale of their larger companies effectively precludes most hostile bids, while vigilance in the Pentagon and

Congress keeps a protective shield around American high technology industries.

Most quoted companies in Britain are vulnerable to takeover. Their owners have few effective forums within which to gather when under threat and to reach a collective judgement; and the advisers to individual shareholders are often in a position of fiduciary trust where anything but acceptance of an enticing offer leaves them vulnerable to legal remedy . . . Suffice it to say that Britain is the predator's natural hunting-ground. Not only is virtually everything for sale but there are few centres where specialist skills in the management of disposals and acquisitions are so highly developed as in London . . .

The logic of a single market must be that any considerations of monopoly and public interest are made first in the context of all Europe, not in that of a single national sector. If we are to bring together the resources of all twelve economies, it makes no sense to start by defining a British company's market share with reference to Britain alone. A proposed merger which combined, say, 50 per cent of the UK market, might command no more than 5 per cent of the European market. The former might be against the public interest by tending to monopoly; the latter hardly so. National governments cannot administer such policies, since each would take the most self-interested view. Imagine a French takeover bid for a British company where it fell to the French to determine whether it was in Europe's interest or not, or vice versa!

There is a balance to be struck: mergers below a certain scale should remain in national hands and those above should be considered by the European Commission . . . At the moment Britain is taking too innocent a view of the takeover climate . . . Sometimes a takeover provides a corrective remedy, achieves necessary rationalization or serves as a discipline to otherwise lax management. But it carries with it dangers that decisions turn on short-term maximization of profit at the expense of the expenditure on research, training or investment on which long-term health and the greatest rewards depend.

If British companies are more available for acquisition than others, it is they that will be converted into branch offices of overseas companies. Some take the view that this does not matter, indeed that further investment will then follow. In the production line and assembly sectors of industry this may be true; but a company owned in Britain will almost certainly have its head office there, and head offices not only have control but also attract a range of service industries around them. British-owned companies will locate their research facilities close to British universities and colleges whenever possible. The spin-off is usually seen locally: innovation grows close to the innovator. When rationalization comes, in recession or under competition, it is the distant factory or branch office which tends to be first in the firing line. No one should expect companies to take unwise commercial decisions in the name of patriotism but nor should anyone assume that company directors are detached from a sense of national obligation. Nor are our fellow Europeans, or other countries anxious to see their companies move into Europe, under any obligation to play by British rules. When only one soldier in a squad is out of step, he is wise to assume that he is the one who is wrong. There is need for a new sophistication in Britain's approach to the ownership of her industrial assets if they are not to be acquired in growing numbers by our rivals as pieces in the game of restructuring European industry.

A final twist in the saga of the multinationals and overseas capital flows has been the advent of the 'screwdriver' assembly plant, pioneered by Japan. Unlike the major American investors in Europe, these plants are said by their detractors to be for the basic assembly of parts manufactured in Japan, endowing the minimum in technology transfer, providing only low-skilled local jobs and retaining a corporate leadership that consists almost exclusively of Japanese whose loyalty to the parent company and authority is never in doubt. The purpose of such operations is to take advantage of local incentives, cheap labour and, above all, to duck under protectionist fences and gain access to local markets.

The claims may be exaggerated, but there is certainly some truth in them, as also to the argument that, by under-cutting local producers, they may in fact be destroying more jobs than they are creating. If this stimulates inefficient local producers to be more productive, it may be a good thing. In Japan's case, industry has been assisted by a mass of uncompetitive practices that make it open to doubt that their success stems from greater efficiency alone: for example, the close relationship between Japanese industry and the banks permits it to benefit from much lower costs of financing than a Western competitor: bank lending to industry was characterized in Japan by virtually non-existent interest rates for a long time.

Japan's investment policy abroad bears this out: the establishment of Japanese local plants overseas began in direct response to protectionism. For example, the Voluntary Restriction Agreement on Japanese car exports to the USA stimulated the setting up of major assembly plants in America by Honda in 1984, Mazda in 1986, Mitsubishi in 1989 and Nissan in 1987, as well as the Toyota-General Motors joint venture. These 'voluntary' agreements limited Japan's sale of imported cars to some 2.3 million in the United States in 1987; the Japanese went for high-priced cars to circumvent this. The average price of American cars rose by $1,300 as a result.

In Europe the restrictions were much tougher. Compared to Japanese penetration of some 23 per cent in the United States, Britain limited protection to some 10 to 12 per cent of the market, France to 3 per cent, and Italy to just 2,750 cars and 750 four-wheel-drive vehicles. In addition, the EC resorted to more justifiable protection against dumping, imposing duties on a wide range of goods from outboard motors to ball-bearings, electronic typewriters and photocopiers.

Protectionism has been sharply on the rise: in 1975 only 8 per cent of American imports received some form of protection. By 1984 the figure had risen to 21 per cent, and by 1986 to 25 per cent. Japan initially had very small interests overseas: only 2 per cent of its manufacturing output was offshore in 1983, rising to just 5 per cent in 1986, before mush-rooming. The Japanese strategy to begin with was to start up wholly-owned manufacturing subsidiaries using non-union labour in govern-ment-supported greenfield sites in economically deprived areas. Komat-su's purpose in having a $12.5 million assembly plant in Britain was clearly to avoid 26.6 per cent anti-dumping tariffs on imported exca-vators. Toshiba's $1.2 million video recorder plant in Britain was to dodge import surcharges; and so on.

There were initially only a small number of Japanese acquisitions of plant (as opposed to acquisitions of real estate, which was on a much larger scale); those accelerated sharply in the late 1980s to 95 totalling $9 billion. Many of the acquisitions were in the firms supplying materials to the car plants – for example, Kawasaki Steel purchased 50 per cent of California Steel, and Nippon Kokan took a 50 per cent stake in Wheel-ing, Pittsburgh. The Japanese companies have introduced radical in-novation in the management technology techniques they use in the West, which has seriously undercut local products. Among these were computer-integrated manufacturing, incorporating flexible manufacturing systems, computer-aided design and computer-aided engineering, robotics, numerically controlled machine tools, sensors and telecommunications, which allowed smaller batch sizes in continuous flow to be produced, without large inventories of components and huge stocks of finished product. One observer, Barrie James argues that:

> The 'new' manufacturing not only allows companies to monitor the flow of materials but also the flow of information needed to manage production from delivery of raw materials, through to shipping out finished products. This helps firms to operate in smaller manufacturing plants and increasingly to customize product ranges through small production runs. At the same time they can reduce their breakeven point and lower their unit costs. Labour in these highly automated systems has become a far less important component of cost.
>
> Japanese companies have been quick to spot the advantages of the 'new' manufacturing and to adopt these new techniques, which allow them to move away from countries with low labour costs to the developed consuming markets without the old penalty of incurring higher labour costs. Japanese companies have also pioneered totally new approaches to manufacturing – for example, 'mechatronics', which combines mechanics and electronics to eliminate mechanical parts by replacing them with electronic components. This has not only eased manufacturing complexity, but also provided better precision, more reliability, lower costs and led to better customer features.

In addition, backing the new overseas companies, is Japan's enormous financial muscle: Sumitomo Bank, for example, is the largest banking company in the world. Six of the world's top eleven banks and fifteen of the top twenty-five are in Japan: these can give a major boost to Japanese companies abroad that undercuts local competition, which is forced to rely on more conservative methods of financing: drawing on unlimited credit, Japanese companies can produce cheaper goods in order to gain market share.

The Japanese have also been notoriously tough about driving hard bargains in the countries where they settle. By going to depressed areas, they secure non-union agreements and workers at below union rates (as for example Mazda in Detroit, which negotiated with the United Auto

Workers' Union). Energy, raw materials, land and labour are all more cheaply available abroad than in Japan. One Japanese company operating an assembly plant for robotics in Britain imports all its engineered spare parts, thus ensuring the least transfer of technology and the least training for the British workforce, whose jobs are limited to simple functions, in a virtually colonial style of manufacturing.

The Japanese newcomers have provided thousands of jobs; but they have also caused thousands to be lost. For example, Ford and Vauxhall announced redundancies of 2,400 jobs early in 1992 because of 'significant challenges' from the Japanese. The cuts were designed to reduce Ford's workforce to 4,500 producing some 45,000 cars a year; this is to be compared with Nissan's workforce of 4,500 at Sunderland, producing 270,000 cars a year, and Toyota's workforce of 3,300, producing 200,000 cars. By the mid-1990s Japanese car makers were producing some 600,000 cars a year in Britain. Output per head in the British plants is roughly a quarter below that of Japanese plants.

There can be no doubt that Japan's attitude to inward investment remains rigorously restricted. Foreign companies have only some 2 per cent or 3 per cent of shares in Japan, compared with 10 per cent in America and some 20 per cent in West Germany, France and Britain. James argues, convincingly, that the employment generated by the new plants is likely to do no more than compensate for a part of the employment lost by local manufacturers, as a result of increased Japanese sales. In his view, 'To many critics Japanese manufacturing investments in the West are synonymous with exporting low value-added metal-bashing and assembly operations which offer marginal if any quality in investment.' He goes on:

Japanese companies have long practised market subsidisation using the cash flows generated in Japan, a high-priced market heavily protected from Western competition, to subsidize the penetration of Western markets. Both the US and the EEC regard cross-market subsidization or 'dumping' as unfair competition and have imposed fines, duties, tariffs and restraint agreements to protect local companies.

In the current climate of increasing protectionism and high yen values export price subsidization has lost much of its viability. However, the new globalized approach of Japanese companies offers indirect opportunities to maintain cash-flow subsidization. With highly developed networks sourcing, shipping, producing and assembling on a global scale, Japanese offshore units became part of a complex logistics system. This provides the opportunity to leverage the flow of raw materials, semi-processed and finished materials, components, sub-assemblies and even finished products between the various manufacturing, assembly and sales operations in different countries. The permutations to continue cross-subsidization of country market share battles with global cash flows, to support product positions, are almost endless given the complexity of global logistics systems – and almost impossible to identify.

What this means is that on a global scale it is possible to practise the kind of market manipulation that the *zaibatsu*, and then the *keiretsu*, have long since carried out at home. Further, the Japanese are adept at exploiting local subsidies in depressed areas in the West: There are no guidelines in the US or EEC which limit the incentives available to investors. So Japanese companies find themselves the targets of different communities outbidding each other to draw them in. For example, Britain's Department of Trade and Industry is believed to have increased its subsidy from £2 million to around £7 million in an effort to attract a new NEC plant to Telford instead of to Hanover in West Germany.

Such incentives are escalating: in 1982 Honda was given grants of around $16 million to build a plant in Ohio, while Toyota was given some $125 million in incentives for its car plant in Kentucky in 1985. The West in fact has huge potential bargaining power with Japan: America and Europe consume more than nine-tenths of its trade surplus between them. Thus Western governments would be wise to insist that potential investors persuade them of the real value of their investments. In fact, this has happened in much of Asia, where Japan is treated warily.

The solution is for much tougher controls to be imposed on Japanese inward investment. Incentives can be linked to the level of local content and paid after a period to ensure that the company complies. Training grants could be made available only for programmes which create or upgrade genuine skills. Or the level of grants could be linked to the level accorded to foreign firms in Japan. This would require Western co-ordination. It seems obvious that this approach is preferable to gut protectionism or exclusion, which can only create inefficiency, would anger the Japanese, and reduce world trade.

It can hardly be clearer that the Japanese are determined to maintain an ever-increasing overseas investment strategy. The Economic Planning Agency stated baldly in its programme for the year 2000 that:

In a long-term view of the future of the economy, it is inevitable that Japan will take the route from being a major trading partner to being a major power in direct investment. There are a number of forces at work, including the relatively rapid increase in international standing of Japanese companies in terms of financial, technological and management strength, and the difficulty of acceptance of trade from a single point for those major export items in which Japan has established a leading position. The increase in real incomes from Japan's relatively high rate of economic growth (a rise in wage and service prices), the possibility of a sustained increase in the yen exchange rate, and the relative increase in production costs in Japan, will be the forces making for overseas direct investment henceforth.

In 1989, Japan's direct investment abroad had grown from just $8 billion in 1975 to $154 billion, placing it third in the world foreign investment league, behind the United States with $373 billion and Britain with $192 billion. Of this, the bulk was in America and Europe. In 1990, for example, Japan invested $27 billion in North America, $14 billion in Europe, $7 billion in Asia and some $4 billion in Latin America. However, the bulk of foreign manpower employed by overseas Japanese firms was in Asia – some 474,000, compared with 354,000 in North America, 120,000 in Europe and 114,000 in Latin America.

Where are the multinationals going today, and is their impact likely to be as trouble-free as in the first two or three decades of their operations? Their role, while more parochial and less dominant than once predicted, has been quite formidable. Their principal attraction stems from the fact that the Third World was so devastated and shell-shocked by its first major encounter with global capitalism – the debt crisis – that it turned in despair to multinational investment as a saviour.

Without such investment, there would be precious little capital at all for the Third World. In a sense, the debt crisis softened up the previously proudly nationalistic and independent developing countries into abandoning their hostile attitude towards the multinationals.

Howard Perlmutter's dire predictions that by now 200–300 companies would control four-fifths of the non-communist world's productive assets has fallen far short of the mark. It is reckoned that some 35,000 multinationals – on a broad definition of the term – exist around the world, controlling some 170,000 affiliates. Of these, the top 400 multinationals account for some $3 trillion of world assets. Anything up to half of all cross-border assets are controlled by the top 100. *The Economist*'s editor, Bill Emmott, calculated in the early 1990s that the top 100 control about 16 per cent of the world's productive assets, and the top 300 around a quarter (although I would put it at closer to a third). This, as he remarks, is not dominance.

But it does represent colossal global power. For just 300 global corporate oligarchies between them to control more than 25 per cent of the productive wealth of the entire world is astonishing, leaving them dwarfing many nation states in wealth. Japan's *keiretsu*, which control around a third of Japanese business, nevertheless dominate Japan's business scene. As proved there, when smaller firms are fragmented and often act as suppliers of the big boys, the domination of the latter is quite secure.

The table opposite gives a list of the top fifty – among them monsters like General Motors, with total assets of $180 billion, Exxon and IBM with $88 billion apiece, Mitsubishi with $74 billion, Toyota with $56 billion and Siemens with $50 billion.

In October 1993, a $33 billion merger between the Bell Atlantic Telephone Company and Tele-Communications (TCI), America's largest cable corporation, was announced. The new company was America's sixteenth largest with $60 billion in assets and $16 billion in revenues, reaching more than 40 per cent of American homes. 'Baby Bell' had in effect swallowed America's largest cable company.

Just by comparison, the total production of a medium-sized economic power like Britain was $960 billion in 1991 and the size of its state sector was $180 billion. For the biggest developing economy, Brazil, the figures were $450 billion and $65 billion respectively, and for a medium-sized developing country like Thailand, they were $180 billion and $9 billion respectively. Thus the assets of General Motors are two times greater than the entire annual production of Thailand, a fifth of the annual production of Britain, and as great as its entire public sector. That is power indeed.

The unelected, anonymous, self-appointed bosses of General Motors, Ford, General Electric and Royal Dutch can and do look upon the great majority of world political leaders patronizingly, *de haut en bas*, because they serve larger enterprises (although of course the politicians represent many more people).

Even within the UN's 35,000 multinationals, there is considerable concentration. Half are based in America, Japan, Germany and Switzerland. Further, as much as a third of all world trade is concentrated within

The top 50
Largest non-financial multinationals 1990, ranked by foreign assets*

Rank		Industry	Country	Foreign assets $bn	Total assets $bn	Foreign sales $bn	% of total sales
1	Royal Dutch/Shell	Oil	Britain/Holland	n.a.	106.3	56.0†	49
2	Ford Motor	Cars and trucks	United States	55.2	173.7	47.3	48
3	General Motors	Cars and trucks	United States	52.6	180.2	37.3	31
4	Exxon	Oil	United States	51.6	87.7	90.5	86
5	IBM	Computers	United States	45.7	87.6	41.9	61
6	British Petroleum	Oil	Britain	39.7	59.3	46.6	79
7	Nestlé	Food	Switzerland	n.a.	27.9	33.0	98
8	Unilever	Food	Britain/Holland	n.a.	24.8	16.7†	42
9	Asea Brown Boveri	Electrical	Switzerland/ Sweden	n.a.	30.2	22.7‡	85
10	Philips Electronics	Electronics	Holland	n.a.	30.6	28.6‡	93
11	Alcatel Alsthom	Telecoms	France	n.a.	38.2	17.7	67
12	Mobil	Oil	United States	22.3	41.7	44.3	77
13	Fiat	Cars and trucks	Italy	19.5	66.3	15.8	33
14	Siemens	Electrical	Germany	n.a.	50.1	15.1‡	40
15	Hanson	Diversified	Britain	n.a.	27.7	5.6	46
16	Volkswagen	Cars and trucks	Germany	n.a.	41.9	27.5‡	65
17	Elf Aquitaine	Oil	France	17.0	42.6	12.2	38
18	Mitsubishi	Trading	Japan	16.7	73.8	41.2	32
19	General Electric	Diversified	United States	16.5	153.9	8.3	14
20	Mitsui	Trading	Japan	15.0	60.8	43.6	32
21	Matsushita Electric Industrial	Electronics	Japan	n.a.	59.1	16.6	40
22	News Corp.	Publishing	Australia	14.6	20.7	5.3	78
23	Ferruzzi/Montedison	Diversified	Italy	13.5	30.8	9.1	59
24	Bayer	Chemicals	Germany	n.a.	25.4	21.8	84
25	Roche Holding	Drugs	Switzerland	n.a.	17.9	68.8‡	96
26	Toyota Motor	Cars and trucks	Japan	n.a.	55.5	26.3	42
27	Daimler-Benz	Cars and trucks	Germany	n.a.	48.8	32.7‡	61
28	Pechiney	Metals	France	n.a.	14.3	9.2	65
29	Philip Morris	Food	United States	12.5	46.6	15.2	3
30	Rhône-Poulenc	Chemicals	France	12.2	21.4	10.4	72
31	E.I. Du Pont de Nemours	Chemicals	United States	11.9	38.1	17.4	43
32	Hoechst	Chemicals	Germany	n.a.	23.8	14.1‡	50
33	Michelin	Tyres	France	n.a.	14.9	9.1	79
34	Dow Chemical	Chemicals	United States	10.9	24.0	10.3	52
35	Total	Oil	France	n.a.	20.8	18.2	77
36	Thomson	Electronics	France	n.a.	20.7	10.4‡	75
37	Amoco	Oil	United States	10.6	32.2	8.5	30
38	Saint-Gobain	Construction	France	9.9	17.6	8.3	65
39	ENI	Chemicals	Italy	n.a.	60.5	7.9	19
40	Electrolux	Electrical	Sweden	n.a.	11.7	12.5‡	89
41	Petrofina	Oil	Belgium	n.a.	12.3	5.7	33
42	Générale des Eaux	Miscellaneous	France	n.a.	27.9	5.9	29
43	Hitachi	Electronics	Japan	n.a.	49.3	10.5‡	21
44	Chevron	Oil	United States	8.4	35.1	9.8	25
45	Sandoz	Chemicals	Switzerland	n.a.	10.1	6.3‡	70
46	C. Itoh	Trading	Japan	n.a.	47.8	19.1	13
47	Toshiba	Electronics	Japan	n.a.	32.7	8.5	29
48	Xerox	Office machinery	United States	8.0	31.5	7.5	42
49	Stora	Paper	Sweden	n.a.	15.0	8.9‡	84
50	Texaco	Oil	United States	7.8	26.0	18.0	44

Source: United Nations * where not available, foreign assets have been estimated for ranking
† outside Europe ‡ including export sales

multinational companies. By 1991, the European Community countries, including Sweden and Switzerland, were the world's biggest global investors, with stock totalling $634 billion, more than Canada's total gross national product.

One striking feature of the multinationals in the past was the way their investment moved away from the developing countries during the 1970s debt boom, and into the developed countries. Recently the bias has been the reverse. The multinationals behave like imperial powers in targeting their investment into four geographical regions. Thus, while there are major flows between America and Europe, and from Japan into America and Europe – with little going back into Japan – each of the three giants has its 'clusters'.

For America, the satellites are Latin America (with the exception of Brazil), Bangladesh, Pakistan and the Philippines in Asia, and Papua New Guinea and Saudi Arabia elsewhere. The Europeans prefer Chad and Morocco in Africa, Brazil in Latin America, India, Sri Lanka and Vietnam in Asia and a clutch of Eastern European countries. Japanese favourites in Asia are South Korea, Singapore, Taiwan, Thailand and Fiji. The tendency of the multinationals is to dominate a handful of preferred countries.

Broadly, of course, they invest in those with a favourable economic climate: openness to investment, incentives and orthodoxy in economics and politics. The multinationals are in a buyer's market: they can pick and choose locations favourable to them, which pursue the economic policies they like.

Another major trend among modern multinationals is the propensity to form alliances – joint ventures, supply deals, research groups and licensing agreements: this suggests that the trend is towards a cartel system, with firms exchanging favours for each other and mapping out turf rather than competing for the benefit of the customer. Such alliances are particularly prevalent in biotechnology and information technology, and are prompted by the expense of research and innovation, the need to gain access to markets, or to carve up a market.

Bill Emmott of *The Economist* argues that this is probably no more than a trend: 'Like anything else, international business is prone to fads and fashions. Unsure of what to do, many simply follow the herd, and in recent years the stampede has been towards the alliance – which is almost always called "strategic" in order to make it appear long-lasting, serious and vital. Nobody ever calls its alliances tactical.'

But the phenomenon is more than a passing one. In a classic free market, a firm arrives in a new market, competes with existing firms and thus improves the range and quality of goods and lowers prices for the consumer. This still sometimes happens, particularly with the arrival of Japanese firms, who use aggressive pricing and production to drive local firms out of business. But in most countries it is far easier for a major foreign firm to enter a deal with a major local one, in which each tacitly accepts what their market is going to be than for them to engage in a furious price war which serves neither of their interests (although it might serve the consumer).

In such alliances, the consumer and the free market will be the loser. While it suits the big firms to preach the virtues of the free market, it is in their interests to practise cartelization. That is what is happening on a global scale now. If this seems something less than monopoly – the classic adversary to free-market thinking – it is not all that far off.

In terms of direct control, moreover, in a number of key sectors, there is an astonishing domination by just a handful of companies. Only five companies sell nearly 70 per cent of the world's total supply of consumer durables. A similar number of companies carve up 60 per cent of world air travel; five aerospace companies control over half the world's production of aircraft while the same tiny number dominate its electric components industries; five in excess of half its electronic and electrical equipment industries; five at least half of world personal computer production; five over 40 per cent of the global media; five a third of world chemical production; and five some 30 per cent of world insurance.

These are staggering concentrations which, spread across the globe, far eclipse the powers of national regulators to control them. In addition, Boeing and Airbus dominate civil airline production, General Electric, Rolls-Royce, Pratt and Whitney and SNECMA carve up aero-engine production between them, and Intel and Motorola the production of microprocessors.

It would be naïve not to imagine that these colossi are going to maximize their profits in their own interests, whether through domination of the markets or alliances to carve up the market, although occasionally relations will degenerate into a ferocious war over turf or prices which might benefit the consumer. Of course, other tough-minded companies often try to break the hold of the giants, and occasionally tunnel through; for example Laker and Richard Branson's Virgin Airways confronted British Airways' dominance in Britain. Laker lost, while Branson survived British Airways' avowedly underhand attempts to crowd him out. Only the very toughest can hope to prevail against the huge power of the big corporations using their bureaucratic, monopolistic and anti-competitive practices to dominate.

There is now a serious political backlash to the power of the multinationals. It would be wrong to believe that the lid had been raised from this particular pressure cooker. The developing world eased its old takeovers of multinational subsidiaries, which peaked in the early 1970s, because they were so obviously counterproductive. In money-starved developing economies, debt was the alternative way of raising capital from abroad; they had no choice but to go cap in hand to the multinationals, and, indeed, invite them in by, for example, privatizing and selling off state assets. IMF conditionality made this necessary and emphasized the need for balanced budgets and reduced state intervention.

Huge swathes of admittedly badly run state industry were bought up by the multinationals at knockdown prices: in 1990 alone more than seventy countries had privatization programmes and had sold assets of $185 billion. The need to improve efficiency and raise capital is powering this move, and it is proceeding more successfully than the doomsday theorists predicted. But that does not rule out a potential backlash against the sale of national assets, pollution, the exploitation of resources, the corruption of local politicians or simply pushing around local governments.

That may yet come. True, the multinationals are less obviously bullying, less concentrated, more sensitive to local needs and have expanded more slowly around the world than expected by a few soothsayers. But still the trend has been unmistakable, and the political reaction, although much slower, may occur in a very dangerous form from countries already experiencing intense suffering as a result of the debt crisis.

CHAPTER 26

THE FIGHT FOR MARKETS

The fourth area in which the world economy is becoming globalized is, of course, trade. The explosion in world trade since the Second World War has brought enormous benefits in terms of global economic growth, expanding the range of products available to consumers throughout the world and improving competitiveness to the benefit of the consumer. From this it is easy to draw the iron conclusion that free trade is a good thing, as virtuous as being against sin. The obverse of free trade is protectionism, which helped to lead to the world slump of the 1930s and which, by excluding foreign products, limits consumer choice. Protectionism hampers economic growth and permits the erection of inefficient industries behind high tariff walls, which allow a country to slip behind its competitors, and, when an economy has to compete in the global marketplace, ultimately leads to impoverishment and industrial collapse.

The one cornerstone of free-market economics that has never been dislodged is the faith in free trade – justifiably so. What, however, the theory does not touch upon is what to do in conditions of imperfect free trade: that is, when some countries do not abide by the rules. The classical theory of free trade is also flawed in one respect: it is in fact possible, and may even be necessary, for a newly industrialized nation to build up highly competitive industries behind tariff walls. The argument here is that a country, in order to develop its major industries, needs them to have a large share of the domestic market: this is unlikely to happen if already efficient external competitors are pouring in goods which local industries are only just beginning to manufacture.

In fact, this has been the pattern for virtually every major country in the early stages of industrialization: Britain, as the first, had no need to be protected and became, unsurprisingly, an ardent advocate of free trade for its own products. Germany and France both built up their domestic industries from behind tariff walls, as did the United States, all of which opened up their economies and themselves became proponents of free trade as they became more confident they could compete abroad. Exactly the same technique has been practised by Japan and the Far Eastern countries over the period since the 1950s, as well as by Brazil. One of the world's foremost free-market theorists, Brazil's former Finance Minister Roberto Campos, told me in 1994 that tariff protection was permissible in the early stages of industrialization – provided that it was export-driven, and therefore local goods were competitive with overseas products. Indeed, a cycle occurs in which a country embarks upon a highly competitive export drive from behind tariff walls, which goes unnoticed for a while, then leads to demands for less protectionism by countries at the receiving end of the exports; in turn this leads to an opening up by the newly industrialized country's economy and, usually, a conversion of that country to the free trade camp.

With Japan, however, something rather different has happened, and is threatening to throw the whole theory of beneficial free trade into disarray. First, Japan has been repeatedly accused of maintaining hidden barriers towards imports and foreign investment – which seems to be borne out by the relatively small penetration of either into Japan. The Japanese retort that the problem is simply that ordinary Japanese – who are, it is true, somewhat xenophobic – shun foreign goods. Their competitors reply that there exists a whole network of barriers – from cartels, to a loaded distribution system, to a refusal to accept foreigners on company boards – that discriminates against them.

The second charge is that Japan's economy is rigged to promote exports in a way no other Asian economy is, for example through links between banking and industry which permit Japanese goods to be sold at a very low price or even below the cost of production for a time, with the banks absorbing the risks, in order to see off the competition. Both of these are formidable charges. With the Japanese retorting that they have no substance, a remarkable thing has occurred: the Japanese are now the world's prime advocates of free trade, while its old proselytizers, America and Europe, are increasingly dubious about its virtues.

In America, free trade is no longer the totem it once was. Robert Heilbroner, a leading economic historian at the New School for Social

Research in New York, argued that 'all trading nations' will go down the path 'of some form of managed trade'. Clyde Prestowitz, the former American trade negotiator, has been blunter still.

> It is not unfair for other countries to have a different view of industrial or antitrust policy than the United States. If the Europeans want to subsidize Airbus, and if the Japanese want to target supercomputers, that is their business. Lambasting them as unfair will only poison relations. The United States should, however, be prepared to offset the negative effects of their policies on its own industry.
>
> Americans should always be willing to negotiate, but they must be prepared to act unilaterally with countervailing subsidies or other measures – not out of moral outrage, but for self-preservation.
>
> The same holds for structural asymmetries. That the Japanese, for example, have a different market structure is not wrong. Americans should not blame them or insist that they become more like Americans. At the same time, the way the Japanese (and others) do business does sometimes put important US industries at an unacceptable disadvantage.
>
> The long-term solution to this problem is, of course, structural convergence. Since it will not come quickly, however, Americans must reconcile themselves to a certain amount of trade management with Japan.

The more extreme argument brought to bear against free trade today is that because of accelerated global transactions the rich become poorer while the poor suffer massive dislocations. In rich countries, competition with low-wage economies has forced wages and benefits down and caused huge trade imbalances. In America recently more and more families have been forced to rely on two incomes, while insurance for workers has been reduced and pension funds have often been raided in the course of corporate mergers. As the American commentator William Pfaff observed:

> High tariffs certainly contributed to the Great Depression of the 1930s. But it is equally clear that low tariffs are contributing to the great recession of our times – the competitive austerity and disinflation, and competitive unemployment and 'social dumping' of the

1990s. Industrial specialization in the poor countries has too often tended to turn them into low-wage suppliers of goods that they remain too poor to consume, while weakening or destroying their agricultural self-sufficiency and undermining their social stability.

The French-British financier and sometime corporate raider Sir James Goldsmith, whom no one has ever accused of bleeding-heart liberalism, recently published (in the Paris newspaper, *Le Figaro*) a powerful social as well as economic argument against further GATT tariff liberalizations. Writing for a European audience, he said that Europe is essentially self-sufficient in economic terms, and added: 'Let us recognize, once and for all, that economic growth is valuable only to the extent that it reinforces the stability of our societies and augments the well-being of our people.'

Sir James further asserted that the impact of free trade has been 'to impoverish and destabilize the industrial world at the same time that it cruelly ravages the Third World'. John Gray, an LSE academic, argued against 'the quasi-religious devotion to securing a GATT agreement'.

GATT is designed to create a global free market in all goods and services, including agricultural products. Such a global free market can only enhance the destructive radicalism of market institutions, which is the principal danger of the post-socialist age. The globalization of market forces has already undermined local and regional ways of life in many parts of the world. For the Third World, global free trade means the destruction of agrarian communities and peasant traditions, as local farming practices are undercut by mechanized Western agribusiness. This in turn means the accelerated migration of impoverished agricultural workers to swollen mega-cities whose social and economic sustainability is questionable. The prospect of over a billion ruined peasants being peacefully absorbed into the cities of the Third World will be taken seriously only by those whose support for market institutions is fundamentalist in character.

In truth, the GATT agreement promises to complete, under the auspices of laissez-faire liberalism, the desolation of peasant life wreaked by communist governments throughout the world. For the developed world, global free trade means a massive increase in structural unemployment as workers try vainly to compete with the low-wage economies of the newly industrializing countries. In both Third and First worlds the GATT proposals are a recipe for social upheaval and political instability on a vast scale. The world envisaged by the GATT proposals is, in fact, a fantasy of economic rationalism, as utopian and as dangerous as its mirror image in Marxism.

Against this have to be set the staggering benefits of free trade: in the last forty years exports of manufactured goods have risen more than twenty-five times, the volume of trade has increased twelve times and world output has jumped six times.

The United States has indeed moved sharply in the direction of protectionism, passing the Omnibus Trade and Competitiveness Act in August 1988, 'a wide-open door for protectionist legislation', according to Martin Feldstein, a former chairman of the President's Council of Economic Advisors. The share of American imports subject to quotas or official restraints has risen from 10 per cent to 25 per cent. The emphasis has now been placed in Washington on 'fair' rather than 'free' trade. President Bush the Younger's imposition of electorally convenient steel quotas in 2002 was the most blatant example yet.

In 1991, President Bush the Elder paid a visit to Japan and a deal was sought by which the Japanese agreed to limit their exports to the United States in certain key areas: this represented a step towards 'managed' trade – barter – which could leave third parties like Europe at a disadvantage and violate the customer's right to buy goods from across the world as he wishes. It was denounced as such by the European Commissioner responsible for trade, Sir Leon Brittan. European restraints on Japanese exports, such as cars, remain high, with Europe demanding 'reciprocity' in trade.

There are also increasing signs of a trade war between Europe and America, with the 1988 European ban on $150 million worth of American hormone-fed meat imports, and in 1992 the row over American restraints on steel exports. Charges of 'Fortress Europe' have been flying about. In official pronouncements, the virtues of free trade remain paramount.

Both America and Europe believe Japan is flouting the rules. The Americans are retaliating through managed trade, thereby flouting the rules themselves, and the Europeans are likely to retaliate in the one area where free trade remains a reality – European–American trade. There is no need to be too pessimistic about this: handled with firmness and flexibility, these huge frictions need not degenerate into catastrophic trade wars. But the ideal of genuine free trade remains very far from being realized.

The globalization of trade, of course, has had an immense effect on the autonomy of individual countries. On the one hand it can lead to improved competitiveness in a country subject to foreign imports; on the other to the decline of domestic industries and the loss of jobs. The flows of money that accompany it are also important: a large Japanese trade surplus, for example, serves as a brake on growth in the rest of the world economy, particularly if the rest of the money is not put to increase Japanese demand for goods produced abroad. If the money instead flows out to fund Japanese purchases of foreign assets abroad – as it has – this greatly increases Japan's hidden 'power' in other countries.

The purchase of American treasury bills to fund the US budget deficit gives Japan huge leverage in any argument about trade with America. Certainly, this leverage has to be used carefully: a sudden major withdrawal of Japanese money would lower the value of the dollar and diminish the value of the rest tied up in bonds and property. But it places a major weapon at Japan's disposal should the American administration get too angry about the trade deficit. As with every other example of the globalization of the world economy, the power of national governments to impose their will upon events is steadily diminishing. The huge authority vested in the World Trade Organization is absolute proof of this.

CHAPTER 27

THE END OF SOVEREIGNTY

Two huge consequences flow from the transcendence of the power of the nation state by these huge economic forces. To the ordinary person, the forces that control his destiny seem bigger and more impersonal than ever. He can vote for the party he wants: but governments are increasingly forced to follow much the same policies, and are inevitably buffeted by larger external economic forces. In other words, just as the principles of free enterprise, personal rights and liberal democracy are making steady strides forward, they are being eroded by much larger forces that elected governments have very little control over – a directly contradictory phenomenon. It is not much use having the right to vote, and to be an entrepreneur, if your government has no freedom of action, or you cannot in practice compete against the big boys.

The second consequence goes back to the basic tripod political theory outlined earlier based upon the individual, the strong and government. The latter, in a properly balanced democracy, exists to prevent the powerful depriving the ordinary man of his freedom – while permitting the strong enough freedom to help create the wealth of the nation. In a global marketplace and economy, the powerful corporations have escaped the control of governments, endowed with legitimacy by popular mandate: in other words, we are back to the state of nature which, as Hobbes argued, was less libertarian than any for the ordinary individual – if not for the strong.

To some free-market theorists, this is entirely desirable (very few recognize the inherent contradiction in arguing passionately for the freedom of the individual consumer or businessman, while espousing a world in which his electoral choice counts for less and less). There is a thread running through much free-market theory which asserts that central banks should be independent of governments, which decide things for 'political' reasons, and that technical economic decisions are far too important to be left to corrupt and ignorant party hacks, interested only in grubbing for votes. The government that governs best governs least. The market is self-regulating with an ingenious mathematical equilibrium that irons out every distortion. Governments only damage delicate natural mechanisms if they interfere; leave the market alone and it will look after itself.

Pure free-market economics is the mirror image of communist economics – the reason why it is so attractive to so many of the old proponents of the latter, seeking another perfect mathematical formula to fit pseudo-scientific theories. Both display spectacular ignorance of human nature: the self plays no part in their calculations. To communist theorists the state had to have control of everything and history fitted a pattern of scientific inevitability; to free-market theorists, economics will automatically determine the best order of things if left alone.

In fact free-market theorists perform much the same role for the power system they justify – the big corporations – that communist economists performed for the all-powerful state. While communism represented the perversion of the power of the state to its zenith, free-market economics represents an idealization of the power of the strong. Set the strong – the large industrial and economic conglomerates, the banks and financial institutions – free of irksome government interference (which in communist countries was deeply inefficient and unproductive, while in democratic societies represented the valid concerns of ordinary electors) and wealth would be maximized.

In the world economy the strong have already been set free because they largely escape government regulation – except for that of the three global superstates swirling together: the Americas; Europe; and Eastern Asia. These giants, in fact, are fast becoming the strongest of the strong and are thus best placed to secure their own interests in the international state of nature, where there is no supreme state authority. For behind the ideal global free market lies the reality that it best serves the interests of those who are strongest.

When, in the 1980s, the United States wanted to expand its defence budget while cutting taxes (a 'supply side' economic theory at some variance with personal motivation), it was able to increase its budget deficit and raise interest rates to attract funds, crippling its smaller European partners – simply because, in the jungle of the money markets, it was the biggest animal. European countries had to follow the rise in American interest rates to avoid a run on their currencies. This had nothing to do with classical free-market theory – that exchange rates set themselves at the levels justified by the state of the economies concerned – it just had to do with the largest economy throwing its weight about and the rest proving too small to resist.

On a smaller scale, German interest rates surged absurdly high in the early 1990s for slightly more defensible domestic political reasons and smaller Western European economies, from the cautious to the profligate, suffered accordingly. The currency markets are increasingly flawed judges of a country's economic viability. Interest rates are the main determinant of currency flows and these bear only an indirect relevance to the state of an economy: for example, high German interest rates may have actually done damage to that country; in Britain, the perception of a 'petro-economy' early in the 1980s contributed to an unusually strong pound – unreflected by the real economy – that helped to bankrupt thousands of enterprises.

The upshot of all these developments is the same: the old nation state has been bypassed, and no longer controls the huge flows of international trade, investment and finance that determine the fate of nations today. Nation states are increasingly democratic and responsible to the people: the giant interests that manage these flows are not, and are more powerful. A world in which people, far from gaining control over their own destinies through the spread of liberal democracy, are in fact losing it through the globalization of non-responsible economic forces is surely one moving in a dangerous direction. In fact, it is in the very same direction that the communists moved for more than seventy years. As ordinary people become more aware that the governments they elect exercise no real power, but merely stage a sham political theatre while being buffeted by larger economic forces, resentment is exploding – in the form of political anger, such as demands for trade protection or the exclusion of foreign investors.

The issue of the transcendence of politics has to be addressed. To some free-market theorists, as noted, it is eminently desirable that the old nation state should have increasingly less power in the face of giant economic forces and that politicians' choices should be restricted and even frustrated by the wider economic forces they face. On this theory, although absolute state interference is worst of all, even limited state intervention is bad, determined by 'crowd-pleasing' and populism and grubbing for votes rather than the necessary technical adjustments imposed by the markets. In Latin America, in particular, the 1970s was the decade of the 'technocrats', men who believed that authoritarian military regimes would permit the sometimes unpopular policies of economic liberalization necessary for economic growth and stability.

The emphasis on monetary policy and taking central banks out of political control is another example: by handing one of the key institutions of economic control to the 'experts', the temptation by politicians to inflate will be reduced. And so what if the globalization of economics removes economic policy from the hands of elected governments? If governments are increasingly forced to follow prudent economic policies because to do anything else would result in financial disaster, what is the harm in that? If an incoming Democratic administration, like Bill Clinton's in America, or a Labour government in Britain is quietly forced to renege on its election promises and follow policies not unlike those of its Conservative predecessors, is this not a good thing?

This argument is flawed in most of its key aspects. To begin with it must be recognized as an essentially authoritarian, anti-democratic argument. Just as communists argued that only they saw what was in the true interests of the people – the latter were too ignorant to know – so the technocrats argue that they alone enshrine economic wisdom which ordinary people are too stupid to understand for themselves; the voter does not know his own true interests.

The argument also asserts that the market is pure and all-knowing. As we have seen, the market is certainly a formidable force, but it obeys rules all of its own, which sometimes are no more than the fashions of the day: there is no such thing as an objectively 'correct' economic policy, as the enduring arguments on the subject attest. We may be groping towards greater understanding, objectivity and judgement, but we do not have all the answers. An economist or central bank governor is just as likely to be flawed in his judgement as a voter.

Further, this theory of expertise obscures the key point that economics is about priorities and choices. It is certainly true that there is an objective body of economic laws that seems to hold true in most economic situations. For example, if a country's money supply expands faster than its productive capacity, or if wages are allowed to rise much faster than output, or if the government increases public spending but does not raise taxes, inflation will result.

But that may reflect a conscious choice on the part of voters: if a left-wing government is elected after a long period of right-wing rule it may be because voters are now more concerned with the quality of public services or the fall in real wages than they are about inflation. The rightists would try and convince them otherwise, arguing that inflation will in the long run make them worse off. But if the voters have a different set of priorities, they cannot be forced to change them. Or if voters prefer high taxes and high public spending to low taxes and low public spending, a rightist can argue against this; but, again, it is a matter of the voters' own perceived self-interest. If voters prefer to spend money on social services rather than defence, a rightist politician's job is to try and persuade them of the importance of the latter; but he cannot impose his choice.

In a democratic society, we respect the choice of ordinary voters, even if we believe it to be wrong, and seek to persuade them through argument. If crowd-pleasing is so bad, why not do away with the whole tiresome business of democratic elections, and let the experts get on with running the show? The theory that the gentlemen in Whitehall know best has much more in common with classical socialist theory than with the free market, and leads inexorably towards totalitarianism: a free society is founded on the free rights of the people, including the right to make wrong choices.

A tyranny which disregards the rights of the people may in theory make wiser decisions, but precedent is not encouraging: usually authoritarian governments simply impose the choices of the clique in power upon the people. In an authoritarian society people may be told to do the 'right' thing (although the authorities, as often as not, get it wrong), but it is not the people's own preference; hence the sense of alienation from government that, throughout the centuries, has resulted in an explosive assertion of the self. Liberal democracy in its present form is not an ideal system; but it is increasingly the only form of government that can persuade people to give their peaceful assent to state policies and actions.

Leaving matters to the 'experts' can seriously distort matters. In 1990, Germany's democratically elected government, for electoral purposes, promised a one-for-one exchange of good West German marks for worthless East German ones. In the absence of high taxes this was highly inflationary, and the independent expert, the Bundesbank, had to raise interest rates to squeeze inflation out of the system.

Was that the right policy? Possibly, although it might have made more sense to permit a modest degree of inflation to cope with the once-and-for-all phenomenon of German unification rather than strangle Germany's economic recovery, and most of the rest of Europe's as well. The Bundesbank should not be blamed: its job was to maintain the value of the currency, and it did exactly that. But its independence reduced the flexibility of German economic policy. It was really up to the elected government to decide whether to permit a degree of inflation as part of the price of reunification. Instead, it was able to wash its hands of responsibility for the policy of high interest rates, and blame the Bundesbank.

To the expert central banker, inflation is viewed as an unmitigated evil in quasi-religious tones – this is understandable, as his job is to prevent the currency being debased. Yet inflation is in its own way no more than a form of disguised – some would say dishonest – taxation. The German government's mark-for-mark policy was in reality a tax upon West Germany to subsidize the East: that would have been the most honest way of presenting it. The most recent example is the European Central Bank, basically a child of the Bundesbank. Endowed with a mandate to impose scrupulously rigid economic policies, it has succeeded in throttling European economic growth since the creation of the single currency. Now that even its German father and French mother are having to break its stifling rules, at last the currency union may be able to have the flexibility of the US 'fed' to tighten and ease when necessary.

To argue that experts should be left to run economic policy in a democratic society is like saying that foreign affairs should be left to the diplomats. The purpose of diplomacy is to negotiate between nations, to avoid war, and to lubricate the sometimes rough edges of national interests as they grate against each other. This is not to belittle a difficult and highly professional activity which generally provides the best solution available. By making concessions, just about any war can be avoided. But a political judgement must be imposed to say, thus far and no further; this is wrong, the people will not stand for it; even war is preferable to the further surrender of national interest, or of justice to aggression. Similarly, the level of inflation, taxation or health spending people will stand for is a political choice which technocrats are singularly ill-equipped to judge, because most of them have very little contact with any but the most restricted circle.

CHAPTER 28

APOLOGISTS OF MIGHT

At this stage it bears noticing that historically a great deal of economic theory has been an authentication, or justification, of political choices. After the Second World War there was a surge of support for welfare policies which benefited left-of-centre political parties with the rationale provided for this by the economic theories of Keynes and his disciples. With the free-market reaction against this in the 1980s, orthodox economic theories were trotted out to press for such things as lower taxes, lower spending on the social services and low inflation.

There was something to be said for each set of policies at its particular moment in history. But economic laws, unlike scientific ones (although even these are increasingly seen in terms of probability) are not subject to iron rules of cause and effect, and economics is really the art of rationalizing and justifying particular political choices. Economics also involves analyzing a constantly innovating and changing economic environment: who could have foreseen the credit boom that followed financial deregulation and the house price boom of the late 1980s?

A quick glance at the history of economic theory bears this out. John Kenneth Galbraith argues persuasively that the wealthy throughout the ages have needed theoretical justification for their being better off than their fellow men – particularly in view of Christianity's essentially egalitarian message – and that economists have for the most part been employed to provide this.

A first foundation of economic thought was that with the introduction of real money, coins of fixed weight and purity in place of weighed amounts of metal, it was morally incumbent on governments not to debase the value of the metal, otherwise they would be guilty of nothing less than fraud. 'Who then would trust the prince who would diminish the weight or fineness of money bearing his own stamp?' asked the first theorist of monetarism, Nicholas Oresme. Indeed, some of the moral indignation of today's monetarists can be traced back to this fundamentally puritanical attitude towards money.

With industrialization, which in place of unchanging rural stagnation and poverty offered the possibility of escape and improved living standards – although for most this took a long time to materialize – further theories were required to justify the differences in living standards between factory owner and worker. Adam Smith, however, was justly accorded his later fame because he was no mere apologist for the factory owners but an independent, impartial observer in the early stages of Britain's Industrial Revolution.

An Inquiry into the Nature and Cause of the Wealth of Nations was published in 1776 and, although rambling, was a brilliant work. On the one hand it legitimized the force of self-interest as the prime mover in the creation of wealth:

> It is not from the benevolence of the butcher, the brewer, or the baker that we expect our dinner, but from their regard to their own interest. We address ourselves, not to their humanity but to their self-love . . . [The individual] is in this as in any other cases, led by an invisible hand to promote an end which was no part of his intention . . . I have never known much good done by those who affected to trade for the public good. It is an affectation, indeed, not very common among merchants, and very few words need to be employed in dissuading them from it.

He was also fairly hard-nosed in his attitude towards pay: this was merely the cost of bringing a worker into the workforce and keeping him in his job. Smith was a passionate advocate of freedom of internal and international trade, based on his observation that the specialization on which the Industrial Revolution depended would be impossible if they were not free. Every worker would otherwise have to concentrate inefficiently on duplicating separate products; instead, each should specialize in making what he could do best, purchasing from another what he could do best through the market.

For Smith the division of labour, and hence economic efficiency, was limited by the size of the market. The wider the market, the greater the division of labour, and the greater economic efficiency. As industry transcends crude specialization, and as markets grow to vast size, this clearly does not apply today – which has not stopped some ardent admirers of Smith still believing it. Here he can be faulted, rather unjustly as his powers were not divine, of not foreseeing the distant future.

Smith goes on brilliantly to attack mercantilism – the idea of protection to ensure a country's stock of precious metals. He asserts, almost incontrovertibly, that a nation's wealth should not be measured in its stock of silver and gold. Instead national wealth is:

> The annual labour of every nation [that] is the fund which originally supplies it with all the necessaries and conveniences of life . . . wealth is created by the skills, dexterity and judgement with which its labour is generally applied; and secondly, by the proportion between the number of those who are employed in useful labour and that of those who are not so employed.

He vigorously criticized two of the restrictive practices of his times – colonial preference and monopolistic practices. He observed caustically that:

> People of the same trade seldom meet together, even for merriment or diversion, than the conversation ends in a conspiracy against the public, or in some contrivance to raise prices. It is impossible . . . to prevent such meetings, by any law which either could be executed, or would be consistent with liberty and justice. But though the law cannot hinder people of the same trade from sometimes assembling together, it ought to do nothing to facilitate such assemblies, much less to render them necessary.

He loathed the professionally managed company in words which resonate down to the big corporations of today:

> Being the managers rather of other people's money than of their own, it cannot be well expected, that they should watch over it with the same anxious vigilance with which the partners of a private company frequently watch over their own . . . Negligence and profusion, therefore, must always prevail, more or less, in the management of the affairs of such a company.

Smith was truly a revolutionary, and the popularizer of the new individualists, anxious to justify their new fortunes.

The era of the professional economist now began. Jean-Baptiste Say, at the beginning of the nineteenth century, argued, with terrible consequences for later economics, that demand was inevitably exactly equal to supply: if goods are produced, the return in wages, profit, interest or rent is sufficient to buy that product. Even if money is saved, it will eventually find its way back into the system to balance the economy.

This theoretically attractive but nonsensical view was to be the orthodoxy for more than a century, and was later to return to haunt the late twentieth century. It was the father of the view that, since the economy automatically balances itself, nothing must be done by government to interfere with the market. The elegant equations of economics would balance themselves. It is easy to see how seductive this view was to nineteenth-century capitalists seeking to minimize the calls for their regulation: all intervention is damaging.

This argument ran directly counter to the economic evidence that from the earliest stages of the Industrial Revolution, cycles of boom and bust began to repeat themselves. At some moments there was too much demand in the system, at others too little; governments actually had to take action, otherwise the economy would overheat or suffer serious slump.

Another baleful economic influence was Thomas Malthus, who argued that the lower classes' insatiable appetite for procreation was the source of their misery. As they bred without control, the only thing that would keep their numbers down was hunger and starvation. So employers and governments were ill advised to help the poor: all that would happen would be even more breeding, and more misery: it was laissez-faire with a vengeance. The existence of such grim theorists, to justify the most callous and brutal of capitalist attitudes towards those who helped to create their wealth through their work, was a remarkable feature of the Industrial Revolution. As Galbraith comments:

> Among the many who sought to put the poverty of the poor on the shoulders of the poor – or remove it from those of the more affluent – none did so more completely than Malthus.
>
> David Ricardo, the other economic guru of the age, argued that the amount of labour used to produce a product decided its worth. He went on to say that wages 'are the price which is necessary to

enable the labourers, one with another, to subsist and to perpetuate the race, without increase or diminution'.

Thus, just as chillingly as Malthus, he argued against a benevolent employer or government improving the conditions of the workers, because this would merely increase their numbers.

However, by urging that the amount of work involved would decide the value of a good (which is actually not true: the value of a precious stone has nothing to do with the labour involved in its extraction) Ricardo was an unwitting forerunner of Marxism: for why should anyone not doing any work benefit from any profit over and above his 'Iron Law of Wages' and 'Labour Theory of Volume'? Other exponents of the classical school were three Austrian economists: Ludwig von Mises; Friedrik von Hayek; and Fritz Machlup; who, in understandable revulsion against the communists at the very gates of their country, took the view that all state intervention was a compromise with socialism.

However, by the late nineteenth century, both in Britain and Germany, there was a growing concern among the better-off about the impact of industrial capitalism upon the huge new working class. In Germany, Bismarck decreed laws to provide for accident, sickness and old age. In Britain people like Robert Owen, George Bernard Shaw, the Webbs, the trade union movement as a whole and, above all, Lloyd George in 1911, pushed through schemes for unemployment insurance and sickness pay. None of this had anything to do with economic theory: it was the response of people disgusted with the plight of the working class – and in great measure it improved their lives without the dire consequences predicted by arid economists.

These straightforward measures to bolster the conditions of the working class were given a further boost, and their first theoretical justification, with the Depression of the 1930s. When this occurred it became impossible to argue, as the classical economists had, that supply and demand inevitably balanced each other. Perhaps they did in the end, but there were huge time-lags, and meanwhile terrible economic recession in which workers lost their jobs and lived on the breadline. 'In the long term,' as John Maynard Keynes wryly observed, 'we are all dead.'

Keynes was the economist who discovered the obvious: he argued in essence that the modern industrial economy did not find its equilibrium with full employment; it could live with unemployment. There could be a shortage of demand, and government had an obligation to step in to prevent this – even if this involved excess spending. In fact his views were extremely cautious, and were elaborated in response to the virtual collapse of classical economic theory. Keynes argued more boldly in favour of government stimulation of the economy – something then happening only in Germany and Sweden – as a substitute for the collapse of domestic demand, through the reluctance of savers to invest their money in a productive economy.

In this he was surely right: the major problem in any slump is to find a reason for those with money to put it back into the system either by spending – which many are reluctant to do at a time of insecurity and uncertainty – through investing in enterprises which seem likely to generate profits, or, if interest rates are high enough, investing in bonds. Keynes argued that governments should subsidize the economy with public works programmes if private investment was sluggish, a standpoint which was widely denounced as socialist, in some way merging with left-wing calls for greater public spending on social security and state control of the economy. This was almost certainly the reason why America, at least, emerged from the recession under Roosevelt. Keynes, on the contrary, believed he was saving capitalism from its own destruction: he was a committed believer in the capitalist system. His right-wing critics believed he was bent on destroying it.

He turned out to be right in the 1930s; and in the 1950s, with the introduction of the welfare state in much of Europe and to a lesser extent in America, the pendulum appeared to move decisively his way. In fact, the 1950s in Britain could be described as economically the most successful period of modern times; although accompanied by the usual hiccups, labelled 'stop-go', the economy grew steadily while both unemployment and public spending were kept at historically low levels. Derailment was to occur when the Labour government of Harold Wilson added a major new twist to public spending at just the moment when it should, probably, have been brought under control. The result was diminishing productivity and higher inflation, which in turn resulted in a backlash, a reversion by Conservative governments in the 1980s to the economic orthodoxies of the century before.

The prophet of the new order, an economist almost as important as Keynes, was the Chicago economist Milton Friedman, who preached that, allowing for time-lags, prices were entirely dependent on the supply of money in an economy. Control that, and you controlled everything.

Friedman also clung to the reductionist view of the state and did not believe government intervention, either positive or negative, achieved anything. The theory was as mathematically ingenious as it was crude in human terms, and represented a reversion to the laissez-faire philosophies of Say, Malthus and Ricardo. Let business get on with it, let government keep out, the market will inevitably and miraculously work things out for the best – provided the supply of money is controlled.

It is, of course, a truism that if there is less money in the economy, there will be lower inflation; but this completely obscures the more fundamental problems in an economy, such as the power of certain groups to secure a greater share of the available money – employers and unions alike. Moreover, monetarism was incredibly crude as an instrument, permitting governments to hand over power to financial managers and central banks. Finally it was overwhelmed by the inability of the market – in particular in exchange-control-free economies – to control the money supply, in an age of international financial flows and booming credit.

By the late 1980s, Friedmanite monetarism had been rendered obsolete by the very force it had set free – financial liberalization. Moreover, far from being a solution to all ills, the creed soon became a kind of abdication of responsibility, abandoned by even its most ardent practitioners, such as Britain's Mrs Thatcher in about 1987. Galbraith has written an eloquent passage on the subject in *The Culture of Contentment*:

> No tax increases would be necessary nor any curtailment of public expenditure. Nor would there be any enlargement of government function; all monetarist policy could be accomplished by the central bank, in the United States the Federal Reserve System, with only a negligible staff.

> For some, monetary policy had (and has) another, even greater, appeal, which was curiously, even unforgivably, overlooked among economists: it is not socially neutral. It operates against inflation by raising interest rates, which, in turn, inhibit bank lending and resulting deposit – that is, money – creation. High interest rates are wholly agreeable to people and institutions that have money to lend, and these normally have more money than those who have no money to lend or, with many exceptions, those who borrow money. . . . In so favoring the individually and institutionally affluent, a restrictive monetary policy is in sharp contrast with a restrictive

fiscal policy, which, relying as it does on increased personal and corporate income taxes, adversely affects the rich.

Conservatives in the industrial countries, especially in Britain and the United States, have given strong support to monetary policy. Their instinct in this matter has been far better than that of the economists, who, along with the public at large, have assumed its social neutrality. The applause for Professor Friedman from the conservative affluent, which has been great, has been far from unearned.

As the 1970s passed, inflation persisted. High taxes, lower public expenditures, direct intervention on wages and prices, were all ruled out as remedies. As sufficiently observed, only monetary policy remained. So in the latter part of the decade, by the ostensibly liberal administration of President Jimmy Carter in the United States and the avowedly conservative government of Prime Minister Margaret Thatcher in Britain, strong monetarist action was initiated. The Keynesian Revolution was folded in. In the history of economics the age of John Maynard Keynes gave way to the age of Milton Friedman.

Supply-side economics, judged by results, should be entirely discredited today. Federal spending grew from 21 per cent of national income in 1980 to around 23.5 per cent in 1990. The federal budget deficit grew from 1.8 per cent to 3.6 per cent. Government borrowing caused net national savings to be halved, from 7 per cent to 3.5 per cent of GNP over the period. Government spending rose during the Reagan administration, although the median marginal tax rate fell from 24 per cent to 15 per cent. It is reckoned that America's capital stock was some 7 per cent below what it would have been without supply-side economics, according to a report prepared by the Federal Reserve Bank of New York. In 1990, America's capacity to produce goods and services was some 3 per cent lower ($165 billion) what it would have been without supply-side economics. In almost every sphere the impact of supply-side economics was the reverse of that intended.

The most immediately damaging aspect of all this was, in Galbraith's view, the creation of an underclass with little stake in the economy. In the past, he argues, the well-off were in the minority and were constantly uneasy about the plight of the majority, whom they feared might turn against them. Now the very wealthy are still in the minority, but the great majority beneath them are comfortably off and share a common interest in such things as low taxes, high interest rates on invested income and so on. The great majority have no interest in the fate of the class beneath them, from which they perceive no threat, believing they are secure precisely because they are the majority.

The pattern then is of a new globalization of capitalism that is making a mockery of the decisions of elected governments, save in the very biggest units – the United States, Japan, the European Union – whose views can make themselves felt by virtue of their size. Capitalism is becoming not just remote and non-responsible to ordinary people, but to whole nations. It is escaping the bounds of control and regulation, leaping across frontiers with equanimity. In this unregulated world, the new global jungle, Hobbes's state of nature has returned.

Large industrial plants are closed and moved if conditions in the host country become unsatisfactory; News International buys newspapers and influences foreign governments; chocolate factories launch bids for rival companies in order to close them down; banks pour money into non-performing loans, bankrupting whole countries and hence starving them of funds; currency speculators destroy the policies of democratically elected governments overnight. If this brave new world seems brutal and anarchic, that is because it is, and increasingly so. As with the great issue of international security after the Cold War, the framework for regulating the new international economic order is not in place. Fortunately, there is much that can be done, a subject which will be returned to in the last section of the book.

CHAPTER 29

THE NEW PRINCES

There is another major factor that is alienating the greatest wealth-creating machine in human history, the free-enterprise system, from its roots, from the very people it exists to serve: and that is the evolving structure of the modern corporation. The changeover, starting in the eighteenth century, from the one-man entrepreneurial business – which still occasionally re-emerges – to the limited liability company, managed by professional managers on behalf of shareholders, marked a turning point. Western business has tended to raise capital largely from the stock market (and a little from the banks), with short-term financial results as the most important factor. In practice, unless there are a few dominant stockholders, most major businesses have been run by the management as self-perpetuating oligarchies.

Within these oligarchies there have been tremendous battles for territory: for example, the old domination of the industrial managers often gave way to that of the marketing men, and then to that of the financial and legal departments, as management buy-outs and asset-stripping became the fashion. Almost certainly, this has been an unhealthy trend. Both in America and Europe, the prime purpose of much corporate raiding has been to strip assets off an undervalued company, or in some cases to crush a competitor, rather than to improve performance, and the main response has been to make a firm as unattractive – as unprofitable – as possible to a raider. None of this has anything to do with a company's real performance.

The other main 'players' – the employee and the consumer – remain very much the underclass: in very few Western companies do the workers have any form of management participation, and their underlying strength lies in threatening some form of union militancy. Consumer rights have vastly increased in recent years, particularly in America, which has a healthy tradition of anti-trust legislation. Yet their real bargaining power remains light, particularly in certain sectors dominated by cartels.

In fact, the average Western company is an autocratic, self-perpetuating institution, which is fine, indeed inevitable, for small firms competing vigorously, but more disturbing for giant conglomerates in the global marketplace. In their secretive management culture, their often immensely bureaucratic way of doing things, the penchant for promotion by protégé, their anonymity, their *de haut en bas* seniority systems (nowadays often disguised behind a common corporate culture which refers to all employees by their first names and permits them to eat in the same canteens), the giant international company of today in fact resembles nothing so much as its defeated communist adversary.

Of course, there is one massive difference: the capitalist giant is subject to the disciplines of the marketplace. If his products don't sell, he goes under, whereas a communist enterprise had a captive market. The difference is more apparent than real: when one looks at any of the strategies adopted by big firms – cutting up markets between them, cartelism, undercutting small competitors, then raising prices when the market is secured – many resort to tactics that are plainly anti-competitive, and can get away with it just because they are so large. In the 'state of nature', as in the jungle, it is size and strength that count for survival rather than the production of inherently better or more competitive products. Of course, the difference still counts enormously: a truly uncompetitive player, as were most of the major industries of the Soviet Union, will go under in the global marketplace. But that is as far as responsibility to anyone stretches.

This should not be seen as too condemnatory: virtually any autocracy, from feudalism to a military regime, to communism, is usually led by well-meaning oligarchs and responsible elders who believe they are doing the best for the people beneath them: large capitalist corporations are no exception. Some degree of authority, as stressed at the beginning of this book, is necessary. This chapter seeks to examine these issues.

The modern corporation is distinguished by its size. In Japan the concentration of capitalism into a handful of giant *keiretsu* – cartels – is becoming increasingly observed by the outside world: vast traditional concerns like Mitsui and Mitsubishi, have been joined by a number of new companies – Sony, Sharp, Canon and so on – expressly groomed for their role by government, with their own banking, marketing and trading groups. These big corporations run a staggering third of the Japanese economy, and dominate another third through their hold on, for instance, much smaller supply firms and retail outlets. Through their privileged access to finance, as well as the government support they enjoy, the *keiretsu* are today being singled out by Western governments for criticism as monopolistic, cartelistic and anti-competitive.

Yet on a smaller scale Western companies are also sinners. In West Germany, the relationship between banking and the big industrial groups, although less close, gives cause for concern, as does the concentration of industry. In France the ties between major industries, a traditionally *dirigiste* central government and banking are worrying. In Britain there is more of a commitment to a free market and a distinction between banking and industry, as well as a much more developed stock market and financial markets in the City. However, in certain areas such as supermarket prices and, above all, in the over-concentrated banking sector, it is hard not to believe that cartelism and price-fixing operate, albeit unofficially, and never on the wrong side of the law.

In America, home of free enterprise, the economic concentration and clout of the major corporations may come as a surprise. In the 1930s it was established that the 200 largest non-banking corporations possessed about one-half of all non-banking corporate wealth, or a quarter of total national wealth. It is now reckoned that the largest 500 non-banking firms in the United States are responsible for 60 per cent of all production there.

An ideal world of thrusting middle-sized firms conjured up by free enterprise enthusiasts sadly does not exist. Cartelism, price-fixing, big firms using their clout in the market to secure their interests – these are the main features of markets around the world. Of course there also exists a large medium-sized sector, and many hundreds of thousands of small firms alongside the giants. But the latter usually get their own way when they want.

Size confers a tremendous advantage. The classical economies of scale are well known. In addition, in terms of corporate strategy, size confers power. To take two basic examples: a major supermarket chain that decides to slash its prices can do so for quite a while without running into trouble because of its stock of capital and creditworthiness; a smaller competitor, without these advantages, can be forced out of business. Or again, a major firm faced with troublesome competition from a smaller one can expand its range of products in a manner that the smaller one cannot, thereby becoming more attractive to customers at a stroke.

A typical case was that of the battle between Honda and the Japanese motor-cycle company Yamaha. Honda dominated the Japanese motor-cycle market in the late 1950s through the classic Japanese strategy of borrowing massively from the banks in an effort to undercut its competitors' market share. The leader in the field at the time was Tohatsu, a conservatively managed group with double Honda's after-tax profits and a debt-to-equity ratio about five times lower. Because of Honda's aggressive strategy, within four years Tohatsu's market share fell from 22 per cent to 4 per cent, while Honda's soared from 20 per cent to 44 per cent. Tohatsu was all but defeated and made huge losses. By February 1964, it had gone bankrupt.

In 1967 Honda decided to enter the automobile market at a time when the market itself was terrified of the new wave of international competition; finance, technical capability and the best managers were directed towards the new venture. Yamaha, a relatively new entrant into the motor-cycle field, saw its chance to stage an ambush while Honda's attention was elsewhere; Yamaha's President Koike claimed that: 'At Honda sales attention is focused on four-wheel vehicles. Most of their best people in motor-cycles have been transferred. Compared to them, our specialty at Yamaha is mainly motor-cycle production . . . If only we had enough capacity we could beat Honda.'

Honda's share of the market had fallen from 65 per cent in the late 1960s to just 40 per cent in 1981; Yamaha had increased its sales from 10 per cent to 35 per cent over the same period. In offering new models, Yamaha had also begun to pull ahead of Honda. In 1981, Yamaha announced plans to build a factory that would allow it to double its production of motor-cycles. Koike declared triumphantly: 'The difference between us and Honda is in our ability to supply. As primarily a motor-cycle producer, you cannot expect us to remain in our present number two position forever . . . In one year we will be the domestic leader. And in two years, we will be number one in the world.'

The following year Honda's President Kawashima told his share-holders without delicacy, 'Yamaha has not only stepped on the tail of a tiger, it has ground it into the earth. We will crush Yamaha!' The two methods adopted were massive price cuts of around a third on their motor-cycles, and the introduction of a huge new range of models – more than eighty, while Yamaha could only produce thirty-four – in the space of eighteen months: both companies had only produced around sixty models altogether before that. Yamaha sales collapsed by around half; the company soon had a year's sales of motor-cycles on the stocks; it struggled furiously to stay afloat, not to expand as Honda had done, and its debt to equity ratio shot up from three to one to seven to one in 1983.

In January of that year, Koike surrendered: 'We cannot match Honda's product development and sales strength . . . I would like to end the Honda-Yamaha war . . . From now on I want to move cautiously and ensure Yamaha's relative position (as second to Honda).' He was replaced, dividends were slashed, employees dismissed and production plummeted from a projected 4 million units at the height of Yamaha's ambitions to just 1.5 million. Desperately, the new Yamaha management begged for mercy, as Honda ruthlessly continued to grow by producing thirty-nine new models compared with Yamaha's twenty-three: 'Since Yamaha is considered responsible for the present market situation, I would first like to study our position and develop a more co-operative stance towards other companies . . . Of course, there will still be competition . . . but I intend it to be based on mutual recognition of our relative positions.'

The main reason for Yamaha's humiliation had been that Honda had carefully waited until its rival was at its most exposed – having invested heavily in a new plant that was not yet producing – before striking. Japanese companies were geared not just to producing goods but to fighting each other in almost a military fashion. Yamaha had dared to challenge the natural hierarchy of the motor-cycle industry and was massacred by the bigger company. That is one of the keys to Japanese efficiency – intense competition beneath the overall constraints of government planning.

Another Japanese-style example of big companies crushing competition was the price war raging in Britain's quality newspaper market. Rupert Murdoch's decision in 1994 to slash the cover price of The Times – with no change in quality – possibly funded by his other operations caught his competitors on the hop. The slightly less liquid Telegraph group was forced to follow suit, while the much smaller Independent teetered on the verge of drowning.

Major companies are divided into three types – single-product, conglomerate and diversified. The first speaks for itself; the second, after the recent merger mania sweeping America and Europe, is increasingly common; a collection of random companies brought together to maximize the profit of the controlling group. A diversified company is one consisting of closely interrelated industries which fertilize each other through, for example, common research and development or the manufacture of common components. That is the pattern in Japan, and it appears to be gaining ground in the West.

A further feature of the large corporation is its lack of a competitive character – except towards those aspiring to take its place. The marketplace, far from consisting of a host of furiously competing enterprises, is itself characterized by big companies that by mutual understanding do not stray on to each other's turf, preferring negotiated deals on territory and prices to wars that may be injurious to both: better to conspire against the customer with higher agreed prices than battle each other to lower them on his behalf. Of course, this is not always the case: wars do break out (for example, the British newspaper war), aggressive smaller companies break through to the big league; but it is the standard position.

The modern big corporation is not responsible to anyone but itself. There are four possible sources of accountability for the capitalist organization: the owners – those who put up the capital for a venture; the customers, to whom the product must appeal or the company will go bankrupt; the workforce – those who actually make the product; or the management. In practice, the only one that counts is the last.

According to classical economic theory the managers were primarily responsible to the owners – the shareholders – and their purpose was to maximize profits. But a famous study by Adolf Berle and Gardiner Means, *The Modern Corporation and Private Property*, established the point, as far back as 1932, that the shareholders had very little influence in most major companies. The management for the most part was responsible for informing the board of directors, which supposedly represented the shareholders. The latter, who stood at one remove from the affairs of the company on the stock market, tended to be uninterested in the daily management of the firm provided the share price went up and dividends were maximized. The stockbroker, acting for the shareholder, would investigate companies to assess their viability, but that was often the limit of accountability. Annual general meetings of shareholders were usually pure formalities.

This has been the position in the United States and Britain, countries with highly developed capital markets. In Japan, and to a lesser extent Germany, the prime suppliers of capital were the banks, rather than shareholders; in addition, government, which stood behind the banks, had a major say. Kenichi Ohmae, Japan's best known management strategist, outlines this quite frankly:

In the immediate postwar era, capital was very short. The Japanese people were and are assiduous savers, but the future of most corporations was then so uncertain that they lacked the confidence to invest their savings in private enterprise. Instead, they put it into the banks, which enjoyed infallible credibility. It was through the banks that corporations with dynamic growth plans borrowed money. Freed from the need to justify complex growth plans to individual stockholders or prospective investors and from the need to worry about keeping the stock price high, corporate executives could devote all their energies to business: people, production and products. They were convinced that by doing a superb job on these three P's they would earn the fourth P – profit – needed to repay the debt. And they were right. Had they been obliged to worry about making their financial performance look better in order to get the financing, they would have fallen into the vicious cycle of cosmetic financial management, opting for short-term profit maximization and neglecting long-term investment.

Again, sequencing was critical. Thanks to the integrative Japanese management style and governmental system, these corporations were not forced to perform before they were ready.

Another big helping hand in corporate finance came from the Japanese government's foreign capital phobia. The Ministry of Finance (MOF) and MITI, for example, in their determination to keep foreign capital from acquiring massive chunks of Japanese corporate stocks on the Tokyo Stock Exchange, did their best to encourage institutional stockholding. Although this stance is now gradually being relaxed, nearly seventy per cent of Japanese corporate shares are still institutionally held. This helped Japanese companies tremendously, not only because stock prices were less affected by the transactions of individual stockholders but also because these institutional owners were, like the banks, much more understanding of the long-term strategies of the companies in which they invested. And mutual holdings within a group of companies made it impossible to exercise short-term buying and selling options.

Thus, the distribution of power is slightly different in Japan. The banks and institutional investors do indeed have a more powerful role than the thousands of individual investors who make up the owners and capital providers of major companies in Britain and America, because they are large commercial interests with more clout. However, the banks, while providing the bulk of the money, do not actually own the company, and as Japanese industry evolved, with the major companies accumulating large capital reserves of their own, they became less dependent on the banks. Indeed, with so little of the company's capital put up by shareholders, the management owned the company in all but name.

By the 1980s, the fact of management control of major corporations had become so blatant that, in the United States, a war took place for control of the major companies. On the one hand corporate raiders moved in to buy out passive shareholders, in a bid to seize control of companies; on the other, management fought back through buyouts to secure their position. Both did so by borrowing large sums of money against the corporations themselves, mainly through the issuing of 'junk bonds', themselves of dubious reliability.

In each case huge debts were loaded on to the firm: in some cases management did so deliberately in order to make the firm less attractive to the predator. This channelled funds away from the firm's real objective – developing and selling products in the marketplace. In order to meet these huge debts, the profitable parts of the business were often the first to be sold off. Finally, many of the investors in the junk bonds went bust, while large profits were made by the various legal and financial advisers. The new refinement of this has been pursuit of a high share price which benefits management through stock options and other inducements. Share prices in the long term usually reflect a company's value. In the short term, creative accounting and other techniques can vastly inflate share prices, reaping rich rewards for managers, which have nothing to do with a company's real success, and leaving long-term investors in the lurch.

The whole exercise contributed to productive enterprise and competition in some cases, but it did untold damage to the corporations concerned in others. The corporate raiders, left in charge of successfully acquired large companies, tended to sell off parts of the business to maintain their profits. Having no intrinsic loyalty to the company itself, they tended to judge the acquisition purely by short-term financial results, accentuating the worst features of the stock market. The successful management buyers confirmed their role in real control of their own companies and in many cases improved efficiency. But their role was far from disinterested.

What is the logic of this pursuit of share prices? Toro-Hardy has a brilliant passage:

> The answer may be reduced to a simple consideration: short-term profit. The need to respond to the short-term expectations of a gigantic group of anonymous stockholders has become in fact the fundamental reason for the economic process now in course. Within this context the large corporations fiercely compete among themselves to win the attention of stockholders, shedding themselves of anything that might weigh down their chances of attaining higher yields.
>
> This leads to another question: who is this nameless stockholder upon which everything depends: he (or she) is none other than the 'common man': the factory hand, office worker, middling executive, widow, housewife, etc. That is the same common man who is threatened by the market forces which he nourishes. The same common man who lives with the anxiety of seeing himself forced to join the swelling ranks of the great counter-society of our day. Through his investments in and search for maximum yields from pension or mutual funds, or by means of his direct investment, however small, in the stock market, he has turned himself into the axis of the very economic process which frightens him and limits his life. Thus following a curious circular process, the 'common man' has become his own enemy, fiercely and pitilessly preying upon himself.

In 1980 it was estimated that the chief executives of the biggest 300 American companies had incomes some thirty times as great as those of average manufacturing workers; in 1990 the figure was ninety-three times as big! A survey by Britain's conservative *Sunday Telegraph* in 1993 found that there was no correlation between mushrooming levels of pay for top management, bolstered by lucrative share option schemes and the performance of the company. The survey, undertaken by Professor Graef Crystal, concluded that there was no relationship between company size and performance and boardroom pay, and that the top five bosses in Britain were overpaid by some £7 million between them.

Britain's highest paid executive then was Mr Robert Bauman, chief executive of Smith Kline Beecham, who took home nearly £2.8 million in pay and options, although his company's size was a long way short of being the biggest in Britain and its performance, while impressive, was by no means exceptional. Crystal calculated that Bauman's real worth was little more than £500,000. Britain's second highest paid executive, Greg Hutchings of Tomkins, who was paid more than £2.6 million, according to Crystal, was only worth a little less than £1 million to his company. Glaxo's Sir Paul Girolami was paid a touch over £2 million, but should have been paid a little under £700,000.

One of Britain's most successful industrialists, former BTR chairman, Sir Owen Green, commented acidly of the highest paid businessmen, receiving some thirty-eight times more pay than average workers:

> I wonder how many of them honestly believe they are worth that money. For these people are neither showbusiness stars nor entrepreneurs. The true creators of wealth are entitled to reward for their labour . . . It suggests an almost papal separation of the leader from his flock. This distancing means executives lose touch with the people who actually do the work. It is not that the executives are objects of envy, though they may be. What they have lost is respect.

The issue of overpaid management in essentially management-run companies is a potentially explosive one.

It follows that the question of whether management is accountable to the workforce can be dismissed quickly. In virtually no enterprise is management other than authoritarian towards the workforce, except in small family enterprises. Sometimes management can be benevolent and paternal, and the more enlightened and self-interested are. Ohmae argues this persuasively:

> If we analyse the characteristics of excellent companies in Japan or elsewhere, we find that what distinguishes them is that they are human. These companies have entered what I call the new era of activated enterprise. The strategy and the organization of such a company are in harmony. Everything is geared to execution. That is how these companies achieve excellent results.
>
> In short, the most successful large corporations today, regardless of nationality or industry, display a number of common characteristics. They offer job security, tenure-based promotion, and internal development of people instead of global recruiting campaigns. They provide endless opportunities for employee participation. They regard their people as members, not mere employees. They promote

a common value system. Knowing the critical importance of the corporation's long-term well-being, they display a real commitment to the businesses they are in instead of pursuing strictly financial objectives with only the stockholders in mind.

Again, Toyota provides a good example. Toyota's suggestion box is certainly not unique to Japan. Back in the early 1950s, the company's 45,000 employees turned in only a few hundred suggestions annually. Today, Toyota gets 900,000 proposals – twenty per employee on the average – per year, worth $230 million a year in savings. Even for a company the size of Toyota, that's not an insignificant sum.

But the purpose is to secure maximum profits and loyalty to the firm: the workers are in no sense owners of the firm. Such rights as they enjoy are handed down by law, not by companies – protection against unfair dismissal, compulsory redundancy payments and so on. Promotion, consultation and pay are entirely within the firm's discretion: the modern company worker enjoys no greater rights than a paid agricultural labourer on a large estate hundreds of years ago. The system is entirely hierarchical and authoritarian. Promotion can take place because of superior ability, or because a worker gets on with his boss: the mentor-protégé relationship is perhaps the most common in the corporate hierarchy.

With recent industrial relations legislation in Britain, coupled with a decline in the power and membership of trade unions worldwide, the control by management has, if anything, increased. Not that the unions were ever much of a check, or a particularly benevolent one: in a situation where workers had no rights at all, they would band together to form an adversarial relationship with management, based on their power to hurt the company through the withdrawal of labour.

This, of course, was damaging to the company and not exercised with particularly good sense; in many cases unions became politicized, dominated by extremists and themselves undemocratic. But it was entirely natural that unions should form when workers were treated so poorly by management; unfortunately, there are few signs that it has learnt this lesson, and there is a danger that the recent period of union retrenchment is being used to extract more for less from the workforce, leading possibly to greater social unrest and industrial militancy in the future.

Finally, there is the question of management accountability to the greatest arbiter of them all, the marketplace, the customer. This, above all else, is cited as the main difference between a large capitalist corporation and a large communist one. The communist ones were accountable to government to meet ambitious production targets, with each being allocated resources by central planning.

In practice, it has been hard for a communist corporation to judge whether targets are being met or to estimate the right distribution of resources; shortages, bottlenecks, corruption and mismanagement develop as mistakes are made. In addition, without the discipline of balancing one's cash flow week by week, a communist corporation can lapse into self-satisfied sluggishness, aware that mismanagement makes little difference to its surival. The contrast between a medium-sized private enterprise and a communist bureaucracy could hardly be more complete.

But a giant private corporation is not so different from its communist equivalent. To begin with it can manipulate the marketplace, as already discussed, so that the benefits of free competition and the disciplines of producing to satisfy a customer may be absent. Further, if a corporation in fact has a captive market – as many major producers of particular goods have – it need not concentrate its attention on diversification, improving or selling its products.

In fact, a corporation's managers can devote themselves increasingly to the business of office politics, power struggles within the organization and maximizing their own pay and perks – just as happened inside the giant communist bureaucracies. Bureaucratic struggles, moreover, are the same in any big corporation, capitalist or communist: they are struggles for control of the largest number of people in the organization, competition for the key jobs and often an attempt to extend empires. The control of men is the key – not any particular ability to produce a product which the marketplace wants. To return to a point made earlier, the communist bureaucracies actually modelled themselves on the giant capitalist enterprises, with their strict division of labour and their social hierarchy, which themselves were probably loosely based on a military model.

The prime analyst of the modern organization was Max Weber, who argued that bureaucracy was the dominant form of organization in the twentieth century, whether in a communist or capitalist enterprise. Weber's analysis has never been convincingly challenged, although he was undoubtedly too pessimistic in the grimness of his vision of bureaucracy which reduced men to automatons, and he failed to foresee the greater flexibility of some late-twentieth-century forms of organization, particularly those making use of new technology.

Bureaucracy was dominant, Weber believed, because of its 'purely technical superiority over other forms of organisation'. He was no enthusiast for this: he mourned the loss of the individual freedom of action it entailed and described bureaucracy as an 'iron cage'. He went on to define the fifteen commandments that are common to bureaucratic organizations. First, they are based on specialization. 'Task discontinuity is achieved by functional specialization. Tasks are specific, distinct and done by different formal categories of personnel who specialize in these tasks and not in others. These official tasks would be organized on a continuous regulated basis in order to ensure the smooth flow of work between the discontinuous elements in its organization.'

This specialization required someone to organize and control the various different divisions. So it becomes necessary, second, for action to be authorized within the organization. Third, this leads inevitably to the establishment of hierarchy: someone has to do the authorizing, and be obeyed. Within the organization, people's responsibilities must be defined; so, fourth, relationships must be contractualized.

Fifth, people's positions are determined by their experience and credentials. Sixth, the existence of a structure means that individuals have to climb it, so there is a trend towards careerization. Seventh, to denote one's status, perks and pay are different, so organizations tend to get stratified. Eighth, the organization is clearly divided between super-iors and subordinates. Ninth, because of the size of the organization, formal rules have to be established.

To enforce these rules, tenth, there is a tendency towards standardiza-tion. Eleventh, in most organizations there is also a tendency towards centralization. Twelfth, action taken on behalf of the organization must be appropriately legitimized. Thirteenth, power belongs to the office, not to the holder: this Weber calls the officialization of organizational action. Fourteenth, because of the same feature, action by the organization tends to become impersonal. Fifteenth, the organization must be run along disciplinary lines.

If all this sounds a little abstract, in fact most or all of these features are visibly present in any bureaucracy, from that of a large corporation, an army, a school to a government department. Weber was over-pessimistic: the best organizations today are flexible, the most rigid and rule-bound less efficient (although this does not apply in every case, particularly in basic assembly operations, for example). Many new companies now structure themselves by handing out franchises, performance-related bonuses and offer independence and freedom of action to motivate individuals. Yet the bulk of big organizations cannot run themselves without these bureaucratic principles, or they fear chaos would ensue.

This poses huge problems for free-market theorists. Friedrich Hayek, the prophet of capitalist organization, bitterly opposed what he took to be the communist bureaucratic model. For him the market was necessarily the best source of 'order' because it brought together the disconnected motives of millions of disconnected individuals – something no planner, he believed, could ever forecast. However, contradictorily, he regarded corporate bureaucracies as acceptable impositions of order and planning because their objective was to secure profit from the market. Adam Smith would surely have shuddered.

Hayek seemed to ignore the point that a huge degree of planning and assumptions about the market are necessary for any large private corporation – which is just as eager as the state to get its own way. Moreover, most private organizations seek to limit the freedom of their employees in much the same way that the state does.

Ordinary workers serve a company for a combination of reasons: pay, recognition, and satisfaction, sometimes loyalty – or even coercion. In a pure free market, workers do not need to stay with a company that treats them badly. In practice, in many areas there may be no alternative but to abide with an existing employer, and not just for geographical reasons: many people, for example, professionals, may be in fields where there are only a handful of employers, and if they wish to practise their chosen profession, there may be no other option but to stay with their firm. Again, the insecurity and upheaval involved in changing jobs is often enough to make workers put up with even a difficult employer: psychologically, change is more difficult for most people, particularly as they grow older, than smoothly functioning free markets allow for.

Unskilled or semi-skilled employment may offer a larger variety of opportunities for mobility than jobs in other fields. A secretary or a building worker may, in reasonable market conditions, find another job fairly easily; not so someone in advertising, or a lawyer seeking a partnership, or someone doing a specialized job particular to one industry. Here there is an element of coercion involved; and many employers will not forgive employees who desert them for another firm, who find themselves dissatisfied and then seek to return. Long-accumulated perks and pay schemes may be at stake. In a recession, the difficulty of finding another job may compel a worker to stay with a firm he dislikes.

Loyalty is a better stimulus to stay in a job, but it must be observed to be returned. Pay, while the common reason for holding a worker, or for his changing jobs, is far from being the only stimulus to mobility of labour, and it presupposes a perfect economy where there are plenty of other similar jobs going. In fact, this is the exception rather than the rule: alternative jobs may be hard to get and people usually think very hard about changing them.

Stewart Clegg pinpoints the difficulty free-market theorists have with the giant corporation that actually dominates the capitalist business world:

> In the vast majority of the advanced industrial societies economic transactions take place either in or between organizations. The greatest volume in monetary terms are controlled by the very small number of very large organizations. Given this then the existence of organizations rather than markets as the major *loci* of economic action is a major embarrassment for the economics of neoclassicism. For one thing, where economic action occurs in organizations then the 'freedom' of the market as a solution to malfeasance or mistrust disappears. While one can easily transfer one's action from one horse-trader to another in a country fair or bazaar, it is somewhat more complex (particularly under the labour market conditions of deregulation favoured by neoclassical economists) as easily to reorder one's employment relations or to choose not to buy some essential from some monopoly or oligopoly supplier.

If a major corporation is accountable in only a limited way to the marketplace, barely at all to the shareholders, and not at all to its workforce, who is it accountable to? The answer is to those who control the firm: senior management.

As corporations have evolved over the last century, they have developed a set of values and characteristics that set them quite apart from the rest of society; as the giant corporation is as dominant a feature of the contemporary social and economic landscape, it is worth analysing these. I would expand Weber's list of fifteen characteristics of the bureaucratic organization by adding a further eight more modern ones.

First, major corporations now lay a premium, Japanese-style, on collective decision-making. Few managements are bold enough to rely on the single entrepreneurial or management genius. Rather, proposals are made by the driving executives in any company – usually in their forties and early fifties, and duly ratified by the dozen or so senior executives, usually in their late fifties or sixties.

This system has the virtue of diluting responsibility: if a mistake is made, it is everyone's mistake, and a company cannot fire all its senior executives; if the right decision is made, all share the credit and a particular manager does not get too big for his boots. The nominal principle, of course, is that 'two heads are better than one'. The danger of this system is that the need for consensus makes decision-making painfully slow, and can result in corporate paralysis. Most big corporations, far from being dynamic, are extremely cautious.

A second feature of the modern corporation is that they have their own internal logic and 'ideology'. Enormous emphasis is attached to sometimes quite trivial things because companies pride themselves on the professionalism of that particular skill, often obscuring much more important matters. Indeed, people's ascent in the corporate hierarchy often depends on the extent to which they can spot the internal arguments that really matter to their superiors and adopt the 'politically correct' positions on them. In another company the same essentials of dogma might not matter at all, but entirely different ones would.

A third feature of the modern corporation is its system of self-selecting hierarchical promotion. Few modern companies are meritocratic in the sense that pure ability will lead to promotion: it is important to have the best possible qualification on joining the company; and, once employed, a high-flyer will have to identify himself (or herself) with an up-and-coming mentor, preferably one of the firm's senior managers.

The bright young thing will be put through years of experience, sometimes in quite lowly jobs, being rotated from one part of the organization to another, to get to know the business, before being promoted; but he (or she) will have been identified from the beginning, and provided he does not make too many mistakes and always proffers the appropriate degree of respect to the company, his chance will come.

In his climb he will always have to show deference to his bosses and organization – coupled with a little bit of acceptable cheek, to show he is human after all. It is not hard to see that this system reinforces the tendency of corporation bureaucracies to play safe, to deviate only marginally from orthodoxy, and by the time a high flyer's time has come, he will be unlikely to have much reformist zeal or critical and original thought left in him.

A fourth feature of the modern corporation is its emphasis on secrecy and loyalty. This is usually unashamedly self-serving: human nature decrees that ambitious and forceful people, particularly if talented, while away their spare time filling in job applications to other firms. But the loyal core of management that make up the backbone of a firm convince themselves that this is not so. If evidence is found of a particular person seeking another job or doing down his company or colleagues to an outsider, the punishment can be quite severe. As a result, and to encourage others not to stray, a loss of corporate status may occur, even sometimes loss of the job itself.

A fifth feature of the modern corporation is its cult of anonymity. Top management are rarely flamboyant or interesting personalities in their own right: the tendency has been to subordinate their will to that of the company while pursuing – or appearing to pursue – its interests with a greater determination than their peers. A perfectly serious handbook for senior management advises anyone being promoted to check that he is moving to a department about to produce good results; he will receive the undeserved credit for them; otherwise, the book advises, he should decline the promotion, or he will receive the undeserved blame.

Giant companies, like any bureaucracy, are jealous and suspicious of personalities and success, except on behalf of the company: the fear is that a particular person might have his own interests, rather than the company's, at heart, or that he may be publicizing himself in order to secure employment elsewhere. If an employee does not have a reputation in the outside world, it is less likely that he will be headhunted to another company and he or she will be dependent on, and therefore more controllable by, the company.

The ideal manager is a man well known within his own corporation, but unknown in the outside world. In addition, a person who is too individualist or too independent in thought tends to challenge company orthodoxy: where decisions are usually made by consensus or commit-tee, an individualist may make his peers feel uneasy. In the tired Japanese phrase, 'the nail that sticks out must be hammered down'.

A sixth feature of modern corporations is their obsession with pay, perks and status. In the closed world of a corporate hierarchy, managers often seem to forget that a world exists outside their own. One major multinational has a pay grid containing more than a hundred grades, with three possible levels of remuneration within each grade; it resembles nothing so much as a school hierarchy of promotion by merits and demerits. The bureaucracy involved in promoting a man is staggering.

In most large modern companies, there is scrupulous attention given to such matters as the sizes of offices and indeed the desks in them and the proximity to the boss's office. Whether or not an employee has a secretary, a company car, an expenses-paid holiday and is invited to weekends in a country house hotel with management are also important matters of status.

Another key badge of status is access. The modern company generally makes much of the boss's accessibility to all, and in the better-run companies the boss will not just know the names of many of his employees, but will give them a friendly nod and smile as he passes. In the most badly run companies, the boss reserves his smiles for those he considers most senior or most worthy and ignores or frowns at the rest. Yet in all firms, any junior who makes too many demands on the time of his boss, or who importunes him at an inappropriate time, or fails to observe the courtesies, is unlikely to go far.

A seventh major feature of the modern corporation – a relatively recent innovation – is the growing tendency to what might be called 'Victorian values', if not outright priggishness and puritanism. A large variety of things, even a culture, is present here. Most companies invariably demand that their employees are well-dressed – which in dealing with outside customers is wholly reasonable; they prefer members of staff to be married; they frown on philandering or homosexuality – particularly between members of the staff; and they increasingly dislike smoking and frown upon drinking – both of which are actually banned in many premises and canteens.

Jollity of the right kind is permitted, but not over-boisterousness, or poking fun at the company itself – not within earshot of a manager, anyway. Understandably, a premium is placed on punctuality, cheerfulness, willingness to do the job, long hours and so on, regardless of the ability or otherwise of the individual concerned. The modern corporation thus takes itself very seriously indeed and is quite uninhibited about placing restrictions on adult lifestyles which, if the state attempted them, would be denounced as a serious infringement of individual liberties.

Finally, an eighth feature – again a fairly recent innovation – of the modern corporation is its increasingly self-conscious commitment to a kind of internal egalitarianism (this probably originated in Japan). Thus all members of staff have to wear ID cards, even easily identifiable bosses, and they frequent the same canteens. They are on first-name terms – managers and workers alike; they refer to each other as colleagues rather than bosses or subordinates; and – perhaps the most recent innovation of all – they increasingly share 'open-plan' offices. It is remarkable how often companies resort to crude social engineering, even though they would secure best results by leaving people to their foibles provided they deliver the goods.

The totalitarian temptation to make people conform to a model is as much a capitalist corporate vice as a communist one. The laudable aim of the open-plan office was probably to make everyone feel more equal, and allow a freer exchange of opinions and information across the table, when in fact it just made them feel more uncomfortable and inhibited. This commitment to equality is, of course, entirely bogus, and is occurring at a time of unprecedented inequality over the thing that matters most to employees – pay. Everyone in a company knows who the boss is, and the fact that he is paid vastly more than themselves, and that they have to watch what they say in his presence. But equality is the trendy corporate thing to do, or, in office-speak, the name of the game.

As with Weber's laws of bureaucracy, so the eight new features of the modern corporation have one striking thing in common: they were also features of the now nearly defunct bureaucratic communist state, as described earlier in this book. Thus, recent communist decision-making was usually collective, not dictatorial; within communist hierarchies, careers were made and broken by internal disputes over arcane points of theory that usually bore no relation to the outside world. Communist promotion was based on hierarchy and the protégé system; loyalty and secrecy were virtues second to none in communist systems. The cult of anonymity was imperative except for those at the very top; perks and status were central to the communist system of internal reward and communist systems could be very priggish – while ruthless towards their enemies. Finally, of course, communism paid immense lip-service to a phoney cult of equality.

There is a ninth and fundamental similarity between the modern corporation and the now moribund communist system: empire-building and turf wars. Just as at the top of the communist hierarchy there was vigorous competition between the major components of the system – the party, the bureaucracy, the army, the security forces – so at the top of major private corporations there is fierce infighting between its key bureaucracies, usually its industrial, marketing, personnel, finance and legal departments.

Broadly speaking, the age of the industrial manager, running his company to produce what the market wants, is over. Personnel was never traditionally strong, and is weaker now that the union challenge has diminished. The marketing side is enjoying a renewed moment of glory, as this was briefly seen as the key to whether a product sold or not; but all too often marketing in the past was treated as a little flamboyant by stodgy corporate bureaucrats. The finance department is now extremely powerful, both because of the current obsession with free-market economics and because it wields the axe in a recession.

The Japanese have convincingly shown that huge finance departments are not only an expensive luxury in themselves, usually outweighing any savings they make, but a major hindrance to corporate growth – not a view shared by the West. Finally, legal departments are now beginning to boom, as so much of corporate affairs is determined by the legal minutiae of takeover battles.

Within these bureaucratic wars, only the industrial managers and marketing men (plus sales, always on the lowest corporate rung) can be said to be primarily concerned with what ought to be the main purpose of a company – to produce competitive goods that people want to buy in the marketplace. The rest are parasites. As with the much bigger communist bureaucracies, the day of the local cadres who actually represented the wishes of the people has long been eclipsed. The modern corporate boss is as divorced from the men who pay his huge salary – the customers – as any communist boss from his cadres.

Three huge questions remain: in spite of all the similarities, why is the modern corporate bureaucracy a much more competitive animal than its communist counterpart ever was? Unlike the latter, why does the corporation appear to be thriving? And, given the similarities, is there a real danger that capitalist corporations may go the way of their communist rivals?

The capitalist corporation is undoubtedly more efficient, seriously flawed in some respects perhaps, but its state counterpart was more so. There are three key differences between capitalist and communist bureaucratic corporations that explain this: the former has ultimately to balance its books; the actual job of its employees is to expand business; and, the existence of competition, while far from pure, does condition the corporate environment.

As already observed, there are qualifications to all three. The bigger a corporation, the easier it is for a department to expand for essentially empire-building motives which have nothing to do with producing and selling goods on the market. Thus, many managers spend the bulk of their time in bureaucratic infighting rather than expanding the business; and competition can be severely restricted or even crushed altogether by size. But if a major capitalist corporation did all of these things – and some have – all of the time, it would eventually be in trouble.

Even such giants as IBM and Coca-Cola have had to cut back as their markets slowed; even these two have had consistently to find ways of expanding their sales, and to become more competitive, after years of dominating their respective markets. The major corporations are ultimately responsible to the markets in the way that the major communist bureaucracies were never responsible to the people – although many short-sighted managers have failed to see this.

The mistake is often made of comparing an idealized small or medium-sized private sector firm with a bloated communist or state sector enterprise. There are four quite distinct types of enterprise, two in the private sector, two in the public sector: the small and medium-sized enterprise struggling in a competitive market; the giant private corporation; the giant state enterprise; and the state-run public service. The 'pure' ideal of private enterprise is represented only by the first.

Michael Heseltine, a successful entrepreneur-owner himself, captures the early days of his own small, but now substantial, enterprise:

There is nothing quite like starting your own business: the sense of independence, exhilaration and confidence that prompts you to the first steps, and the loneliness with which you return again and again to the bank manager. He knows what you are going to say. He has heard it all before. You do your best with arguments that have been rehearsed by others a dozen times that day and often rejected. He makes a judgement about you. Sometimes you are lucky.

Friday is crisis day, when the wages must be paid. The other six days are devoted to selling the product and collecting the cash. The entrepreneur lives on his wits, his nerves and ultimately his determination to see it through. It matters as few experiences can ever matter. There are many ways up but only one way down.

The rules are elementary. The bills can either be paid, or not. The creditors can either be kept at bay, or not. The product either works, or it does not. The scale of the thing seems huge because the stakes and the price of failure are very high.

It is not surprising that attitudes forged in such a climate engender self-reliance and a certain intolerance of advice. You come to believe that if you can survive in this jungle, you must have a destiny. Success creates intolerance of the slower-moving, orderly minds of bureaucrats or of anyone who lives in the non-wealth-creating parts of the economy. You pay the taxes; they spend them. You take the risks; they make it harder for you.

I remain deeply committed to the virtues of a private enterprise system. I have competed in the business world and I know the disciplines it imposes. There is no substitute. Nothing drives an organization to greater efficiency than fear of a lost order. The market-place sorts out men from boys and entrenches power in the hands of the consumer, to whom the producer becomes servant. You work for your crust, or there is no crust.

The giant corporation, which dominates the economic scene, has the three competitive features already described, although it is lacking the immediate pressure of the marketplace. If a giant corporation does make a mistake, then starts to lose money, it will generally, after a long time-lag, be restructured in the interests of making more money, with the emphasis on lower costs, greater efficiency and higher sales.

A classic example was Britain's *Daily Telegraph*, its largest up-market newspaper. As market leader of the 'quality' newspapers, with a circulation of well over 1 million, it was astonishing that, by the mid-1980s, it was not highly profitable. It suffered from three problems: a huge printing bill, derived from the restrictive practices of the printing unions; excess costs from a staff that had grown too large; and massive financing costs on an overambitious, but imaginative, decision to invest in a new printing plant.

Those factors brought it to a low point of vulnerability and financial weakness; the proprietor, Lord Hartwell, was forced to seek funds from an outside investor, Hollinger's Conrad Black, a Canadian. Black made firm the option to put up more money, and secure a controlling stake, unless there was an immediate improvement in the *Telegraph*'s fortunes – a situation which failed to materialize. He took it over, slashed costs, and soon reaped the substantial benefits of the new printing plant, coupled with the end of restrictive practices among printers, following their defeat at Wapping.

This was an example of the 'bottom line' function of the market. When even a large company is about to run out of money, the axemen, the industrial consultants and the outside investors move in. In other respects it showed the deficiencies of the market, too: that matters should have been allowed to get so bad; and that, had the *Telegraph*'s credit been a little more positive at the crucial moment, the takeover would have been avoided. The newspaper's debt was largely the product of a farsighted, if too ambitious, investment project that paid off in the end. Western banks, however, are rarely far-sighted. Certainly the reduction in staff costs helped return the newspaper to solvency, although it may have contributed to a lower quality product in some respects. (Overseas staff were reduced and the *Telegraph*'s offices were moved to the East End from central London, diminishing its contact with the main stories; both these moves proved of dubious benefit to the newspaper.)

Did the product improve, or sell more? It continued slowly to lose circulation and, while toying with a slightly different format, retained many of the same readers as before. Yet within the *Telegraph*, as within any large bureaucracy over time, there were undoubtedly savings to be made: the tendency in times of plenty is to take on more staff than you need, and in times of recession to shed staff. The great capitalist enterprise has this degree of accountability to market conditions at least.

The second way in which the capitalist bureaucracy is different from the communist bureaucracy is in company policy. In good times, a capitalist company is interested only partially in its main purpose of selling goods in the marketplace; the rest of the time it is more concerned with internal squabbles and personalities; the same is true of the communist system's basic commitment to equality and the betterment of peoples' lives. However, when the system is in difficulty, the original goals are the objectives by which performance is measured. The capitalist goal is a highly productive one; the communist goal is unattainable and actually anti-productive.

The corporate bureaucrats, like communist bureaucrats, are more concerned about their own position in the pecking order and their status when things are going well. When things are going badly, their job is to produce and sell, while the job of a communist bureaucracy is much harder to define. The lower echelons in a capitalist corporation will be motivated to produce and sell. The lower echelons in a communist bureaucracy will be motivated to work harder, through coercion, for the 'general good'. It is hardly surprising that the cruder, more basic, more human capitalist motive – self-betterment – wins over the vaguer, more coercive, more unpopular communist one. Carrots always were more effective than sticks (something some managers have not understood). There is thus a significant difference between the systems.

But it does not detract from the fact that the actual structure of the organization is not very different. Nor, in practice, was communism really based on selflessness. The system had long been forced to introduce exactly the same enticements as exist in any capitalist corporation for its executives, the main reason for climbing up the communist ladder being pay, perks, special shops, housing and privileges.

The third and key difference between the bureaucracies is the competitive environment. Where only one contractor – a government one – can bid for a contract supplied by the government, there really is very little reason for him to get his act together. He can settle into a cosy relationship with his client, in which one will accept a shoddy service and the other will provide it. In addition, in such a situation, the company providing the service has not the slightest reason to improve its performance or find other clients; it cannot. Once the job has been done, the employee goes home.

Private industry is, or should be, constantly engaged in the search for new clients. In the private sector, even the giant corporation is run to some extent by the need to find competitive suppliers and to compete for tenders – except in the not infrequent cases where it is in a monopoly, cartel or dominant position. Heseltine's discussion of an early example of privatization is worth quoting at length:

> My eyes were opened by the burden on the defence budget of the two Royal Dockyards at Devonport and Rosyth, where there were clearly severe management problems . . . The urgent need was for effective, accountable management and we decided the best way to achieve it quickly was to keep the land and assets in public ownership, and invite tenders for commercial management . . .
>
> Enthusiasm, I know, can sound like doctrinal obsession, so let me restate what I regard as overwhelming reasons why many organizations should be moved from the public to the private sector.
>
> The first is that, in the public sector, there are few of the commercial challenges and comparisons which show whether the cost of a service, which may be only a routine activity such as building or consultancy, is properly competitive with what the private sector can offer. You cannot know that the price is not right unless there is competition and an arm's-length relationship between customer and supplier. This the Government cannot have with its own limb, the PSA; nor until now could the Royal Navy with the Royal Dockyards, or the Army with Royal Ordnance. The clearest example of the weakness is again in the Dockyards. There was no budget of cost, only a record of what had been spent.

Indeed, an awkward hurdle in the way of bringing in commercial management was the cost of introducing accounting systems.

These were essential to enable proper comparison with the private yards, or pre-contract estimating, to be undertaken.

The second point is that, within such organizations as the PSA and the dockyards, there are skills which are directed solely to the limited objective of serving the Government's purpose, in these cases maintaining either warships or estates and offices. The scale of the job is defined within the limits of one programme and one purse. There is none of that thrusting for wider opportunities which is the natural activity and essential strength of the commercial world . . .

For a measure of the inefficiency that has characterized at least this area of public sector activity, there is no need to look further than the figures for absenteeism. On average each employee in the dockyards was taking four and a half weeks' paid, unauthorized absence a year. That reflects upon the management. The cost of the extra overhead falls on the taxpayer. The attitude to work which absenteeism on this scale reveals and engenders dramatically affects the quality of service that the Royal Navy can expect. It must also have set a style and approach which percolated into the wider local economy.

Private sector stimulus would long since have cured this. After the initial trauma of achieving acceptable levels of efficiency the private sector will seek to expand its business because that is its nature. The nature of the unregenerate public sector business is not to exert itself or change but to remain as it is, inefficient, inert and un-enterprising. That is a burden on local society and the national economy which we can no longer tolerate.

Even the biggest bureaucratic corporation, while prone to many of the same tendencies, is unlikely to find itself in quite such a passive position as a state one (although this has been true, in particular, of the giant American defence contractors). There is a great convergence between the capitalist and communist systems, but the differences should not be minimized.

The final category of organization is the public sector institution. This does not pretend to make money, to balance the books. It does not exist for that purpose. It includes the welfare services, defence, the police and other necessary public services. The difficulty with this category is to find any proper system of accountability: profit cannot be the measure, but this type of spending can be highly inefficient unless properly accounted for and audited – even if the purpose is entirely worthwhile. It is mistaken to apply purely private sector disciplines to the necessary parts of the public sector, much of which is overstretched in its provision of key services. In Britain imaginative steps have, however, been taken towards the creation of an 'internal market' in the health service.

Thus the two bureaucracies – excluding the 'pure' private sector, competitive small and medium-sized enterprises; and the 'pure' public sector, providing real public services – remain fairly similar in structure, but with some differences. There is a considerable convergence of the two systems. Are the giant bureaucratic corporations of the West as much under threat as were the giant communist corporations of the East?

The answer, when taken together with the globalization of capitalism, is yes. Domestically, the giant corporations are getting dangerously remote from their own natural constituencies: the customers, the workers, the shareholders. Internationally, they often behave more like colonial freebooters than the respectable guests of their host countries. On the world financial markets, there is a kind of all-powerful tide crashing about, destroying domestic national economic policies for no apparent reason. This tide is governed largely by speculative movements and guesses, not economic logic. In banking and finance, this has long been the case. This has always been the case in such areas as commodity broking and international trade. Coupled with the breakdown of the Cold War bipolar structure, the threat is of a global Hobbesian 'state of nature', a free-for-all in which the strong are dominant but not all-powerful – global anarchy in place of the tidy, if occasionally frustratingly, ordered post-war world.

What in practice does this mean? What could the increasing escape of the great capitalist corporations from political control and the growing impotence of national governments – even as they become more democratically representative – result in? What are the consequences of America's move to unilateralism, and Europe's failure to fill that gap, for the emergence of more assertive backward nations and for the spread of nationalism, the rogue state, terrorism, nuclear proliferation, and drugs, to name but the major challenges?

It is worth examining a doomsday scenario, because catastrophe is not just possible but probable unless these problems are identified and acted upon. It is time to outline the worst possible case.

PART IV

THE TRIUMPH
OF DEMOCRACY

CHAPTER 30

THE GLOBAL STATE OF NATURE

What could go seriously wrong in the new world panorama? The globalization of capitalism is inherently dangerous. To recap on each of the areas in which this is occurring. There is the impact of currency flows, overriding all but the strongest economies. If this persists, the impotence of the governments of major industrial countries, as well as Third World ones, to pursue their own economic policies will become apparent. A widespread disillusion with the democratic process would not be far behind. Democratically elected governments would, quite simply, be seen to be unable to deliver. They would have to qualify their election pledges with the proviso 'assuming international circumstances permit'.

This is a new state of affairs. Up to now, overseas economic problems have had major repercussions; and of course the Depression in the 1930s ricocheted across the world. But over the past forty years the world economy has been more or less stable, mistakes were usually home-grown, and spendthrift governments were to blame for such things as devaluation and inflation. Today this has been transformed: governments can be more or less silly, but the whim of the international financial markets determines the success or failure of national economic policies.

Conservative governments in Britain, Italy, Sweden and France, a liberal one in Ireland, and a socialist one in Spain were successively picked off in an almost unprecedented volley of crises in 1992–3; it strains credulity to believe that they were all mismanaged and deserved their fate. Perhaps they all had bad governments and mistaken policies –

although these varied enormously. But a far more convincing explanation is that governments were not really in charge: they had been buffeted by forces over which they have no control. This knowledge is liable to discredit leadership in long-established democracies, and all the more so in countries with new democratic traditions. Small wonder that a survey conducted by the European Commission in 1993 found that a record 55 per cent of voters were dissatisfied with the way their country's democracy works. Turnouts have been dropping in many democratic elections, most spectacularly in Britain in 2001.

What are the dangers in practice? Diminishing electoral turnout, decreasing participation in elections, a rise in support for extremist parties, a resort to political violence, direct action or to utopian solutions are a few of the obvious ones. In Germany and Italy these things are already happening. In Britain, France and Spain they are beginning to. Even in America, low turnouts can be partly ascribed to the seeming impotence of government in the face of larger forces.

In the great number of countries that are recent converts to democracy, its fragility is apparent. In much of newly democratic Latin America, Eastern Europe and Asia, it will take only a few years' awareness of the politicians' inability to dominate events for authoritarians to reassert themselves. There is no reason, given the sheer size of arbitrary international flows, to suppose the new democracies will last long. The prospect is of a reversion, for a time at least, to simple-minded regimes.

In the West, the democratic tradition is now so deeply ingrained that this is unlikely. But lesser consequences could flow: in particular the growth of an underclass within America, and to a lesser extent in Britain and Germany, would pose a major challenge to the social order. The danger this poses is of a sharp increase in crime, particularly in the inner cities, the growth of effective no-go areas, and occasional social and political explosions. In the United States, the Los Angeles riots could multiply; in Britain, summers of hatred could be repeated.

Let us turn to the next example of capitalist globalization: the debt crisis. Here, a decade of crisis and falling living standards has yet to produce a major political explosion, which is remarkable. Part of the explanation is the traditional passivity of ordinary people in Latin America and Africa; it is an attitude born of centuries of poverty and repression. But there is also a time-lag involved. People do not take up arms immediately; they hope things will change for the best. The debt crisis, although apparently concluded to the satisfaction of the bankers, continues remorselessly to grind down the living standards of a large part of the underdeveloped world.

Maybe there is no limit to the extent to which people will suffer in silence, especially in Africa: hunger induces passivity. However, with the coming of more representative regimes and democracies, ordinary people began to have more hope that their leaders would indeed represent their interests. It is only when it becomes apparent that their politicians have little real power that the possibility of social explosion exists. If this occurs, the armies waiting in the wings are likely to move out of their barracks. This time, however, military intervention would be different: in Latin America and Africa military intervention has traditionally been seen as the response of the establishment to the failings of democratic populists. If it happens now, after years of moderate democracy, it will be seen as virtual proof that democracy does not work in such societies: armies in Latin America and Africa could be very long in taking their leave.

The third move towards the globalization of capitalism is in the spread of the multinationals. As observed, the difficulties associated with this have been less than devastating so far, falling far short of the prediction of the doomsayers in the 1960s. But this state of affairs may not continue. In America, Britain, large parts of Europe and much of Asia, evidence of resentment towards the multinationals is beginning to mount. The problem already provokes interest on the streets and among political parties in these countries. There is an element of hypocrisy present, in that most of the critics welcome the jobs and prosperity the multinationals bring, while objecting to their statelessness and the local power they wield. The multinationals could become a major target of local anger once again, if economies continue to worsen, even though this would itself help to accelerate the deterioration.

The final major area in which capitalism is becoming globalized is trade. The eruption of trade wars between the three major economic blocs, already under way, has huge political consequences. If increased trade continues to benefit Asia, particularly Japan, at the expense of America and Europe, protectionism seems inevitable, helping to push the world towards economic stagnation, huge job losses, and an effective tax on consumers and efficiency everywhere. The danger of America, Europe and Japan fighting a major trade war against each other is likelier than ever, one in which both America and Japan, incidentally, have an interest in frustrating European integration.

Thus the unchecked globalization of capitalism carries with it the seeds of worldwide political instability: if such instability occurs, the tendency in much of Latin America, such parts of Africa as are democratic, and in Asian countries like South Korea and Thailand, will be to revert to military rule. Elsewhere, there might be a temporary hardening of authoritarian regimes, from Middle Eastern monarchs to Chinese colonial masters in Tibet to Confucianists in Japan.

The huge advances of the 1980s would be reversed, as societies discovered that there were few material benefits in their being democratic because whatever government they voted for was forced to do much the same by international economic circumstances. In places like China and Brazil outright popular anger and demonstrations against the multinationals could not be ruled out.

Anti-globalization protests are already fanning out across the world. These are small and elitist, taking place at gatherings of world leaders and institutions. But the potential for expansion is huge. In a sense both communism and Islamic fundamentalism were and are 'anti-globalization'.

If such a reaction breaks out against the globalization of capitalism, there is every prospect of popular outbursts in the United States and Europe against Asian commerce and investment penetration, leading to trade wars, retaliation and tit-for-tat protectionism to appease the electorate. The dangers of a major contraction in world trade need no underlining. Again, the possibilities of a popular reaction towards overseas investment penetration are considerable.

CHAPTER 31

POLICING THE JUNGLE

Globalization need not mean anarchy – the law of the jungle – nor a return to the state of nature. As already observed it is much more localized than commonly supposed, being two-thirds to three-quarters confined to one of the three great economic blocs: North America, Europe and Japan and their dozen or so favoured economic 'satellites' around the world. However, the globalization of capitalism presents great challenges. There are two entirely separate approaches to the problem. The first is supra-national regulation; the second, the recognition of internal responsibility by the major corporations.

The first is the easier to tackle. The entire history of the development of capitalism has been characterized by the gradual evolution of state intervention to obviate its excesses: anti-trust regulations in the United States, social legislation in Britain and so on. The business enterprise is both necessary and crude: necessary because without it the organization does not exist for the creation of wealth and jobs, crude because the main objective of its owners and management is to maximize profits, and they have no obligations beyond that.

Society has to impose its own obligations through regulation – obliging capitalists not to destroy their local environment through pollution, to house workers in decent conditions, not to employ children, and so on – without destroying the dynamics of capitalist wealth-creation. The global firm has to a large degree escaped national constraints – not in these fields (although major Western firms are much less scrupulous about observing them abroad than at home), but in the way it moves investment about arbitrarily, devastates economies with profligate lending, clobbers them with unfair trading practices, permits globalized industry to be dominated by a few huge firms and, in the field of currency trading, allows speculation that knocks national economies off course, for no better reason than the herd instinct of the market. All these phenomena require new means of control; otherwise the law of the jungle is back, at a time when most countries have become more democratic, because most economic decisions have been taken out of governments' hands.

The key is a decisive strengthening of international regulatory organs. The shape of this is obvious. The world is increasingly dividing into three giant trading and economic blocs – the Americas, Europe and its dependencies, and Japan and East Asia. Only these giant clusters are going to be capable of controlling international flows. Indeed, co-operation among the three may be necessary to harness the really powerful forces – for example, currency movement or multinational investment. It is not impossible to see even Japan allying itself with the other two blocs if the major economic forces cannot be overcome by them acting alone. Of course, the embryo of such co-operation already exists in a host of international forums, such as the G7, the UN, the IMF, the WTO, the World Bank, the OECD and so on.

But, as with the UN in the security field, there is little real commitment to such multilateral institutions. The only real hope lies in deals between the three main economic groupings – the three world superstates. It is already evident that these exist: the American superstate, NAFTA, joins 250 million Americans with 87 million Mexicans and 25 million Canadians. America provides some 85 per cent of NAFTA's GDP, Canada 10 per cent and Mexico 5 per cent, yielding a combined total of $7 trillion a year. The European superstate of some 350 million people produces a combined GDP of more than $6 trillion a year. The Japanese superstate, with its three-quarters share of the output of East Asia, has a population of 126 million and an output of $3.5 trillion.

Some people argue that if China, Hong Kong, Taiwan and Singapore are taken together in a 'greater China' bloc, their exports are equal to those of Japan and could exceed them early in the millennium on the current 7 per cent average growth rate over the past thirty years. The Chinese could outstrip the GDP of either Germany or Japan. However, only Hong Kong joined mainland China in 1997; the others seem likely to retain their independence. China's underlying weakness is exposed by the fact that its per capita GDP is still about a fifth of America's and a sixth of Japan's. It is true that 50 million Chinese who live overseas have a huge share of the regional Asian economy: 80 per cent of foreign investment in China comes from Taiwan, Hong Kong and Singapore. Companies owned by overseas Chinese account for around 70 per cent of the private sector in Singapore, Malaysia, Thailand, Indonesia and the Philippines. But Japanese dominance is currently undisputed.

Let us return to each example of the globalization of capitalism in turn. In terms of currency trading, major reserve currencies are obviously far more powerful than smaller ones. A speculative flow can overwhelm a currency as large as the pound. It can even slightly lower the value of the dollar, the Euro or the yen, although almost invariably changes in these can be ascribed either to deliberate policy by their central monetary authorities, or to entirely understandable phenomena, such as the American twin deficits, or the Japanese trade surplus. In other words, the major currencies are affected by rational movements of money markets, rather than the capricious speculation that knocks about the smaller currencies.

The failure of national governments to control speculative currency flows would not apply to the dollar, the yen and the Euro. The three main currencies could float freely against each other or, more likely, as is already beginning to happen, be managed so that a massive Japanese trade surplus is compensated for by a rise in the value of the yen, as negotiated between the monetary authorities. Currency rates are too unpredictable and fickle to be permitted total freedom: where sudden movements can destroy the export strategy of a perfectly competitive economy, some stability must be introduced.

The world's economy should be managed and monitored as intensively as a national economy: already the embryo of global economic management exists within the G7 group of major industrial nations. A G3 group – America, Europe and Japan – could work much more effectively to iron out destructive currency fluctuations, shortages of global demand, economic overheating and the dangers of protectionism. Recently the world has been experiencing a surplus of liquidity and a shortage of demand – on a smaller scale, the classic ingredients of recession that helped to cause the Depression in the 1930s. This is because of a curious combination of orthodox economics that were fashionable in the 1980s, the implosion of demand in the non-Asian Third World that followed the debt crisis, the deflationary impact of Japan's trade surplus which is sucking demand out of the system, the recessionary impact of relatively high European interest rates needed to pay for German unification, and the straitlaced, stiff-collared policies of the European Central Bank, a promenade of old umbrella-bearers entirely outside democratic control.

It may prove impossible to get Japan to alter course significantly through reflation, although Keynesian tinkering has been tried there in the wake of the bursting of the 'bubble economy'. But in the future it should be possible, for example, for the Americans and Europeans to agree on a concerted increase in demand by both economic blocs. If the Japanese won't play ball and increase their own straitjacketed domestic demand, both Western blocs could indulge in a joint devaluation against the yen that would prevent Japan reaping the export benefits of greater demand in their economies. To some extent this is already happening. This is the kind of global economic management that becomes possible in a world of three superstates, replacing the current free-for-all on the foreign exchange markets. G3 would be much more effective than G7.

The arguments for and against a single European currency are well rehearsed: it will come as no surprise to the reader that the author accepts the single currency as the best means to protect individual nation states against speculative currency flows – and also to end the massive interference with free trade of fluctuating national currencies. One condition must apply to the creation of the Euro: an effective regional and industrial policy that ensures there are no massive transfers of wealth to the centre – a tendency in any superstate. This has not yet happened.

A greater role for the state in Europe requires government structures with much more satisfactory accountability than is provided by the present unelected Commission. The structures of this can be argued about, but their outline is clear: an elected executive, chosen either by the European Parliament or directly by the people; a more powerful parliament containing a senate elected by national parliaments; and a European central bank whose governors would be chosen by the nation states, but which would be accountable to parliament.

It is a matter of semantics whether to label this federalism or not. Ironically in the United States and Germany, federalism was a term implying the decentralization of authority to the constituent states, as opposed to a more centralized confederal state like Canada. In America, that most varied and parochial of societies, there is much grumbling about Washington and the federal government, but few people really consider it a remote and bullying central authority. In American elections there is greater participation in local and governorship races, as well as congressional battles, than in presidential elections. This is entirely healthy: people are concerned about the running of their state more than the remoter political battle in Washington. The same would undoubtedly be true of a European state.

In Iowa and Alabama there is no sense of resentment about dealing in dollars printed in Washington. The reverse is true: people know they are dealing in a strong, hard currency. The same is beginning to apply to the common European currency. In Asia we are already seeing the evolution of a 'yen zone', willy-nilly. As Japan becomes the dominant economic partner in the region, responsible for some 70 per cent of its GDP, and regional trade is increasingly carried out with Japan rather than the United States, the advantages of having local currencies pegged to the dollar are diminishing.

The great advantage in the past was that the exporting countries of East Asia ensured that their products never became uncompetitive in America as their currencies descended with the dollar, while, as the yen rose, they became more competitive in Japan. But as the volume of their trade with Japan increases, so does the disadvantage of being paid in appreciating yen, rather than depreciating dollars, and people are choosing to hold yen to facilitate transactions. The Japanese government, previously opposed to the concept of a yen zone, is now sympathetic.

The problem of creating one is, however, more complex than with Europe. Many fear that Japan's domination of the regional economy – much greater than Germany's in Europe – would create a one-sided arrangement between Japan and little local satellites. Now with the growth of China's economy and the possibility of Korean union, there will be at least two other major economies in the region, with Taiwan and Singapore some way behind. The relationship may become slightly more equal, which makes for an easier one.

APEC, the Asia-Pacific Economic Community, which first met in Seattle in November 1993, has much more modest goals than the European Union: its own internal report circulated in advance of the summit argued that:

The creation of APEC in 1989 represented a critical first step in the process of filling an inter-governmental institutional vacuum. The time has now come to use the organization much more extensively to promote the economic interests of its members. It could thereby promote their security and political interests as well. APEC should adopt a bold new vision for the future of the Asia-Pacific. This would provide a clear – and even dramatic – substantive mandate for the institution.

The proposed Asia-Pacific Economic Community would not seek to replicate the evolution of the European Community. We see neither a need nor a practical possibility of creating a single internal market. We do not envisage a common currency or a common foreign policy. We do not even advocate a customs union.

Nonetheless, few Europeans – and even fewer observers else-where – believed in the 1950s that Europe could overcome its vast cultural differences and tragic history to unite economically. Today we take Europe's common market as an established part of the landscape. It is quite feasible, if difficult and ambitious, for the Asia-Pacific Community to achieve the more modest course we propose in the decades ahead.

The issue of the links between the super-currencies and the countries on their periphery is also crucial. There could be nothing more dangerous globally than if the three superstates become exclusionist, leaving the developing world to the predatory forces of currency speculation which they have escaped. Any global co-operation between the three economic superpowers must provide for the possibility of third countries attaching themselves to the arrangement, and thus enjoying currency stability. This would be crucial to the establishment of a yen zone; the United States has been enlightened in bringing Mexico into NAFTA. A European currency should offer linkage agreements with Eastern European currencies currently outside the community and with Third World countries traditionally associated with Europe.

One key aspect is that the superstates must always be ready to bring in outside countries as they become economically mature enough to benefit from membership. In the long term, the European superstate will reach out to embrace Turkey, much of Eastern Europe and even, possibly, the Ukraine and Russia. The American superstate could reach down into Latin America; and the Japanese one could extend to Indonesia and much of South East Asia. Meanwhile, currency association agreements would bring much stability to those on the periphery.

Sub-Saharan Africa deserves special mention. Africa must be taken in paternalist partnership by Europe. With the end of colonialism, and the passing of proxy wars like that in Angola between the superpowers, it has become the world's neglected, stagnant backwater, sinking – in spite of some commendable local efforts at reform – even deeper into poverty, malnutrition and strife for control of scarce resources. As commodity prices bump along the bottom and the debt burden mounts, large parts of Africa are, quite literally, returning to their pre-colonial past.

The average African today eats a tenth less than he did twenty years ago, according to the UN Food and Agriculture Organization. While African populations have risen by around 3 per cent a year since 1970, annual production of staple cereals has grown by less than 2 per cent annually. The amount of cultivated land per person has fallen by half over the past two decades. Some 34 million Africans in fifteen sub-Saharan countries suffer from what the FAO genteelly calls 'exceptional food emergencies' – virtual starvation. The average Ethiopian eats 1,500 calories a day in food – 300 calories below FAO's minimum recommended intake.

Life expectancy in the two most recent African flashpoints – Rwanda and Somalia – is forty-six years. Four-fifths of Rwanda's population live in absolute poverty, as do three-fifths of Somalia's. The average Somali attends just three months of school, while the average Rwandan spends fourteen months there. Rwanda's average population growth is 3.3 per cent a year, or 8.5 children per woman, in the country which already has the highest population density in Africa. Food production in both countries has plummeted by a fifth in the past decade.

That grim aplogist of capitalism, Malthus, has found his laboratory at last in Africa, where genocide could be classed as at least restoring the food-population balance. In nearby Zaire, law and order has deteriorated to the point where the country is effectively under the control of marauding armed bands of soldiers. The celebrated Kenyan author, Ali Mazrui, has even advocated 'a once unthinkable solution: recolonization . . . Even the degree of dependent modernization achieved under colonial rule is being reversed,' he points out. 'External recolonization under the banner of humanitarianism is entirely conceivable.'

Few would go so far. One self-interested incentive for Africa's northern neighbour, Europe, to help develop the continent is to create more developed populations capable of consuming Western products. Another is precautionary – to help stem the increasing flow of migrants from the continent. But it is also humanely incumbent upon prosperous Europe to assist towards developing a huge continent whose living standards seem to be slipping back to those of the nineteenth century. It was never likely that countries abandoned in a rush by the colonial powers, endowed with only a handful of university graduates, would modernize themselves by their own efforts. It would be a tragic historical irony if continuing neglect causes Africa to look back to the age of colonialism and super-power competition across their territories as a golden age.

The increasingly tempestuous world economy would be radically changed by the establishment of the three main currency blocs (it is already three-quarters there) and a global pact between them to manage their currencies responsibly. The present picture of huge funds sloshing their way about the world leaving devastation in their wake would be transformed. If all three were prepared to agree annual exchange rate targets, based on rational criteria, such as trade flows, interest rates and so on, and were prepared to support each other with the massive reserve funds at their disposal, there would be relative currency stability; the size of the available intervention funds would reduce the margins for speculation considerably. In itself this would greatly facilitate international trade; currency instability has been one of the single biggest obstacles to the expansion of world trade in the post-Bretton Woods period. There would be an end to destructive currency tidal waves.

In addition, the herd, and irrational instincts of the market, would be replaced by more measured economic co-operation. Of course the market would still have a role: where exchange rate targets were out of line – as, given the fallibility of all human institutions they sometimes would be – the market would probably anticipate the necessary corrections. Given the size of the currencies concerned, financial flows would have a relatively small impact, helping to prompt a more realistic readjustment. The wild fluctuations against smaller currencies would be things of the past: size confers stability.

The state of nature would have been brought under control: the biggest beasts in the jungle would have imposed a measure of order in which they no longer grappled fiercely with each other while the interests of the weak went unprotected. The best guarantee of order throughout human history has come when the biggest accepted responsibility for enforcing it. Co-operation between the three biggest animals in the jungle is indeed the only realistic way of bringing order to it.

The second item on the global economic agenda is world finance. International bank lending seems to be recovering slowly from the debt holocaust. With the drying up of financial flows to the Third World, banks suddenly realized that there was such a thing as sovereign risk and stampeded just as stupidly in the opposite direction, refusing to lend money because of the possibility of default, thus creating a financial drought for perfectly good Third World projects. The banks found themselves stranded as huge, inflationary money pumps looking for places to put money.

After the debt crisis, the same team brought the junk bond and secondary banking crisis in America, the splurge of the 'bubble economy' in Japan, the massive inflation of property values in Britain, creating an artificial boom which like all others ended in collapse, the dotcom bubble, and now, just possibly, another South Sea Bubble in overheating China. The flow of international bank lending globally, as of 'hot money' in bond and equity markets, is largely unregulated, and inherently both inflationary and deflationary – inflationary when it pours into a particular country or region, deflationary when it seeks to recover its loans. The solution is to find ways of ensuring that bank lending is channelled to investment or productive purposes – which requires much greater supervision; if the banks are incapable of this, the regulators must step in.

In Latin America, for example, the World Bank and Inter-American Development banks, for all their deficiencies, are ideally placed to pass judgement on whether a particular project loan is likely to be well spent or not. The collapse of the Bank of Credit and Commerce International exposed the scandalous inadequacy of international banking regulation in the global marketplace. Here the problem is to marry banking with fundamentally creditworthy projects in the credit-starved Third World, as well as containing the excesses of banking deregulation and the oversupply of credit in the developed countries.

The first problem is relatively easy to solve, in four practical stages. There needs to be a global resolution of the debt problem, so that commercial banks understand that they can resume lending for viable projects without the risk of these loans being swept away in a national default. This is already being part-achieved through selling Third World debt at a discount, debt-equity swaps, the writing off of debt and so on, mechanisms for which the international banking community has congratulated itself for its ingenuity. Yet because these are so grudging and partial, huge debt burdens remain, which helps to deter productive lending for fear of a repeat of the crises of the 1980s.

Another step forward would be international guarantees of lending for the right kind of projects, permitting banks to take minor risks. This requires proper inspection and regulation of those projects; as already suggested, the development banks are in a good position to provide this. Again, this is already to some extent happening because in practice commercial banks are unwilling to extend new loans except for projects which have the World Bank or IDB seal of approval; other possible supervisors are Eximbank in the United States or Britain's Export Credit Guarantee Department. After the fiasco last time, when lending was left to international banks literally chasing each other to lend money to Third World saints and sinners, some degree of supervision is right and necessary: the 'market' proved to be a disaster.

This calls for an improved and overhauled World Bank, Inter-American Development Bank, Asian Development Bank and European Bank for Reconstruction and Development. The World Bank has in practice amassed a mass of expertise in the Third World but suffers from bureaucracy, political appointments and over-dominance by the United States, as does the IDB. The EBRD got off to an appalling start and, in view of America's domination of the World Bank, needs to be developed to channel funds not just to Eastern Europe – its initial mission – but to the developing world.

One of the biggest global problems is reconciling the surplus of international capital with its productive use. Marx defined colonialism as a product of the search by surplus international capital for a home in the developing world. The contrary is true today: finance-starved Third World countries desperately need such money. The problem is that when the banks fight shy of such countries and channel funds into the industrial nations, they risk merely adding to inflationary pressures unless they are careful in their choice of project: the junk bond boom and the property boom were examples of that.

In fact far more non-inflationary wealth can be created in less developed countries, with their frontier opportunities, than through the expansion of credit in already prosperous countries. In the developing world this can be done through inspected, authorized lending under the eye of responsible banking institutions with experience in the field acting as catalysts for large flows of commercial bank lending. The wasteful spectacle of funds looking for a home, chasing borrowers in the Third World, or in real estate or predatory take-overs could gradually be brought to an end. In its place, capital surpluses could be recycled into commercially viable Third World projects (the developed world needs schemes for recycling capital to its underdeveloped regions; but that is another subject). This would be non-inflationary, and unlikely to result in the depressing cycle of boom followed by bust.

The need for a proper strategy of bank lending in the Third World is an urgent one. At the moment the panacea for most of its ills is acquisition and investment by the multinationals or by 'hot money' in pursuit of equity and bonds.

Of course, this proposal for resumed commercial bank lending guided by, and underwritten by, the major development banks, is far from foolproof: they are far from perfect institutions. But can it be doubted that their supervision would be considerably more sensible than the profligate and naïve lending of the commercial banks during the debt crisis?

Whether the International Monetary Fund has a role in all this remains an interesting question. After the mess, those who mopped up certainly perform a useful role in restoring some confidence. But its tough, unimaginative, and often inappropriate addiction to narrow financial targets for Third World countries has possibly done more harm than good. It should revert to its proper role, not as a kind of totem pole around which the developing countries have to dance, but as an official receiver when things go disastrously wrong. The rule of thumb should be that if one country goes bankrupt while the rest remain solvent, that country is at fault. When a large number of countries go bankrupt, the international financial system is at fault and narrow-minded IMF prescriptions are inappropriate. After the debt crisis, much of the 'hot money' flowing to the Third World took the form of bonds and equity, which are just as liable to sudden panics, as in the Mexican crisis of January 1995. Then, nearly $50 billion had to be stumped up at speed by the official international financial community; the IMF might have a role in raising such money itself from the commercial market, as such cases are likely to be increasingly frequent given the size of international flows.

The third main field for regulation of the global jungle lies in the activities of the multinationals, which has been highlighted by the collapse of Enron. This can best be attained through co-operation between the three superstates, which have the size and market access to overawe even the largest global companies. In addition, as we shall see in the next chapter, the problem of company size and power can be addressed through making large corporations more responsible to their shareholders, customers and employees.

The fourth area for regulation of the global jungle, the global state of nature, is trade flows, and they need not detain us long. The establishment of a tripod of superstates would do much to remove the most damaging aspects of these. If Japan could be brought on a voluntary basis into agreement with America and Europe on the amount of trade that should pass between the three, the biggest problem would have been resolved.

If not, concerted pressure by America and Europe – Japan's biggest markets – should make the country see reason; at present it plays one off against the other, and the Americans, always trying to steal a march on Europe, lend themselves to this. The Japanese trade surplus, although now contracting sharply, has been a huge global problem, acting as a severe restraint on the world economy and is not, as the Japanese contend, entirely a product of their super-efficiency. If this sounds like trade management, so be it, provided it is aimed at removing obstacles to free trade and is not used against weaker trading nations.

The goal must be to dismantle tariffs between the developed and developing world. But where tariffs exist between the big three, a certain toughness is required to force one or another down. In the global jungle, the big three should seek to resolve their differences amicably, or all the animals will suffer: growling will sometimes be necessary, but the big three should be as kind as possible to the weaker animals, which are no threat to them.

A serious danger of this arrangement is that the three economic superpowers might appear to be dictating terms to the rest of the world, arousing anti-colonialist resentment. The extent to which the triumvirate shows itself aware of the danger, and of the importance to be derived from rekindling growth in the Third World, will determine its success.

The biggest problem is, however, the extent to which the global triumvirate itself could become too remote and detached from the ordinary person. If the nation state has been transcended by the forces of international capitalism, the global co-operation needed to control the latter seems almost as remote. Communities of hundreds of millions of people are not likely to be in close touch with their grass roots: the collapse of the Soviet Union seems an awful warning of the remoteness of a major superstate from its people – as Britain's Mrs Thatcher, among others, has often pointed out.

Yet the argument is mistaken: there is certainly a danger of a non-democratic superstate – like the Soviet Union – moving too far from its people. The European Union is a largely non-democratic institution, and so there is also a danger of this in Europe. The answer is not to do away with superstates – which are essential – but to make them democratic. The United States – with some reservations – has shown how extraordinarily successful a superstate can be at retaining its roots, its contact with ordinary people, and avoiding a backlash of the kind which destroyed the Soviet empire.

Several aspects of the American system prevent it from being remote from the ordinary person, and permit a nation of 250 million people, covering an immense geographical area, from not appearing as a distant bureaucratic entity which ordinary people cannot relate to. In spite of the grumbles about Washington, most Americans are intensely patriotic and supportive of their President and proud of their system and way of life. America has many lessons to offer other would-be superstates like Europe and Japan.

The federal system, in particular, gives a remarkable degree of power to the state and local governments. Moreover, America's written constitution and supreme court enshrine a mass of liberties and rights that no one – least of all government – can tamper with. In addition, Congress, in its battles with the executive, encapsulates a division of powers which gives the ordinary voter a feeling that he really matters, and that he is being represented. The administration is constantly being scrutinized and checked. In particular, with the whole of the House of Representatives and a third of the Senate being re-elected every two years, Congressmen could hardly spend more time nursing their districts. With every state sending two members to the Senate, no part of the country, however underpopulated and remote from the centre, feels left out.

The presidency itself, with its sometimes ludicrous over-personalization, with its travelling circus at election times, and with the genuine partisan battles between Republicans and Democrats, serves to defuse suspicion of the central bureaucracy. There has been nothing remote about men like small-town Harry Truman, amiable, shrewd Dwight Eisenhower, glamorous John Kennedy, lived-in Lyndon Johnson, clever, devious Richard Nixon, ordinary Gerald Ford, idealistic Jimmy Carter, communicator Ronald Reagan, preppie George Bush and stumbling Bill Clinton. All supremely professional politicians – as they need to be to survive the gruelling year-long American election – their obvious human failings under the spotlight make them appear close to ordinary people, and far from remote. George Bush was as near to being a bureaucratic politician as any modern president – and he was not that near and did not survive that long.

Finally, the power of the media, and in particular television, helps to knit America together as one nation. America shows that it is possible for a superstate to be in touch with its people – and both Europe and Japan have a lot to learn from this: Jacques Delors would not win an election in the United States.

In case this seems too adulatory, there are some serious defects in American democracy. Institutional paralysis is produced by the interminable battle between President and Congress, which over some issues – in particular foreign policy and the budget deficit – threatens to freeze the system into inaction. The huge range of issues in which co-operation is achieved between executive and legislature dwarfs this; and in foreign affairs presidents have often got away with acting now, explaining later. But over the deficit, Congress reinforces any president's propensity to spend and blocks any attempt by the treasury to save.

In many cases this is not objectionable: deficit financing is preferable to underspending, lack of demand and recession. But when deficit financing occurs through inflation, or through arbitrary or high interest rates, thereby hurting other economies, and becomes institutionalized, there are serious dangers and presidents and congressional leaders have to address them. Others who might imitate the American way should consider whether the balance between executive and legislature is right, or whether the latter, on this key issue, is too powerful. Short-termism is a major problem: with important elections every two years, America's attention span is woefully short.

Another major defect of the American system is more dangerous: while the ordinary American does not feel remote from central government, there is a perilous remoteness between civil society and a large, although in the minority, underclass: previously mostly consisting of blacks from the inner cities and the south, this now includes a large number of first-generation Mexican immigrants, poor southern whites and new European immigrants.

Galbraith, among others, has argued that all that keeps these people from revolting against the system is that they consider themselves better off than their forefathers, but that this will not apply to their children. Because the overwhelming majority of Americans are contented, the needs of the underclass are neglected; they are not a revolutionary class, in a historical sense, because they are a minority. However, the potential for mass discontent among the second generation, trapped in a cycle of poverty, should not be underestimated.

Whether Galbraith is right or not depends on whether American society provides its traditional safety valve of offering opportunities for these people to escape their predicament: the record among inner-city blacks is not encouraging. If he is right, a second Kennedy-style era of emancipation may be necessary to prevent American cities degenerating into riot zones and armed camps, where haves protect themselves from have-nots.

The failings of America should not blind Europe and Japan to the lesson that the superstate can be made to work, if it incorporates some essential features. Neither does, at the moment. The European superstate, because of the reluctance of the nation states to share power with the centre, has a nominated executive, the Commission, which is no more democratic in composition than the leadership of the former Soviet Union. The executive is supposedly checked by a largely impotent parliament for which ordinary voters – unsurprisingly, in view of its lack of authority – show little enthusiasm, and by a fairly threadbare system of personal rights and legal guarantees. The relationship between ordinary people and senior government officials, because of their non-election, is almost non-existent.

Jacques Delors made a fine demon for the British tabloid press as the apparently colourless bureaucratic empire-builder he appeared to be. Until Europe has an elected executive, its authority will be small as Mr Gorbachev discovered in the Soviet Union. Without major and massive institutional reform, the European Union does risk suffering the Soviet fate – becoming a superstate without popular consent.

This is not because it is a superstate or too large: it is because Europe is not democratic. It is perfectly adequate in one respect – the relationship between the nations and the centre; if anything the nations have permitted too much authority to flow to the bureaucracy, while obstructing its democratic development to ensure their own dominance. No serious person can possibly believe Europe will ever override or crush the sovereignty of the nation states, any more than the American federal government does of the states. In a democratic state, this is impossible – it could happen only in an undemocratic set-up like the Soviet Union. The European superstate should acquire control over areas where common action needs to be taken, in order to regain power over the outside forces that have diminished national sovereignty – through, for example, the globalization of the world economy. The nation state should retain sovereignty over the rest.

In Japan, a political vacuum exists because of the country's essentially authoritarian tradition of government behind a democratic façade. This may be changing; but until it does, massive tensions will continue, and the sense of alienation of ordinary people from their government is palpable.

The state of nature, the global jungle, thus needs to be brought under control by the three biggest animals acting under democratic rules, as responsible as possible to their own people because their very size runs the risk of alienating them: the United States has shown it can be done, and so it should by both Europe and Japan – or they run the risk of going the Soviet way.

CHAPTER 32

REFORM FROM WITHIN

B ut there is a second way of imposing order on the state of nature: and that is for the middle-sized powers within it, the major corporations, to become responsible to their own constituencies. This needs immediately to be qualified: this author is not proposing any real change in the structure of what might be called the dynamic private enterprise, the small or medium-sized company competing furiously in the market. For these, the issue is whether they can survive; they are already intensely accountable to the market. To compete they may need the inspired, striving leadership of a dictatorial individual. It is the already established bureaucracies in the giant corporations, barely accountable to the market, that need to be made more responsible, or they risk arousing the same kind of hostile reaction that led to the collapse of communism. At present they are controlled by only one of their three constituencies, and are distantly accountable to another. The collapse of Enron shows the need. Barings, Long Term Credit Management, and Asian Pulp and Paper are other examples. President Theodore Roosevelt got it right a century ago:

> The vast individual and capital fortunes, the vast combinations of capital which have marked the development of our industrial system, create new conditions, and necessitate a change from the old attitude of the state and the nation towards property. More and more it is evident that the state, and if necessary the nation, has got to possess the right of supervision and control as regards the great corporations which are its creatures.

Self-appointed corporate management runs the show, subject to its demonstrable failures in the marketplace – but, as suggested, this is much less likely for a giant company than anyone else. Most managers are obviously motivated by the desire for self-enrichment and status, but it is also true that many have the corporation's interest at heart (although this is not true of today's predators). Most managements cannot be described as ill-motivated, because very often this is not the case, although there are plenty of people about whose purposes are simply to maximize their earnings irrespective of the corporate good.

But, equally, the management clique is responsible to no one. As in a communist bureaucracy, it chooses its own successors, it makes the decisions, it rewards those who respect the system and it punishes those who dissent. In terms of financial size, it may be the equivalent of a small country and, in terms of numbers, of an army. It is unashamedly authoritarian and believes that its efficiency derives from this fact. It has very little contact with the free market: its size enables it to manipulate the market and its bureaucratic structure, where possible, stifles individual initiative. Horizontal and vertical integration increase the bureaucracy and creates huge conflicts of interest.

How then to make it responsible, and to whom? All three constituencies need to be brought into play. The time has long since come for those who provide capital to be given a louder voice. A shareholder today has only two rights: depending on the type of shareholding, the right to a say in the choice of directors; and the right to sell his shares if dissatisfied with the performance of the company. In fact the right of participation in the choice of directors is barely exercised at all by most shareholders. It is difficult for them to attend company annual general meetings, difficult for them to vet the often over-simplified accounts they are presented with, and even more difficult to understand who is responsible for what decision, in the light of the almost total secrecy that generally swathes corporate affairs.

Only very occasionally, when companies have very high profile management or very visible failings, are shareholders motivated to exercise their rights – Britain's Lonrho being one example, Ratner's another (although both were simultaneously victims of boardroom coups). Directors are usually selected by the management, with the shareholders' formal consent – and a docile lot most of them are. They are, however, wholly incapable of ruling the corporate roost and are selected for their importance – or self-importance – and passivity, not for their ability to represent the shareholders vigorously.

So shareholder power, if it exists at all, consists of voting with their feet, abandoning companies in visible trouble, which is why shareholders so often get stung. As already noted, a company's financial results are not necessarily the best guide to its good management and profitability – under-investment or the sale of assets, detrimental to the company in the long run, may be used to puff up a company's annual results. Often the accounts are the last thing to show the company's weaknesses. Perhaps the most classic rip-off by the professional managers of the men who put up the money and then sat back, expecting to reap large profits, has been the experience of many syndicates in Lloyd's of London; devious professionals can sting absentee investors.

That said, there are two things happening in Britain to the stock market which both tend towards greater accountability. The first is the growing power of the institutional shareholder – the pension fund, the unit trust, the building society and so on; the second is the dispersal, through privatization, of millions of shares among ordinary people. The institutional shareholder is no less a corporate bureaucrat than the company he invests in. But he knows what he is looking for, and is unlikely to invest in a company which he views as unsatisfactorily managed.

The small shareholder has very little say at present, and the very atomization of shareholdings makes it easy for the management of the new privatized corporations to ignore him. So far most privatized companies are doing well in terms of share prices and dividends. But if these companies start doing badly, thousands of small investors will be affected, and it cannot be long before they demand an explanation: it is not easy for a bus driver or bank clerk to ring his stockbroker and sell his shares if he scents a whiff of trouble in the financial press. But he can join with his fellows to make his voice heard.

This is heartening at a time when most companies lack any form of accountability to those who put up the money for them. In Britain the Cadbury Committee, reporting in May 1992 on ways to improve company accountability, argued in favour of self-regulation, while accepting the need for legislation if this failed. The committee recommended setting up a nomination committee for each company, dominated by the non-executive directors, with the task of coming up with the names of new directors. They also recommended that an audit committee should be set up for each company consisting of non-executive directors alone, with direct access to the company auditors, reviewing half-yearly results and looking at the internal control systems of companies before they are put to the board. Finally, a remunerations committee for each company should examine the issue of executive pay. They pronounced:

> Shareholders are entitled to a complete disclosure and explanation of directors' present and future benefits, including stock options and stock appreciation rights, and of how they have been determined.
>
> Accordingly, we recommend that in disclosing directors' total emoluments and those of the chairman and highest-paid UK director, separate figures should be given for their salary and performance-related elements and that the criterion on which performance is measured should be explained.
>
> In addition, we recommend that, in future, service contracts should not exceed three years without shareholders' approval . . . this would strengthen shareholder control over levels of compensation for loss of office.

This would safeguard against executives deciding their own pay. Auditors should be encouraged to report their suspicions of fraud to the investigatory authorities. However, the committee accepted that there was concern about the lack of a direct link between auditors and shareholders, and that the need to secure a commission from a company often overrode an auditor's perception of his duty to the stockholders. Auditors should not be able to acts as consultants to their clients. The accountancy profession needs better regulation. Executives should be made to disclose stock transfers and to share information about industry trends.

Both institutional investors and mass investors should demand two more things: that directors be submitted to contested annual re-election by postal ballot – exactly what is now required by law of trade unions; and a much greater access to information about the company than presently available. 'Creative accounting' can obscure the truth about all but the most ineptly managed company: the regulations requiring disclosure of company information need to be much tougher, and the company accounts much more transparent and accessible for inspection by the ordinary shareholder.

As observed, there is little demand for this when things are going well; there will be when they go badly; as in some newly privatized companies they surely will. Finally, chief executives should be appointed directly by the shareholders – not through the directors as at present, because they are effectively chosen by the executives. This will generally be a formality, but could give shareholders power in the event of a major problem.

The second main 'constituency' in a company is the market. For small and medium-sized business, this works fine. Capitalism is at its most efficient, and most impressive, in the efforts of single individuals creating dynamic and thrusting companies against all the odds placed against them by the big boys, the giant bureaucratic firms: entrepreneurs like Crosby's Tim Beardson, who set up from scratch a multimillion-dollar stockbroking company in Hong Kong, or Hugh Ehrman, pioneer-king of Britain's mail order knitwear business. Even within major groups, individuals can sometimes flourish if given enough autonomy and initiative. Yet major companies can manipulate the market to a great extent, although not entirely. The market can be made more efficient, through anti-trust and anti-monopoly legislation, at a global level through action against anti-competitive practices such as predatory mergers or anti-competitive cartelism, and finally through greater consumer action and awareness.

In the United States consumer awareness has actually strengthened competition and corporate effectiveness through increased sales. There is nothing radical or anti-capitalist about insisting upon free competition rather than rigged markets; indeed, this is to return capitalism to its first principles, the ideals of Adam Smith. Modern free-marketeers like Hayek appear to believe that markets are free if left to themselves; in reality, markets have to be supervised in order to preserve the freedom of the many from the predations of the monopolistic few. Consumer legislation is being increasingly recognized as not just beneficial to the consumer, but to the producer.

The modern corporation also has responsibilities to the workforce. Traditionally its attitude to management has been confrontational and, frankly, extremely crude. In response to the employers' attitude that its objective is to provide goods at the lowest possible labour cost, workers banded together to deny employers their labour and demanded better pay and conditions. They also formed the backbone of socialist political organizations devoted to their interests. The struggle was for the most part successful at the beginning of the century and in the immediate post-war period.

However, the massive expansion of the state machine, and the inflation caused by soaring labour costs, provoked a backlash that reversed the tide in the employers' favour, and caused a major erosion of trade union power. The unions are now in decline, their membership falling, reluctant to indulge in strikes in America and across Europe. This would be welcome news, but for the feeling that employers are increasingly reverting to their old high-handed attitude of hiring and firing and squeezing as much labour for as little pay as possible. Technically, innovation has made it possible to maximize productivity, increasing industrial tasks for workers on new machinery for no increase in pay.

The decline in union power has not been so dramatic that it is impossible for employers to overstep the mark. They might take a leaf out of the Japanese example. The latter have introduced new plant into Europe with no-strike agreements: in exchange they offer job security, reasonable pay and facilities to air grievances. This paternalistic approach, while in some ways unsatisfactory, is infinitely preferable to management methods, imported mainly from the United States, where labour is viewed as just one of many disposable costs of production. Labour is the key to any successful business, and the best results will be secured if workers are treated as human beings.

While the organization of any firm requires a chain of command and a clear definition of management authority, some innovations would greatly improve the climate. One is a much greater diffusion of information to the workforce. Unnecessary secrecy can only render management decisions much more difficult to apply. In addition, the presence of one or two directors directly representing the interests of the workforce (not simply able employees who have made it from shop floor to boardroom), but not endowed with any power to block board decisions, would assure the workers' interests were not misjudged or overlooked.

The Japanese practice of offering workers – and management – across-the-board pay cuts instead of compulsory redundancies when a firm is in difficulties would do much to secure the loyalty of a workforce for whom unemployment is a far greater evil than lower pay. This would encounter resistance from traditional unions, of course, whose primary purpose is to secure higher pay for the existing workforce, rather than to represent the interests of all workers in a country, employed and unemployed – unions themselves are a major source of unemployment – but it might be popular among the rank-and-file. These innovations would not, of course, make management responsible to, or representative of, the workforce in any way; a company has to have an authoritarian structure. But they would give the workforce some influence in decisions that directly affect it.

CONCLUSION

These then are the five great areas of change necessary to avoid a state of global political economic anarchy: the establishment of superpower policing to combat terrorism and to prevent conflicts breaking out all over the world, through an efficient system of regional alliances and deterrents, backed up by the threat of major superpower intervention; the widening and deepening of global democracy; the regulation of the global economy through co-operation between the three economic superstates of the next few decades – America, Europe and Japan – in co-operation with regional groupings of the rest of the world; a gigantic government-primed stimulus for demand and development in the three-quarters of the developing world untouched by globalization (a new Marshall Plan, a Powell Plan, perhaps?); and reform from within of the capitalist corporation. The United States must take the lead, as senior partner, chairman of the board, head of the family, head office for a global franchise of autonomous regional offices – but emphatically not as emperor, nor even worse, biggest guy on the block protecting its own interests in an anarchic neighbourhood, nor worst of all, hunkered down in its bunker, scarcely ever venturing out.

The alternative to these changes is hardly worth contemplating. It includes one or more of the following: American unilateralism, withdrawal from its global responsibilities; an uncontrolled terrorist offensive; growing rivalry among the European nations; the spread of a host of ethnic and nationalist conflicts across the globe (already under way); possible confrontation and war between quite major powers – for example, Pakistan and India, China and Japan, China and Taiwan,

Iran and Iraq (again), or either with Saudi Arabia, possibly involving the use of nuclear weapons. And the expansion of narcotics trafficking, with its huge social consequences for the developed world, to uncontrollable proportions.

On the global economic front, there is the prospect of the bitter legacy left by the debt crisis in the developing world erupting into savage confrontation with the developed world. This would involve: the seizure of multinational assets, the collapse of major multinationals, attacks on Westerners, and the degeneration of the world economy into a trading confrontation between America, Europe and Japan, with profound recessionary consequences; the growth of widespread disillusion even among long-democratic electorates; and the reversion of many new democracies to populism and authoritarianism. It might further result in explosions of crime or rioting by the underclass, reinforcing the impression that governments are simply unable to govern; and/or the disintegration of the European Union into a free-for-all in which Germany dominates its weaker neighbours and even perhaps ends up in confrontation with its rivals, France, Britain and Russia.

Global disorder would be in prospect. Many of these things were already beginning to happen prior to September 11. The concept of a 'new world order' is not just some hollow phrase employed by a now discarded American president. It is essential because the old world order – which for all the danger of nuclear confrontation saw the world through a period of relative peace and a surge in prosperity – has collapsed. Without a new world order there will be no world order.

Doomsday – global anarchy, the state of nature, where the strong prey on the weak unchecked, where the powerful neglect their responsibilities and the world becomes a dangerous, unpredictable and inequitable place, the undoing of all the great strides towards international order that over the past forty years replaced a world riven by world war and the murderous ideological disputes of last century – is a real possibility if America and its allies do not rise to the occasion. Thirty years of world wars, economic crises and social disorder followed the collapse of the last world order in 1914. The consequences of not acting in time are terrifying.

This in turn requires political leaders and corporate bosses capable of lifting their eyes above the daily political and economic grind to sense the dangers and take evasive action. There were only a few signs that this was happening in the global jungle of international security prior to September 11, and fewer in that of international economics.

This is the challenge for the planet as the sun rises on the new millennium. Will it be the red dawn of danger, of countless conflicts and economic hardships, or the brightness of a new, gentler, more ordered age for humanity? September 11 provided a ghastly glimpse into the abyss. Provided the United States responds with the measured firmness of the world's leader and only megapower, and its allies make their contribution, the world can be made safer again and the future of uncontrolled global conflict averted. Then the horrific sacrifice of those in New York, Washington and on Flight 93 will not have been in vain.

INDEX